CW01455389

THEATRE AND GOVERNANCE IN BRITAIN, 1500–1900

This book begins with a simple observation – that just as the theatre resurfaced during the late Renaissance, so too government as we understand it today also began to appear. Their mutually entwining history was to have a profound influence on the development of the modern British stage. This volume proposes a new reading of theatre's complex and shifting relation to the state, society and the public sphere. Employing a series of historical case studies drawn from the London theatre, Tony Fisher shows why the stage was of such great concern to government by offering close readings of well-known religious, moral, political, economic and legal disputes over the role, purpose and function of the stage in the 'well-ordered society'. In framing these disputes in relation to what Michel Foucault called the emerging 'art of government', this book draws out – for the first time – a comprehensive genealogy of the governmental 'discourse on the theatre'.

TONY FISHER is a Reader in Theatre and Philosophy at the Royal Central School of Speech and Drama, University of London, where he is Associate Director of Research (Research Degrees). He has published a number of journal articles in both theatre and philosophy, and he is the co-editor of *Performing Antagonism: Theatre, Performance and Radical Democracy* (2017).

THEATRE AND GOVERNANCE IN BRITAIN, 1500–1900

Democracy, Disorder and the State

TONY FISHER
Royal Central School of Speech and Drama

CAMBRIDGE
UNIVERSITY PRESS

University Printing House, Cambridge CB2 8BS, United Kingdom

One Liberty Plaza, 20th Floor, New York, NY 10006, USA

477 Williamstown Road, Port Melbourne, VIC 3207, Australia

4843/24, 2nd Floor, Ansari Road, Daryaganj, Delhi – 110002, India

79 Anson Road, #06–04/06, Singapore 079906

Cambridge University Press is part of the University of Cambridge.

It furthers the University's mission by disseminating knowledge in the pursuit of education, learning, and research at the highest international levels of excellence.

www.cambridge.org
Information on this title: www.cambridge.org/9781107182158
DOI: 10.1017/9781316855966

First published 2017

Printed in the United Kingdom by Clays, St Ives plc

A catalogue record for this publication is available from the British Library.

Library of Congress Cataloging-in-Publication Data
NAMES: Fisher, Tony, 1964– author.
TITLE: Theatre and governance in Britain, 1500–1900 : democracy, disorder and the state / Tony Fisher, Royal Central School of Speech and Drama.
DESCRIPTION: Cambridge, United Kingdom ; New York, NY : Cambridge University Press, 2017. | Includes bibliographical references and index.
IDENTIFIERS: LCCN 2016053238 | ISBN 9781107182158 (Hardback)
SUBJECTS: LCSH: Theater–England–London–History–16th century. | Theater–England–London–History–17th century. | Theater–England–London–History–18th century. | Theater–Political aspects–Great Britain–History–16th century. | Theater–Political aspects–Great Britain–History–17th century. | Theater–Political aspects–Great Britain–History–18th century.
CLASSIFICATION: LCC PN2596.L6 F485 2017 | DDC 792.09421/2–DC23 LC record available at https://lccn.loc.gov/2016053238

ISBN 978-1-107-18215-8 Hardback

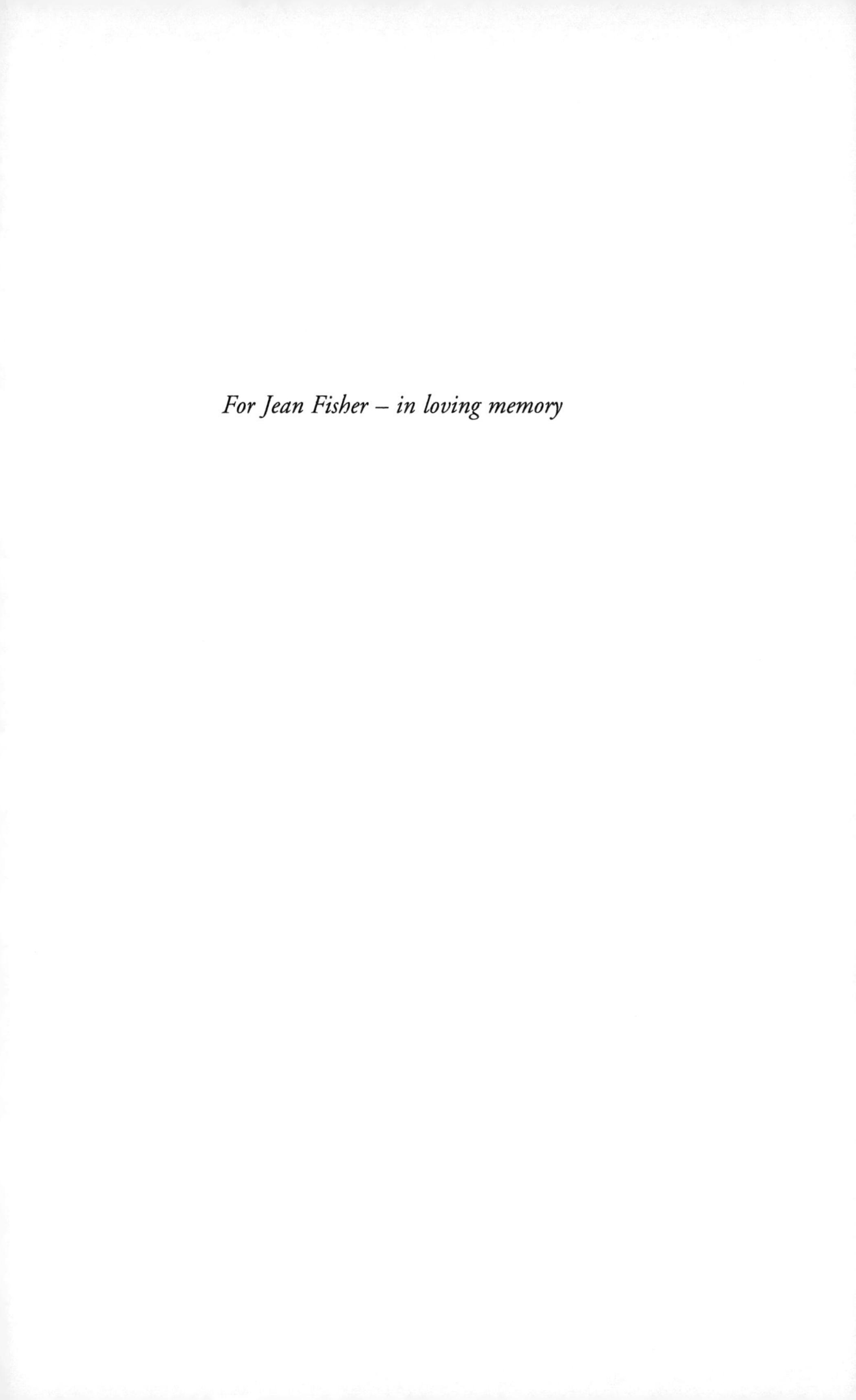

For Jean Fisher – in loving memory

Contents

Acknowledgements

It is almost a decade since I first started work on this study. To be sure, its origin owed more to the vagaries of chance encounters – to the contingencies and serendipities of research – than to any consistent plan on my part at its outset. Indeed, what guided my first foray into the subject was anything but a firm sense of direction, merely a vague hunch that there was something worth pursuing in the development of the theatre and the problem it posed to government. It was only when I broke cover and first exposed what I was working on to colleagues and friends that the project began to take on a coherent shape; and, in truth, without their criticism, guidance and encouragement, I doubt that this book would ever have seen the light of day. Whether that would have been a good thing or not is ultimately for the reader to decide. Suffice it to say, no book can truly succeed without the help of the number of individuals who contribute to it, sometimes without even knowing they have done so; at the same time, in each case it is its author who must bear sole responsibility for its failings – and my book is certainly no exception to this general rule.

In particular, I have benefitted from the scholarly insights and suggestions of Simon Shepherd, Gilli Bush-Bailey and Jacky Bratton, each of whom not only read and responded with great generosity to drafts of chapters, but in the process led me to appreciate the nuances of British theatre history. My gratitude also goes to Robin Nelson for his support during his time at Central. I am especially appreciative of Maria Delgado for her invaluable advice on framing the book's introduction, her astute practical guidance in negotiating the world of academic publishing and her unwavering personal support. Equally, I am grateful to the anonymous reviewers at Cambridge University Press who provided helpful criticism at a crucial juncture, since it was due to their counsel that I was brought back from the morass of sprawling ambition to a more focused discussion of the topic. The expertise and generosity of several close friends were also essential to the writing of the book. Louise Owen very kindly read and commented on Chapter 3, Zachary Dunbar gave useful feedback on Chapter 4, and Joshua Edelman, whose exceptional largesse and candour I hope one day to repay, acted over a number of years as an excellent sounding board. Going above and beyond the call of duty, he provided me not only with perceptive criticisms of several chapters, but also many hours of lively discussions that were both intellectually challenging and great fun. Hing Tsang bears some responsibility for this book, too, since it was during one of our many wrangles over philosophy, that the idea behind this project first lodged itself in my mind.

I have presented papers on the subject of this book at several conferences and research events, and have gained much helpful feedback on those occasions. In particular, I am grateful to colleagues in the Performance Philosophy network and TaPRA's Theatre, Performance and Philosophy working group whose members have engaged with my work over the past few years – Eve Katsouraki, Kélina Gotman, Jim Hamilton, James Corby and Laura Cull have each left their mark on the way the project evolved. I presented a version of Chapter 1 at a research event in Aberystwyth, where Karoline Gritzner and Alison Forsyth encouraged me to continue with their positive responses to the paper; a version of Chapter 2 was presented at Quorum, Queen Mary, thanks to Lynne McCarthy, who from early on was a particularly enthusiastic supporter and friend to the project. The postgraduate research students at Royal Central School of Speech and Drama have endured several presentations on my research over the years, for which I am grateful. I owe a debt of gratitude also to Kate Brett and her team at Cambridge University Press, who could not have been more helpful and supportive throughout the publication process.

On a more personal note, the profoundest thanks of all must go to my family – to Beatrice and Matilda for their joyful disregard of every attempt I have made to impose order on them – long may it continue!; but, above all, to my partner in crime, Amanda Stuart Fisher. Without her unflinching support, love and boundless patience – and, truth be told, cajoling – there would simply be nothing here to read.

Introduction
The Discourses of Theatre and Governance

During its long history the stage has been subject to the hostility of moral and religious commentators, the contempt of philosophers and the ire of governments. It has been taken as a threat to the very existence of the political order: something to be censured, perhaps even suppressed. This study aims to revisit the peculiar discontentment that so infuses the social history of the modern European stage. It aims to tell anew the story of how theatre was thought by those who viewed it as symptomatic of the corruption of society, as expressing the image of the social malcontent, who perceived the stage to be a cradle of sedition – a spur to the grumbling hive – or who feared that it would incite and inflame the degenerate predilections of the vice-ridden multitude. Indeed, by the nineteenth century the theatre becomes a means, among some commentators, of defining and categorising those 'dangerous classes' who could not be assimilated into the vision of a harmonious social totality. And yet this is also the history of those who took a different view of the stage: who saw it as a tool for instructing the people, as something that, through the power of its pedagogical effects, could help found a more virtuous and coherent society. In their hands, theatre became an instrument of reform. It provided a means for sustaining the social order through the cultivation of a national identity – in short, this is also the story of how the stage was assimilated during the modern period to the interests of government.

In spite of this history, it would not be too much of an exaggeration to say that the idea that the stage possesses any profoundly political influence is treated with a fair degree of scepticism in theatre and performance circles today.[1] It may even seem preposterously naive or incredible to think that

[1] See, for example, Alan Read's intricate discussion of theatre's political dimension, structured around the sceptical proposition: 'Theatre is a total stranger to the instrumentality of political effects', Alan Read, *Theatre, Intimacy and Engagement: The Last Human Venue* (Basingstoke: Palgrave Macmillan, 2009), p. 27; Joe Kelleher's *Theatre and Politics* (Basingstoke: Palgrave Macmillan, 2009), p. 72; and Brandon Woolf's 'Toward a Paradoxically Parallaxical Postdramatic Politics', in *Postdramatic Theatre*

such a view was once taken seriously. It is certainly difficult to envisage a time when the stage was held to have had such powerful and influential effects on those who frequented it in previous centuries. The most explicit expression of this line of attack against the pedagogical and political efficacy of the stage is found in a short but controversial article by the philosopher Jacques Rancière, who has popularised the view that the spectator is not, and never was, in need of being emancipated. I will not be detained by that debate here, except to say that for the purposes of the present study my approach is entirely agnostic when it comes to answering the question as to whether or not there is or can be such a thing as a genuinely 'efficacious' theatre.

Nevertheless, the relationship between the stage and politics must be self-evidently implicated in a study whose title is 'Theatre and Governance', and so it obliges me to say something about my view of that relationship at the outset. What I would like to suggest in this book is that far from being mistaken, or jejune, the questions that were addressed to the theatre, throughout its long history, concerning the social, moral and political efficacy of the stage are of profound import to us. The way the stage is governed today is very much a product of this history. It is a history that has shaped the stage in two fundamental senses, both germane to this enquiry. The first permits, through an analysis of its discourse, an explication of the way the theatre is positioned as a social institution. It speaks to the history of the social, political, moral, philosophical and economic influences that have informed the way the modern theatre developed. The second sense, although this is more difficult to discern, shows that the discursive positioning of the theatre had a profound impact on the way theatre was made. It requires an examination of how those discourses are implicated at the level of its shifting practices, to perceive the marks and traces of such discursive effects upon theatre's material surfaces. To the extent that the various discourses on the stage have had an undeniable influence upon it, the proposition behind this study is that no full understanding of the relationship between the theatre and the political sphere will be complete without thoroughly comprehending how these two histories intersect. This brings me to the objective I have set myself in this book: to present a critical history of the discourses of the stage and, in so doing, to account for the haphazard development of European

and the Political: International Perspectives on Contemporary Performance, ed. Jürs-Munby, Carroll and Giles (London: Bloomsbury, 2013), pp. 31-46.

theatre and its practices in light of *another* genealogy – that of the modern practices of government that have influenced and shaped it.

In order to explicate the themes of the book, this introduction begins with a brief overview of the way Plato made use of the image of the theatre in the *Laws*. The reason for this is simple: the issues that recur throughout the discourse on the modern theatre inevitably align, in one way or another, with the Platonic vision of the stage. Having sketched these broad themes, I then consider the methodology of the book, where I return to the problem of governance in more detail, and specifically to Michel Foucault's notion of governmentality, upon which the study draws. In the final section, I turn to the theoretical rationale behind its argument and the exposition of its chapters.

Theme

Plato's Theatrocratic Metaphor

In the third book of Plato's *Laws*, the unnamed Athenian visitor who is at the centre of the dialogue engages his two interlocutors (the Spartan, Megillus, and Clinias the Cretan) in a peregrination that seems at first blush to be quite an incidental and minor issue given their preoccupation with the laws and constitution of states: a discourse over the regulation of music in the ancient Athenian *polis*. It soon becomes clear, however, that far from regaling his listeners with a pleasant if trivial digression into the oddities of a long-since-lapsed Athenian law, what emerges is one of the most fundamental issues confronting any political state. It is a problem that places the theatre, and the problem of democratic licence with which it will be associated by Plato, at the very heart of government. It is therefore fitting that this study, which is concerned precisely with investigating the relationship between the stage and governance, should begin by first situating it in the context of a dispute that can be traced back to antiquity.

What is of concern to the Athenian visitor is the way in which the loosening up of the regulations governing music can be seen as analogous to the more general liberalisation of law that now defines the *polis* of Athens. The purpose of such a proposition is not simply to show how life has become 'progressively freer of controls';[2] it is to assess, more crucially, the consequences of this development for the government of the city. In

[2] Plato, *Laws*, III, 700b.

the past, the visitor patiently explains, the old laws were rigidly imposed and the people adhered to them, living 'in a kind of "voluntary slavery"'.[3] Likewise, the musicians, composers and performers of Athens were subject to strict controls, which were applied through the systematic regulation of the approved categories, genres and forms of music. In this way, music was both tolerated in the *polis* and received the protection of its legislators. Its musicians were permitted to compose hymns, since through them the poet could sing praises to the gods. They could also compose laments, paeans and dithyrambs and, finally, nomes – that class of poems sung to the accompaniment of the lyre and whose name is significant due to its etymological link to *nomos*, the Greek word for law. These categories were known and fixed by legislation; and according to this ancient statute, it was prohibited to alter them or to employ any kind of tune in a composition that derived from a separate category. Since the form of music composition was so closely identified with the law that regulated it, the corruption of one would automatically entail the infringement of the other.

This strict regulation was not confined to composers of music, however; it also applied to the spectators – as the Athenian explains:

> And what was the authority which had to know these standards and use its knowledge in reaching verdicts, and crack down on the disobedient? Well, certainly no notice was taken of the catcalls and uncouth yelling of the audience, as it is nowadays, nor yet of the applause that indicates approval. People of taste and education made it a rule to listen to the performance with silent attention right through to the end; children and their attendants and the general public could always be disciplined and controlled with a stick. Such was the rigor with which the mass of the people was prepared to be controlled in the theatre and to refrain from passing judgment by shouting.[4]

Where once the audience attended a performance in silent and respectful appreciation, now it indulged in the frenzy of applause. It is obvious to the Athenian that a vociferous crowd, which expresses its pleasure or displeasure by braying and howling, is also a disobedient and insolent crowd. What, though, he asks, explains such a stunning transformation in the behaviour of audiences? In fact, what precipitates this lamentable deterioration in their behaviour must be understood in terms of the power of manipulation that the composer possesses through the effects his composition has on them, and which explains exactly why composition must fall under the remit of the law. The problem is this: there came a time when

[3] *Ibid.*, 700a. [4] *Ibid.*, 700c–d.

composers grew tired of the restrictions placed on their art by legislators; they began to experiment, broke the rules, tore up the statutes and deliberately set out to offend good taste. Although one cannot say that these composers lacked talent – quite the contrary – what they did lack was sufficient respect for the 'correct and legitimate standards laid down by the Muse'.[5] The result was cacophony, the pandemonium unleashed by mixing incompatible melodies, rhythms, measures and genres: 'Gripped by a frenzied and excessive lust for pleasure, they jumbled together laments and hymns, mixed paeans and dithyrambs, and even imitated pipe tunes on the lyre. The result was a total confusion of styles.'[6] Not only did they offend against the law that ensured good taste; by abandoning that scrupulous rectitude of composition imposed by law, quite unintentionally they produced an effect that would be far more pernicious in its wider consequences. What these musicians inadvertently proclaimed through their compositions was the idea that 'in music there are no standards of right and wrong at all, but that the most "correct" criterion is the pleasure of the man who enjoyed the performance, whether he is a good man or not'.[7]

I would like to mark the correlation here of good taste in music and good morals, since what the composers did not anticipate was precisely the social catastrophe that their experiments with composition would produce. In suspending the ancient law, they thoughtlessly imposed a new one. Not only did they effectively reject the only sound basis upon which discernment and judgement in matters of taste is founded; most calamitously of all, they delivered the power to judge music to those least capable of doing so – to the common member of the audience.

> Consequently they gave the ordinary man not only a taste for breaking the laws of music but the arrogance to set himself up as a capable judge. The audience once silent, began to use their tongue; they claimed to know what was good and bad in music, and instead of a 'musical meritocracy', a sort of vicious 'theatrocracy' arose.[8]

It is hardly worth asking what this peculiar word, 'theatrocracy', signifies for Plato, for it is quite clear: it denotes the scandal of democracy itself. To be sure, says the Athenian, the oddity of the democratic form of spectatorship would not in itself be troubling if all that it signified was degeneracy in the conduct of audiences at the theatre. Although such a spectacle would be disgraceful and unedifying, no great harm would come

[5] *Ibid.*, 700d. [6] *Ibid.*, 700d. [7] *Ibid.*, 700e. [8] *Ibid.*, 700e–701a.

of it for the state. But at this point an elision emerges in the Athenian's argument that will be endlessly repeated throughout the centuries to come. On the one hand, the degeneracy of the laws over music composition is interpreted as the first sign of a more general slackening of the standards of obedience by which the people's submission to the rule of their governors can be demonstrated. The poor behaviour of audiences in the theatre thus becomes a convenient symptom with which to diagnose the ailments of the democratic form of government. On the other hand, what the composers of the *Laws*, and the poets of the *Republic*, initiate is the effective cause of the theatrocratic state insofar as they promote the general conviction that every man can be 'an authority on everything'.[9] With such disregard for the law, the incipient democratic tastes of the theatre audience usher in a state of uncurbed license; and the former authority of the *polis*, once grounded in true knowledge and the wisdom of an eminent and educated elite, is quickly supplanted and usurped by the authority of 'each and all'. But what kind of authority is it that is grounded in nothing other than the 'assurance engendered by effrontery' and a 'reckless lack of respect for one's betters'?[10] In the revolt of theatrocratic speech, what one finds is not just a total disregard for authority but the collapse of the rule of law as such. This is the vicious condition of government defined by the word 'theatrocracy': it names that government of the ungovernable – a government of the ungovernable by the ungovernable and for the ungovernable – which 'springs from a freedom from inhibitions that has gone much too far'.[11]

The Corrective Use of the Theatre Metaphor in the Laws

It would not be farfetched to say, at this point, that for Plato all is not lost with respect to the theatre, notwithstanding the diabolical degeneracy of the theatrical state he describes. In the *Laws*, there is not only a corrective to the problem posed by the theatre, but also, in an astonishing twist in the argument, a solution that recuperates the theatre, transforming it into the very model of good government. In the *Philebus*, Plato had already prepared the ground for such an image of the theatre by drawing a vivid comparison between the theatrical stage and 'life's tragedies and comedies',[12] but it was not until the end of his life, with the writing of the *Laws*, that the metaphor of the theatre as the very form of the ideal state takes on, for the first time, its comprehensive and familiar shape. It is here that he

[9] *Ibid.*, 701a. [10] *Ibid.*, 701a–b. [11] *Ibid.*, 701b. [12] Plato, *Philebus*, 50b.

employs the famous image 'that each of us living beings is a puppet of the gods',[13] and in book VII he would even go so far as to compare the act of founding the state itself to the genre of tragedy.[14] The statesman is pictured as composing laws, just as the tragedian composes his tragedies, although there is a notable difference between the two in that while the poet trades in pleasing representations designed to pander to the vulgar disposition of the crowd in the *agora*,[15] the statesman crafts his representation in homage to the divine authority on which he models his design. Where the latter speaks of truth and justice, and thereby aims at a state founded on order and perfection, the former, according to the *Republic*'s well-known prescriptions, trades in falsehoods and serves only to undermine public and civic institutions, corrupting the integrity of the *polis* by introducing a plague of disorders.

All the same, these theatrical images come at a price, conjured as they were from a philosophical imagination that was in conflict with itself since it was also saturated by a profound affinity for the very thing it wished to exclude. Because of this the *Laws* might well be seen as an attempt to reconcile the irreconcilable: the image, if not the reality, of the stage with the project of a perfectly regulated state. Even as he appeals to tragic poetry, Plato takes great care to ward off its excesses: theatre is employed as a means to defeat the theatre; or rather, and more precisely expressed, it is invoked to ward off what the theatre itself arouses and encourages: the calamitous state of affairs that befalls the state when theatre rules supreme. Was it by accident that Plato, a philosopher obsessed with symmetry, crafted two metaphorical functions for the theatre? To be sure, if the theatre is invoked by Plato to render philosophy a service, it is only inasmuch as it possesses a metaphorical power, and only insofar as one should, at least according to the kind of rationality that led the Greeks to the discovery of the *pharmacon*, administer poison if one wants to cure a sickness.

Nevertheless, the theatre metaphor proves to be profoundly metastable in Plato's hands; its undercurrents produce deep uncertainties, not least because, according to Plato, and perhaps due to his own suppressed predilections, his very use of the metaphor concedes that theatre has already prevailed – here and everywhere, on earth and in the heavens – and precisely because the metaphor extends the theatrical *topos* to include the entire cosmological order, whose obscure shape and design it comes to define and render visible. And yet the instability introduced by the

[13] Plato, *Laws*, I, 644d. [14] Plato, *Laws*, VII, 817b. [15] *Ibid.*, 817c.

doubling of the metaphor never troubles the *Laws*. For one thing, it is never presented as a simple opposition. Plato does not present the two opposing images of the theatre as a brute juxtaposition: the theatre of the world – the cosmos imagined as a vast theatrical system – and the simulacral and inferior theatre of the tragedians. On the contrary, the theatre metaphor and its double are fixed by a logic of mutual exclusion, as demanded by an ontological and epistemic order whose normative arrangement was implicitly taken for granted. It is to assert that one theatre must necessarily preclude the existence of the other, and vice versa. The theatrocratic state is produced precisely when one disregards the divine provenance of the law, while the well-ordered society demands the suppression of those democratic predilections that lie at the heart of a theatrocracy.

The German philosopher Ernst Cassirer once remarked that, for Plato, '[t]he political cosmos is only a symbol, and the most characteristic one, of the universal cosmos.'[16] What this recalls links the *Laws* to a previous work, the *Timaeus*, which Plato does not explicitly make reference to at this point; the connection was most certainly made by later commentators, however.[17] In the *Timaeus*, Plato developed his cosmological understanding to its fullest extent in the figure of the *demiurge* – the divine fabricator, the 'maker and father of the Kosmos'.[18] The Platonic notion of cosmogony, which casts God in the role of cosmic artist, would have a profound impact, later, on the cosmological imagination of the Renaissance when, during the fifteenth century, Ficino, for instance, would describe God as the 'great artisan'. For my present purposes, it is perhaps sufficient to note that in Plato's *Laws* what is prepared in the image of the theatre of God is a means of connecting a political order, the just state, to a cosmological and divine order. The intrinsic political meaning behind this spectacular design had already been asserted in the *Republic*, and in terms that were designed to show it to be self-evident: 'There is a model [of the *polis*] in heaven, for anyone who wants to look at it and to make himself its citizen on the strength of what he sees.'[19] It is thanks to these peculiarly theatrical images that a form of government is able to be asserted that, insofar as it appeals to an authority that transcends the world, is granted an absolute right to dominate it.

16 Ernst Cassirer, *The Myth of the State*, trans. Charles W. Hendel (New Haven, CT: Yale University Press, 1974 [1946]), p. 66.

17 For a fuller discussion of this, see Lynda G. Christian's *Theatrum Mundi: The History of an Idea* (Harvard Dissertations in Comparative Literature) (New York: Garland, 1987).

18 Plato, *Timaeus*, 3.28.

19 Plato, *Republic*, IX, 592b.

Methodology

Discourse, Theatre and the Idea of Governance

To envisage the image of the theatre as the form that makes the cosmological order perceptible to the human mind is evidently not to speak of theatres in the particular or even of the theatre in general. Still less should Plato be understood to be proposing a 'Platonic theatre' in the manner suggested by Martin Puchner in *The Drama of Ideas* – the putative theatre (or otherwise) found in the Socratic dialogues.[20] Nor should he be seen as providing, even in embryonic form, a blueprint for what would later comprise the rationale by which the national theatres across Europe were developed. Theatre is here grasped as a pure figure of thought, as a metaphor with which to think the discernible arrangement and legibility of the world, immediately available to all those who have an eye for it, in its visibility and representability. In this manner, philosophy understands theatre to have a certain explanatory scope, a certain discursive radius; in short, a certain explicative value for the legislator who would seek to build a state. But it is far from clear where that leaves the actual theatre. If it is the 'theatre of the world' that was henceforth afforded an immense amount of prestige in the minds of philosophers and theologians, the material theatre of the poet entered history, more often than not, accompanied by a prestigious quantity of their condescension and contempt.

But what does history itself tell us about the 'old quarrel between philosophy and poetry', as Plato famously expresses it?[21] Is it quite as polemically rigidified as it might at first appear to be? While theatre scholars are very familiar today with the history of this antipathy from the work of Jonas Barish, the 'anti-theatricalist' thesis he promotes, or such is the view of this study, only tells one-half of the story.[22] And, as it happens, far from being the subject of an anti-theatrical prejudice, when it comes to the development of the modern stage, at least, the European theatre is invested by the polity with the kind of standing that would eventually qualify it for the emoluments of the state. As early as 1690, the first national theatre was inaugurated in Europe in the form of the Comédie Française; and although it would take until 1949 before

[20] See Martin Puchner, *The Drama of Ideas: Platonic Provocations in Theatre and Philosophy* (New York: Oxford University Press, 2010).

[21] Plato, *Republic*, X, 607b.

[22] Jonas Barish, *The Anti-Theatrical Prejudice* (Berkeley: University of California Press, 1981).

Parliament would pass the act that would see the building of a national theatre in London, already by the late nineteenth century the English stage had been taken up by the middle classes and given pride of place in the pantheon of its activities. Might it not be said that despite all the noise and bluster that condemns the stage as a diabolical artifice, the arguments of anti-theatricalists are of rather less significance than commentators such as Barish would have us believe, and that this is borne out precisely by the building of theatres across Europe whose sole purpose lies in promoting the prestige and self-esteem of nations?

There is another possibility, however: might it be the case that the arguments of anti-theatricalists and pro-theatricalists share rather more in common than they think and that such polemical attitudes would have us believe? It is this thought that provides the leading clue for the present effort. Indeed, what has guided me in this study began with the idea that if one moves beyond the level of polemics, and locates such anti-theatrical statements within a wider discursive terrain, as forming part of a broader system of statements concerning the stage, regarding its lawfulness or otherwise, what will be revealed is less the disparity between their respective points of utterance – even less will it be a matter of disagreement between the opinions and beliefs that motivated different speakers – than a question of discerning their structural filiation.

Tracing that filiation belongs to the task of uncovering a discourse. Such a task should not, for all its apparent similarities, be confused with works that seek to establish the meaning of the theatre in its different permutations, through a synoptic history of how the theatre was theorised, as can be found, for example, in Marvin Carlson's dauntingly compendious *Theories of the Theatre*.[23] The task I have set myself is rather more limited in scope. I take the temporal boundaries of the event by which this discourse can be demarcated as commencing in the late sixteenth century and coming to maturity in the late nineteenth century, and the principal geographical locus, for the sake of linguistic convenience, to be primarily, although not exclusively, the London stage. The reasons behind these choices are threefold. First, I have sought to trace the shifts and displacements, continuities and points of rupture in the discursive positioning of the stage in the specific context of the development of modern forms of government. Second, the modern form of government emerges during the sixteenth century, just as the modern European stage is born. In other

[23] Marvin Carlson, *Theories of the Theatre: A Historical and Critical Survey, from the Greeks to the Present* (Ithaca, NY: Cornell University Press, 1993).

words, the study focuses on a period whose significance for any comprehensive appreciation of theatre's relation to its political, cultural and social dimension lies in understanding how that period gave rise to what Foucault called a new art of government: 'The classical age developed . . . what could be called an "art of governing", in the sense in which "government" was then understood as precisely the "government" of children, the "government" of the mad, the "government" of the poor, and before long, the "government" of workers.'[24] This new art of government sees a crucial extension of the meaning of government, beyond its restriction by jurists to questions of sovereignty, to incorporate areas as diverse as household economy, the conduct of the self, the security of the state and the management of populations. Third, the study of the theatre in relation to this history of the development of the problem of governance would be far too onerous were it not possible to delimit it in some way. Given that the London stage found itself frequently at the epicentre of significant developments in the tactics of government, it provides a good basis for a series of case histories, however incomplete they may be.

By the same token, this incompleteness offers a clue as to why the task is undoubtedly challenging. As my objective is not to understand what theatre means, as a set of practices in and of themselves, but rather to see how it was deployed and constituted within a wider field of discourses of governance in general, a substantial portion of these case histories necessarily refers to non-theatrical history. In this sense, what this study shall refer to as the 'discourse on theatre' must be grasped in terms of what Foucault once described as 'a system of dispersion'.[25] To employ a further Foucauldian image: the discourse on theatre might be seen to comprise a 'great surface'[26] where heterogeneous objects, dispersed in both temporal and regional locales, are collected together.[27]

It is a system in which the utterances of legislators, jurists and magistrates converge with those of playwrights, players, critics and theatre

[24] Michel Foucault, *Abnormal, Lectures at the Collège de France, 1974–1975*, trans. Graham Burchell (New York: Picador, 2003), pp. 48–49.

[25] Michel Foucault, *The Archaeology of Knowledge*, trans. A.M. Sheridan Smith (New York: Pantheon, 1972), p. 38.

[26] *Ibid.*, p. 79.

[27] For Foucault, a discourse is not a 'text', it is an event: 'An event is always a dispersion; a multiplicity. It is what takes place here and there; it is polycephalous. By discursive event I do not understand an event that occurs in a discourse, in a text. But it is an event which is dispersed between institutions, laws, political victories and defeats, demands, behaviours, revolts, reactions.' Michel Foucault, 17 March 1971, *Lectures on the Will to Know, Lectures at the Collège de France 1970–1971 and Oedipal Knowledge*, trans. Graham Burchell (Basingstoke: Palgrave Macmillan, 2013), p. 194.

managers. Here, in a move that may well infuriate those who insist on maintaining a stark disciplinary division between the study of 'theatre' and the study of 'drama', I take plays to be a source of discursive statements equal to any found in anti-theatrical pamphlets, or to treatises aimed at teaching the virtues or otherwise of declamatory style in performance. Thus, if one asks: what will count as a statement? I answer, as Foucault does: any unit of the discourse – including thereby sources as diverse as plays, playbills, authorial prologues, prefaces and dedications, along with texts on personal conduct, household economy, treatises on poetry, theatrical criticism, and so on. The discourse on theatre presents a formidably expansive surface upon which the theological and moral concerns over the stage in one age were able to encounter the new economic realities of another – the age of political economy, for instance – only to then become further adopted by an emerging social economy, as part of its agenda of reform. It is a place where innovative modalities of dissemination, such as the development of the printing press and the mass production of pamphlets, procured new domains of influence, enabling the reactivation of ancient thematic concerns over the stage, but in highly differentiated and transformed contexts. In short, the task that I set myself in this study was to describe these complex correlations of statements, separated by profession and background, rhetorical style and purpose, as being nevertheless subjacent and contiguous, whether in reference to the domains of law, theology, criminal justice or political economy, and to do so in terms of the formation of that discursive group for whom the governance of the stage is a matter of the profoundest concern.

Presenting the discourse on theatre as fully as possible has meant reversing the obfuscations that arise by placing undue emphasis solely on anti-theatrical sentiments; but it has also, more profoundly, meant opposing the idea that one must begin with something akin to an anthropological constant in order to assimilate the history of anti-theatrical discourses to it, as though they constituted a kind of opaque datum that would, with enough effort, be forced to reveal their innermost secret – that 'kernel' of the prejudice that 'would seem to reflect something permanent about the way we think of ourselves and our lives'.[28] It is not that I dispute the existence of anti-theatrical discourses, of course – they form a

[28] Barish, *The Anti-theatrical Prejudice*, p. 2: 'The fact that the disapproval of the theatre is capable of persisting through so many transformations of culture, so many dislocations of time and place, suggests a permanent kernel of distrust waiting to be activated by the more superficial irritants' (p. 4). What lies behind the fear and loathing of the stage will turn out to be 'a rage for authenticity' (p. 464), which signals an implicit reduction of the discourses of anti-theatricalism to the

significant part of the discourse on theatre; but I do seek to reverse the logic of the anti-theatrical prejudice – to invert the force of its rhetoric. Thus, whereas Barish argues that the 'specific evils' and 'presumptive effects' of the theatre are to be passed over 'lightly' as 'local considerations' and that the task is to reveal what is said about it in its 'essence', for the purposes of the kind of genealogical study I am engaged in here, such an approach could not be any more egregiously misleading. My tactic has been, on the contrary, to stick to the local effects, to see each statement as a singular event and to set it against the backdrop of a wider field of statements that are to be preserved in their specific locality.

There is one final reason for departing from the orientation set by the anti-theatrical prejudice, and it is this: I seek to displace the thematic concern with the stage away from the standard preoccupation within theatre studies with mimesis and theatricalism in order to refocus the debate on a prejudice that I take to be rather more mundane but that is nonetheless essential to the formation of the discourse on theatre. I call this the 'theatrocratic prejudice', understanding it, in plain terms, as the prejudice against common life. To explain what this shift entails I would like to turn now in more detail to the problem of government in the modern period.

The 'Governmentalisation' of the Stage

In his book *Theatre and Citizenship*, David Wiles presents his reader with a compellingly woven narrative that describes the history of theatre in terms of what he calls the 'social practice' of citizenship, whose ethic of participation theatre is said to embody. Characterising the core mission of theatre in essentially civic terms, Wiles claims that the purpose of theatre is to create communities – a characterisation that at the same time inevitably assigns theatre to a quintessentially pre-modern identity: 'It is, I shall argue, the very nature and purpose of theatre to create communities, and most forms of pre-modern theatre maximised the audience's awareness that it embodied a community that transcended familial and neighbourly relations.'[29]

psychological and existential dimension of the subject who craves 'some form of anti-theatrical self-transcendence in the deepest corner of its own being' (p. 464). At the heart of the anti-theatrical prejudice, then, is a *subjective* fear motivated by the threat of theatricality – that we are not what we appear to be; that our identities are not fixed or stable but are in a constant process of negotiating difference (p. 469).

[29] David Wiles, *Theatre and Citizenship: The History of a Practice* (Cambridge: Cambridge University Press, 2011), p. 8.

Now, it should be said – and Wiles is well aware of this – that modern theatre is far from being self-evidently predicated on the formation of a community. On the contrary, there is something essentially troubling about the modern theatre audience, once placed in relation to the mythic theatrical communitas of the ancient world, upon which Wiles's treatment of his topic rests: the 'pendulum swing towards individualism' has eroded the basis on which a 'communitarian account of theatre spectatorship'[30] might be constructed, where the audience is not merely a passive receiver of experience, but involved actively within a community of 'co-perceivers'.[31] The problem is that the theatre has never been 'less connected to the public sphere of the citizen'.[32] Nevertheless Wiles insists: 'It is in the public sphere that theatre and citizenship converge.'[33] How to reconcile these two statements? On the one hand, it is necessary to reconnect theatre to its original mission, which is that of 'the making of an active citizenship';[34] and on the other, one must invoke the ancient power of the stage in order to invigorate and reanimate a moribund public sphere. In this way, what becomes visible is the considerable ambition behind Wiles's project: 'only in the domain [of the public sphere] can the practice of theatre coalesce with the practice of citizenship.'[35] There are, nevertheless, significant obstacles confronting such a project and not least the obstacle of the public sphere itself.

First, it is true to say that without the kind of democratic openness identified with the formation of the public sphere, it is hard to speak with confidence of the institutional solidity of the modern democratic state and its processes. Wiles is right to claim that 'it becomes increasingly irrelevant to talk of democracy in the absence of a functional "public sphere".'[36] In *The Structural Transformation of the Public Sphere*, Habermas had already theorised the causes behind the dysfunctional failures of the public sphere. By the late 1800s, two related tendencies had already become discernible, or so that book argued, both symptomatic of the breakdown of the public sphere. The first is that it lost its 'political function'; the second is that it lost sight of its founding principle: that publicity should be critical.[37] By the twentieth century the collapse of the public sphere was all but consolidated with the development of mass consumerism and the colonisation of the life-world by the instrumental forces unleashed by late capitalism.

[30] *Ibid.*, p. 21. [31] *Ibid.*, p. 15. [32] *Ibid.*, p. 10. [33] *Ibid.*, p. 208. [34] *Ibid.*, p. 208.
[35] *Ibid.*, p. 21. [36] *Ibid.*, p. 208.
[37] Jürgen Habermas, *The Structural Transformation of the Public Sphere*, trans. Thomas Burger (Cambridge: Polity Press, [1962] 2008), p. 140.

These conspired to produce a systemic crisis triggered by the massive expansion of the bureaucratic administrative apparatus of the modern state – what Habermas called a 'legitimation crisis'.[38] Now subject to the manipulations of a populist press that reinforces public misconceptions, recidivist sentiments and prejudices, the public sphere can no longer be said to engender that sense of communal identity, critical reason or civic responsibility essential to the construction of that civic-minded person, that critical individual, once designated by the term 'citizen'.

All the same, several questions intrude upon the grounds of this debate. It might be asked in the first instance whether such a rational sphere of public discourse ever truly existed – something that seems to me to be highly questionable. It might also be asked whether, in order to comprehend the full extent of the dilemma confronting a project hoping to construct a modern citizenry, it is necessary to confront the prior question of how subjects are formed within the modern practices of governance: is the political project of modernity founded on the presupposition of an autonomous public sphere, populated by autonomous agents, or upon something else? If so, what of this something else that resides within the recesses and furrows of the discourse of the public sphere – its subjects and their apparent autonomy? This leads to the following series of subsidiary questions: by what historical derivation does the meaning of the term 'the public' emerge? Through what discursive mechanism was something like 'public man' first able to make his appearance on the world stage? According to what strategic imperatives and determined by what regulative ends was the 'freedom of speech' endorsed and encouraged? Located within which precise limits and interests was 'opinion' first invested with the power of criticism over matters of public economy? And finally: in terms of what instruments of inclusion and exclusion was a public sphere able to be constituted? These issues will be addressed in detail in Part II of the book when I consider the context of eighteenth-century theatre publics; suffice it to say here that the problematic way in which a public is constituted will have an inevitable impact on how Wiles's assertion is to be understood: that the theatre was 'for centuries a place of public encounter where opinion was shaped and relations of power negotiated'.[39] As shall be seen in Chapters 3, 4 and 5, there are several reasons Wiles's reader should pause before accepting such an assertion. Excepting a few well-chosen examples, it would seem that the idea that theatre is a place for

38 See Jürgen Habermas, *Legitimation Crisis*, trans. T. McCarthy (London: Heinemann, 1976).
39 Wiles, *Citizenship*, p. 208.

'the making of an active citizenship' has always been something of an aspiration rather than a reality.

In order to put this aspiration fully into relief, I propose to situate the development of the modern European stage in the context of a twofold historical movement that comes into being during the eighteenth century. The first is centripetal and draws the theatre increasingly towards a new centre of power, constructed around the formation of a unique and powerful discursivity – the public of *Homo economicus*. The other is centrifugal. It enacts a twofold displacement and marginalisation, not to say discursive exclusion – first of the old centre of court power and its broader radius of influence, associated with the system of nobility, secured by landed wealth; and second, through the disciplinary confinement of the labouring population, along with the corresponding patriarchal confinement of women to the domestic and private sphere. It is no accident that just as the public produces an exemplary historical figure in the form of protean economic man, it simultaneously finds its mirror image reflected back to it in the ghastly shape of *Homo penalis*, a figure of shame and ignominy, who will become the disciplinary subject of the new penitentiary system of the eighteenth and nineteenth centuries.

To be sure, Wiles by no means endorses an uncomplicated idea of the public sphere any more than does Habermas, who identified the structural contradiction at its heart in the equation: 'homme = citoyen = property owner'.[40] But what this points to is an unresolved tension in citizen debates, particularly insofar as they rely on the ideal formation of the public sphere. On the one hand, the citizen is understood to occupy a space of public reason whose rationality is in no way meant to be occluded by the opacity of the specific historical conditions of emergence of this individual. The citizen is in principle the agent of free, rational debate and choice, unalloyed by the material context by which he is historically constituted. On the other hand, the citizen is indelibly associated with the historical context that saw his emergence onto the world stage, just as the medium for that appearance – the public sphere – is itself shot through with all the contradictions that supported and necessitated its discovery. Those contradictions are not merely incidental, but fundamental. Both the public sphere and public man are tied historically to the domination of civil society through the new conditions of ownership and the legal apparatus that supported the development of private property. It is for this reason, too, that theatre must find itself also subject to the selfsame

[40] Habermas, *Structural Transformation*, pp. 55–56, 87; Wiles, *Citizenship*, p. 209.

double-bind that benights the history of a reasoning public. It is, in Wiles, both a historically constructed space determined by wider forces that condition its mode of appearance, and the ideal site of the 'face-to-face' encounter, where the dream of citizenship wins its privileged place – notwithstanding the backdrop of pillage that made it possible.

One thing, then, remains axiomatic for Wiles: regardless of the historical contradictions at play within its history, theatre still produces a space of universality, where a public can enjoy the arts of public reasoning – of 'communicative interconnectedness involving the mutual recognition of truth claims'.[41] The theatre retains this promise, located at its point of origin, which was never quite lost in its passage through modernity: 'theatre,' says Wiles, 'remains a uniquely valuable testing ground for citizenship both because it brings citizens face to face in an interactive space, and because of its history.'[42]

It seems to me, though, that this final clause, '*and* because of its history', introduced by a subtle grammatical cut, whose peculiar effect is to relegate history to the status of an afterthought, reveals the underlying tension in Wiles's argument: in short, it reproduces that caesura that indicates the fundamental misalignment of these two *topoi*, which the connective 'and' cannot quite conceal. What this misalignment indicates is a conflict between, on the one hand, the space opened up by philosophy and, on the other, that opened by history itself. What is disclosed is the existence of a contradiction between the 'interactive space' of citizenship – where theatre is grasped as a pedagogical practice, designed to inculcate civic virtues in its audience, or cultivate an ethic of communal responsibility, and so on – and the material history of the stage itself and what that history actually reveals regarding the pedagogical uses made of theatre, when viewed in terms of the problem of modern governance.

I would like to touch briefly on the nature of that contradiction by showing how the fate of the stage is inexorably bound by its own history to the logic of modern governance. In Rousseau's notorious attack on the stage in the *Letter to Monsieur D'Alembert* an intriguing puzzle emerges. Rousseau argues that the stage can never be employed as a means of cultivating civic virtue; and yet nevertheless he offers the following maxim: 'when the people is corrupted, the theatre is good for it, and bad for it when it is itself good.'[43] How can the theatre be good for a corrupted

[41] Wiles, *Citizenship*, p. 211. [42] *Ibid.*, p. 223.
[43] Jean-Jacques Rousseau, *Politics and the Arts*, trans. Allan Bloom (Ithaca, NY: Cornell University Press, 1960), p. 65.

people, if the theatre cannot instil civic values in them? What is proposed here should not be dismissed as one of Rousseau's rhetorical contrivances; in fact, it goes to the heart of the problem, confounding the aspiration to produce a political culture founded on a participatory ethic. The answer to the question brings the debate on citizenship back precisely to the problem of modern governance, which Rousseau perceptively identified in the third book of the *Social Contract*. In large modern states and cities, the brute numerical facts of population mitigate against any meaningful participation of citizens in the running of the state. There is, simply put, no assembly large enough to contain it; therefore, in such a state the people can no more exercise their sovereignty than they can exert any tangible influence over the policies and decisions of government. The idea of modern governance, moreover, corresponds precisely to a new political logic founded on this calculus of population that, with the invention of statistics, soon became the principal tool of political economy. It sees a fundamental shift in political organisation away from a polity based on notions of citizenship and freedom, towards a polity based on domination of the population by means of policy. Foucault termed this process the 'governmentalisation of the state'. What he meant by this somewhat ugly formulation can be simplified to the following idea: that the art of government encourages the citizen to live outside the dimension of the political but not outside the dimension of governance. This is the meaning of the term 'domination' – the cultivation of a passive, politically inert and docile citizenry for the sake of better economic management of the population and the productive resources of the state.

It is in light of this art of calculation, by which government equates to the best result according to the most expedient and pragmatic means, that Rousseau's maxim on the role of modern theatre is to be understood. By the same token, I would suggest that what Rousseau describes, albeit at a very early point in the process, is what I shall refer to in this study as 'the governmentalisation of the stage':

> in a big city . . . the police can never increase the number of pleasures permitted too much or apply itself too much to making them agreeable in order to deprive individuals of the temptation of seeking more dangerous ones. Since preventing them from occupying themselves is to prevent them from doing harm, two hours a day stolen from the activity of vice [by attending the theatre] prevents the twelfth part of the crimes that would be committed.[44]

[44] Rousseau, *Politics and the Arts*, pp. 58–59.

This governmentalisation of the stage, which I explore fully in Part III of this book, is an inexorable consequence of the historical development of the discourse on the theatre in the modern period of government. Notwithstanding the contradiction that permits the polemical division of this discourse into pro-and anti-theatrical statements, both aspects will therefore be understood here as colluding in the same process of governmentalisation: both contribute to the discovery of the uses and abuses of the modern stage, by which it will be regulated and managed; and, inevitably, both must be understood in terms of their insertion into the broader field of discourses of governance that motivate them.

The Theatrocratic Prejudice

To return to the Platonic theme with which I began, my primary subject in this book is the development of the discourse on the theatre insofar as it belongs to a wider field of discourses whose concern lies at the heart of the problem of modern governance. It is a problem that proliferates around two mutually intersecting yet irreducible poles, those of 'order and disorder', which both play constitutive and limiting roles in the formation of modern society. For the sake of convenience, I will collectivise these discourses under the rubric of 'theatrocratic discourse'. The concept of theatrocracy has, of course, been studied before, but it has never been approached with a view to grasping it in terms of the historical problem of governance that lies at the centre of this study. What is peculiar about this fact is that, for Plato, theatrocracy is understood explicitly as a problem for and of government. In *Stay Illusion! The Hamlet Doctrine* by Simon Critchley and Jamieson Webster, while this is fleetingly acknowledged, the theatrocratic problem is no sooner raised than it is subsumed under the Debordian crisis engendered by a post-modern politics of the spectacle: 'political power passes through theatrical display.' Theatrocracy thus denotes a politics 'that legitimates itself through the production of theatrical or mediatic illusion that gives the impression of legitimacy without any genuine substance'.[45] The problem with this interpretation is not that it is entirely wrong but that it too hastily embraces the standard Platonic idea of representation that combines theatre as conceit with the politics of deception and illusion – that is to say, it threatens to reduce theatrocracy to the phenomenal and immaterial dimension of ideology, thereby

[45] Simon Critchley and Jamieson Webster, *Stay Illusion! The Hamlet Doctrine* (New York: Pantheon, 2013), p. 15.

overlooking the material level of discursive practices that are identified by Foucault with the techniques, strategies and tactics of government. A similar reading can be found in Samuel Weber's *Theatricality as Medium* where a theatrocracy of the mediated spectacle produces those 'dividuals' whose identity is constitutively split by their participation in the spectacle. They are the consumers of television who find themselves caught in a perpetual cycle of mediatic interruption:

> 'Give me a break!' (from the break) – this is the unsung plaint of theatrocracy today. The media respond by interrupting their programs to bring a special announcement. The more catastrophic the message, the better, so long as it fills the 'break' that separates viewers of the broadcast media today and enables them to 'survive' the spectacle they behold.[46]

A quite different and more historically nuanced approach to the problem of theatrocracy can be found in Martin Puchner's intriguing if heterodox interpretation of Plato, in *The Drama of Ideas*. For Puchner, theatrocracy is the 'rule of the audience over a production',[47] which he then develops to incorporate the problem of democracy that is central to the present study:

> Plato's attack on tragedy and his view of theatre also have a strong political valence. Tragedy, with its emphasis on a chorus composed of citizens and its mode of presentation in front of a good portion of the citizenry of Athens, was closely associated with democracy. Hence Plato's critique of the democratic audience as a 'theatrocracy', a kind of mob rule caused by playwrights who, without proper philosophical knowledge, incite the baser emotions of the audience.[48]

Puchner, however, wishes to rescue Plato from any suggestion of anachronism resulting from Plato's anti-democratic pronouncements. If Plato takes an 'anti-democratic' stance, it is not due to any propensity towards elitism, Puchner insists. On the contrary, a more nuanced reading will show that Plato held an 'ideal of a fragile educational process that is in principle open to anyone' and that he was against the 'conspiratorial rule of the few, a class-based oligarchy that meets behind closed doors'.[49] Puchner later argues that Plato's own form of 'anti-tragic' drama anticipates the 'widespread sense that the modern world, with its belief in human agency, progress, and democracy, is fundamentally at odds with the harsh world-view of tragedy'.[50] In 'dramatic Platonism' – Puchner's name for Plato's theatricalised dialogues – tragedy is transformed into 'something new and

[46] Samuel Weber, *Theatricality as Medium* (New York: Fordham University Press, 2004), p. 53.
[47] Puchner, *Drama of Ideas*, p. 26. [48] *Ibid.*, p. 28. [49] *Ibid.* [50] *Ibid.*, p. 73.

better'.[51] It is for the sake of understanding what this new and better drama might be, writes Puchner, that 'Plato must be rescued from the friends and enemies of the theatre alike'.[52] Insofar as both misunderstand the Platonic attack on the stage, both misunderstand Plato's intentions – namely, that Plato was 'not an enemy of the theatre but a radical reformer'.[53]

But in fact there are two ways of understanding the issue of reform historically. The first asserts the stage itself is in *need* of reform; the second is that the stage is an *instrument* of reform. While it is far from clear what that reform entails for Puchner, it is clear that, within the history of the discourse on theatre, a reformed and reforming stage correspond to the increased influence of government over the stage – an influence whose provenance is indeed Platonic. This influence was most explicitly felt over the seventeenth and eighteenth centuries when, under the weight of the neo-Stoic revival during the period, Plato was translated into several European languages for the first time. An abridged works appeared in English in 1701; a French translation of the *Republic* – *La Republique de Platon; au de juste, et de l'injuste* – appeared in 1726, with English translations in 1763 and 1800. It is hardly surprising, then, to find, during the same period, a wave of Socratic plays being written, some for production, but many for literary consumption such as George Stubbes's *A Dialogue on Beauty in the Manner of Plato* (1731). It is worth remarking how Stubbes himself characterised his dialogue as a 'not uninstructive entertainment for young Ladies, even of the highest Rank'.[54] His dialogue will lead its young female reader, he asserts, 'with Pleasure thro' a System of Beauty entirely new to her, and discover to her View the Secret Foundations of Moral Excellence'.[55] What this brief example makes visible is three things: the moral nature of reform; that it requires a pedagogical approach; and that its aim is the cultivation and improvement of the student. It is due to this insistence on combining moral improvement, reform and education that eighteenth-century writers were drawn to Plato. In his 'Discourse on Plato', Henry Spens, the translator of the English edition of the *Republic*, published in 1763, would proclaim:

> Education is here represented as the foundation of government, and the finer arts as the handmaidens of virtue. The least attention to such

[51] *Ibid.*, p. 10. [52] *Ibid.*, p. 7. [53] *Ibid.*, p. 5.

[54] George Stubbes, *A Dialogue on Beauty in the Manner of Plato* (London: W. Wilkins, 1731), p. vi.

[55] *Ibid.*, p. vii. For an interesting reading of Stubbes's play, see Michael Prince, *Philosophical Dialogue in the British Enlightenment: Theology, Aesthetics, and the Novel* (Cambridge: University of Cambridge Press, 1996), pp. 175–79.

> principles as these, may help promote the taste for true politeness; and a more thorough acquaintance with them may give us the knowledge of ourselves, and raise the mind to the sublimest contemplations.[56]

If the translation of this 'philosophic play', as Spens labels it, is to 'recommend philosophy to the politer part of mankind',[57] one also finds a more explicitly political meaning in its characterisation of the impolite part of the community. The *Republic*, says Spens, serves to warn of the dangers of democracy for those who possess a genuine interest in lawfulness – that is, for those who wish to live by the 'wise institutions of government, and just maxims of virtue'.[58] The problem is that in 'every Democracy the people are enemies of the good'[59] and not least because, as was the case in Plato's Athens, the 'credulous multitude' fall under the baleful influence of the stage: 'The common people had a set of instructors, of their own, who served them at an easy rate; namely the poets; and their rehearsers, and expanders, the rhapsodists.' On the other hand, insofar as 'the poets wrote to please the multitude', they fell under the baleful influence of the audience and consequently became 'the great supporters and promoters of the religion of the vulgar'.[60]

It is in Spens's use of the word 'common' that the fundamental object of concern that unceasingly feeds the discourse on the theatre asserts itself most prominently. In its most direct and unambiguous sense, this object will be equated with the people themselves who are the subject of theatrocratic discourse – that 'monster with innumerable heads',[61] but it will also refer to democratic phenomena more broadly, assuming multiple and diffuse forms, where democracy will be characterised not as a mode of government but as disorderly phenomena, and identified most explicitly with 'the disorders of the stage [and the] licentious impunity' it encourages.[62] What lies behind the discourse on the theatre, in other words, is less a pathological hatred of the stage, an 'anti-theatrical prejudice', than it is an irreconcilable and profound contempt for common life – an anti-theatrocratic prejudice. It is in this sense that the suspicion with which democracy is almost ubiquitously viewed is to be comprehended. It is, writes Spens, 'like a ship, perpetually tossed by the billows of popular sedition'.[63]

*

[56] Henry Spens, 'Introduction', in *The Republic of Plato. In Ten Books*, trans. Henry Spens (Glasgow, 1773), p. vi.
[57] *Ibid.* [58] *Ibid.*, p. xi. [59] *Ibid.* [60] *Ibid.*, p. xi. [61] *Ibid.*, p. xxxi. [62] *Ibid.*
[63] *Ibid.*, p. ix.

It is, then, this anti-theatrocratic prejudice that I pursue through the pages of this book in seeking to trace a genealogy of the governmental discourse on the theatre. Acknowledging the complexity of the subject, however, as well as the considerable historical breadth of the study, I have tried to facilitate the reader's journey through the book by dividing it into three broad parts. Part I deals with the embryonic formation of the discourse on the theatre during the early modern period, covering the years prior to the English civil war when the public theatres flourished, before picking up the threads of the debate following the interregnum with the reopening of the theatres during the Restoration. Specifically, Chapter 1 seeks to identify the origin of the discourse on theatre amidst the tumult and chaos of early modern London, where an itinerant population, comprising swathes of the dispossessed rural peasantry, began to descend on the capital stoking fears of disorder, vagabondage and criminality. With 'masterless men' drawn to the new public theatres, the stage provides the locus for an emergent discourse of government that began to associate the democratic licence of the audience with the vices of the multitude. Rather than accounting for this discourse on the government of the theatre as resulting primarily from Puritan opposition to the stage, I draw attention instead to a more complex array of forces and sundry influences that frame theatrocratic discourse as a discourse on the government of common life. Three particular areas are of interest insofar as they coalesce in forming the nascent discourse on the theatre: first, the development in Italy of a novel conception of government, with the appearance of the theory of 'reason of state', which quickly spread throughout Europe, and in which it is the people rather than the prince and his court who constitute the primary goal for political intervention; second, the appropriation of forms of religious moralisation by governmental logics, exemplified by the anti-theatrical discourses of the period; and third, the figure of multitude that will be used by contemporary commentators to characterise the audience with its base and unruly disposition.

Where the first chapter commences my narrative with the need to master the multitude in early modern London and its theatres, Chapter 2 proceeds to consider a different set of needs, agendas and calculations – in short, a changed set of governmental problems and initiatives, shaped by the new context of the theatres following the return of the monarchy in 1660. Here I chart a move from the earlier debates focused on the necessity of governing an unruly multitude to a cognate necessity: of how to govern the unruly individual, and the extent to which individual freedom of conduct is a threat to civic order. A key moment in this debate, as far as the theatres are concerned, is the Jeremy Collier stage controversy. The chapter situates Collier's critique of the stage in relation to its wider discursive context – paying particular attention to the increasing grip that new forms of patriarchal power exerted over the family. I argue that the notoriety of the Restoration stage, with its exemplary figure, the libertine, can best be understood in the context of a discursive struggle against the emergent governmentality that sought to exercise control over the conduct of individuals. It is in relation to this notion of the government of individual conducts that I identify a novel form of governmental power, unique to the modern form of government, which – in modifying Foucault's analysis of the Christian pastorate – I designate 'deontic power', thus signifying the profoundly moral nature of modern governance.

In Part II, I turn to consider the political constitution of theatrical and other publics during the eighteenth century. Chapter 3 provides a broad contextual background for the two more focused case histories that comprise Chapters 4 and 5, by placing a particular emphasis on the agonistic milieu that characterised the emergent bourgeois public sphere. The stage is situated in Chapter 3 at the forefront of a fiercely contested struggle over what constitutes the appropriate limit for political criticism – of what can and cannot be said through satire – as well as its proper site and location. The social position of the stage, its catachrestic forms of speech, the ambiguity of its effects, so difficult to control or to predict, as well as its fluctuating audience demographics, make the theatre a wholly inappropriate place to engage in political criticism – arguments that culminated in the licensing act of 1737 and that were central to Walpole's successful attempt to remove forms of satirical criticism from the stage.

The chapter's remit is also wider: it is to show how theatrical publics came to be delimited by forms of discursive exclusion. It shows how the figure of the plebeian, in particular, came to represent the external limit through which the identity of the public was confirmed. The mob who lined the route to Tyburn crystallised in particular this image of a dangerous and uncontrollable plebeian throng; it comes to exemplify, within discourses of governance, what I call the 'excluded commons', whose amplification in discourses on crime and violence, during the century, produced the paradoxical effect of rendering that commons ever more visible. In Chapter 4, I pursue this notion of a theatricalised commons in a case history on what is perhaps the century's most notorious, yet popular, play: *The Beggar's Opera*, first performed in 1728. The chapter shows how theatrocratic concerns over the stage were intensified by the figure of Macheath, who substitutes the highway robber for the aristocratic libertine of Restoration drama. If *The Beggar's Opera* represents, for the discourse on theatre, the worst excesses of theatrocratic licence, George Lillo's domestic tragedy *The London Merchant* provides a diametrically opposite example: the model for a theatre capable of reforming its audience. Thus the topic of Chapter 5 is the identification of a theatre that will be entirely consistent with the ends of government. I draw on feminist readings of the play to show how a discourse of government, aimed specifically at inculcating an ethic of work within London's apprentice classes, was promoted through the play's advocacy of exclusively male homosocial relations. In homosociality one finds the appropriate form of conduct in the government of recreational time for 'men of business'.

Part III takes up the problem of the legislation of the stage, with significant developments in governmental control over theatres occurring throughout the course of the nineteenth century. My argument in Chapter 6 turns on the question not of how theatre, but rather of how *theatres*, should be governed: how notions of both extending the franchise and controlling the 'multitude' are practically worked out through the ongoing legislative debates about copyright, censorship, monopoly and the extent of the theatrical market – and even the possibility of deciding, through normative prescription, what should be the preserve of the 'national drama' (and what forms of theatre should be refused such an honour). While the normative issues proved difficult to resolve, the chapter shows how they were nonetheless useful in settling many of the practical complexities thrown up by debates over how the theatres should be governed. In particular, it permitted the demarcation of the theatre from the music hall, thus instituting a legislative apparatus predicated on a clear understanding of social distinction. The consequences of these legislative debates are explored in Chapter 7, when I attend to the material *dispositif* of the theatre, which emerged from the ways in which the discourses on theatre and democracy came to be imbricated in the architectural designs of theatre buildings, particularly those repurposed as bourgeois-friendly venues in the final decades of the nineteenth century. The book concludes by showing how the theatre *dispositif*, made possible by new forms of local government administration, provided the means for resolving the ongoing controversy over theatre censorship – something forcefully advocated by George Bernard Shaw during his appearance before the Select Committee of 1909. Although the contentious issue of censorship continued to dominate debates well into the twentieth century, I suggest that in Shaw's remarkable intervention we can nevertheless identify the culmination of the discourse on theatre, both its terminal point and lasting effect on the modern stage. What Shaw's involvement crystallises is the thought of the eclipse of the discourse on theatre; and while he does not exactly announce its abrupt end, he nonetheless fully articulates the beginning of its eventual disappearance as 'discourse'. This is revealed through Shaw's rather shocking demand: that government involvement in theatre governance should be limited to providing a practicable legal framework in which the theatre can be permitted to be *immoral.* The discursive import of this argument is twofold: first, that it overturns the entire deontic logic that had to this point dominated the discourses of the stage; second, that while it demands that the stage be liberated from arbitrary interference by government, at the same time it accepts the settlement – central to the theatre *dispositif* of the nineteenth century – that would see the consolidation of the anti-theatrocratic prejudice through the permanent exclusion of common and vulgar tastes from the theatre. This is the paradoxical price Shaw's 'immoral theatre' was, of course, prepared to pay for its cerebral autonomy; but it is also – I would suggest – part of the lasting legacy of the genealogy of the discourse on the theatre, continuing to influence the way theatre governance is understood today.

PART I

Origins of the Discourse on Theatre

CHAPTER 1
The Theatre of the Multitude

Introduction

When London's public theatres began to emerge during the 1570s they did so during a period of rapid development and growth for that city and against a backdrop of widely circulating fears and incipient threats to the state over food security, public health, crime and the 'evils' of vagrancy, and the multiple disorders associated with indigence. To understand the scale of the socio-economic problems that confronted London's municipal authority at the time, one need merely remark that between 1520 and 1600 London's population expanded from 60,000 to 250,000,[1] when it accounted for 5 per cent of the entire population of England, and produced a city whose size was 'without parallel in contemporary Europe'.[2] By 1650, the population had risen further to an estimated 400,000 people. It is in relation to this wider context of demographic crisis provoked by an unprecedented growth and urban concentration of population that this chapter seeks to understand the emergence of the discourse on the theatre in early modern England, and to discover its principal 'object of enunciation'.[3] That object was not simply the theatre per se, but the theatre given the nature of its audience and its possible effect upon them. If the theatres were immensely popular among those new inhabitants who swelled the retinue of the city's suburbs, it is also true to say that it was those selfsame inhabitants as much as, if not more so than, the presence of theatres in the city that provoked the wrath of its citizens, its governors, aldermen, Justices and magistrates. What London's first theatres produced was thus far more than a merely religious controversy over the 'morality' of the

[1] D.B. Grigg, *Population Growth and Agrarian Change: An Historical Perspective* (Cambridge: Cambridge University Press, 1980), p. 95.

[2] Robert Allan Houston, *The Population History of Britain and Ireland 1550–1750* (Cambridge: Cambridge University Press, 1995), pp. 20–21.

[3] Foucault, *Archaeology of Knowledge*, p. 194.

stage, as is commonly believed: they produced the first articulation of that modern discourse belonging to a newly emergent field of government.

This is to say that the discourse on theatre belongs to a discourse and indeed a practice of government that is very much discovered for the first time during this period. The pervasiveness of the new discourse on governance is reflected not only in the way it was used to condemn the stage; it was also invoked in arguments by those who sought to defend it. In the anonymous pamphlet petitioning for the reopening of the theatres in 1643, a year after their closure, the attempt is made to reassure government that theatres pose no threat to the Commonwealth and precisely because they themselves are already circumscribed by government. For these pamphleteers, the governmental suppression or restraint of the stage is unnecessary and heavy-handed, since the theatres, unlike the bear gardens, which incidentally remained open to 'rioting companions resorting thither with as much freedome as formerly', are 'well reformed' and the 'disturbers of the publike peace . . . dare not be seen in our civill and well-governed theatres, where none use to come but the best of the Nobility and Gentry'.[4] The stage, notwithstanding the specious sanctity of this proclamation, is something that can and ought to be subject to governance – something that both detractors and supporters agreed upon, even if for opposing reasons, with divergent motivations, and with conflicting ends in mind.

It is by no means simply the factual problems associated with population growth that account for the development of the discourse of government, however. The abundance of governmental discourses in the late Renaissance testifies to something else, something discernible only beneath the level of apparent fact: that an epistemic upheaval had occurred that began to transform the very concept of government and the way it was to be practiced. The sudden profusion of discourse about government not only signalled a shift in how government was to be thought; it also pointed to an underlying event that made the very appearance of a modern discourse of government possible at the same time as it invalidated a concept of government that had dominated the West over the previous millennia. The theatre was more than circumstantially connected to this event. During the early modern period, the image of government frequently invoked the metaphor of '*theatrum mundi*' – the idea, as discussed in the introduction, that terrestrial government rested on a divine order

[4] *The Actor's Remonstrance, or Complaint: for the Silencing of Their Profession, and Banishment from Their Severall Play-houses* (London, 1643).

where the government of the world was viewed as a vast celestial theatre. *Theatrum mundi* represented the very image of order, fixity and security. It consigned to man both his place and his purpose, so that 'in this most glorious theatre', as Calvin was to put it in his *Institutes of Christian Religion*, 'he may be a spectator [of the works of God]'.[5] Order is thus made visible as theatrical spectacle: 'being placed in this most beautiful theatre, let us not decline to take pious delight in the clear and manifest works of God.'[6] But order is not simply divinely ordained spectacle; it is also to be observed (and reflected) in the social hierarchy. For Thomas Elyot, in *The Book Named the Govenour*,

> Forasmuch as Plebs in Latin, and Commoners in English, be words only made for discrepance of degrees, whereof procedeth order: which in things as well natural as supernatural, hath ever had such pre-eminence, that thereby the incomprehensible majesty of God, as it were by a bright beam of a torch or candle, is declared to the blind inhabitants of this world. Moreover, take away order from all things, what should then remain? Certes, nothing finally, except ... Chaos, which of some is expounded, a confuse mixture.[7]

And yet it is precisely this theatrical image of the government of the world that will be increasingly called into question during the period, just as order will be endlessly invoked and interrogated within the theatre itself. One small remark of Bacon's is perhaps sufficient to demonstrate at this point how easy it was, by the early seventeenth century, to puncture the bloated pretensions that had prolonged and maintained the cosmology underpinning the image of theatre conveyed in the *theatrum* metaphor throughout the medieval period and well into the Renaissance: 'But men must know,' he wrote, 'that in this theatre of man's life it is reserved only for God and angels to be the lookers on.'[8] What is signified here is as radical as it is subtle. In Bacon, it is as though the theatre metaphor has suddenly been stood on its head and with such alacrity that the whole of reality has been carried along with it, as though in a state of dumbfounded stupefaction.

Except it is precisely because it is not reality, but its 'idolum', that Bacon's commonsense locution '[b]ut men must know ...' is able to seize, with such apparent ease, the world by its roots in order to shake the entire

[5] John Calvin, *Institutes of Christian Religion*, trans. Thomas Norton (London, 1561), p. 86.

[6] *Ibid*., p. 156.

[7] Thomas Elyot, *The Book Named the Govenour* ((London: John Hernaman and Ridgeway and Sons, 1834 [1564]), p. 3.

[8] Francis Bacon, 'The Advancement of Learning', book II in *The Works of Francis Bacon*, vol. 2 (London, 1740), p. 508.

edifice, in order to strike at its very foundations. 'But men must know ...' – as if they did not already – that the world in which they had for so long laboured was nothing but a sham, an empty husk from which nothing of any real worth could ever grow. Where does Bacon's 'great instauration' leave the figure of 'man' if not thrown back upon his world and his own finite resources; and where does this leave the theatre if not, through a complete inversion of its meaning, reduced to the hollow of a world that has been abandoned to itself? No longer does the thought of the world answer to those fixed and eternal forms that Bacon calls the 'shadows of resemblance'; one must abolish those misconceptions,

> which have crept into men's minds from the various dogmas of peculiar systems of philosophy, and also from the perverted rules of demonstration, and these we denominate idols of the theatre: for we regard all the systems of philosophy hitherto received or imagined, as so many plays brought out and performed, creating fictitious and theatrical worlds.[9]

For this reason, not only does the discourse on theatre emerge during a period of profound epistemic crisis; in many respects it articulates that crisis at its most extreme point of torsion. It is in this sense that the theatre, understood in metaphorical terms, as a paradigm of government, as a 'Platonic theatre', cannot escape the collapse of that regime of knowledge to which it had owed its prestige during the middle ages. At the same time, the period sees the emergence of a new kind of theatre – the public theatres that grew up around the outer fringes of London – that increasingly became the locus of concerns over population that would be central to the new logic of government, which in many respects that epistemic crisis necessitated.

My aim, over the ensuing pages, will be to flesh out some of these wider issues so as to uncover the peculiar discursive shifts that inform the conceptual and historical emergence of the modern discourse on the stage at its point of origin. The chapter is concerned not so much with the practicalities of governing the stage, which I shall consider in later chapters, but with drawing a connection between the development of government (emerging as a specific problem in the modern period) and the impact such a revolution would have on the image of the theatre at the time. What the chapter describes is not just how that image responded to what might be called the new 'logic of government' that began to assert itself over the

[9] Francis Bacon, 'Novum Organum Scientarium', in *The Works of Francis Bacon*, vol. 4 ([1620] 1815), p. 16.

social and specifically urban sphere during the period – but how and why, at a certain point in its history, a profound transformation occurred in the way the metaphor of the theatre was experienced, a transformation whose meaning I suggest draws the theatre into the orbit of a new 'mentality' of government and which produces the first articulation of the modern discourse on the theatre.

Theatrum mundi and the 'Theatre of the Multitude'

So far, I have suggested that there are two images through which the theatre was thought during the Renaissance, and whose juxtaposition makes visible the principal theme of this study at its point of emergence. The first image is nowhere more explicitly asserted than in what is perhaps the most famous theatre of the age – the Globe Theatre – and relates Elizabethan and Jacobean theatre to the Renaissance commonplace, the 'theatre of the world'. It is referenced in the poem that provides the preface to Thomas Heywood's *An Apology for Actors*, written in 1612 – his defence of the English stage in response to the slandering of the theatre by its critics:

> [Then] our play's begun,
> When we are borne, and to the world first enter,
> And all finde *Exits* when their parts are done.
> If then the world a Theatre present,
> As by the roundnesse it appears most fit,
> Built with starre-galleries of hye ascent,
> In which Jehove doth as spectator sit,
> And chiefe determiner to applaud the best,
> And their indevours crowne with more then merit;
> But by their evill actions doomes the rest,
> To end disgrac't, whilst others praise inherit.
> He that denies then Theatres should be,
> He may as well deny a world to me.[10]

Although Heywood's poem does not mention the Globe Theatre explicitly, it is easy to draw the connection, as Frances Yates once did, for without doubt the Globe Theatre makes reference to the sacred drama intended by the theatrical *topos* as described here and, by implication at least, is meant to share in its piety. As such, Yates argued that the Globe Theatre must be grasped as a 'religious and moral emblem'.[11] Just as

[10] Thomas Heywood, *An Apology for Actors* (London: Garland, 1973 [1612]).
[11] Frances Yates, *Theatre of the World* (Oxon: Routledge, 1987), p. 162.

Heywood 'sees the cosmic theatre as the great moral testing ground on which all men play the parts of their lives in the presence of God',[12] so must the Globe, according to this image, conform to the selfsame moralism with which the metaphor was imbued after two millennia of Christian and stoic thought. With Jacques's melancholic speech on the senselessness of life in *As You Like It*, Shakespeare himself would appear to endorse the basic precepts of the Christian Stoic tradition, with its disdain for common and worldly life. The world is a stage and men and women are merely players upon it. The Globe Theatre itself provides verification of Yates's interpretation. Its motto, which adorned the entrance to the building, was 'Totus mundus agit histrionem'. Moreover, as Ernst Curtius first pointed out, it was borrowed from the *Policraticus*, placing the theatre 'under the banner of the medieval English humanist' John of Salisbury, who it is reckoned was the first to coin the phrase 'theatre of the world'.[13] It is hardly surprising, therefore, that Yates should have arrived at the view that the Globe Theatre epitomised the highest sensibility of the Renaissance, where *theatrum mundi* still 'expressed the world in its groundplan'.[14] In the image of the Globe is a theatre 'the plan of which expressed in simple geometrical symbolism the proportions of the cosmos and of man, the world music and the human music'. It is for this reason that the stage of the Globe is, in her estimation, 'worthy' of Shakespeare's 'genius', for it articulates 'man's destiny in its cosmic setting'.[15]

But there is also another image of the Globe Theatre that is diametrically at odds with the presentation of the theatre regarded as the embodiment of the Renaissance and Neo-Platonic vision of the cosmos. It is located in the image of the audiences who attended public theatres such as the Globe Theatre, and which I will designate 'theatre of the multitude'. In fact Yates's image of the theatre already contains this other image with which it is correlated, an image that is conjured up only so that it may be quarantined: it is the image of a theatre 'disturbed by crowds of people'.[16] It is this other theatre, busy, bustling and teeming with life and bodies, where the theatre of the multitude is understood as existing in opposition to that serene image of an eternal and immobile theatre of the world. The theatre of the multitude is theatre viewed from the perspective of the groundling, thus in relation to the milieu of its audience – evoking an

[12] *Ibid.*, p. 164.

[13] Ernst Curtius, *European Literature and the Latin Middle Ages* (Princeton, NJ: Princeton University Press, 1990), p. 141.

[14] Yates, *Theatre of the World*, p. 171. [15] *Ibid.*, pp. 134–35. [16] *Ibid.*, p. 160.

image of the theatre where performance and actors are autochthonous. I shall return to this second image later on, more thoroughly examining it in using contemporary depictions of those auditors who attended London's public theatres, but in order to do this I would like to first provide a context for the discussion by tarrying a little longer with the idea that the theatre represents 'the world'. First, because one can truly understand an image only once one has grasped what was involved in arriving at its discursive construction, and second, because in order to make way for the second image, in order to understand historically how it resonates more widely with governmental discourses, one must understand the significant transformations in the underlying political rationality of the period. What shall be seen is that the image of the theatre of the multitude, utterly at variance with that transcendent order upon which the first image rests, renders the former meaning of the theatre metaphor increasingly anachronistic and, finally, illegible for the modern age.

It is not just that the image of the theatre is – in this way - deprived of its explicative power, according to which the affairs of men, inserted into the mystical correspondences of macrocosm and microcosm, came to resemble God's providential plan by conforming to preordained notions of hierarchy and order. It also, thereby, signifies the key problem that will be central to the embryonic discourse on the stage as it emerges during the modern period: if, for the modern period, the stage represents a pre-eminently governmental problem, it is not simply because, for the early moderns, it represented the crisis of transcendence, provoked by that vast epistemic rupture that inaugurates modernity. More precisely, it embodies the consequent problem of *immanence* – that is to say, of a world restricted to material and sensuous existence, defined by economy, labour and the market, that will increasingly characterise the conditions of life in the modern epoch. How governmentality slowly emerged as a response to that problem of immanence, and how the stage came to be caught in its web of stratagems, techniques and discursive structures, is the subject of this book. For now, I simply wish to distinguish this new dimension of governance by designating it according to the element within which it moves and where it becomes operative: the logic of government, insofar as it will be conditioned by the field of immanence.

One can quickly understand the significance of this new logic of immanent government by contrasting it with what it is not: the prevailing theory of government during the period in which political power was thought in terms of the exercise of sovereignty. Seventeenth-century political theory was almost exclusively concerned with debating the extent and limits of the Prince's power, the authority and prerogatives of the sovereign, and the nature of constituent power – that is, the extra-juridical rights of the monarch to change or amend the constitution. The theory of sovereignty reaches its clearest formulation during the century in the doctrine of absolutism. It is succinctly summarised by Jean Bodin in his compressed verdict: 'This power is absolute and sovereign, for it has no other condition than what is commanded by the law of God and of nature.'[17] But insofar as the theory of sovereignty conceives political power through the rubric of the legitimacy of the sovereign, as determined by the personage of the Prince and his relation to the law ('a king cannot be subject to the laws'[18]), it is quite incapable of accounting for the discovery of an entirely new object of government, and therefore of that entirely new dimension of governance of concern here. It is an object that, falling 'beneath the sovereign', as Foucault writes, 'eludes him, and this is not the design of Providence or God's Laws but the labyrinths and complexities of the economic field'.[19] What this signifies, in its broadest sense, is that in contrast to transcendent power, configured around the unassailability of the king grasped as the terrestrial representative of the divine, what is announced with the new governmentality, with government by 'means of economy', is the development of *immanent power*. Still, if the discovery of a form of power operative in the field of immanence required a wholesale transformation of the way in which government in the Classical period would need to be exercised, then it is necessary to ask: what exactly constitutes the 'labyrinthine' field of economy? And what, specifically, does that nascent governmentality, which circulates this new and unfamiliar form of immanent power, uncover as the objects of governance?

Theatres of Immanence: The New Logic of Government

Although the immanental turn would eventually come to define the functioning of the modern state, nevertheless, already something like an immanental logic of government had begun to develop during this period that would entirely displace the older cosmological conception of government. To understand the crisis that the immanental turn provoked in the way government was conceived, I would like to briefly turn to the scandal

[17] Jean Bodin, *On Sovereignty*, trans. Julian H. Franklin (Cambridge: Cambridge University Press, 1992), p. 8.

[18] *Ibid.*, p. 12.

[19] Michel Foucault, *The Birth of Biopolitics, Lectures at the Collège de France 1978–1979*, trans. G. Burchell (New York: Palgrave MacMillan, 2008), p. 292.

of Machiavellianism that swept through Europe during the late 1500s and 1600s. What lay at the heart of this scandal is succinctly expressed by Machiavelli's opponent, the ex-Jesuit Giovanni Botero, who claimed to have been 'moved to indignation . . . to find that this barbarous mode of government had won such acceptance'. What Botero, and many others like him, found objectionable in Machiavelli's short tract, *The Prince*, was its advocacy of a form of government that was 'brazenly opposed to Divine Law'.[20] Although he was opposed to it, Botero did not simply reject the Machiavellian doctrine; on the contrary, in his book *Della ragion di stato*, published in 1589, he sought to improve upon it, remedying what he saw as its immoral and disreputable aspects, at the same time as recognising that in 'reason of state', as he called it, Machiavellianism could be adapted to the new conditions of government that had begun to develop during the late Renaissance. It is likely that Botero's intervention was a belated acknowledgement that the impact of reason of state was irreversible: as he concedes in his dedicatory epistle, it was already 'a constant subject of discussion' in the courts of Europe. Noel Malcolm has suggested that, notwithstanding the prevailing demonisation of Machiavelli, a 'great popular vogue' for reason of state had already swept across Europe, influencing the development of political thought.[21] If it was a vogue, however, it would have far-reaching consequences – not just on the way it transformed the practices of government, but in terms of what it signified for the way government itself was to be conceived. In order to highlight the wider significance of reason of state, with its bearing on the period's sense of epistemic crisis, it is worth noting Foucault's perceptive observation that reason of state contains no 'reference to a natural order, an order of the world, fundamental laws of nature, or even to a divine order. Nothing of the cosmos, nature, or the divine is present in the definition of *raison d'Etat*.'[22]

In other words, what the doctrine of reason of state signifies is the emergence of a logic of government founded not on transcendent 'order' but on immanent or 'worldly' principles. It is a doctrine that is quite unconcerned with questions regarding the legitimacy or otherwise of the sovereign, and which pays little or scant attention to the theological and

[20] Giovanni Botero, *Reason of State*, trans. P.J. Waley and D.P. Waley (London: Routledge & Kegan Paul, 1956), p. xiv.

[21] Noel Malcolm, *Reason of State, Propaganda, and the Thirty Years' War* (Oxford: Oxford University Press, 2010), p. 92. I am indebted to Malcolm's nuanced reading of reason of state in this section.

[22] Michel Foucault, *Security, Territory, Population, Lectures at the Collège de France 1977–1978*, trans. G. Burchell (New York: Palgrave Macmillan, 2009), p. 257.

moral foundations of the political order. Consequently, reason of state must be differentiated from the essentially juristic concept of sovereignty, where the action of government aims at the *summum bonum* or the *bonum commune* of theological thought, and requires that the Prince act on the basis of what is most virtuous ('If advantage is at odds with honesty, it is only reasonable that honor should prevail').[23] In reason of state, by contrast, government is determined not by 'honestum', but by interest: by what is most practicable or useful given the strategic interests of the state. For the first time, politics, as Malcolm expresses it, 'becomes decipherable and legible'.[24] In this sense, government founded on the interest of the Prince or the state implies a rather more pragmatic and flexible approach, one adapted to the exigencies of governing, which eschews the pious concern for incontrovertible principles of law: 'in the decisions made by princes interest will always override every other argument.'[25]

For instance, Justus Lipsius, in a work that would be translated into English in 1594, explicitly rejected the idea that government must be founded upon theoretical precepts. Government, and specifically civil government, requires 'experience' of the world: 'we give best credit to things tryed by experience.'[26] Although Lipsius was concerned to develop a concept of practical government that combined *honestum* with a notion of interest, nevertheless, the emphasis placed on experience suggests that it matters little whether one's precepts are good or bad since if they cannot be 'determined by art', that is to say, if they cannot be made practicable, then they are 'without the reach of wisdom'.[27] This is not to say that reason of state should be viewed as simply an attempt to communicate the practicalities of government; rather, it signals, in Malcolm's terms, a different evaluative standpoint; one that reflected 'something quasi-normative, a value, a ground for justification – not a moral value, however, but one which operated on a different basis (profit, utility) and became most noticeable precisely when it conflicted with morality'.[28] The question asked is not what is right, given the conscience of the Prince, but what is of benefit to states; what is to their advantage – in short, what should fall under the 'interest of the state'?

[23] Bodin, *On Sovereignty*, p. 33. [24] Malcolm, *Reason of State*, p. 96.
[25] Botero, *Reason of State*, p. 41; cited in Malcolm, *Reason of State*, p. 94.
[26] Justus Lipsius, *Sixe Bookes of Politickes or Civil Doctrine*, trans. William Jones (London: William Ponsonby, 1594), p. 13.
[27] *Ibid.*, p. 59. [28] Malcolm, *Reason of State*, pp. 93–94.

The answer to these questions is, quite simply, economy. René de Lucinge thus proclaims: 'we shall therefore concern ourselves only with profit, which we may call "interest".'[29] While Lipsius would argue: 'Ciuill life consisteth in societie, societie in two things, Traffique and Gouernment.'[30] The early modern notion of economy, or 'traffic', should not be understood in terms of the narrow meaning that characterises the activities of contemporary economists, who develop highly speculative mathematical models and rarefied market products. Economy, here, belongs to a different heritage, and should be grasped in relation to something rather more concrete and practical, as signifying 'a level of reality and a field of intervention for government'.[31] It is summarised by Guillaume de la Perrière's axiom: 'Government is the right disposition of things arranged so as to lead to a suitable end.'[32] In short: government will be grasped as economic government, and economy, correlatively, as the government of 'men and things':[33]

> There is not a thing of more importance to increase a state, and to make it both populous of Inhabitants, and rich of all good things; than the Industrie of men, and the multitude of Artes; of which, some are necessary; some commodious for a ciuile life; others some for a Pompe and ornament; and others for delicacy, wantonnes, and entertainment of idle persons by the meanes whereof doth follow, concourse both of mony and of people, that Labour and worke, or trade that is wrought, or minister and supply matter to Laborers and worke-men; or buy, or sell, or transport from one place to another, the artificious and cunning parts of the wit and hand of man.[34]

It is in relation to this wide-ranging economic rationality that reason of state can be said to initiate a new logic of government in which the monarch will no longer be the primary point of reference or the centre of political gravity. Instead, government will be directed towards a new set of objects that are to be acted upon in the interests of the prudent management of the state's resources. The ends of government can therefore no longer be seen as external to the principality; as Mitchell Dean writes, they are now wholly 'immanent to the objects of government'.[35] As a consequence of the collapse into immanence, government will find its necessity exclusively in the mundane objects of day-to-day existence with which it is concerned.

29 Quoted in *ibid.*, p. 94. 30 Lipsius, *Sixe Bookes*, p. 4.

31 Foucault, *Security, Territory, Population*, p. 95. 32 Cited in *ibid.*, p. 96. 33 *Ibid.*

34 Giovanni Botero, *A Treatise Concerning the Causes of the Magnificencie and Greatness of Cities*, trans. Robert Peterson (London, 1606), p. 48.

35 Mitchell Dean, *Governmentality, Power and Rule in Modern Society* (London: Sage, 2010), p. 104.

Seen in terms of these immanent objects of government, at the heart of reason of state, in fact, one finds, broadly, two interconnected objects of fundamental concern to government, but also, in relation to these two objects, two corresponding *limits* on government. One will be defined broadly by economic activity – the government of 'things', which it will be the duty of governments to encourage rather than frustrate, hinder or impede – as is discovered through the influence of mercantilism on early modern government (economic activity must be given the greatest possible latitude and thus be subject to *less* government intervention). The other object might be termed 'demographic', the 'government of men', where instead there should be rather *more* government. That men require more government has, without a doubt, everything to do with the expansion of the new urban population. In this sense, government becomes, for reason of state theorists, nothing but its own necessity: a necessity founded on the need to preserve order in the face of man's vicious inclinations – and vices. To comprehend the nature of this second limit on the art of government is to understand in what sense demography defines a unique problematic of government; it is to understand that demography becomes an intramural problem for government, core to its very *raison d'être*. One finds this idea in Hobbes, who writes that since 'the Actions of men proceed from their Opinions . . . in the wel governing of Opinions, consisteth the well governing of mens Actions, in order to their Peace and Concord'.[36] What this signifies for the new logic of government, which exercises political power in an increasingly secular sense, is an understanding that the art of government corresponds to a set of knowledges, teachings and practices that will inevitably bring government, perhaps for the first time, into the closest possible proximity to the governed. To govern the people, one must know them. Lipsius offers precisely this advice to Princes: 'Whosever then thou art, that desirest to attaine to wisdom and dexterity in matter of gouernment, thou oughtest to knowe the nature of the common people, and by what meanes the same may be discreetly gouerned.'[37] While the consequences of ignoring such advice is developed in an exemplary way in Bacon's short essay *On Seditions and Troubles*, which opens with the startling, one might even say 'Shakespearean' image: 'Shepherds of people had need know the calendars of tempests in state.'[38]

[36] Thomas Hobbes, *Leviathan*, cited in Malcolm, *Reason of State*, p. 115.

[37] Lipsius, *Sixe Bookes*, p. 67.

[38] Francis Bacon, 'On Seditions and Troubles', in *Essays Moral, Economical and Political* (London: T. Payne 1800), p. 63.

The significance of this issue is dramatically exemplified in the second part of Ulysses's speech in Shakespeare's *Troilus and Cressida*, where Ulysses, after having expounded on the cosmological foundations of a secure political order, reflects on the principal cause of disorder in states:

> . . . but when the planets,
> In evil mixture, to disorder wander,
> What plagues, and what portents, what mating,
> What raging of the sea, shaking of earth,
> Commotion in the winds, frights, changes, horrors,
> Divert and crack, rend and deracinate
> The unity and married calm of states
> Quite from their fixture!

It is not, for all its deployment of cosmological images, the itinerancy of nomadic planets that causes cosmic cataclysm and disorder to befall and corrupt states, according to Ulysses's speech. Quite the opposite: something rather more mundane lies behind the collapse of order, and Ulysses swiftly exchanges the lofty imagery of the cosmos for rather more terrestrial imagery in order to vividly envisage the symptoms and causes of the degeneracy that gnaws away at the very foundations of states. What corrupts both order and degree is something quite unknown to either: a 'democratic' appetite – those vices and inclinations whose energy and dynamic is powerful enough to consume states, and whose evil influence, if left untended, results in the malaise of that theatrocratic *lack* of government which produces the 'government of the ungovernable':

> . . . O! When degree is shak'd,
> Which is the ladder to all high designs,
> The enterprise is sick. How could communities,
> Degrees in schools, and brotherhoods in cities,
> Peaceful commerce from dividable shores,
> The primogenitive and due of birth,
> Prerogative of age, crowns, sceptres, laurels,
> But by degree, stand in authentic place?
> Take but degree away, untune that string,
> And, hark, what discord follows! Each thing meets
> In mere oppugnancy: the bounded waters
> Should lift their bosoms higher than the shores,
> And make a sop of all this solid globe:
> Strengths should be lord of imbecility,
> And the rude son should strike his father dead:
> Force should be right; or, rather, right and wrong
> (Between whose endless jar justice resides)

Should lose their names, and so should justice too.
Then everything includes itself in power,
Power into will, will into appetite;
And appetite, an universal wolf,
So doubly seconded with will and power,
Must make perforce an universal prey,
And last eat up himself. Great Agamemnon,
This chaos, when degree is suffocate,
Follows the choking.
And this neglect of degree it is,
That by a pace goes backward, in a purpose
It hath to climb. The general's disdain'd
By him one step below; he, by the next;
That next, by him beneath: so every step,
Exampled by the first pace that is sick
Of his superior, gnaws to an envious fever
Of pale and bloodless emulation (I.iii)

What is expressed in Ulysses's discourse is not only fearfulness at the prospect of a looming collapse of order, but also an acute recognition that it is a collapse into a state of pure immanence. There is, to be more precise, at the level of its governing statements, a profound sense of epistemic crisis underpinning this speech and that is why one finds such an intense anxiety over the repugnant prospects for the once well-governed state. After all, the condition of immanence is unequivocally equated by Ulysses with the disorders and injustices that arise from the emancipation of earthly (democratic) appetites.

Nevertheless, the question that reason of state will pose, in response to the crisis of immanence that confronts the political order in the late Renaissance, will be entirely practical and realist in orientation: given that the government of modern states obliges us to rethink the art of government around the problem of governing men, how might one nonetheless preserve and secure order in society? How, in short, *should* one 'govern men'? This pre-eminently pragmatic question in no way concerns itself with the problem of whether degree is legitimately founded or not, any more than it will, conversely, attempt to answer the question by proposing the solution of democratic equality through the greater participation of the majority of men (and women) in the affairs of government. For reason of state, order still entails degree. What differentiates it is not that it develops a different concept of order founded on egalitarian principles; order, degree, hierarchy are to remain intact. Rather, what it initiates is a new logic of governance in which order, hierarchy and degree are to be preserved on immanental grounds, that is, *by means of* the 'government of men'. It is precisely this necessity of governing men – the common populace – that brings me, at this point, back to the discourse on the theatre and to the task of paying off my earlier debt by now interrogating the second image of the theatre, the 'theatre of the multitude'.

Formation of the Early Modern Discourse on Theatre

A Discursive Orientation: The Actor's Scourge, or, 'Puritan' Manners of Speaking

There is a tendency in scholarly debates around the developing discourse on the theatre during the English Renaissance to characterise it primarily in terms of Puritan opposition to the stage.[39] G. Blakemore Evans nuances this view somewhat by suggesting broadly two kinds of 'anti-theatrical' antagonists:

> the attacks were limited basically to two groups: those who objected to plays as incitements to vice of all kinds and who found their voice in a number of Puritan extremists (men like John Northbrooke (c. 1579), Stephen Gosson (1579), Philip Stubbes (1583), and William Rankins (1587); and those like the City Fathers (the Lord Mayor and Aldermen of London and other towns), who saw plays and playhouses as breeding grounds of civil riots and disease.[40]

It would be wrong, no doubt, to dismiss the claim that a large number of anti-theatrical statements were issued by those whose fulminations against the stage were expressive of sincerely held Puritan convictions. Nevertheless, it is moot how far one can sustain such a sharp distinction between the City fathers and those Puritan ideologues who objected to the stage. The City fathers were staunch Sabbatarians, after all, while it is believed that Stephen Gosson was hired by them to write his *School of Abuse*. Margot Heinemann has persuasively argued that there are innumerable ways of complicating the idea that anti-theatricalism during the period is motivated simply by the Tertullian moralism of a group of religious fanatics. 'To see all Puritans as automatically hostile in principle to the theatre and the arts generally is,' she writes, 'to misunderstand the depth

[39] One noteworthy example of this tendency, of course, is Jonas Barish's chapter 'Puritans and Proteans', in *The Anti-theatrical Prejudice*, pp. 80–131.

[40] G. Blakemore Evans, 'Introduction', in *Attitudes Toward the Drama in Elizabethan-Jacobean England*, ed. G. Blakemore Evans (New York: New Amsterdam, 1990), pp. 3–17 (p. 3).

and complexity of the intellectual and social movements that led to the upheavals of the 1640s.'[41] Not only were Puritans such as Milton or the Third Earl of Pembroke (Shakespeare's patron) by no means opposed to the existence of the theatre, but equally, anti-theatrical sentiments were just as prevalent in the Catholic world during the period of the Counter-Reformation.[42]

While I do not have space to examine the intricacies of this controversy here – to gesture towards it will have to suffice – there is nevertheless a substantive point to be made that will help orientate an understanding of the kinds of statements that this discourse produced at the time. It is, certainly, easy to be distracted by the shrill tone adopted in many anti-theatrical tracts; Jonas Barish exemplifies this when he writes of William Prynne's notorious *Histrio-Mastix*: 'It is as though he were himself goaded by a devil, driven to blacken the theatre with lunatic exaggeration and without allowing it the faintest spark of decency or humanity.'[43] But what if the specific beliefs and opinions that motivated those individuals to express their views in the way that they did was of rather less importance than is commonly assumed; while of rather more importance was the way in which those statements were organised and structured by the kind of discursive rationality that is of central concern in this study: how might such statements be understood against the emergent rationality of government?

If one takes the example of Prynne, a particularly iconoclastic figure, to be sure, but one frequently held up as the most extreme – and perhaps the most pathological case when it comes to anti-theatrical fundamentalism – several things become quite clear on closer inspection. In the first instance, it is soon obvious that Prynne's objections to the stage are by no means simply expressive of his so-called Puritan beliefs. For Prynne, objections to the stage are not at all reducible to Puritan doctrine, and he argues that both Protestant and Catholic can agree that no Christian state should tolerate the stage.[44] Theatre is intolerable not only to Protestants and Catholics *alike*, he points out, but also to many others:

> Pagan Writers, Emperors, States, and Magistrates; together with the primitive Christians, Fathers, and Christian Writers of Forraigne parts; but even

[41] Margot Heinemann, *Puritanism and Theatre: Thomas Middleton and Opposition Drama under the Early Stuarts* (Cambridge: Cambridge University Press, 1982), pp. 21–22.

[42] *Ibid*., p. 27; see chapter 2, pp. 18–47, of that book for a fuller discussion.

[43] Barish, *The Anti-theatrical Prejudice*, p. 87.

[44] William Prynne, *Histrio-Mastix: The Player's Scourge, or Actor's Tragedy* (London: Edward Allde, Augustine Mathewes, Thomas Cotes adn William Iones, 1633), p. 483.

> our owne domestique Writers, Preachers, Universities, Magistrates, and our whole State it Selfe in open Parliament, both in ancient, moderne, and present times [all] have abandoned, censured, condemned Stage-playes and common Actors, as the very pests, the corruptions of mens mindes and manners; the Seminaries of all vice, all lewdness, wickedness and disorder; and intolerable mischiefs in an civill or well-disciplined Common-weale.[45]

It might be objected that this overlooks the interminable quantity of religious commentary found in Prynne's book; that its rhetorical gestures are a reflection of authorial persuasions that are indeed directed by the dictates of a conscience inspired by faith; that it should be understood, more broadly, in relation to the desperately fractious and apprehensive context of pre-revolutionary English public life. All of this is true; nevertheless, one should take care not to conflate an author's religious and political convictions, or even circumstances, with discursive structures, especially in a period when there was a preponderance of religious discourse (and indeed little else). To adopt an alternative viewpoint: the religious dimension of the discourse (here and elsewhere) might be seen as a kind of skein or surface – a tropology – on which the statements of the discourse on the stage and government were able to make their appearance. Such statements will be located in a space of discourse whose threshold is determined by its historical specificity, and in which religion constitutes both the condition of possibility for their enunciation as well as a limit beyond which that discourse cannot yet reach. The significance, I would suggest, of the *Histrio-Mastix* would not be found by looking to Prynne's religious beliefs any more than its relentlessness should be explained on psychological grounds – as evidence of his putative 'megalomania'.[46] Instead (as the above quote indicates) it lies in its form of argument, with the way the burden of proof is understood within the anti- (and pro-) theatrical discourse of the period, how its designations are determined by a set of highly localised conceptual codes and apodictic strategies.

What does it mean, after all, to 'prove' the anti-theatrical case, or the pro-theatrical case for that matter? In fact, everything depends on a particular discursive game that requires opponents to trade blows with one another through tit-for-tat citation of traditional authorities.[47] There are seven authorities enumerated by Prynne at the outset of his book, which would have been utterly familiar to anyone reading it, and unquestionably accepted: (1) scriptural sources – for instance Deuteronomy;

[45] *Ibid.*, p. 497. [46] Barish, *The Anti-theatrical Prejudice*, p. 84.
[47] See, for example, Heywood's reliance on traditional authorities in his *Apology*.

(2) the primitive Church; (3) the Church authorities: its counsels, as well as canonical and papal constitutions; (4) the Church Fathers – authorities such as Augustine; (5) modern Christian writers – the 'divines'; (6) the ancient 'heathen' sources of Greek and Roman philosophy, oratory, history and poetry; and finally (7) the acts of states, irrespective of whether they are Christian or 'heathen'.[48] Each of these constitutes a kind of evidentiary space, and – in the order of Prynne's discourse – an authoritative point of reference that secures and validates it as discourse.

If there is something remarkable and excessive in the way in which Prynne goes about his task, producing a book of 1,000 pages, it owes everything to the *style* of this kind of discourse, with its methodological insistence that the act of demonstration equates to the certified appropriation of reputable sources. To argue, in other words, is to display one's erudition. What does systematic citation demonstrate if not the qualification of the author to enter into the enunciative space of discourse; that by demonstrating mastery over one's sources one testifies to the authority of one's own 'speech'? If Prynne's extraordinary text yields a vast and tremendous commentary – a kind of glossomania (if one is to speak in terms of pathology here) – it is because it attempts an impossible feat: to suture the very space of discourse. It is as if the struggle over the stage can be won by the sheer capacity and volume of citation; by the display of an encyclopedic and totalising knowledge of those authorities. This volume of discourse is not the speech of a lunatic or fanatic, then, but a consequence and result of Prynne's mode of argument, which, resting on the validity of his sources, comes down to one fundamental line of attack: "if all of these great and 'unanswerable authorities'[49] – both Christian and Pagan – should deem it prudent to suppress the stage, then must not we ('lest we prove farre worse then Pagans'[50]) do the same? Should not we, who count ourselves Christians, heed this 'army-royall of Play-condemning Authorities'?"[51]

Moving now beyond the problem of *how* one demonstrates that theatre is unlawful – the style, modality and form of the argument – there is the further question of *what* this discourse seeks to demonstrate, and this is precisely *that* the stage is unlawful; that theatre goes against all the 'Statutes of our Kingdome'. It is for this reason that Prynne's entrance into discourse is to be grasped, not simply as a religious diatribe against the stage, but as falling precisely within the compass of the discourse on governance. The stage is a matter of grave concern to government for the simple reason

48 Prynne, *Histrio-Mastix*, p. 8. 49 *Ibid.*, p. 718. 50 *Ibid.*, p. 454. 51 *Ibid.*, p. 719.

that theatre 'endanger(s) Church and State at once'.[52] What Prynne invokes in the combining of Church and Stage is quite typical of the period and reflects a broadly instrumentalist view of religion. One also finds this approach promoted by theorists of reason of state, as well as political philosophers such as Hobbes; 'religion aids in the proper function of the state', as Katherine Ibbett puts it.[53] Religion, in short, provides a pragmatic means of controlling the people. This governmental aspect to Prynne's 'Puritan' discourse is quite explicitly embraced when he announces time and again that plays go against the 'rudiments of civill policy'. Thus, if one asks in what way the theatre poses any kind of threat to the 'well-ordered Christian Republike', or why it should be a matter of concern and urgency, Prynne's answer is that the theatre is a corrupting influence on the *disposition* of the people:

> [as] the happinesse; honor; life and safety of every Common-weale consists in the ingenuity, temperance, and true vertuous disposition of the people's mindes and manners; so the distemperature, malady, and confusion of it always issues, from the exorbitant obliquity, the uncontrolled dissoluteness, and degeneracy of their vitious lives, which bring certaine ruine. Whence the most prudent Princes and Republiques in all ages, have constantly suppressed all such pleasures, as might either empoison the younger people's manners, or pervert their minds.[54]

Discursive Imbrications of the Stage and Multitude

Thus, I suggest, understanding this discourse on the theatre as *discourse* is to release such statements from their reduction to historical positivities; it is to say that they cannot be grasped by filtering them through the subjective perspective of speakers engaged in highly sectarian disputes (as valid and interesting as the histories of religious disputes may be on their own terms). Instead they will be grasped here as located within a pre-subjective discursive event, at the heart of which one finds a set of concerns over whether or not the theatre is conducive to a well-governed state – whether or not the theatre can be considered lawful. There is, granted, a sense of urgency within the rhetoric of these statements: but what that rhetorical urgency signifies should not be

52 *Ibid.*, p. 5.

53 Katherine Ibbett, *The Style of the State in French Theatre 1630–1660: Neoclassicism and Government* (Farnham: Ashgate, 2009), p. 69.

54 Prynne, *Histrio-Mastix*, p. 448.

thought merely as a kind of moral panic on the part of Christian zealots over the perceived immorality of the stage. In order to reverse the polarity of this perspective, I would say instead that Christian piety, moral panic and concerns over the immorality of the stage are directed by governmental discourses, motivated in turn by the emergence of an ever-expanding urban and suburban population. Behind this discourse, one cannot locate a dim or obscure existential threat, gradually brought into being, by repeated exposure to the stage, but the myriad socio-economic and demographic transformations that give rise to the question of how to govern the population. It is a question that is encapsulated, during this period, in the formation of a specific object, the protean multitude.

But perhaps it will be thought inappropriate to suggest that the discourse on the theatre is *also* a discourse on the problem of multitude; or that the discourse on the stage is *also* – as I have been arguing – a discourse of governance. Am I not in danger of multiplying discourses exorbitantly and needlessly? Quite the reverse – for as I have already said, the discourse on the theatre can be understood only by situating it within a wider discursive field, mapping the network of discursive relations through which its statements are distributed as imbricating sets that cut across one another; that overlay, supplement and extend one kind of knowledge in one field of discourse (for instance, theology), with reference to another found elsewhere (for instance, the knowledge possessed by the judiciary). What this permits is the development of complex objects of discourse in a highly heterogeneous field. Thus in speaking of the theatre of the multitude, already it should be understood that the discourse on the theatre is constituted in the foreign milieu of other discourses, with which it is matrixed. What these matrices make conceivable are precisely objects conjured into being through the equivalences that can be drawn across the discursive field in which they will be articulated.

Above all, during the early modern period, the discourse on the theatre is correlated with the discourse on multitude precisely through a set of shared discursive practices that enumerate common objects of concern. Take, for example, the Queen's edict, issued in 1601, directed against that 'great multitude of base and loose people' 'dispersed within our city of London, and the suburbs thereof', where the series of objects that appear within concerns over the multitude converge seamlessly with concerns to do with the morality of the stage – as is well documented: government statutes against plays and players fell *within* statutes directed against acts of vagrancy[55] (the act of 1597, for example, classifies 'comon Players of Enterludes and Minstrells wandring abroade' as 'rogues and vagabonds'). What is a vagrant? It is a person who 'neither haue any certaine place of abode, nor any good or lawful cause of businesse to attend hereabouts'. The vagrant, like the actor, is without stable vocation and unlocatable within the order of the Commonwealth – a point I shall return to later, but which almost certainly places discourses on vagrancy within the scope of what I have called theatrocratic discourse. Having no fixed employment, the vagabond is immediately to be suspected, becoming an object within the discourse on law and order, since he is likely to 'enter into any tumult or disorder'. Such a person is also inherently treacherous, 'spreading false rumours and tales'; they are a likely cause of sedition (invoking a discourse on state security). What is also particularly noteworthy in this proclamation, albeit that it is by no means exceptional, is the way in which it extends the individual figure of the vagabond (a figure to be feared, shunned and finally subject to punitive discipline) as a means of determining the basic characteristics of the new population of the city as a whole (in contrast to its 'legitimate' citizens): these are dangerous 'refuse and vagabond people' who 'continually flocke and gather to our City' and are the principal cause of disorder in London. Thus constituted, this vagabond people present government with a virtual horizon of incipient criminality and degeneracy.

A previous proclamation, issued two years earlier, also aimed at 'suppressing … the multitudes of idle vagabonds, and for staying of all unlawful assemblies, especially in and about the Citie of London', invoked a further set of discourses that were put into circulation during the Elizabethan period and trained on the growing problem of indigence. Once again, it is the presence of the poor, whose ranks are now swelling the City's streets, that incites a discourse of multitude, albeit that the specific context in which this proclamation appears seems to be motivated by the rise in beggary among demobilised soldiers – those 'multitudes of able men, neither impotent nor lame, exacting money continually upon pretence of service in the warres without reliefe'. Particularly worthy of note are the questions that it raises. First, how should the undeserving vagrant, prone to idleness, be distinguished from the genuinely deserving

[55] See various acts and statutes: 1530/31, 22. Hen. VIII, ch. 12; 1572; 14 Eliz., ch. 5; 1597/98; 39 Eliz. chs. 3, 4, 17; 1601, 43 Eliz. ch. 9; 1603/4 1. Jac. 1. ch. 7; 1609/10 Jac. I, ch. 4; 1662, 14 Car. II, ch. 12; 1698/99 II Wm. III, ch. 18; 1706, 6 Anne, ch. 32; 1714, 12 Anne 2, ch. 23. Vincent J. Liesenfeld, *The Licensing Act of 1737* (Madison: University of Wisconsin Press, 1984), pp. 160–63, appendix A.

poor – those who are in some way incapacitated and unable to work? Second, for those who are able to work but refuse to do so – those distended multitudes of idle vagrants – how can they be compelled to become more productive; to submit to the discipline of work? The proclamation, naturally, attempts to answer these questions: mobilising the city authorities, the officers of the Justices of the Peace, and the watch to clamp down on the multitudes of 'idle people'; ordering the imprisonment of able-bodied vagabonds; returning the lame, under poor-law statutes, to the 'countrey' (to despatch them to places of birth or to last places of residence); while for the more 'notorious offenders' – those who refused to be reformed – to confront them with martial law, sending them 'without delay . . . [to the] Gallows'.

In James's proclamation of 1603 'against inmates and multitudes of dwellers in strait rooms and places in and about the citie of London', a further discourse is invoked: the discourse of public health, specifically around fears to do with the 'great confluence and accesse of excessive numbers of idle, indigent, dissolute and dangerous persons' now living in crammed living conditions (called 'strait roomes') in London's suburbs. It is not simply fear of plague that motivates this particular declarative statement. On the contrary, by speaking of the 'pestering' of the multitude and of those places and houses 'pestered with multitudes of dwellers', its discursive function is to explicitly associate the multitude with infection, pestilence and disease, while pointing, at the same time, to a primitive epidemiology whose object will be urban deprivation. What this reveals is the chronic nature of the problem posed by the multitude to government, and that, notwithstanding the attempts made to suppress the urban poor, it becomes increasingly intractable as the century proceeds (an act of Parliament on 5 March 1646, for instance, calls upon the Justices, the Lord Mayor, commissars, and Quarter sessions courts to enact the existing laws in preventing 'the multitude of Beggars, poore, and vagabonds in and about the Cities of London Westminister and in other parts of this Kingdome' – to punish 'Beggars, Rogues, and Vagabonds' and provide 'reliefe of the poore').

One might cite many more instances that testify to the growing 'discourse on multitude', but these examples suffice in indicating something of the complexity of the discursive field during the period with its multiple discourses on poverty, crime, public health, housing, idleness and the problem of productive employment. Furthermore, they show that within this discourse one finds everywhere that necessity of government of which I spoke earlier. Nowhere is that necessity more acutely felt than in the discursive construction of the common figure of the vagabond, insofar as he acts as a kind of cipher for an essentially ungovernable commonality. At the same time, if a vagabond people enables a governmental discourse on multitude to emerge, then equally the figure of the *monstrum multorum capitum* finds its *locus classicus* in the emergent discourse on the stage, whose disorders I would now like to turn to through an examination of the discursive figure of the theatre of the multitude.

The Theatre of the Multitude

The theatre of the multitude can be found in a thousand scattered references to the actual experience of the Elizabethan stage – the hundreds of missives, tracts and petitions, eyewitness testimonies, diplomatic reports, poetry, Church sermons, as well as, of course, the countless instances in which it featured within plays written during the period. Stephen Gosson in his *Playes Confuted in Five Actions* (1582) offers, however, perhaps the most apposite characterisation of the theatre of the multitude, when he says: 'The ancient Philosophers . . . called them a monster of many heads . . . The common people which resorte to Theatres being but an assemblie of Tailors, Tinkers, Cordwayners, Saylers, Olde Men, young Men, Women, boyes, Girles, and such like.'[56]

Presiding over this multitude (the artisans, 'country clownes', misfits, fishwives, old lags, sailors and callow youth, and so on) are the players, who, in Gosson's words, are to be looked upon as: 'Lords of misrule or the very schoolmasters of these abuses . . .', and he goes on to proclaim: 'were not players the mean to make such assemblies . . . such multitudes would hardly be drawn into so narrow room.'[57] To swell the ranks of the multitude further, one might also add to this strange inventory: the apprentices, clerks, labourers and serving men, who (or such was the assumption of the discourse on the stage) regularly skipped work to catch a play, flagrantly breaching the 'Statute of Artificers' which was meant to strictly regulate their working day, and which, if it had worked as it was intended to, would have altogether prohibited their attendance at public theatres.[58] These are the 'youthes' who go to the theatre to see

[56] Quoted in Andrew Gurr, *Playgoing in Shakespeare's London* (Cambridge: Cambridge University Press, 2004), p. 249.

[57] Gosson quoted in Muriel Clara Bradbrook, *The Rise of the Common Player: A Study of Actor and Society in Shakespeare's England* (London: Chatto & Windus, 1962), p. 100.

[58] See Alexander Leggatt, *Jacobean Public Theatre* (London: Routledge, 1992), pp. 29–30. Despite the fact that the 'working classes were regulated by the Statute of Artificers', which attempted to police

and be seen, who 'carry theire eye through every gallery'.[59] There were also the irreverent gallants – those young men who regularly attended the theatre not because they had a love for poetry but, on the contrary, because they were in pursuit of amorous adventures. The gallant's pastime involved visiting harlots, whores and courtesans; or, if he was actually paying attention to the theatrical proceedings, it was in making a spectacle of himself by sitting on the stage and mocking the actors – something Ben Jonson would complain about in *Every Man Out*. The gallant, he says, 'sits with his armes thus wreath'd, his hat pull'd here, cryes meow, and nods, then shakes his empty head'.[60] Finally, wherever there is a crowd, one will always discover a criminal element: traders of black-market goods such as tobacco, as well as the cutpurses, knaves, 'coseners', 'coney-catchers' and pilferers who circulate through the audience, preying on the unsuspecting victim. All of these types, villainous, licentious, or just plain idle, feature in descriptions of the public playhouse audience and provide a vivid image of what the theatre of the multitude was meant to look like.

But it is equally telling to consider those who were not counted among their rank, as the anonymous author of *A Refutation of the Apology for Actors* (1615) did in his response to Heywood. According to this vituperative commentator, one would not expect to see 'an ancient citizen, a chaste matron, a modest maid, a grave senator, or a wise Magistrate, a just judge, a godly Preacher, a religious man not blinded in ignorance' attending a theatrical production.[61] If the adjectives chaste, modest, grave, wise, just and godly specified the qualities of the true community, founded on Christian virtue, then membership of the community of the theatre of the multitude was to be defined by a symmetrical lack of quality. The 'vulgar sort' who run 'madding unto playes' are those without 'counsel, reason, or discretion'.[62]

If, then, these figures provide a vivid image of the regular constituents about which the discourse on the multi-headed monster of the theatre of the multitude was to be composed, the next question is: how did the stage extend that image of multitude by imbuing it with a peculiar

the working day, limiting the amount of available leisure time, if anything in order to favour attendance at church, 'all the evidence that the non-elite should not have attended the playhouses is countered by a substantial body of evidence that they went anyway' (p. 29).

59 Gosson in Bradbrook, *Rise of the Common Player*, p. 100.

60 Ben Jonson, 'Every Man Out of His Humours', in *The Works of Ben Jonson, in Nine Volumes*, vol. 2, ed. W. Gifford (London: W. Bulmer and Co, 1816), pp. 18–19.

61 Anon., *A Refutation of the Apology for Actors* (London: W. White, 1615), p. 63.

62 *Ibid.*

symptomatology; and how did the emerging discourse on the theatre identify, in the abuses of the stage, the vices of the commonality?

The Disorders of the Stage and the Vices of the Multitude

There are several forms of abuse that are commonly associated with the theatre during the period. Since these appear in numerous statements, dispersed across different contexts and activated at different times (the period ranges from the opening of the theatres in the late 1500s to their closure in the early 1640s) I shall concentrate on organising them, not in terms of the chronological order by which they appeared, but by thematic import. It will be a general assertion of the discourse on the stage, during the period, that theatres encourage 'all manner of mischeefe',[63] and so the task here is to simply provide some sense of what that assertion meant insofar as the disorders of the stage might be seen to be indicative of the so-called disposition of the people.

To say the stage encourages 'all manner of mischief' is to characterise it, according to the language of the period, as 'seditious'. Sedition will be understood by the early modern discourse on the stage in two senses – one rather more grievous than the other. First, at its most extreme, the act of sedition will refer to a practice of agitation or intriguing – to a 'conduct of speech' directed against the authority of the state and church. Second, it denotes acts designed not to stir up rebellion, mutiny or discontent but to breach the public order. The stage will be thought seditious in both senses. Henry Crosse, for example, in *Virtue's Commonwealth*, was particularly concerned at the prospect of 'nocturnal and night plays, at unseasonable and undue times [since] more greater evils must necessarily proceed of them, because they not only hide and cover the thief, but also entice servants out of their master's houses whereby opportunity is offered to loose fellows, to effect many wicked stratagems'.[64] Lurid accounts of how London's theatres stoked the incipient flame of rebellion in servants and apprentices indisputably exaggerated and distorted the facts.[65] Some

[63] Petition to the Privy Council from the inhabitants of Blackfriars, 1596, in Gurr, *Playgoing in Shakespeare's London*, p. 217.

[64] Reproduced in Bradbrook, *Rise of the Common Player*, p. 103.

[65] In fact, the only known case of sedition, involving an actual plot that implicated Shakespeare's company, occurred in 1601, when conspirators associated with the Earl of Essex commissioned a performance of *Tragedie of King Richard the Second* at the Globe Theatre: if they had hoped to stir a rebellion in the theatre-going crowd, they were disappointed; the plot failed, and several of the conspirators (many of whom had attended the performance) were later executed. See Louis Montrose on the Essex plot, *The Purpose of Playing, Shakespeare and the Cultural Politics of*

historians have even rejected the idea that the public theatres catered to anyone but the most privileged playgoers. Ann J. Cook argued, for instance, that 'few apprentices, day labourers, or servants had either time or money to spend on the theatres' (and if that is true they could hardly have had time to engage in seditious activities).[66] Even so, this is to miss the point: what these reports did was pander to the fear of the authorities and the reading public that theatre involved the misuse and manipulation of the power of public assembly for questionable political ends. If theatre appears abusive, in the sense that it provides an opportunity for people to agitate against the state, it is because it exemplifies, as M.C. Bradbrook once observed, the 'danger of any open assembly'.[67]

No doubt the fact that the theatres were located 'out of the Citiees iurisdiction' did not help. Away from the prying eyes of the city's magistracy, theatre provided opportunities for 'vagrant persons, masterless men, thieves, horse-stealers, whoremongers, cozenors, coney-catchers, contrivers of treason, and other idle and dangerous persons to meet together'[68] where they might hatch 'confedericies & conspiracies, which ... cannot be prevented nor discovered'.[69] It is not, however, the point that the theatre of the multitude was factually seditious, but rather that, thought in a state of permanent discord, it constituted for the juridical imaginary of the time both a persistent opportunity for and potential source of rebellion. As is made clear in a remarkable document (a letter from the Lord Mayor of London and the Aldermen to the Privy Council, on 28 July 1597), what should be of particular interest 'for the good government of this [the Queen's] city' is not simply that the stage induces its audience to engage in intolerable behaviours, which it encourages and inspires, but rather, that it can do so only because the audience itself is already *predisposed* to such

Elizabethan Theatre (Chicago, IL: University of Chicago Press, 1996), pp. 66–70. For an interesting discussion of the political content of plays, such as Samuel Daniel's *Philotas* (1605) and its suppression by the Privy Council following the Essex rebellion, see Heinemann, *Puritanism and Theatre*, pp. 18–47. See also Jonathan Dollimore, *Radical Tragedy, Religion, Ideology and Power in the Drama of Shakespeare and His Contemporaries* (Basingstoke: Palgrave Macmillan, 2010).

66 Anne J. Cook, *The Privileged Playgoers of Shakespeare's London* (Princeton, NJ: Princeton University Press, 1992), p. 18.

67 Bradbrook, *Rise of the Common Player*, p. 102.

68 Official Letter from the Lord Mayor of London and Aldermen to the Privy Council, 28 July 1597, reproduced in Evans, *Elizabethan-Jacobean Drama*, p. 5.

69 1592, February 25, the Lord Mayor to John Whitgift, the Archbishop of Canterbury, reproduced in Edmund K. Chambers, *The Elizabethan Stage*, vol. 4 (London: Clarendon Press, 1923), p. 307. There appears in a petition of the precinct inhabitants of Blackfriars to the Lord Mayor, circa 1619, the same warning of 'danger ... occasioned by the broils, plots or practices of such an unruly multitude of people' (Document 27, reprinted in Irwin Smith, *Shakespeare's Blackfriars Playhouse* (New York: New York University Press, 1964), p. 490).

'faults and vices' – those 'evil-disposed and ungodly people that are within and about this City [who] assemble themselves [at the theatre] to make their matches for all their lewd and ungodly practices'.[70]

Who are these people? The letter is adamant – the lower orders – those such as the:

> divers apprentices and other servants who have confessed to us that the said stage-plays were the very places of rendez-vous, appointed by them to meet with such other as were to join with them in their designs and mutinous attempts, being also the ordinary places for masterless men to come together and to recreate themselves.[71]

Recalling Lipsius's advice to princes, that one must get to know the 'nature of the common people', the question here is: in what way are the common people to be constructed as an object of discourse and knowledge? Lipsius himself provides an answer that is wholly consistent with the prevailing view on the multitude during the period: 'The common people are unstable, and nothing is more unconstant then the rude multitude. They are given to change, and do suddenly alter their determinations like unto tempests.'[72] Just as in Bacon, who also employed the iconography of the tempest, the multitude is constituted as a quasi-natural phenomenon: capricious, unpredictable and highly intemperate. It must be approached with great care and caution: the sea swells, as Bacon puts it, and imperceptibly a storm gathers. One should be under no illusions, says Lipsius, the multitude is 'desirous of new commotions: light headed; seditious, and quarrelsome, coveting new matters, enemies to peace and quiet. Especially if they have a leader [such as the player] . . . so the people, who of their owne disposition are quiet, are by the persuasions of seditious persons stirred up, like violent tempests.'[73]

*

If the primary threat of theatre was that it provided the context and occasion for a potentially insurgent multitude, the second form of sedition threatened to menace the state in rather more anarchic and unpredictable ways: the public theatre encourages abuses of public (dis) order. Not only does the theatre of the multitude provide, as Gosson would say, a 'generall market of bawdrie', but for Anthony Munday it

[70] Lord Mayor of London and Aldermen to the Privy Council, in Evans, *Elizabethan-Jacobean Drama*, p. 5.
[71] *Ibid.* [72] Lipsius, *Sixe Bookes*, p. 68. [73] *Ibid.*, p. 69.

promised, as a consequence, to bring the 'whole Common-weale into disorder'.[74] Fear of anarchic disorder during the period would find its correlate in an equally obsessive desire for an order that was nevertheless elusive. What exacerbated the sense of crisis was no doubt prompted by the immense social, political and economic upheavals that had volatised the entire social structure of England since the close of the medieval period, and which, as has been known since Marx, was the result of the massive expropriation of peasant and ecclesiastical property during the Reformation. The theatres appeared to attract many of London's itinerant day labourers, becoming a meeting point for the emergent class of workers who sprang from the evicted rural peasantry and who, descending on the city in their droves, prompted precisely those fears already mentioned over increasing vagrancy and vagabondage. Thus the discourse on the theatre of the multitude, which sees the theatre as one of the 'ordinary places of meeting for all vagrant persons and maisterless men',[75] provided one of the most acute expressions of the growing alarm felt by the city's burghers and citizens at the increased visibility of the dispossessed and pauperised 'third estate' in London. Theatre's power, as a minute from the Privy Council in 1597 was to warn, lies in its virtually magnetic facility to 'draw a concourse of people out of the country, thereabouts pretending herein the benefit of the towne, which purpose we do utterly mislike, doubting what inconveniences may follow thereon . . . when disordered people of the common sort wilbe [*sic*] apt to misdemeane themselves'.[76]

Of these misdemeanours, there were broadly speaking three kinds. The first were those disorders that might be classified under the general category of social pathogens, with theatres providing a breeding ground for all manner of criminal activity – primarily theft, but also antisocial behaviour, from brawling to rioting. Apprentice riots were not uncommon during the period, and at times threatened even more serious acts of public disturbance – as a letter from William Fleetwood, the 'reader of London', to Lord Burghley makes clear, following an incident that occurred in the vicinity of the Curtain Theatre: 'Upon these troubles the prentices began the next day, being Tuesday, to make mutinies and assemblies, and did conspire to have broken the prisons and to have taken further the prentices

[74] In Chambers, *Elizabethan Stage*, p. 209.

[75] From a letter, dated 3 November 1594, from Lord Mayor to Lord Burghley (in Gurr, *Playgoing in Shakespeare's London*, p. 210).

[76] In Chambers, *Elizabethan Stage*, p. 321.

that were imprisoned.'[77] Only through a timely piece of intelligence were the authorities able to thwart the plan and arrest the ringleaders of the plot. A second set of misdemeanours might be termed moral disorders and were exemplified by the Puritan preoccupation with sexual degeneracy, vice, prostitution, as well as with theatre's so-called effeminating effects – something I shall return to in the next chapter. It would lead the author of the *Refutation* to paint a sensationalist account of theatre's permissiveness, concluding that it is 'licentiousness . . . which most pleaseth the multitude'.[78]

If theatre's appeal to the multitude, according to this author, had to do with its inherently dissolute and impious nature, there was nevertheless something rather more profound at stake: a different kind of vice, and in fact a different dimension of disorder altogether, one that has long aggravated the authorities wherever theatre has been an object of concern to the governing polity. This third 'abuse' is rather more impalpable: unlike the riot, the theft of a wallet or the trade in prostitution, one cannot simply point to it. Where it arises is in the question of what effect the stage has in terms of disturbing what might be called the 'government of time'. This disordering of the government of time becomes apparent precisely where disquiets arise over the questionable influence of the theatre on work, insofar as theatre-going encourages the vice of sloth. The spectators who attended the theatre, are – it will be said – the rabble who pursue 'vnlawful artificiall Pleasures, whereby they might passe away . . . the most precious time of their life . . . idlely and fruitlesse, without any profite to the Church, or Common-wealth wherein they live'.[79] Underpinning such suppositions was the thought that theatre substitutes one form of time – essentially productive time – for another temporality that is utterly profligate and wasteful. In the *Anatomie of Abuses*, Philip Stubbes was to decry those 'idle lubbers and buzzing dronets [who] suck up and devoure the good honie, whereupon the poor bees should live'. And when Thomas White remarked, 'Looke but upon the common playes in London, and see the multitude that flocketh to them and followeth them: behold the sumptuous Theatre houses, a continual monument of London's prodigalitie and folly,'[80] he had in mind the prodigality that is born of the investment of so many in a passion for idleness inculcated by the theatre.

[77] William Fleetwood, letter to Lord Burghley (18 June 1584), printed in Evans, *Elizabethan-Jacobean Drama*, p. 8.

[78] Anon., *Refutation*, p. 27. [79] *Ibid.*, p. 3. [80] In Chambers, *Elizabethan Stage*, p. 197.

From this it might be surmised that it is not just that theatre leads to 'the corrupcion of youth',[81] as the well-known, if jejune objection goes; but, rather, that the corruption of the young harbours a far greater magnitude of corruption within it that should be of grave concern to the guardians of Commonwealth and State. Thomas Nashe would complain: to the extent that they 'withdrawe Prentises from their worke', the theatres 'corrupt the growth of the Citte'.[82] The prevailing view of the theatres, over this period, is one entirely oriented by these kinds of negative economic effects – theatre acts as a spur to the scourge of indolence that begins to infect the industrious members of the community: they promote a taste for idleness; they embolden the work-shy; they lure people without vocation into the city; and they persuade 'apprentices and other servants' to abandon their work, thus depriving their masters of valuable hours of productivity.[83] The seriousness with which the problem of the governance of workers and the young was taken becomes clearer when it is recalled that order during this period, as Anthony Fletcher and John Stevenson explain, 'rested on the family and household, on schooling and apprenticeship and on the formal and informal institutions of control in the parish'. In a period when law enforcement was haphazard, to say the least, 'the maintenance of a well-regulated society' was very much dependent on intramural relations 'between husbands and wives, parents and children and heads of households and their dependents and servants' (rather than exercised through extramural relations with barely existent state agencies, e.g., the poorly paid parish officers who were charged with the enforcement of laws).[84]

*

The question with which the city elders, the churchmen and the apprentices' masters endlessly taxed themselves was this: Is it not the case that the theatre will substitute for the discipline of work, the ill-discipline of leisure? What it revealed in their eyes, while it may not be the most palpable, could nonetheless be construed as the most pernicious abuse of

[81] 1592, Court of the Guild of Merchant Taylors in *ibid.*, p. 309.
[82] Thomas Nashe, 1592, in Gurr, *Playgoing in Shakespeare's London*, p. 209.
[83] Lord Mayor of London and Aldermen to the Privy Council in Evans, *Elizabethan-Jacobean Drama*, p. 5.
[84] Anthony Fletcher and John Stevenson, Introduction, in *Order and Disorder in Early Modern England*, ed. A. Fletcher and J. Stevenson (Cambridge: Cambridge University Press, 1985), pp. 31–32.

them all insofar as 'time-devouring Stage-playes' undermined the foundation upon which rested the authority of both Church and State through the corrupting of the government of time.[85] This anxiety is precisely what lies behind the well-known antipathy of religion to the theatre, insofar as it was seen to substitute play for sermon, player for priest, and playhouse for ministry – hence the vitriolic response to the presumptuous claims found in defences such as Heywood's that the theatre performed an educative function, traditionally the preserve of the Church. Prynne warns explicitly of the 'prodigall mispence of much precious time, which Christians should husband and redeeme to better purposes'.[86] In this 'profuse mispending of our Masters Stocke of time', he asks, 'how many millions of pounds' have been lost through theatre-going[87] – 'where thousands spend the moitie of the day, the weeke, the yeere in Play-houses, at least-wise far more houres then they imploy in holy duties, or in their lawfull callings'?[88]

Accordingly, if one asks in what way the theatre posed a challenge to traditional authorities such as the Church and the State, the answer is not simply that it is thought to encourage open rebellion, or inspires forms of social unrest, or provides the occasion for a disturbance of the peace. More fundamentally, for the discourse on the theatre, what theatre flouts is the temporal basis of government authority. In the end, by challenging the government of time, theatre cannot but challenge the power of the authorities to determine and decide what is just and equitable within the Commonwealth as a whole – and thereby, its capacity to instil order through the regulation of work. What the theatre of the multitude called into question was, quite simply, the very legitimacy of the political and social order; and no doubt, in doing so, it pointed to the glaring inequality which held sway, separating individuals and privileges according to rank, aptitudes and qualities – that is to say, insofar as order rested upon the immutable fixing of social relations predicated on the hierarchical distribution of vocations, rewards and entitlements.[89] In a society where order derives from the strict regulation and division of the social body, specifically through the allotment of roles, occupations and correlative privileges, the ultimate disorder, which is identified with the subversive power of indolence, must stem from the

85 Prynne, *Histrio-Mastix*, p. 310. 86 *Ibid.*, p. 302. 87 *Ibid.*, p. 304. 88 *Ibid.*, p. 307.

89 For an extended discussion on this point and one that has certainly informed my argument see Jacques Rancière's *The Philosopher and His Poor*, chapters 1 and 2. See also, the discussion of Plato in Jonas Barish's *The Anti-Theatrical Prejudice*, chapter 1, pp. 5–37.

squandering of those selfsame aptitudes and abilities upon which the virtuous and just order or Commonwealth is founded – its 'body politic':

> Whether he bee as a hande, an eye, a finger, or a foote of a Commonwealth: knowing that every Common-wealth is a bodie politique, compared to a bodie natural. And as the head is the cheifest part, the guide and superior governour of the bodie, and all the members are as officers under the same; some of a higher qualitie and authoritie then others, as the heart, the eyes, the hand, and Legges, which are principall members, servants in office to the superiour; so are the fingers and toes, &c. peitie officers unto the former, every one of them being bound to his next superior: and so all by a naturall dutie, are servants to the head, and that for all the preservation and supportation of the entrails and maine bodie; which is so much the more safe from danger, by how much every member hath ablenes, and skill to performe his place, in true dutie, not one part whereof is void of some necessarie function . . . So is our superior Magistrate, the head and governour of us, who being many in member, make up a complete bodie politique.[90]

In the final analysis, it was not just that the playhouses were a 'great hinderance of traides';[91] the underlying inconvenience was that the theatre of the multitude came to represent to the conservative city's magistracy what must have appeared as the growing self-assertion of the labouring classes who sought, through the medium of the theatre, an equality and freedom they could not find beyond its walls. The theatre becomes the means to escape the prison-house of work. If one recalls that under the Statute of Artificers, an act designed to 'banish idleness', the terms of employment for apprentices, servants, artificers and labourers amounted to little more than legislation in favour of an oppressive and intolerable condition of bondage or indentured service, then the opening lines of Shakespeare's *Julius Caesar* suggest not so much a 'theatrical in-joke'[92] as a wry acknowledgement of the predicament of the poorest part of the audience:[93]

[90] John Norden, *A Christian Familiar Comfort* (London, 1596), pp. 53–54.

[91] Lord Mayor to Privy Council, 1597 in Evans, *Elizabethan-Jacobean Drama*, p. 5.

[92] Leggatt, *Jacobean Public Theatre*, p. 30.

[93] The composition of social classes in Shakespearean England was rigidly defined in Holinshed's *Chronicles* in 1577, when William Harrison identified four basic classes: the first, comprising the class of nobles and gentry; the second, citizens and burgesses; the third, the yeomanry or rural smallholders; and the fourth, the artisans, labourers and apprentices – beneath the latter, the underclass of vagabonds and beggars – see Gurr, *Playgoing in Shakespeare's London*, chapter 3, pp. 49–54, for an extended analysis.

> Hence! Home you idle creatures, get you home.
> Is this a holiday? What! Know you not,
> Being mechanical, you ought not walk,
> upon a labouring day, without the sign
> Of your profession? – Speak, what trade
> art thou? (I.i)

Thus does the tribune, Flavius, admonish the Roman rabble with words whose meaning the Globe's audience – at least those standing in the yard – could hardly have misunderstood since they explicitly referenced them. One can imagine the response of the theatre crowd to Flavius's question: "our trades? We are the 'tailors, shoemakers, carpenters, brickmakers, masons &c'[94] – in short, we are the artisans of London; together we comprise the 'great swarmes of idle serving men',[95] those drones to whom you would deny the pleasures of the theatre!"

In this sense, the discourse on the theatre of the period comes down, perhaps inevitably, to the ancient question posed by the presence of the artisan, the worker, the artificer, the labourer within the political space of the Commonwealth. The question has a long history, originating in Greek political thought, but the scandal of the Elizabethan and Jacobean theatre, with its particular disorders, opened a suppurating wound on the body politic of London that provoked many to ask it once again: what of the multitude? Not only did the theatre provide a highly visible and contentious locus for this question, which had resurfaced with the renaissance of the theatre during the Elizabethan period; but, more significantly, it was the theatre that pre-emptively answered the question in a way that confirmed all the gravest fears of the City's legislators – as though the worst of all Platonic nightmares was about to come to pass. This is not to say that the theatre of the multitude placed any political demands on the legislature; it did not. But what it did do was far more disturbing. Those few workers who took the theatre as the occasion to assert their right to leisure time, without asking anyone for permission to do so, assumed thereby in the eyes of the prevailing order the spectre of a democratic community that could only prove intolerable to it.

Hence the indefatigable hatred of those in authority for the community of the audience: this is what makes the image of the 'theatre disturbed by crowds' so radical; partly, because it was conjured out of a genuine fear of the theatre, and that was sufficient to produce a crisis of reality within the political discourse of the age; partly, because that fear found some

[94] William Harrison, 1577, in Gurr, *Playgoing in Shakespeare's London*, p. 53. [95] *Ibid.*

confirmation in the audacity of the poorest part of the audience to abandon work in pursuit of a pastime that was in all but name prohibited to them.

Theatre's Two Communities

It is the presence or intrusion of the multitude within the discursive field of the age, then, that locks both the discourse on the theatre and the discourse on government into an intractable dispute over two opposing concepts of community. One will be a community that is founded, in various ways, on a principle of unity and order: a commonweal grounded upon a 'true' principle of sovereignty constituting the authentic body politic; the other is a community that is in truth nothing short of an anti-community made up of the aggregated individuals who comprise the *multus* of the multitude – the many who become, through the sovereignty of sheer numbers, and through the brute and contingent arithmetic of a head count, the illegitimate community of the audience.

Two kinds of political community, each implacably opposed to the other – but what exactly is at stake in the antagonism that fundamentally divides these two communities, such that they must be seen as irreconcilable? To answer this question, I would like to return to the point where the discourse on the theatre founds itself and the point where the good community of the well-governed Commonwealth is instituted at the cost of excluding the community of the audience. It is in Plato's *Republic* that the poet and the theatre are, as everyone knows, expelled from the *polis* – although it is worth recalling that in sixteenth- and seventeenth-century London the playwrights and players were not so much expelled as denied entrance to the City in the first place. For Plato, if there was a reason to exclude the theatre, it was because it threatened to undermine the only principle capable of securing the foundations of the *polis*: that of justice. One might reasonably wonder what place the theatre has in a philosophical discussion about justice, of course. What is crucial to recollect here is how Plato defines justice as 'keeping what is properly one's own and doing one's own job'[96] (what Norden, above, referred to as that 'ablenes, and skill [each needs] to performe his place, in true dutie'). Platonic justice both founds and is founded upon the order of vocations. It is determined by the scale of social rankings, where each is to find his place according to the just distribution of aptitudes, capabilities and talents: 'we aren't all

[96] Plato, *Republic*, 433e–434a.

born alike, but each of us differs somewhat in nature from the others, one being suited to one task, another to another.'[97] It is this principle that each is suited to do one thing and one thing only that assures, for each of its citizens, that the *polis* remains ordered – and ordered justly – where each is awarded his due in proportion to his or her contribution.

The society based on the theatre could not be more contrastive: not only do actors blatantly contradict the principle that one should do one thing and one thing only, thus undermining the idea of a hierarchy founded on the fixed divisions and distributions of labour; it also encourages each to forget his place in order to pursue *more* than is his due. What it thereby invokes is the counter-paradigm to the very idea of order and justice that structures and governs the celestial theatre that is the 'theatre of the world'. What the theatre of the multitude comes to represent, according to the counter-paradigmatic view of the discourse on theatre, is the negative exemplar of the disorderliness of embryonic democratic society. The reason is simple: the principles governing theatre and democratic society are essentially the same for Plato: both '[treat] all men as equal, whether they are equal or not'.[98] What results as a consequence of the example of the theatre of the crowd is precisely the anarchy of theatrocracy. This is the warning Socrates wishes to impart to his interlocutors when he argues: theatre not only 'destroys the better sort of citizens'; it also 'strengthens the vicious ones and surrenders the city to them'.[99] Theatrocracy, in sum, cedes the city to government by the multitude.

It was precisely Plato's point that if the common and uncultivated man were to get a taste of those 'unnecessary' pleasures that exposure to theatre seemed to excite, then the good society based on the discipline of work would soon be imperilled, for such men would be quick to relieve themselves of the shackles of austerity which they had imposed upon themselves. They would rapidly descend from a society premised on collective obedience, duty and restraint into a society of individuals driven solely by the pursuit of private pleasures – as Plato says, if there is any equality in democracy it is only an 'equality of pleasures'.[100] What results is both 'disregard for all laws'[101] and a 'general permissiveness [which] eventually enslaves democracy'.[102] It is this idea that democracy promotes lawlessness, permissiveness and a general disrespect towards all authority that allows Plato to associate its disorders with the disorders of the theatre and, more importantly, to equate thereby the dissolute state of a people

[97] *Ibid.*, 370a–b. [98] *Ibid.*, 558c. [99] *Ibid.*, 655a–c. [100] *Ibid.*, 561a. [101] *Ibid.*, 563d. [102] *Ibid.*, 563e.

living within a democratic system with the theatre of the multitude, that is, with the contingent and barbaric community that is represented by the audience. Here Plato's arguments find more than a passing similarity to the objections of early modern opponents to the theatre: in fact, they endorse his critique point for point – although nowhere more so than in his denigration of the theatre crowd and its crown prince, the poet who must inevitably pander to them (or player, as was the case in Elizabethan and Jacobean England):

> [The player] doth conjecture somewhat strongly, but dares not commend a playes goodness, till he hath either spoken, or heard the *epilogue*: neither dare he entitle good things *Good*, unless hee be heartened on by the multitude: till then hee saith faintly what hee thinks, with a willing purpose to recant or persist: So howsoever hee pretends to have a royall Master or Mistresse, his wages and dependences prove him to be the servant of the people.[103]

What is specifically at issue here is not just that poets are forced to flatter the people;[104] it is rather what such flattery implies: the questionable legitimacy of the power of popular sovereignty entailed thereby. Under the sovereignty of the audience, as Plato will argue in the *Laws*, each comes to believe he has as much right to pass judgement on the theatre spectacle as any other, regardless of the fact that the multitude who constitute the assembly of spectators are without 'counsel, reason, or discretion'. The lesson is plain and clear: just as the theatre crowd who judge the performance do so in sheer ignorance of its merits, without the least competence, skill or understanding, and only on the basis of an authority that derives from their combined or aggregated power, so in a democracy the power of political decision devolves to the ignorant majority: those who 'take no part in politics and have few possessions', simply because they are the most numerous in the assembly[105] – the vulgar multitude, in short. This confusion of status, rank and persons of quality with those without status, rank or any quality whatsoever is the absurd price of universal suffrage, which theatrocratic egalitarianism demands, and which provides the target for Dekker's satirical remark:

> Sithence the place is so free in entertainment, allowing a stool as well to the farmer's son as to the Templar; that your stinkard hath the same liberty to

[103] J. Cocke (1615), 'Satyrical Essayes Characters and Others', in Chambers, *Elizabethan Stage*, p. 256.

[104] See Bradbrook: 'In the common theatre, the audience gradually realized that the offering was addressed to them all; that each was a Chief Spectator'; thus each felt 'himself entitled to resentment or applause as lord of the show' (Bradbrook, *Rise of the Common Player*, p. 100).

[105] Plato, *Republic*, 565a.

> be there in his tobacco-fumes which your sweet courtier hath; and that your car-man and tinker claim as strong a voice in their suffrage, and sit to give judgement on the play's life and death, as the proudest Momus among the tribe of critic.[106]

Notable in this passage are Dekker's choice of words: 'free', 'liberty' and 'suffrage' – signifying that, within the theatre at least, all are considered equal; thus does the theatre provide him with the means to ridicule democratic society. It is for this reason that the discourse on theatre reveals more than a merely Tertullian suspicion of plays, grounded in Christian piety and moralism; it must ultimately be understood beyond its Puritan rhetoric as a *political* phenomenon, that is, in light of the formation of a developing discursive power, driven on by fear of the rudimentary power of the multitude.

It is the latter – the multitude itself – which the discourse on theatre of the period incessantly speculates on and whose character it attempts to deduce through an analysis of its disorders, seditions and immoralities. In this sense, the discourse on the theatre correlates with the discourse on multitude, whose object must ultimately be understood in terms of the discursive function it serves within the development of immanent power, during the period of epistemic crisis that belongs to the formation of modern practices of government. If the discourse on multitude prefigures the notion of population upon which a new art of government would increasingly be imposed – indeed practised – it is because it already signifies, in an inchoative form, this emergent phenomenon, which it indelibly associates with the expansion of the commonality. In other words, and to conclude: the principal object of enunciation for the discourse on the stage will be nothing other than common life itself – its pleasures and its vices.

[106] Thomas Dekker, *The Gull's Hornbook, or Fashions to Please All Sorts of Gulls* (London: J.M. Gutch, 1609), p. 46.

CHAPTER 2

Revolts of Conduct on the Restoration Stage

Introduction

I have said that governmentality corresponds to the emergence of a novel form of power, which I designated in the previous chapter by the term 'immanent power' – a power directed at the government of common forms of life. The aim of this chapter is to show how this novel form of power, addressed to the field of immanence, began to take shape in the late 1600s, to show how it was circulated – by what agencies, instituting what kinds of relationships and with what end in view. But the objective of the chapter is also rather more specific: it is to understand the evolution of the discourse on the theatre during the period of the Restoration, when London's theatres reopened following the long interregnum of Cromwell's republic. How does immanent power enter into considerations over the governance of the stage during the late 1600s, beyond earlier debates inspired by multitude, to incorporate a wider set of objects and concerns? The Restoration stage occupies an important moment in the development of theatre governance in England: it marks the moment when the theatre began to undergo something of a 'moral' turn under the influence of new forms of governmental reasoning – a process that accelerated in the period following the 'Glorious Revolution' of 1688–89. Although I am not able to look at this political transformation in any depth – the focus of the chapter is more concerned with analysing the peculiar form of power that developed at the time – nevertheless the profound impact of that revolution on English life should be acknowledged at the outset. In the words of Steven Pincus, it is 'important not because it reaffirmed the exceptional English national character but because it was a landmark moment in the emergence of the modern state'.[1] The revolution 'created a new kind of modern state' in

[1] Steven Pincus, *1688: The First Modern Revolution* (New Haven, CT: Yale University Press, 2009), p. 6.

which government would take a 'more active role'. Crucially, it was a vision of government that promoted the values of economic participation, religious tolerance and 'liberty', in which the 'tools of the state' were employed to 'accelerate economic growth and shape the contours of society'.[2]

But it is also important to recall the broader understanding of government: its wider sphere of influence, its application beyond the operation of executive authority – in short, government grasped as a general 'mentality'. Here I return to Foucault's invocation of governmentality that, he says, aims to 'structure the possible field of action of others'. For Foucault, government is defined as a mode of power, whose practical exercise aims at the economic administration of common life; and in terms of the specificity of this practice, he writes, government

> is a set of actions on possible actions; it incites, it induces, it seduces, it makes easier or more difficult; it releases or contrives, makes more probable or less; in the extreme, it constrains and forbids absolutely, but it is always a way of acting or being capable of action.

Government thus understood does not refer to diplomacy between states, the act of declaring or prosecuting territorial wars, or to the juridical activities of legislators. Rather, it refers to a set of consuetudinary practices whose aim, often subliminal, is to direct the behaviour of individuals. It develops into what Lisa A. Freeman has helpfully described as 'a new epistemology of public practice'.[3] And yet, as Foucault also points out, the exercise of government 'of men by other men' implies a peculiar ambiguity insofar as governmental power can only be exercised over free subjects. To speak in terms of governing the conduct of men is to acknowledge that alternative forms of conduct are always available to them – that the subject operates within a margin of (limited) freedom, in which the potential of 'freedom's refusal to submit' will be one of the conditions of possibility for the exercise of power.[4]

The intransigence and obduracy of freedom will be of specific import in this chapter in seeking to understand the way the discourses on the Restoration stage developed, particularly given the rather contumely language of Restoration comedy and the peculiar outbreak of so-called

[2] *Ibid.*, p. 9.

[3] Lisa A. Freeman, 'Jeremy Collier and the Politics of Theatrical Representation', in *Players, Playwrights, Playhouses: Investigating Performance, 1660-1800*, ed. Michael Cordner and Peter Holland (New York: Palgrave Macmillan, 2007), pp. 135–51 (p. 136).

[4] Michel Foucault, 'The Subject and Power', in *Power, Essential Works of Foucault 1954–1984*, vol. 3, ed. James B. Faubion (New York: New Press, 2000), p. 342.

anti-theatricalism that it occasioned. The controversy over the Restoration stage would find its centre of gravity in Jeremy Collier's *A Short View of the Immorality, and Profaneness of the English Stage* of 1698, which although by no means the only contribution to this debate concentrates objections to the stage in a way that will be influential and far reaching (the controversy lasted for several years; Collier himself wrote several 'vindications' of his *Short View* in response to a number of critics).[5] Sister Rose Anthony once described Collier's book as one of the most important publications of 1698[6] and not least because of the impact it would have on later perceptions of comedy, while Matthew Kinservik has more recently confirmed this view, arguing that the Collier stage controversy set out the discursive conditions that paved the way for the licensing act of 1737.[7]

My interest in Collier's intervention is determined by a different set of imperatives, however, insofar as it provides a means of understanding the way in which the Restoration stage became implicated in a conflict provoked by the new governmentality – at the centre of which is found, precisely, the problem of freedom and individual conduct. In order to prepare the ground for this discussion, the chapter first seeks to provide an answer to the following cluster of preliminary questions: around what existing social structures was this new art of government able to operate, according to what underlying principles of governance and in light of what authority was it to be rendered tenable?

The 'Great Game of Conduct'

To begin to answer these questions is to begin to understand what was seen as essential to the establishment of the new bourgeois concept of order as it emerged in the seventeenth century. Viewed in terms of the problem of government, during this period order is concentrated almost entirely on the economic management of the family. But from this assertion a second related problem of government emerges that is not unconnected with the family and that may very well serve to undermine it: the problem of the government of individuals. If there is a problem with respect to the

[5] See, for instance, Jeremy Collier, *A Farther Vindication of the Short View of the Prophaneness and Immorality of the English Stage in which the Objections of a late Book, Entitled, A Defense of Plays, are considered* (1708).

[6] Sister Rose Anthony, *The Jeremy Collier Stage Controversy 1698–1723* (New York: Benjamin Blom, 1966 [1937]), p. 26.

[7] Matthew J. Kinservik, *Disciplining Satire: The Censorship of Satiric Comedy on the Eighteenth Century London Stage* (Lewisburg, PA: Buchnell University Press, 2002), pp. 25–26.

government of individuals, it is because the individual is to be governed with respect to their freedom: to what extent must one value the individual's freedom and to what extent must one restrict that freedom in order to restrain its effects? Individuality, for all its celebrated qualities today, was a far more controversial prospect in the late seventeenth century, no doubt because of the concept of liberty that it implied. On the one hand, good governance equates to a valorisation of the power and productive capacity inherent in the structure of the family, which requires for its most favourable organisation a firm understanding of all the principles of sound economic management, which will be essential to its flourishing; and on the other, there is the enterprising power of the individual embodied in the new figure of *Homo economicus*, who will be essential to the development of a competitive market. The power of the latter, however, will need to be carefully calibrated to the needs of the social body if its dynamism is to be harnessed as a productive force. This is because, at its extreme limit, the individual turns out to be anything but 'productive', and in the case of virulent ultra-individualism, motivated by self-interest and venal egotism, he or she represents a dangerous threat to the order of the state and to the institution of the family. It is hardly surprising that the seventeenth century, which gave birth to the individual, should also give birth to a type of wayward behaviour whose name, libertinism, associated with the likes of notorious figures such as John Wilmot, the Earl of Rochester, would represent all that was excessive and destructive in the concept of the individual.[8] It is the libertine who would seize the stage during the closing decades of the seventeenth century and thus provoke all that was intolerable to the discourse on theatre. To men such as the nonjuring cleric Jeremy Collier, who was only the most vocal and well known of theatre's many opponents at the time, it was the libertine-rake hero who would come to epitomise the essential evil of theatrocracy. These good citizens had every reason to be alarmed, because what emerges with the libertine is not simply an extravagant immorality at odds with the tenets of Christianity, but rather the forceful assertion of Plato's principle of theatrocratic egalitarianism – the 'equality of pleasures' – an equality, moreover, as it now comes to be expressed, that picks up the distinct cadence of Hobbes's

[8] The destructive aspect of the libertine is examined in Harold Weber's 'The Rake-Hero in Wycherley and Congreve', *Philological Quarterly*, 61:2 (1982, spring), 143–60. Weber remarks that in Dorimant we find a rake who is no longer motivated by the pursuit of pleasure, but has 'subordinated sensuality to aggression and discovers in sexual pursuit the triumph of the will and the celebration of the ego' (p. 148). In Congreve, Weber argues, the playwright seeks to secure the rake's 'creative vitality', transforming him from a 'dangerous predator to a valuable member of society' (p. 158).

vision of anarchic nature, since in his individual pursuit of gratification and in his utter disregard of the needs of the majority, the libertine not only endorses the vice of excessive *amour propre* but in so doing actively promotes the war of all against all.[9]

Nevertheless, there is another side to the story of the libertine that needs to be taken into account in order to fully understand the nature of his rebellion. To acquire a sufficient grasp of what is politically at stake in the discourse on theatre during the Restoration is to locate the libertine in relation to the three elements contained in the questions that were posed above, and around which the new governmentality was to first articulate itself: the economic structure of the family, the principles of its governance and enhancement, and the source of its authority. It will be the argument of this chapter that the Restoration stage was provocative not because it endorsed the philosophy or behaviour of the libertine: some playwrights did, but many did not. Rather, it was seen to be provocative because it used the figure of the libertine to probe and question those structures and principles upon which the new governmentality was to rely. How it did so was by placing the problem of 'conduct' at the centre of the dramatic action. It might be objected that conduct is hardly a new word in the lexicon of the English stage; nevertheless, in the Restoration it takes on a singular import and meaning – so much so, in fact, that the libertine's rebellion may well be thought of as a kind of 'revolt of conduct', to employ an expression first coined by Foucault. In order to understand what is novel and innovative in the Restoration playwright's use of conduct, compare it with the Shakespearean drama that preceded it where the term 'conduct' can be found scattered throughout Shakespeare's work, but where it signifies little more than the act of being conveyed from one place to another: to be conducted is to be escorted. A more pertinent use of the term occurs in *King Lear* where, following Cornwall's death, it is asked: 'Who is the conductor of his people?' To which Kent replies: 'As 'tis said, the bastard son of Gloster' (IV.vii). In this brief exchange two key aspects of conduct emerge. First, it refers to the act of leading men. To conduct is to govern a people. But in declaring Gloster's illegitimacy, conduct is also grasped in relation to his character and whether his character befits the office of the conductor of men. Construing the point more broadly, what is revealed here is a theme that was of primary importance to Shakespeare

9 The influence of Hobbes on libertine thought is well documented and has a long history – most notable here is Dale Underwood's *Etherege and the Seventeenth-Century Comedy of Manners* (New Haven, CT: Yale University Press, 1957). See, in particular, pp. 10–28.

in his tragedies: the interrogation of the conduct of the Prince and his courtiers.

What, then, is significant and novel in the multiple uses of the word and concept of conduct in the Restoration play? No doubt it would be wrong to assume writers such as Dryden, Etherege or Otway simply changed its meaning – as the following examples show: when in *The Wives Excuse, or Cuckolds Make Themselves* a question is raised over her husband's honour, Mrs Friendall, in order to protect his reputation, commands him: 'In other things you have a good opinion of my conduct; pray let me govern here' (II.ii). In Etherege's *She Would If She Could*, Lady Cockwood, seeking to conceal her infidelity from her husband, makes the following appeal to him: 'If you moderate yourself according to my directions now, I shall never conceal anything from you, that may increase your opinion of my conjugal fidelity' (IV.i). To conduct means to lead, to direct or to govern, as much as it refers to the object of that action, the modification of an individual or collective behaviour. What has changed here is not the denotative sense of the word but its social context and usage: on the Restoration stage, conduct is no longer a matter of Princes and the court; it refers instead to what could be termed the public dimension of private conduct. For the Restoration dramatist, conduct is a matter for the government of the civic person, whose theatre is not political but civil society.

It is precisely this contextual reframing of conduct that accounts for the specificity of Collier's attack on the Restoration poets: for it soon becomes obvious that what is scandalous to Collier regarding the theatre of the Restoration, as his *Short View of the Immorality and Profaneness of the English Stage* (1698) makes clear, is that conduct has now become the target of *satire*. No longer will conduct testify to the dignity of kings or to the elevated and ennobling grandeur of the tragic fate that befalls the great and the good. Instead, the stage diverts its auditors by indulging in 'idle and sensless . . . Conduct'.[10] What is more, in a terse and severe appraisal of Aristophanes, although with his own contemporaries very much in mind, it is the poet's own 'want of Conduct' that becomes the focus of Collier's derision.[11] This *ad hominem* attack owes everything to Collier's understanding of the purpose of the theatre: if for Collier the theatre is essentially tragic theatre, it is because its purpose and principal end lies in the

[10] Jeremy Collier, *A Short View of the Immorality and Profaneness of the English Stage* (London: S. Keble, 1698), p. 43.

[11] *Ibid.*, p. 44.

instruction of the audience; and it is because Collier can conceive of theatre's legitimacy only in terms of its pedagogical function – because the theatre must either educate or lead astray – that it becomes incumbent upon poets that they too are to be 'govern'd by the Maxims of Morality'. Only insofar as the poet is '[obliged] to Sobriety of Conduct' can he 'assign a proper Fate and Behaviour to every Character'; only because he is unimpeachable in his own conduct can he assure the audience of 'a just distribution of Rewards, and Punishments';[12] and only because those transgressions requiring redress will be committed by characters who are authorised to appear on the stage – and who are authorised precisely because their nobility is intrinsically heroic, assuring the audience that sublime *hubris* at the heart of the tragedy will not corrupt but edify – in other words, *only because the sanction of the moral law internal to tragedy falls upon the heads of one's betters* can the poet be assured that the 'strokes' of conduct will be experienced as something 'admirable'.[13]

What could be further from this tragic determination of conduct than Lady Plyant in Congreve's *The Double-Dealer*, who calls herself a 'Woman of . . . Conduct' (II.i) in order to signify that she is a woman of society, in which – if I can so put it – the 'great game of conduct' is perpetually afoot? At the centre of this game – this 'comedy of manners' – what is at stake, what is gambled and risked, what is speculated upon and ventured, is not one's life; it is far worse: it is nothing less than the honour and reputation of its players. When Lady Fidget urges caution on Wycherely's rake, Horner, in *The Country Wife* – perhaps the most notorious of pre-revolutionary Restoration comedies – it is because, as she tells him: 'you must have a great care of your conduct, for my acquaintance are so censorious . . . that perhaps they'll talk to the prejudice of my honour' (IV.iii). While Etherege's *A Man of Mode* provides its auditors with a brutal demonstration of the play of wit and of how the surface appearances of conduct are worked to mitigate in favour of a rake's reputation – for conduct implies a masquerade – it is a play on appearances, and in two senses. First, in a literal sense in that characters often employ vizards, or masks, in order to conceal their identity – the vizard is a familiar trope in Restoration plays; but second, the mask takes on a rather more

[12] *Ibid.*, p. 151.

[13] *Ibid.* Collier will develop these ideas in his later *A Defence of the Short View of the Profaneness and Immorality of the English Stage* (London: S. Keble, 1699) – his reply to Congreve and Vanbrugh's attempt to defend themselves: 'Comedy is distinguish'd from Tragedy by the Quality of Persons . . . the Business of Tragedy is to represent Princes and Persons of Quality, Comedy ought to be confin'd to the ordinary Rank of Mankind' (pp. 6–7).

metaphorical meaning – as happens with Dorimant, the 'frigid Machiavellian seducer'[14] of the play, who brilliantly conceals what he would rather not have exposed to public scrutiny. It is Dorimant who cultivates friendships simply because it is strategic to do so, not for the sake of companionship, but because the right friend will be expedient to the furthering of his enterprise: the seduction of women. When he is challenged to explain his reason for befriending the young Bellair, who is 'tolerable' but does 'not abound in wit', what Dorimant confesses to his bemused friend and fellow rake Medley is quite unashamedly mercenary: Bellair has 'honorable intentions of marrying' and that makes Dorimant, by virtue of acquaintance alone, appear in a better light than he otherwise would. Dorimant exploits Bellair's good reputation for dishonourable purposes, in order to gain access to the women of quality upon whom he preys: they 'judge', he says, 'more favourably of my reputation. It makes him [Bellair] pass upon some for a man of very good sense, and I upon others for a very civil person' (I.i). In terms of advancing the game, Bellair has a strictly tactical function, and that is to provide Dorimant with an ostensible air of respectability, a 'front'; for friendship with the decent and highly regarded Bellair gives Dorimant the necessary cloak of decorum beneath which he can pursue his real objectives.

If the rake's game of wit requires him to be a master strategist, it is because his game transforms the terrain of conduct into a battleground – a theatre of war.[15] In order to prosecute this war against polite society, against the codes of civility, against the laws of probity and sobriety, the rake will need to turn conduct against conduct. To do so he will exploit the two symbolic registers that conduct makes possible. First, in turning 'conduct against conduct', he opens up the world of manners to a host of confusions and duplicities, insofar as the rake acts in seeming conformity to the expectations of social conventions in order to defy them; the man of wit understands conduct in a way that his victims do not, as the skein of social intercourse and civil practices in which the self unwittingly finds itself entangled and where – if it is witless enough – it is entrapped in the snares and folds of its own modes of public presentation.

[14] Harold Weber, *The Restoration Rake-Hero: Transformations in Sexual Understanding in Seventeenth-Century England* (Madison: University of Wisconsin Press, 1986), p. 4.

[15] In fact, war metaphors abound in Restoration plays – for example, in Etherege's *She Would If She Could*, the rake, Courtall, encourages his comrade, Freeman, to engage Sir Oliver as follows: 'thou wilt find 'em tired with long fight, weak and unable to observe their order; charge 'em briskly, and in a moment thou shalt rout 'em, and with little or no damage to thyself gain an absolute victory' (II.i).

Next, in cynically tapping into the undercurrent of suppressed desires that propriety conduct must disavow, wit turns social discourse back upon itself in a game that exploits language at its meta-discursive level, most notably in the play of the lewd metaphor (see, e.g., Horner's famous play on the word 'China'). Crafty wit forces its dim-witted opponent into a kind of unsuspecting collusion that is ultimately corrupting, exposing the victim to the rake's charge of hypocrisy, since to acknowledge wit is to acknowledge precisely what conduct forbids. If libertine wit has the supreme advantage of being able to manipulate language, it is precisely because those who appear to the rake to be fair game are those who do not grasp the ontological significance of conduct; that conduct should be grasped – just as the rake grasps it – as no more than conventional discourse. They are those who for one reason or another fail to see that adhering to conduct is to confuse what distinguishes being from seeming. These are the pavonine fops, who embrace modish fashion without the least understanding of why it makes them appear so ridiculous.

Sir Fopling Flutter, for example, is a tedious importer of the latest continental fads, whose lack of irony belies his superficiality; Sparkish in *The Country Wife* is a pretentious imitator of wit, 'the greatest fop, dullest ass, and worst company' (I.i). Equally guilty of bad faith, if not more so, are the 'persons of quality' who become victims of the rake because their coarseness, naiveté and downright stupidity makes them easy prey – the countless gullible husbands, for example, who are befriended by rakes only then to find themselves cuckolds; or their wives who, out of an excessive concern for their 'virtue' and 'honour', fail to understand that their conduct is no more than a representation, beyond which all their virtue, honour and reputation possess no real substance. This ontological, perhaps even 'existential', dimension of libertine thought, which shows up as a kind of proto-nihilism, is most explicitly stated in one of Rochester's well-known poems, *Upon Nothing*:

> Great Negative, how vainly wou'd the wise
> Enquire, define, distinguish, teach, devise?
> Didst though thou not stand to point their dull Philosophies?[16]

It is this nullity at the heart of conduct that attests to the libertine's terrible 'truth', and it is nullity that exposes the vanity of the wise, who seek

[16] John Wilmot, *The Works of John, Earl of Rochester: Containing Poems on Several Occasions*, 4th edition (London: Jacob Tonson, 1732), p. 69.

through their dull philosophies to teach, that is to say, to conduct other men. Thus the great game of conduct, at least as it is played by the rake, must be, according to libertinism's own precepts, a zero-sum game. And yet this game cannot be played without running up against a spectacular paradox. On the one hand, what his truth reveals will strike the rake as the greatest irony of all, since it is what everyone already secretly understands: that nothing exists beyond one's reputation. In losing a carefully cultivated reputation, one loses everything. It takes cunning, wile and a steely nerve to play this game – something Horner demonstrates with aplomb in his extraordinarily risky stratagem of declaring to the town that he has become impotent: 'Now may I have by the reputation of an eunuch, the privileges of one; and be seen in a lady's chamber in a morning as early as her husband . . .' (I.i). On the other hand, it cannot be possible to win the game without a thoroughgoing contempt and disregard, not for the mere superficialities of social convention, but for everything that such convention represents. But now a second and indefatigable irony must strike the libertine: while he is at war with conduct, it is a war he cannot afford to win, even if it is a game he cannot afford to lose. I shall return to the point later; suffice it to say here that, ultimately, even for the rake, the great game of conduct is a game that can be played only in bad faith. The reason why is certainly known to the rake better than to anyone else: conduct is never simply reducible to behaviour. Even where it does refer to the dimension of behaviour, this proposition is not to be understood in merely psychological terms. On the contrary: where conduct is at stake, so too is an entire apparatus of governance – and so too is the social ontology underpinning it.

Two Versions of Immanent Power: Pastoral and Deontic

To expand a little upon this idea that conduct is not behaviour but a social power, in order to better situate the response to the rake's revolt, I have proposed, so far, two ways in which conduct is central to Restoration plays. First, conduct represents the field of operations, the theatre of combat, which the Restoration playwrights identified as the object of their satire. Second, conduct is employed as a dramaturgical tactic in prosecuting the great game of conduct – through the use of masks and deception, and as a play of wit against the stultification inherent in social discourse. Conduct understood in this twofold sense, as a dramaturgical tactic and as the strategic field, will constitute the two dimensions of the libertine's revolt against the society of conduct. But what is this apparatus of governance that takes as its object the conduct of individuals, and what social power does it promote? An answer to these questions can be found by looking more specifically at what offended the enemies of this restored theatre. It is well known that the institutions the libertine stage offended against were first and foremost those of the church and the institution of marriage. But what is more important to determine is the nature of the power that these institutions seek to produce and, insofar as they are invested with it, the power through which they are able to be reproduced. It is against this power, after all, that the libertine rebels, while it is for the sake of preserving this power that the counter-offensive of the discourse on theatre is launched. Clearly, the kind of power operative through Church and family is neither sovereign power in the strictly juridical and political sense; nor is it, broadly speaking, disciplinary power in the sense popularised by Foucault. But, of course, Foucault did provide a name for this third type of power and he did so when specifically referring to the political adaptation of the Christian pastorate to the new governmentality of population that emerges in the seventeenth century. He called it 'pastoral power':

> in Christianity the pastorate gave rise to an art of conducting, directing, leading, guiding, taking in hand, and manipulating men, an art of monitoring them and urging them on step by step, an art with the function of taking charge of men collectively and individually throughout their life and at every moment of their existence.[17]

Power understood in this pastoral sense is nothing less than, as Foucault expresses it, 'an action upon action'.[18] A power that governs and directs conduct is a power that is 'co-extensive and continuous with life'[19] and intimately linked to the 'truth of the individual himself'.[20] In the new governmentality, the exercise of power directs itself essentially to the 'conduct of conducts' where it 'operates on the field of possibilities in which the behaviour of active subjects is able to inscribe itself'.[21] It is also for this reason – to employ Mitchell Dean's astute observation – that governing becomes an 'intensely moral activity'.[22] In its generalised form – which is to say, regardless of whether it takes on a religious or a secular character – I would like to suggest that pastoral power is, in fact, best understood as a mode of 'deontic power', as I shall call it here. By deontic power I mean any form or mode of power that exerts an influence over the

[17] Foucault, *Security, Territory, Population*, p. 165. [18] Foucault, *Subject and Power*, p. 340.
[19] *Ibid.*, p. 233. [20] *Ibid.* [21] *Ibid.*, p. 341. [22] Dean, *Governmentality*, p. 19.

subject – not through the application of physical force, but through the use of moral force. Moral force is a power in the sense that it commands obedience, but it is distinct in the sense that whereas disciplinary, juridical or sovereign powers command by means of the force of law and thus through the techniques and instruments of state or juridical violence, moral force derives its power from the demand of the good (where 'good' is to be here understood in terms of what counts as a socially accepted good). It might be objected that juridical power also produces individuals through the conferral of rights on individual subjects. But this overlooks the fact that juridical power is primarily concerned with the individual as the passive recipient of rights and who is abstracted under the law, as a subject bearing duties and responsibilities. In the case of disciplinary power, on the other hand, while it is true that it takes the body in its singularity and thus produces an individual 'subject', what it denies to that subject is precisely freedom: 'discipline produces subjected and practiced bodies, "docile" bodies.'[23] This is not to say that individuals within a disciplinary regime have no capacity to resist the will of the sovereign; rather, it is to say that within the discursive space of disciplinary and sovereign power, no freedom is recognised – or at the very least, it is not essential to its operation. (The point of disciplinary power, as Foucault insists, is not to govern individuals in respect of their freedom, but to divide 'normal from the abnormal'.)[24] In the case of deontic power, by contrast, the freedom of the individual is a fundamental presupposition without which it could not produce its effects – in other words, produce individual subjects, specifically, at the level of an individual's conscience. This is why deontic power always has the subject's morality – their 'conduct' – and their freedom as its primary concern.

And for this same reason, deontic power has traction over the individual because it 'implies a knowledge of the conscience [of each 'soul'] and an ability to direct it'.[25] In this sense, its exercise first and foremost *individualises* the subject. Individuality is what spiritual direction produces, above all else, insofar as it attempts, as psychoanalysis will seek to do in the twentieth century, to penetrate the closed interiority of the subject. On the other hand, if deontic power operates on the conduct of individuals – shaping, forming and moulding behaviours – it also circulates 'socially' within intramural contexts, establishing what might be called, borrowing from

[23] Michel Foucault, *Discipline and Punish, the Birth of the Prison*, trans. Alan Sheridan (London: Penguin, 1991), p. 138.

[24] Foucault, *Security, Territory, Population*, pp. 56–57.

[25] Foucault, *Subject and Power*, p. 333.

Luc Boltanski and Laurent Thévenot, 'orders of worth'.[26] Deontic power thus aims at regulating the spheres of life: spheres of common existence – for example, the domestic sphere, the civic sphere, the public sphere and the sphere of work. Within each sphere one can locate appropriate deontic qualities to which individual conducts should conform. To act appropriately within the civic sphere, for instance, is to conform to a certain set of values, organised around notions of the common good, duty and patriotism; the value set of the domestic sphere, by contrast, places the emphasis elsewhere – on obedience, respect for authority, chasteness and so on. What these interlocking spheres produce is a nexus of dependencies, of mutual responsibilities, of forms of recognition of worth, status and position, as well as forms of censure and exclusion.

To refine this notion of deontic power in the specific context of the Restoration, I would like to look more closely at the figure of the pastor. The pastor, according to Hobbes, belongs to the magisterium of the Church – the part of the Church invested with the authority to teach. His function, however, should not be restricted solely to an evangelical purpose – he is not simply an 'envoy of the Gospel'. The pastor's function, rather, is one of 'superintendence'.[27] In the *Reformed Pastor* (1655), Richard Baxter likewise writes that the pastor's task is not simply to 'feed the church' but to 'perform every branch of pastoral oversight' – '*pastorem agere*: to do the work of a Pastor or Shepherd to the flock'.[28] Pastorship is the practice of 'personal inspection';[29] its objective, the salvation of the flock: 'A minister is not only to be employed in public preaching to his people, but should be a known counsellor for their souls.'[30] What does pastoral oversight, inspection or superintendence entail? 'The *Pastoral* task,' says Hobbes, '[is] to teach, strengthen and govern the minds of those who already [believe].'[31] But this pastoral task of teaching, guiding, directing, counselling – 'conducting souls', as Foucault puts it – makes an extraordinary demand on the pastor: as Baxter exhorts his reader – before the pastor can 'take heed to all their FLOCK' they 'should take heed to themselves'.[32] Due diligence requires that the first duty of the pastor will be to examine their own personal conduct.

[26] Luc Boltanski and Laurent Thévenot, 'The Sociology of Critical Capacity', *European Journal of Social Theory*, 2:3 (1999), 368.

[27] Thomas Hobbes, *On the Citizen*, ed. Richard Truck and Michael Silverthorne (Cambridge: Cambridge University Press, 2010), p. 222.

[28] Richard Baxter, *The Reformed Pastor* (London, 1888 [1655]), p. 29.

[29] *Ibid.*, p. 40.

[30] *Ibid.*, p. 41.

[31] Hobbes, *On the Citizen*, p. 223.

[32] Baxter, *Reformed Pastor*, p. 2.

Thus Baxter will insist that in order to perform the function of pastor, pastors are 'diligently to watch over ourselves; our own conduct and behaviour, our heart and life: all our tempers, words, and actions'.[33] There are three reasons that make this requirement of permanent self-examination necessary. First, pastoral power does not primarily operate from the sanctuary of the pulpit; it is above all a practical endeavour that aims to form the proper conduct of life *in* the pastorate. The pastor must come down from the pulpit and engage the pastorate directly, and for that reason, administering to the flock must be an all-consuming vocation:

> A practical doctrine must be practically preached. We must study as hard how to live well, as how to preach well. If the saving of souls be your end, you will certainly attend to it out of the pulpit, as well as in it; you will LIVE for it, and contribute all your endeavours to attain it ... You have very great need of the strictest care over your conduct.[34]

Second, and precisely because his is a practical vocation, the pastor must also abide by the law of the gospel – in the strictest sense, he must follow it to the letter. Only in this way will the pastor's own conduct be beyond reproach – and only in this way can the pastor lead the flock by his example: 'All that a preacher does is a kind of preaching.'[35] Therefore the pastor is warned: 'Take heed of your conduct, because the success of all your labours does very much depend upon it.'[36]

The third reason ties the pastor to pastorate by means of a theatrical metaphor:

> When you live a covetous or careless life; when you drink or game, or waste your time, &c. by your practice you preach these sins to your people ... for they take the pulpit to be but as a stage; a place where preachers must shew themselves and play their parts ... They will not much regard it if you do not shew, by your conduct amongst them, that you meant as you said.[37]

The stage is invoked not in order to suggest that the power of the pastor is merely a kind of ploy, a deception, a kind of empty theatrics, but because the church, like the theatre itself, is invested with the power of demonstration. It shows the flock (or audience) how they should behave with respect to the specific example that it stages. What one demonstrates in a church, what is rehearsed there, no less than in the theatre, is conduct. This shows that the audience of the actor and the pastorate of the pastor share a fundamental susceptibility to being influenced by the power of the example. It is as a kind of analogon that the pastor must stand before his

[33] *Ibid.*, p. 3. [34] *Ibid.*, p. 20. [35] *Ibid.*, p. 24. [36] *Ibid.*, p. 28. [37] *Ibid.*, p. 24.

flock, representing for the entire pastorate the very model of Christian virtue. 'Watch therefore, brethren,' advises Baxter, 'over your own hearts'[38] because the pastor's conduct will only be seen to be unimpeachable, if it *is* unimpeachable. Those who lead are susceptible to the same temptations as other men, but they will be judged more harshly where they transgress: 'Take heed to your conduct, because your sins are attended with more heinous aggravations than those of other men.'[39]

Still, if the pastor must perform the role of the exemplar, if he must be able to stand before his flock as *persona exemplaris* – as someone fit for imitation – the question nevertheless is why on earth he should matter to them? Why should they care? In short, if the pastor has no disciplinary means to physically sanction and coerce his flock, then what power does he possess over them? What exactly is the nature and source of pastoral power? First, for the Christian pastorate at least, the source of pastoral power derives directly from the authority of Christ with the bestowal of pastoral duties upon the Apostles;[40] but as to its *nature*, it is the power, as Hobbes puts it, to remit or retain sin: a 'power of losing and binding'.[41] In other words, the pastor is the one whose investiture by Christ gives him the authority to secure for the penitent sinner the salvation they seek; equally – for the impenitent, he has the authority to exclude them – to banish them from the Christian community. It is here that pastoral power asserts itself most explicitly in distinguishing itself from sovereign or disciplinary power, insofar as it works through the regard that every pastor must have for each member of his flock: 'Does not a careful shepherd look after every individual sheep, and a good physician attend every particular patient?'[42] What could be more particularising than directing a sinner to the point of recognising that atonement is needed if they are to repent their sins and escape damnation? To repent is to be 'singularised' by submitting to the charge of one's own conscience. It is to own the offence, but in so doing, it requires *owning up to it*. It is for this reason that in order to repent a sin one is necessarily required to submit to the authority and power of someone authorised to pass judgement upon one's errancy. In a sense, it requires a twofold performance: in the first place one must be able to demonstrate that one has ceased one's rebellion against Christ; and thus,

[38] *Ibid.*, p. 26. [39] *Ibid.*, p. 21. [40] John 20:21.

[41] '*Pastors have the power to truly and absolutely remit sins*, but only *to the penitent, and to retain them but only to the impenitent*' (Hobbes, *On the Citizen*, p. 225).

[42] Baxter, *Reformed Pastor*, p. 40.

the penitent sinner must also be able to make a show of his obedience by submitting to the will of the pastor.[43]

For this reason, repentance must always be accompanied by a declarative speech act. It requires a confession; only through a public act in which one condemns oneself can the penitent demonstrate that he has been duly and sincerely humbled, that he has come to know what sin *is*. And only by exposing himself to the absolving gaze of the pastor can the act of penitence be truly and finally verified. One finds this exigible form of pastoral power at work in repentance in the extraordinary account of Rochester's less than elegiac death-bed recantation of his 'former wicked life', in *The Libertine Overthrown: Or a Mirror for Atheists* (circa 1690) – witnessed by his wife and family chaplain:

> For the benefit of all those who I have drawn to sin by My example and encouragement, I leave to the World this last Declaration, which I deliver in the presence of the Great God, who knows the secrets of men's hearts, and befor whom I am now appearing to be judged.

Rochester's confessional atonement by all accounts was met with profound bewilderment across the town. Nevertheless, two essential things are revealed about the nature of pastoral power insofar as it exerts an influence over his final words. First, for the pastorate, where there is conduct there is always the prospect of the bad example, of a form of conduct that promotes sin. 'I have been,' Rochester confesses, 'an Open enemy of Jesus Christ.' His is the example that leads astray. And yet in his prodigality, the bad example becomes – and precisely because it was the worst and most egregious of all possible examples – the most exemplary and the most exceptional. As the authors of the book proclaim, Rochester's case demonstrates an 'eminently and sincerely penitent death'.

*

Repentance and reform, then, are the two watchwords of the counter-offensive of the discourse on theatre against the revolt of the libertine, a counter-offensive, however, that must be understood beyond the

43 Foucault describes this as 'a relationship of submission, but not submission to a law or a principle of order . . . It is a relationship of submission of one individual to another individual, correlating an individual who directs and an individual who is directed' (Foucault, *Security, Territory, Population*, p. 175).

response of a few religious zealots to the provocations of a cluster of plays; rather, it should be understood relative to the rapid expansion of the pastorate and its appropriation to the field of deontic power during the closing years of the seventeenth century. Deontic power, I have suggested, is the general form of power constitutive of a new governmentality whose core features can now be more precisely demarcated. First, deontic power is above all an 'interpellative' power in that it is capable of producing the individual in his singularity – it *personalises* him, calls upon him to give an unreserved account of himself. In Christian terms, it is the power that interpellates each individual subject before the authority of God and his ministry, and in prospect of the subject's possible salvation, excommunication and even damnation. It is a power of examining the subject through the evidence of their personal conduct, but for this reason, second, while deontic power is not sovereign power, it has a quasi-juridical capability in that it exhibits a dual performativity: it *prescribes/proscribes*. It thereby possesses the authority to regulate, that is to say, set limits on what is permissible in the conduct of individuals according to pre-established norms, and to judge individual transgressions in relation to those norms. Related to this, third, it is a power that always takes a *conventional* form – one that operates through social and civic relations, and therefore it exposes individual conduct, on the one hand, to the possibility of public censure, disapproval and reproach, and, on the other, it honours, pays tribute to and praises virtuous behaviour. When one speaks of an individual's 'moral conduct', what is meant is that the personal conduct of an individual is always subject to a communal understanding of socio-cultural norms as mediated by the social practices it is expected to perform. Thus in its performance deontic power *mediates* the individual's relation to the group. Fourth, and finally, deontic power *predisposes* the individual, in that it saturates the entire social field through the forms of cultivation by which the individual through circumstance and education is inclined in one way or another to act. Thus, deontic power is a pedagogical power that *cultivates* subjects.

In the case of the Restoration play, then, it is deontic power, insofar as it determines conduct through the mediate form of 'manners', that is challenged, satirised, flouted and defied on the stage; and it is in terms of the rejection of its prescriptions, conventional mediations, forms of cultivation and modes of personalisation that one can begin to understand more specifically why the libertine revolt is not just a 'revolt of conduct', but a revolt that will need to be suppressed.

Conduct, Counter-conduct and Revolts of Conduct

To get a better purchase on this revolt of conduct, I would like to return momentarily to Foucault. Wherever pastoral power is exercised, it will inevitably produce forms of resistance, dissidence, disobedience and insubordination – and not least because there is 'an immediate and founding correlation between conduct and counter-conduct'.[44] These 'specific revolts of conduct' take the form of 'movements whose objective is a different form of conduct . . . wanting to be conducted differently, by other leaders (*conducteurs*) and other shepherds'.[45] To be sure, it might be objected that seventeenth-century libertinism hardly constitutes a movement in the sense Foucault had in mind – for instance, he spoke most frequently of nonconformist religious movements, the 'dissenters' such as Methodists and Anabaptists.[46] Notwithstanding this fact, I see no justification for restricting the concept of a revolt of conduct to religious dissident groups, and neither, I believe, does Foucault – counter-conducts can be extended to incorporate the behaviour of the delinquent, the deviant, the mad and the ill. Indeed, delinquency is arguably one of the forms of counter-conduct that the libertine engaged in, as this remarkable description of libertine counter-conduct, recounted in Pepys's diary, illustrates:

> [The Rake Sedley was seen] coming in open day into the Balcone and show[ing] his nakedness – acting all the postures of lust and buggery that could be imagined, and abusing of scripture and, as it were, from thence preaching a Mountebanke sermon from the pulpit, saying that there he hath to sell such a pouder as should make all the cunts in the town run after him – a thousand people standing underneath to see and hear him. And that being done, he took a glass of wine and washed his prick in it and then drank it off; and then took another and drank the King's health.[47]

[44] Foucault, *Security, Territory, Population*, p. 196. [45] *Ibid.*, p. 194.

[46] An alternative defence could be mounted on the basis of scholarship that seeks to establish a relationship between religious dissidence and libertinism. For example, Sarah Ellezweiz, 'The Faith of Unbelief', *Journal of British Studies*, 44:1 (2005), 27–45, argues that Rochester's libertinism was the 'inheritor of revolutionary religious radicalism' (33) and 'a continuation, in modified form, of the radical sectarianism of the interregnum' (32). Ellezweiz cites Christopher Hill, who suggests a 'link between the sexual and religious libertinism of the Rutters' (32). Gillian Manning argues that Rochester's poem *Satyr against Man* inspired an animated debate on atheism throughout the 1670s, although was not a refusal of all forms of spirituality – 'Rochester's Satyr', *Seventeenth Century*, 8.1 (1993), 107. Jeremy Webster also argues for the connection between libertinism and those radical Christian heterodox sects who 'not only glorified in sex and sinful behaviour as evidence of grace but also denied the immortality of the soul'; Jeremy Webster, *Performing Libertinism in Charles II's Court: Politics, Drama, Sexuality* (Basingstoke: Palgrave Macmillan, 2005), p. 7.

[47] Pepys quoted in Webster, *Performing Libertinism*, p. 4.

It should also be noted that after flirting with the term 'revolt of conduct', Foucault goes on to reject it in favour of what is perhaps a less voluntarist concept: that of a 'counter-conduct'. A counter-conduct specifies the form by which an individual resists deontic power; but that resistance by no means entails an act of explicit or wilful rebellion. There are many subtle ways of rejecting the instructions, the values, the obligations and duties of the pastorate; of refusing to be led to one's salvation; and of subverting, perhaps even incapacitating the authority of the pastor – in short, of exerting a counter-will to the 'official governmentality of society'.[48] A specific counter-conduct may even take the form of the symptom, as is the case with mental illness where the language of insurgency would seem misplaced. With libertine counter-conduct, however, there is a sufficient level of 'revolt' to merit retaining the term. Moreover, the political implications of his revolt justify its use. For the libertine's resistance, above all else, is a resistance to the 'intrication of the pastorate', as Foucault puts it at one point, in all forms of civil governance.[49] In the seventeenth century, this intrication of pastoral power and private life – this entanglement of personal conduct and civil power – is most clearly associated with the instrument of matrimony. It is for this reason, without doubt, that marriage tends one way or another to be located at the very heart of the Restoration comedy of manners; and thus the specific force of libertine satire is most derisively felt when it is directed against the civic power that matrimony – its institution, its underlying principles and its authority – symbolises.

Hence the reason behind the attack Collier launched on Vanbrugh's *The Provok'd Wife* (1697):

> I perceive we should have a rare Set of *Virtues* if these *Poets* had the making of them! How they hug a Vicious Character, and how profuse are they in their Liberalities to Lewdness? In the *Provok'd Wife Constant* Swears at Length, solicits Lady *Brute*, Confesses himself Lewd, and prefers Debauchery to Marriage.[50]

Vanbrugh's play provides an interesting case in point, and not least because he attempted to defend himself against Collier's attack, arguing that the play 'tends to the Reformation of Manners'.[51] Collier had misunderstood the 'Nature of Comedy' whose business 'is to shew People what

[48] Foucault, *Security, Territory, Population*, p. 199. [49] *Ibid.*, p. 203.
[50] Collier, *Short View*, p. 143.
[51] Vanbrugh, *A Short Vindication of the Relapse and the Provok'd Wife, from Immorality and Prophaneness* (London: H. Walwyn, 1698), p. 49.

they shou'd do, by representing them upon the Stage, doing what they Shou'd not'.[52] Vanbrugh – and Congreve with him – who wrote in the wake of the revolution of 1688, had embraced the 'moral turn' of the age. To represent the libertine on stage was, for Vanbrugh, by no means to endorse his conduct. On the contrary, he writes: 'I have shew'd *Constant* upon the Stage . . . I have laid open his Vices as well as his Virtues.'[53] In this sense what *The Provok'd Wife* attempts to do is both to make thematic what is essentially at stake in the libertine attack on matrimony and to ameliorate some of its excesses.[54] Nevertheless, while it is true that Collier cynically misreads the play, he rightly intuits that what is held in contention in the play, what is made controversial there, and subjected to the scrutiny of wit, is precisely the value of virtue within a marriage that is in reality nothing but 'a tawdry façade'.[55] This fact alone is enough for Collier to view it as indistinguishable from the rest of the libertine stage with its general attack on the value of marriage. In *She Would If She Could*, to offer a quick survey of some examples, Sir Oliver protests: 'a pox of this tying man and woman together, for better, for worse! Upon my conscience it was but a trick that the clergy might have a feeling in the cause' (I.i) – suggesting that not only do the clergy have a vested interest in promoting the business of marriage, but perhaps, more scurrilously, they have an interest that is sexual. Rashley, in Thomas Durfey's *A Fond Husband* (1677), expresses the central contradiction in the institution of marriage, namely that it promotes duty and virtue over sensual pleasure and love:

> Marriage acts only the decrees of duty; love has the least share in't. In this age, a husband with a wife is like a bully in a church: the only pleasure he takes is to sleep away the hours should be employed in conjugal duty (IV. iv, 224).

It is for this reason that, in Otway's play *The Soldier's Fortune* (1680), Sylvia declares that 'of all creature's a husband's the thing that's odious to me' (I.ii). And Goodvile, in *Friendship in Fashion*, laments on 'that domestic plague called wife' (IV.i), while his wife, Mrs Goodvile, spends

[52] *Ibid.*, p. 45. [53] *Ibid.*, p. 46.

[54] One could also cite Vanbrugh's *The Relapse*, for example, and in particular the exchange of wit between Berinthia and Worthy:

> *Worthy*: She runs . . . into the common mistake of fond wives, who conclude themselves virtuous because they can refuse a man they don't like, when they have got one they do.
>
> *Berinthia*: I think 'tis a presumptuous thing in a Woman to assume the name of virtuous, till she has heartily hated her husband (42).

[55] Michael Cordner, 'Marriage Comedy after the 1688 Revolution: Southerne to Vanbrugh', *Modern Language Review*, 85:2 (1990, April), 273–89 (p. 289).

her time hatching a plot to show the world 'how dull a tool a husband is, compared with that triumphant thing, a wife, and her guardian angel lover' (V.i). In *The Provok'd Wife*, the play's preoccupation with the problem of virtue leads Constant – Lady Brute's would-be lover – into an extended discourse on the nature of virtue in an effort to convince her to abandon it:

LADY BRUTE: 'Tis an offence, a great one, where it would rob a woman of all she ought to be adored for, her virtue.
CONSTANT: Virtue! That phantom of honour, which men in every age have so condemned; they have thrown it amongst women to scramble for.
LADY BRUTE: If it be a thing of so very little value, why do you so earnestly recommend it to your wives and daughters?
CONSTANT: We recommend it to our wives, Madam, because we would keep them to ourselves; and to our daughters, because we would dispose of them to others.
LADY BRUTE: 'Tis then of some importance, it seems, since you can't dispose of them without it. (III.i)

What is implicitly satirised here through Constant's cynical attitude towards virtue is, of course, essential to the libertine satirising of marriage itself: it is the way women are determined by their position in the family as the property of men. A husband will protect his wife as he might protect his goods and chattels. A similar sentiment is expressed by Collier in his criticism of the libertine: 'I have sometimes wonder'd why a Lewd Person is not as infamous as a Thief. Is Domestick quiet, and the Securities of Blood and Marriage, less valuable than a little money? I say, why is not he that steals a woman's Honour as uncreditable as a common surprizer of property?'[56] In an essay on 'whoredom', he will be even more explicit: 'Has a Man no Property in his Marriage?'[57] Needless to say, in the case of daughters, a virtuous reputation is required if they are to enter into a profitable marriage arrangement, where the point of marriage will not be the happiness of the spouses, but the increase in the wealth and prestige of an estate.

For the Restoration playwright, then, the internal dimensions of marriage could be satirised effectively only if they were drawn in relation to the problem of virtue – and correlatively in the sense that, insofar as it targets virtue, libertine satire implicitly threatens the founding institution of social

[56] Collier, *Short View*, p. 123.
[57] Jeremy Collier, *Essays upon Several Moral Subjects, Part III* (London: George, Strahan, 1720), p. 116.

order with theatrocratic disorder.[58] The reason for this becomes clear once it is seen that virtue is grasped less in terms of the play of manners and instead as intrinsically linked to the exercise of deontic power that is invested in the institution of marriage (and by extension, the family). In this sense virtue is not something anyone can aspire to have or possess: one is not and cannot *be* virtuous. Rather, virtue – like Hobbesian honour, which is 'not in the person being honoured but in the person who honours'[59] – is likewise something that must be performed. Strictly speaking, there is no such thing as 'virtue'. On the one hand, there are only virtues: precepts to govern one's action, and, on the other, there is the *observation* of virtue in the sense intended by J.S. Mill when he spoke of the 'cultivation of the love of virtue'[60] which *predisposes* individuals to act rightly. For this reason, the administration of virtue, understood as something to be cultivated within each individual and as the set of rules governing their private conduct, will constitute the apparatus of governance that will be exercised over the social institution of the family.

Governance and the Family: The New Patriarchy

That the family should become the locus of this kind of governmental scrutiny, this regime of deontic power, in the seventeenth century, is hardly surprising: the family was already viewed as a kind of microcosm of government, a 'model' of government; but also, it thereby becomes the primary site for the cultivation of individuals, and thus the primary site of pastoral instruction. In this way, deontic power binds the fate of the family to both Church and Commonwealth: all three constitute a form of ethical unity, a kind of *Sittlichkeit*. In his *Of Domestical Duties* (1622) William Gouge would argue the point explicitly:

> Besides, a family is a little church, and a little Commonwealth, at least a lively representation thereof, whereby trial may be made of such as are fit for any place of authority or of subjection in Church or Commonwealth. Or rather it is as a school wherein the first principles and grounds of government and subjection are learned: whereby men are fitted to greater matters in Church or Commonwealth.[61]

[58] Maximillian E. Novak writes, '[i]t should be obvious that the appeal to the virtues in wildness is related to the Libertine ideal of man the animal – man purged of the corruptions and restraints of society'; 'Margery Pinchwife's "London Disease": Restoration Comedy and the Libertine Offensive of the 1670s', *Studies in the Literary Imagination*, 10:1 (1977, spring), 1–23 (p. 17).

[59] Hobbes, *On the Citizen*, pp. 175–76.

[60] John Stuart Mill, *Utilitarianism* (London: John W. Parker, 1864), p. 57.

[61] William Gouge, *Of Domesticall Duties* (London: George Miller, 1622), p. 11

For this reason, Gouge writes, a 'conscionable performance of household duties' will be 'accounted a public work'. It is also for this same reason that Baxter asserts that 'a general reformation' cannot occur unless the reformation of the family 'is first procured'[62] – arguing that the 'life of religion, and the welfare and glory of church and state, depend much upon family government and duty. If we suffer the neglect of this, we undo all.'[63] A reformation of the family will require nothing less than its remodelling on the basis of pastoral power. This correlation of pastoral power and household governance is asserted in Bunyan's *Christian Behaviour* (1674), where he argues that 'the master of the family [has] a work to do for God, namely, the right governing of his family'.[64] What this entails is made perfectly clear through an analogy: in his house the master is *as* a pastor is in the house of God – a conductor of souls. Thus Bunyan decrees:

> A pastor must be sound and uncorrupt in his doctrine ... so must the master of a family.[65]
> A pastor should be apt to teach, to reprove, and to exhort; and so should the master of a family.[66]
> A pastor must himself be exemplary in faith and holiness ... [as] should the master of a family.[67]

Baxter designates this pastoral form of family governance, typical for the age, a 'Christian Oeconomics'.[68] The doctrine of Christian economics will link together the Greek concept of *oikonomia* and the Christian concept of pastoral power. In the first place, it promotes an economic logic of good and prudent governance of the household, an *oikonomia*, in its standard sense – that is, the art of managing the individuals, the wealth and goods in one's estate – administering the affairs of the household in order to ensure its prosperity; and then, second, there is an understanding of *oikonomia* now inextricably associated with the idea that the master of the household, as its 'steward', bears an additional responsibility: he has the duty of pastoral oversight within the family. Consequently, he will be responsible for the moral guidance and direction of his wife, children and servants. The basic principles of the economic government of households will be

[62] Baxter, *Reformed Pastor*, p. 46. [63] *Ibid.*, p. 43.
[64] John Bunyan, *Christian Behaviour* (London, 1674), p. 32. [65] *Ibid.*, p. 33. [66] *Ibid.*, p. 34.
[67] *Ibid.*, p 34.
[68] Richard Baxter, *A Christian Directory*, vol. 2 (London: R. White, 1673). '*Domus & Familia*, a *Houshold and family*, are indeed in Oeconomicks somewhat different notions, but one thing. *Domus* is to *familia* as *civitas* to *republica*, the *former* is made the *subject* of the latter, the latter the *finis internum* of the *former*' (p. 490). See also Foucault on the 'economy of souls', in *Security, Territory, Population*, p. 192.

indistinguishable from the moral governance of the family. William Whately's *Bride-Bush* (1617) advises, for instance:

> For as the Ministers must watch ouer the soules of their flocke for their profite and saluation, not for their own priuate wealth and aduantage: so must the husband deale with his wife . . . so that as hee must aime at her good, so must hee effect it, by gouerning in a right manner, to the nourishing and encreasing of whatsoever virtue, rooting out and weakening of whatsoever corruption hee shall meete with in her.[69]

Good economic management of the household requires the directing, instruction and, where necessary, correction of the conduct of each member of the household, according to their place and duties within it: 'The Husband must undertake the principal part of the Government of the whole family, even of the Wife herself.'[70] He must be 'acquainted with the End to which he is to conduct them'; and with respect to the wife, he must be 'her teacher in the matters that belong to her salvation'.[71] A husband's 'knowledge must be used for the Instruction and sanctification of the Wife'.[72]

Correspondingly, the wife's duty will be twofold. She is to 'follow the conduct' of her governor and to live in 'voluntary Subjection and Obedience'.[73] This form of patriarchal organisation, at the heart of Christian economics, determines the duties women were expected to perform, as well as the virtues to which they were meant to conform. These are repeated endlessly in the conduct books of the seventeenth century.[74] The *English* Housewife (1675) – a kind of practical guide to household economics for women – provides a compendious account of the practical tasks that fall to the mistress of the house. It offers advice on the preparation of medicines, for example, on gardening, on appropriate forms of habiliment and on cookery. But also it advises her on her 'inward vertues'. The 'office of our English House-Wife', the author writes, 'hath her most general imployments within the house; where from the example of her vertues, and the most approved skill of her knowledge, those of her family, may both learn to serve God and sustain man in that Godly and profitable sort, which is required of every true Christian'.[75] Similar moral

69 William Whately, *A Bride-Bush, or a Wedding Sermon Compendiously Describing the Duties of Married Persons: By Performing Whereof, Marriage Shall Be to Them a Great Helpe, Which Now Finde It a Little Hell* (London, 1617), pp. 21–22.

70 Baxter, *Christian Directory*, p. 529. 71 *Ibid.* 72 *Ibid.*, p. 499. 73 *Ibid.*, p. 531.

74 In *A Man of Mode*, Medley will mock conduct books such as Hannah Woolley's *The Gentlewoman's Companion* (1675), which he describes in the play as 'The Art of Affectation' (II.i).

75 Gervase Markham, *The English Housewife; Containing the Inward and Outward Virtues which ought to be in a Complete Woman* (London, 1675), pp. 1–2.

prescriptions can be found in Brathwaite's *The English Gentlewoman* (1631), a complete taxonomy of genteel conduct for women, which counsels its reader: 'know then (noble Gentlewoman) that your Honour, be it neuer so eminent; your Descent, be it neuer so ancient; lose both their beauty and antiquity, if virtue haue not in you a peculiar souveraignty.'[76]

This ceaseless advocacy of virtue was not a merely rhetorical device, an effort to convince both men and women to accept the restrictions of domestic life; nor is it therefore simply reducible to the prescriptions of an ideology that would be, as it were, cobbled together from existing religious doctrine by the new patriarchy. It is misunderstood if it is thought simply as a form of exhortation – as a kind of mass manipulation of minds – just as libertine satire is misunderstood if it is seen merely as an attack on the superficial 'manners' of the society of conduct. It is necessary rather to see how both relate to the exercise of deontic power, to understand that practices of governing one's conduct are, above all else, practices of governing one's self. The author of the *Applause of Virtue* (1705), for instance, will admit quite candidly: 'Reputation is the Bridle, wherewith God useth to repress all sorts of Vices.'[77] Virtue grasped in this way refers not to qualities of moral excellence – chastity, prudence, temperance, fortitude and so on – but to the practice of governing oneself according to precepts aimed at determining not just how one should act, but how one's actions should conform to the duties one is expected to fulfil in order to be counted as a subject within the Christian Commonwealth. It is not simply a matter of ensuring a standard of moral correctness and probity at the level of one's private conduct. Rather, it is a matter of inculcating in the individual, by means of instruction or discipline, a new governmentality, in which what is to be produced is a subject who will be obedient to the broader polity, and whose 'moral qualities' will be measured, precisely, in terms of how well they perform their duties, whatever those may be, given their rank, position and social status.

Several things are important to clarify here. First, there is the question of what this practice of self-governance demands of each individual self. Second, how does the governmentality of the self procure through a 'reformation' the objectives of a broader governmentality? Third, why do these practices produce the contradiction of libertinage insofar as they take

[76] Richard Brathwaite, *The English Gentlewoman* (London: B. Alsop & T. Favvcet, 1631), p. 193.

[77] Frances Norton, *The Applause of Virtue, Consisting of Several Divine and Moral Essays Towards the Obtaining of True Virtue* (London: James Graves, 1705), p. 98.

the self of the individual and, specifically, the self in its freedom, as their material? I will address these issues *seriatim*.

(1) What is demanded of the self in practising Christian virtue is the discipline of mortification. Baxter would write an entire treatise on the subject, but the idea is simple enough to grasp: 'brutish inclinations'[78] must be 'subdued' and 'governed' by reason: 'the appetite and all the senses [were] made to be ruled by reason.'[79] Practising Christian virtue means observing 'temperance and modesty' in all matters of one's conduct.[80] This doctrine of mortification is really what lies at the heart of the discourse on theatre during the period, and emerges most explicitly when it is juxtaposed with the conduct of the libertine. Collier will complain, for example: 'Thus we see what a fine time Lewd People have on the English Stage. No Censure, no mark of Infamy, no Mortification must touch them.'[81] The 'only valuable qualities' to be found in plays, he remarks sarcastically, are the opposing qualities of 'Libertinism and Profaness, Dressing, Idleness, and Gallantry'[82] – these are 'the Standard[s] of Behaviour' that libertine characters such as Wildblood, Horner, Bellamy, Harcourt, Mellefont and Valentine set for the audience insofar as they are elected 'the Masters of Ceremony and Sense'[83] by the English Stage. The author of the *Applause of Virtue* is equally uncompromising with respect to the task of expurgating vice through mortification of the flesh; but she also draws upon the affective and psychological dimension of sin to make her point against the libertines:

> Libertines have no other Aim in the World but the Contentment of Nature, which unavoidably engageth in all manner of Vice. In all Pleasures we shall find so little Contentment that the Vanity of the Possession will soon reprove the Violence of the Appetite ... A longing after Sensual Pleasures, is a Debauching of the Spirits of a Man, and makes it ... unapt for Noble and Spiritual Imployments ... The Nature of Sensual Pleasure is vain, empty, and unsatisying; biggest always in Expectation, and a meer vanity in the Enjoyment, and leaves a Sting and a thorn behind, when it is gone.[84]

Does the author of this book write from personal experience – the disappointment and bitterness of thwarted and expended passions? Perhaps. Nevertheless, and possibly with the theatre of Vanbrugh and

[78] Baxter, *Christian Directory*, p. 144.
[79] Richard Baxter, *The Practical Works of Richard Baxter in Four Volumes*, vol. 1 (London: Arthur Hall, 1847), p. 301.
[80] Baxter, *Christian Directory*, p. 144. [81] Collier, *Short View*, p. 148. [82] *Ibid.*, p. 145.
[83] *Ibid.*, p. 148. [84] Norton, *Applause of Virtue*, p. 99.

Congreve in mind, she is assiduous in her defence of the cause of matrimony against the corruptions of the libertine: 'The nearer you are to God, the better shall you be united: such an Union will not allow so much as an unchast Thought . . . much less the freedom in polluting the Marriage-Bed, which this Corrupted Age pursues, nay, makes Boast of.'[85] And as if to counter the defilements of the theatrical stage, she declares: 'God hath given us the whole stage of our Lives to exercise all the Active Virtues of Religion.'[86]

(2) The exercising of the active virtues of religion points to the second question regarding the object, purpose and end of this form of pastoral governmentality. In the first instance this end approximates to the problem of how to ensure 'moral hygiene' within the polity. For the discourse on theatre, the ends of virtue will be expressed through the doctrine of mortification. What it says amounts to a quasi-Platonic prescription against one of the fundamental evils identified with the theatre: its purported effeminacy. The anonymous author of *Remarques on the Humours and Conversations of the Town* (1673) – a book warning a young man from taking up residence in London – seeks to establish a stark contrast between the 'innocent and manly' 'divertisments of the Country', such as horse-riding and hunting, which preserve ones 'health' and 'vigour',[87] and the 'effeminacy' of the pleasures of the town, such as the theatre: 'it is a double indiscretion, to soften and charm our Youth with luxuries and Pleasures . . . degenerating the antient Vertue of the English.'[88]

What exactly is meant here by effeminacy? First, effeminacy is the state that results when one shuns the practices of mortification, when one lives, as the libertine does, solely by rule of one's appetites. It signifies a kind of perverse wilfulness that is simultaneously an expression of the individual's rebellion against the rationality of the will, a refusal of subjection to the authority of reason, and a kind of disobedience towards the precepts of Christianity. Hence effeminacy will indelibly mark the association of atheism and libertinage: 'Live therefore like men, and not like beasts; like Christians, and not like atheists and epicures.'[89] Second, insofar as it signals the submission of the will to the affective dimension

[85] *Ibid.*, p. 48. [86] *Ibid.*, p. 13.

[87] Anon., *Remarques on the Humours and Conversations of the Town* (London, 1673), p. 29.

[88] *Ibid.*, p. 66. '[The] life of a young Gentleman [in the Town] is for the greater part vicious, sottish, and prophane, and not only degenerated below the precepts of ancient gallantry and generosity; but beneath that prudence, sobriety, and discretion, which ought to be found in all who pretend to man-hood' (*Remarques*, p. 2). See also George Ridpath, *The Stage Condemn'd* (London, 1698), p. 38.

[89] Baxter, *Practical Works*, p. 406.

of the body, to its sensuality and thereby its infirmities and corruptions, it will be symptomatic of the mortal weakness in man – expressed otherwise, it discloses the presence of sin: a 'base unmanly thing it is', says Baxter, 'to be a slave to a fleshy appetite.'[90] Indulgence, intemperance and emasculation – all will be associated with the effeminising influence of the theatre of the libertine; but also, insofar as effeminacy is associated with physical sensibility that typically characterises women as inferior to men in the seventeenth century, it will signify a kind of betrayal of the manly virtues required to build a strong and vital nation. The author of the *Remarques* understands the counter-conduct of the stage precisely in this way when he says: 'those who debauch and effeminate Nations, may be pleasing, but they can never be wise and generous Directors.'[91] In fact, one finds this peculiar assertion everywhere in the discourse against the theatre – that in threatening to weaken the morals of the nation, theatre threatens the very polity itself: 'what well-form'd Government or State can last, when wit has laid the people's Virtue wast?'[92]

To understand why such views were so prevalent, consider how the purpose and end of deontic power will turn precisely on the formation of the kind of ethical unity mentioned earlier. A 'commonwealth [civitas] and a church [ecclesia] of the same Christian men', writes Hobbes, 'are exactly the same thing under two names.'[93] They comprise the same material, the same bodies and souls, obligated to one another according to the same precepts and laws: it is this co-belonging of all to one Church that forms the unity of the polity within a Christian Commonwealth.[94] It is also why the figure of the atheist is so problematic. To be an atheist is to refuse to be counted as a subject within such a Commonwealth ('All the rest we should

[90] *Ibid.*, p. 405. [91] Anon, *Remarques*, p. 65.

[92] *Ibid.*, p. 5. See also Sir Richard Blackmore, *A Satyr against Wit* (London, 1697). Blackmore's critique of theatre pre-empts by several years Collier's better-known attack. In the preface to his heroic poem *King Arthur*, Blackmore will write, primarily against Dryden: 'And tho' these mischievous ways of writing are still endur'd, to the great prejudice of Religion and good Manners, yet if ever the English Nation recovers its ancient Vertue ... most of those writers who have often been esteem'd and applauded ... will be rejected with Indignation and Contempt, as the Dishonour of the Muses, and the underminers of the publick good' (pp. vi–vii). For a more general attack on the theatrocratic nature of libertinism, see Edward Reynell's *An Advice against Libertinism* (London: Roper 1659) – where again, the libertine phenomenon is identified as a threat to the State: 'so is Libertinisme a sin framed out of all manner of sins, to annihilate the most sincere part of Christianity. It draws along with it, a great train of vices, and corruptions, which tend directly to the utter desolation of Kingdoms and Empires' (p. 28).

[93] Hobbes, *On the Citizen*, p. 221.

[94] A well-governed church, says Baxter, makes 'a happy State and Commonwealth' (Baxter, *Christian Directory*, p. 514).

call not subjects but enemies of God').[95] The point will be treated with the utmost severity by political philosophy. Locke will declare: 'To disobey God in any part of his Commands (and 'tis he that Commands what Reason does) is direct Rebellion; which if dispensed with in any point, Government and Order are at an end.'[96] It is also why the libertine attack on marriage will be simply unconscionable to such a polity, where one finds the rationality of the state of marriage to be essential to the very rationality of the state itself. In *The Lawes Resolutions of Women's Rights* (1632) this rationality is expressed in terms of the two causes of matrimony. The first is the 'increase of children' – a cause that will find support in the mercantilist doctrine that to increase the wealth of the nation it is necessary to increase its population. The second is the 'quitting of fornication and uncleanliness'[97] – a cause that will set the new 'moral' classes on the path to political dominance in the following two centuries. It is thus possible to discern here, despite all the brashness of its rhetoric, the motivating force of the discourse on theatre during the Restoration: it pits two opposing 'virtues' against one another in mortal combat. On the one hand, there is a virtue that would associate sexual health and prudent government with the preservation of wealth and the accumulation of new capital; and on the other hand, there is the 'virtue' of the libertine, which promotes – to borrow Claire Blencowe's apposite expression – 'the previous aristocratic privilege' of heredity power.[98] The aristocrat belongs to a class whose power, in short, derives from previous accumulation, and whose self-assertion takes the peculiar form of a 'revolt of conduct', in the theatrics of the excessive sexual expenditure of the libertine, who prefers fornication to procreation.

(3) The final point concerns the freedom of the self – a freedom that binds both pastor and libertine together in a peculiar, even bewildering contradiction. Where deontic power is exercised, one must admit a basic presupposition that infinitely complicates how it must be exercised: that within the discursive space occupied by deontic power the individual is at liberty to refuse its specific forms of governance; the individual is free to choose not to be so conducted and can even elect not to be saved. The contradiction can be expressed as a paradox: deontic power must allow

95 Hobbes, *On the Citizen*, p. 172.

96 John Locke, *The Reasonableness of Christianity: as Delivered in the Scriptures* (London: Awnsham and John Churchill, 1696), pp. 14–15.

97 *The Lawes Resolutions of Women's Rights: or, The Lawes Provision for Woemen* (London, 1632), p. 63.

98 Claire Blencowe, *Biopolitical Experience: Foucault, Power and Positive Critique* (Basingstoke: Palgrave Macmillan, 2012), p. 70.

what it disallows. For this reason, Baxter will concede that there must be two ideas of freedom and liberty: 'There is a holy, blessed liberty, which no man must deny ... [and] there is a wicked liberty, which no man should desire.'[99] Of this 'holy liberty', Baxter says, it is the freedom to 'be freed from the power of sin ... and the accusations of a guilty conscience'. It is directly opposed to the wicked liberty of the libertine, which is nothing more than 'liberty from righteousness'[100] and a 'freedom from salvation'.[101] And, of course, the libertine's freedom has its implications for legislators since 'it is part also of this sinful, miserable liberty to be free from the government, and officers, and good laws which rule the Church and Commonwealth'.[102]

Where the liberty of the individual is at issue, then, once again, what is apparent is the spectre of theatrocratic disorder and the question of how much liberty is tolerable to those who wish to maintain the good order of the Commonwealth. Denouncing the excessive liberality of the theatre will nevertheless not resolve the paradox of freedom at the heart of deontic power. The question is more fundamental: if one is to save souls, will it not be the case that this perplexing duality of freedom and liberty must entail that where some are saved, others will be lost? And that they are lost precisely because they are able to freely choose the path of rebellion and sin? This is what Hobbes meant when, referring to the art of the pastor, he spoke of 'binding' and 'losing' souls. And yet it is not enough to say that this is an occupational hazard for the pastor/shepherd; for the pastor is the one who works under the injunction: let one sheep pass, and risk your own damnation.[103] Foucault will put it this way: 'the shepherd must keep his eye on all and on each, *omnes et singulatim*, which will be the great problem both of the techniques of power in Christian pastorship, and of the ... modern techniques of power deployed in the technologies of population.'[104] For this reason the freedom of each and every individual is not simply incidental to deontic power: it provides the very material upon which it must obsessively work. But precisely owing to this fact, freedom also circumscribes deontic power with the threat of an insufferable permissiveness, which it will experience, each time it surfaces, as a call to arms. Which is precisely why the discourse on theatre is so virulent and hostile to the criminal excesses of the stage: if it expresses its alarm at the counter-

99 Baxter, *Reformed Pastor*, p. 407. 100 *Ibid.*, p. 426. 101 *Ibid.*, p. 427. 102 *Ibid.*, p. 427.

103 Saint Benedict declares: '[The pastor/shepherd] must strive with all his sagacity and know-how not to lose one of the sheep entrusted to him', in Foucault, *Security, Territory, Population*, p. 169.

104 Foucault, *Security, Territory, Population*, p. 128.

conducts of the Restoration stage – at those false conductors of the people, at the poets of the stage 'who pretend to direct whole Generations'[105] and at the 'mighty Directors of our Vertue'[106] who seek not so much to 'rule, as to destroy'[107] – it is because it perceives in the liberty it promotes the sign of an evil that threatens to extinguish all possibility of order.[108] The counter-conduct of the stage, then, is not simply an affront to the Church but a direct and dangerous competitor in the struggle for souls; nevertheless it is also a struggle that must confront pastoral power endlessly with the nagging possibility of a refusal of the demands of the pastor by the pastorate. Collier knows this full well: his adversary is a dangerous one precisely because his case is so compelling. The 'advantages are now in the Enemies hand'. He knows, also, that in this struggle it will not be enough to simply ban or suppress the theatre as other, less sophisticated opponents of theatre will insist. For Collier, there is really only one way to counter the 'mischief' of the playwright and that will be to use the power of theatre against itself; one must fight it at the level of discourse: 'To confound them in Speech is the way to confound them in practice' – why? Because 'in a great measure [things] are Govern'd by words'.[109] In this struggle one must appeal directly to the consciences of men: by argument and by counter demonstration, one must persuade them, employing all the rhetorical tricks of the preacher; but above all, one must pit the true speech of the pastor against the false rhetoric of the stage – that '*ignis fatuus* [false light] of our own fancies'.[110] Only in this way can the discourse on theatre counter the 'Disorders of Liberty' promoted by the stage, and only in this way can it 'expose' the 'Singularities of Pride and Fancy [and] make Folly and Falsehood contemptible'.[111]

The Shoemaker and the Libertine

But there is one more possibility that needs to be considered. If the paradox of freedom cannot be easily resolved, perhaps there is a way in which it can be dismissed as an illusion; might not the struggle of the pastor be, precisely, a struggle against the illusions promoted by a counterfeit freedom? Jeremy Collier will argue that the Restoration stage presents society with a stark choice. Either one accepts that virtue is

105 *Remarques*, p. 63. 106 *Ibid.*, p. 58. 107 *Ibid.*, p. 63.

108 This same idea will be repeated later in Collier's warning: 'our Poets steer by another Compass: Their aim is to destroy Religion, their Preaching is against Sermons' (Collier, *Short View*, p. 124).

109 Collier, *Short View*, unpaginated. 110 Reynell, *Against Libertinism*, p. 29.

111 Collier, *Short View*, pp. 12; 1.

vitiated by the freedom promoted by the libertine, in which case all social distinction becomes little more than a play of manners, a mere performance, or one accepts that virtue has an authentic substance after all, and provides a ground for conduct, in which case the libertine's freedom will surely prove to be chimerical. The choice should not be too difficult to make, since 'To exchange Virtue for Behaviour is a hard Bargain.'[112] But I would like to probe a little deeper into what is involved in this choice since in a sense it forces us to confront a problem that has been gnawing away at the edges of the debate from the beginning. What has been discussed so far would seem to present something of an anomaly within the discourse on theatre, insofar as the Restoration stage is primarily the theatre of the aristocratic elite. In which case, should it not be said that the discourse on the theatre of the Restoration cannot properly speaking be called 'theatrocratic', if theatrocracy denotes a correlating of the identity of the theatre with the assertion of *democratic* vice? But in fact one need not look too far to discover, beneath the turmoil wrought by the libertine's misadventures upon the good society of orderly conduct, the social problem that arises with the division of the Commonwealth into classes. It might also be said that it is here, around the issue of social class, that Collier has one final trick up his sleeve, which he plays with such subtle ingenuity that one might easily overlook its devastating consequences for the libertine stage. The problem can be posed as a question to Etherege, which arises when Medley says to Dorimant's shoemaker in *A Man of Mode*: 'Whoring and swearing are vices too genteel for a shoemaker' (I.i). To which the shoemaker's complaint that '[p]oor folks can no sooner be wicked, but th' are railed at by their betters' receives the following blunt answer from Dorimant: 'Go, get you home and govern your family better.' So the question is whether or not it will be possible for a humble shoemaker to be a libertine. And of course the answer must be: it will not be possible, for the poor do not enjoy the privileges of the aristocrat and cannot be awarded the same freedoms.

The point that Collier will make in his own way will be the same: libertinism promotes liberty, but it dares not promote equality. It is this objection that Collier levels at the internal logic of the libertine in order to expose his fundamental contradiction. To be sure, anyone who has read the *Short View* will know that one of Collier's principal objections to the Restoration playwrights is that not only does the profanity of the stage degrade human dignity by sinking it into base appetite, but it also, and

[112] Collier, *Short View*, p. 287.

more alarmingly, degrades the dignity of man by breaking down his distinction – the very thing that separates him from beasts. The effect of this degradation will be twofold: one is that it will lead to a degradation of language itself – 'Goats and monkeys . . . would express their Brutality in such language as this';[113] the second is that this degradation of language encourages indistinction between the classes:

> 'Tis a very Coarse Diversion, the Entertainment of those who are generally the least both in Sense and Station; the looser part of the *Mob*, have no true relish of Decency and Honour, and want Education, and Thought, to furnish out a gentile Conversation. Barrenness of Fancy makes them often take up with those Scandalous Liberties.

The problem, in other words, is that by making the upper classes the target of their satire the Restoration poets drag what is noblest in humanity down to the level of what is most ignoble: 'To treat Persons of condition like the *Mob*, is to degrade their Birth, and affront their Breeding. It levels them with the lowest Education.'[114] The key word to be emphasised here is *levelling*: an excess of liberty and a satire on reputation and breeding will lead to the widespread decline of obedience amongst the lower classes and a 'lessening' of political authority in the upper.[115] 'One would think,' Collier says, 'these poets went upon absolute Certainty, and could demonstrate a Scheme of Infidelity. If they could, They had much better keep the Secret. The divulging it tends only to debauch Mankind, and shake the Securities of Civil Life.'[116] The political implications of what Collier means here by infidelity go to the heart of the contradiction of libertinism, but also recur to the paradox identified with deontic power itself. If the pastor is susceptible to the contradiction of having to permit the impermissible, can the libertine really avoid falling victim to the same contradiction: must libertinism not also, by its own logic, allow what it disallows: that lowly shoemakers might be libertines? Thus Collier's sardonic remark, 'I hope the poets don't intend to revive the old Prospect of levelling, and Vote down the House of Peers.'[117] The point is made even more forcefully in Collier's *Essays* and, in particular, in the exchange between Eulabius and Crito. When Crito asks: 'But what do you think of those who appear in Defense of Immorality, endeavour to Blast the Credit of Virtue, and reverse the Notions of Good and Evil . . .?,' Eulabius (aka Collier) replies:

[113] *Ibid.*, unpaginated. [114] *Ibid.*, p. 205. [115] *Ibid.*, p. 129. [116] *Ibid.*, p. 190.
[117] *Ibid.*, p. 176.

> I think such writers ought to be pursued with Satyr, and Infamy; to be check'd in their Sallies upon Religion, and lie under Publick Discountenance ... Atheism strikes at the Vitals of Government; and destroys the Securities of Trust. Without a supream Being and a future Account, Appetite and Humour are absolute; and all things must be govern'd by Convenience. Infidelity sweeps away all Distinction, and is the best Leveller in Nature; for what Pretence to Authority, unless 'tis given from above?[118]

Levelling, then, will be the ultimate consequence of libertine philosophy. Levelling in the sense of the equality of *all* pleasures, an equality the aristocratic rake would do well to discountenance – this is the concealed cost of the rake's 'liberty', and the price he must pay for his atheism. In order to justify his freedom, after all, the libertine cannot but deny the ultimate authority of God. The problem will then be: if one denies the ultimate basis for authority, is that not tantamount to making all earthly authority merely contingent? Freedom is either the illusion promoted by a cabal of privileged men, who seek to justify their exemption from morality, but brands them as hypocrites, or it is the possession of all men – and then shoemakers no less than libertines will enjoy the same privileges. Libertine atheism thus gives freedom an absolute licence and what results can be nothing less than democratic disorder – a theatrocracy:

> [Atheism] gives appetite an unlimited range, and dissolves Property, and would be a most admirable *Charter* for the *Mobb* to hold by ... if a man sees a Horse he likes, his Fancy has transferr'd the Title, and he may take him away without Money or Theft. And thus Apprentices, and Soldiers, and Subjects, may change their Masters, and desert when they Please.[119]

There is here a lesson for the would-be libertine behind Collier's gambit. Given that the libertine's freedom is in truth a freedom of exemption that owes everything to the privilege of his class, and that in order to preserve his privilege, the rake must, in fact, end up opposing himself to the very thing he promotes, the only way to escape the bad faith implicit in his stance will be a return to the fold – to give up all claims to specious and corrupting liberty. The vulgarity of the poor can be tolerated, even if it is not exactly acceptable – for lacking education they know no better. But the rich should and do know better and must, as

[118] Collier, *Essays*, p. 51.

[119] Collier, *Essays*, p. 144. Collier also makes the same point elsewhere: 'where there's no Conscience there can be no Law, and where there's no Law there can be no Property', p. 52.

Collier will remark, conduct themselves accordingly: 'The Favours of Providence are particular to Persons of Condition: Their knowledge exceeds that of the Vulgar, and their Example is more drawing and prevalent. Upon this account, their liberty is rather less, and their Misconduct more criminal and provoking.'[120]

[120] *Ibid.*, p. 148.

PART II

Theatre and Its Publics

CHAPTER 3

Theatrocracy and the Public Sphere

Introduction

It is at the very beginning of the eighteenth century that a general consciousness of the problem of governance first appears. This general consciousness – which is to be understood here not as something belonging to a specific group of individuals but as the enunciative form of embryonic civil society to which they belonged – is inextricably bound to the new economic and political interests of the age, interests that warranted a share in the administration of the state and its economic policy. In his landmark essay *The Structural Transformation of the Public Sphere*, Habermas attributes the birth of this nascent governmental consciousness to the moment when the private sphere of civil society breaks free of the forces that restricted it to household *oikonomia*, resulting in one of the great concessions of the state to those new social forces that were to oversee the emergence of bourgeois political economy. Habermas writes:

> Civil society came into existence as the corollary of a depersonalized state authority. Activities and dependencies hitherto relegated to the framework of the household economy emerged from this confinement into the public sphere. ... The economic activity that has become private had to be orientated toward a commodity market that had expanded under public direction and supervision; the economic conditions under which this activity now took place lay outside the confines of the single household; for the first time they were of general interest.[1]

This 'general interest' has multiple points of origin: it arises in the struggle of economic interests between the power of established wealth, founded on territorial possession and the ancient estates system, and the new wealth based on commerce, commodity markets and mercantile trade. It emerges

[1] Habermas, *Structural Transformation*, p. 19.

with the problem of who has political influence over monetary policy and public revenue. And it is articulated as the right of the new middle-class proprietors to partake in civic authority more generally. But the problem of origins is of less importance to my argument than the peculiarity of its modalities of enunciation, the forms of speech by which it gets articulated, and, specifically, its highly agonistic character. In England, the agonic and plural nature of the public sphere was uniquely visible at a time when absolutist regimes were still the norm in Europe. Following the Glorious Revolution of 1688, these multiple struggles converged on the development of an embryonic free press, providing every opportunity for private individuals to prise open the hitherto closed space of autonomous speech. It is in regard to this that the Jeremy Collier stage controversy should be understood as one of the first great disputes of the eighteenth-century public sphere. But, of course, there were others. Notably, in the year after Collier launched his attack on the Restoration stage, Matthew Tindal would fire a warning shot across the bows of those who would seek to constrain the freedoms of the public through the offices of a licenser of the press, fuelling thereby one of the century's most protracted debates. 'The greatest Enjoyment that rational and sociable Creatures are capable of,' he would write, 'is to employ their Thoughts on what Subjects they please, and to communicate them to one another as freely as they think them; and herein consists the Dignity and Freedom of human Nature, without which no other Liberty can be secure.'[2]

How might the significance and meaning of this development of autonomous speech through which a society of private individuals was able to evolve a political discourse distinct from the legislative discourses of the state be comprehended? In the first instance, it should be understood that the new discursive surface opened up by the public sphere corresponds to the development of a liberal rationality that would increasingly call for a new style of open, transparent and accountable government. Second, the new 'governmental consciousness' would therefore begin to materialise as an emerging liberal consciousness that is very much concerned with the preservation of its freedoms, while at the same time being acutely aware of the need to regulate public dispute by insisting on the duties, rights and obligations of individuals insofar as they are determined as autonomous, rational and responsible subjects. It is also for this very reason that the

[2] Matthew Tindal, *A Letter to a Member of Parliament Shewing, That a Restraint on the Press Is Inconsistent with the Protestant Religion, and Dangerous to the Liberty of the Nation* (London: J. Darby, 1700), p. 24.

advent of the discourses of liberalism begins to oversee the assimilation of deontic power to a properly secular form of government – for if government is understood here as a set of discursive practices that aim at forming, shaping and influencing human conduct, as it emerged in the previous chapter, then the locus of nascent liberal government will be the public insofar as the public comprises subjects who are free to think, act and behave in a variety of different ways. The aim of liberal governance, in short, is to ensure that the autonomous individual conforms to the ends of government, and its problem will therefore be how to develop techniques of influence, guidance, direction and persuasion that are consistent with those ends. This is exactly what is at stake in the controversies instigated by Collier and Tindal, and not least because the questions they raise anticipate the broader disputes and preoccupations of the early eighteenth-century public sphere: what constitutes the limit of freedom? How far do the freedoms of individuals extend? How might freedoms be exercised legitimately? How might they be constrained without infringing the basic rights of individuals, without coercion, and without contradicting the very principle of autonomy upon which those rights are founded?

One place where these questions would be intensely debated is in the highly public arguments over the theatre in the years leading up to the licensing act of 1737, which were played out not just in parliament but on the stage itself as well as in newspapers such as the *Craftsman* and the *Daily Gazetteer*. And yet, what those debates reveal is not simply that the statutory regulation of the stage represents the point whereby the freedoms of the public sphere encounter their limit, that a margin of tolerance has been reached beyond which liberalism will not be able to proceed. Rather, it will be the argument of this chapter that the discourse on the theatre, during the 1730s, reveals two structural limits by which the public sphere is able to be constructed as a liberal identity. In other words, what will be discovered within the articulation of these limits is by no means to be thought of as constituting a challenge or threat to that identity, any more than the assertion of limits should be seen to contradict it. On the contrary, they are formative for it, and precisely to the extent that they make that identity what it *is* – 'liberal'.

The first of these constitutes an internal limit, which specifies the appropriate conduct of individuals who are engaged in public dispute. What the discourse on the theatre will epitomise (for the disputing public) is the problem of determining the optimum amount of licence permitted within the public sphere, while sustaining its agonistic character. The argument over the stage is therefore not so much about delimiting the content of political dispute per se – albeit those in favour of the stage would make that claim – as it is about determining the proper form and context of political disputation. The licensing act resolves the dispute decisively by declaring the stage to be an inappropriate place for carrying out political disagreement; politics must be kept off the stage. The broader question is why that should be so. This brings me to the second aspect of the discourse on the stage, during the period, and to a further limit set upon the public sphere – a limit that articulates what I will call its disavowed theatrocratic supplement. What the stage designates and comes to define is an 'external limit' that establishes a horizon of antagonism by which a rational, liberal and free public – associating itself with codes of moral governance, civility and taste, reason and self-constraint – will constitute itself in relation to an anomic, irrational, violent, immoral and illiberal exterior.

Where is that exteriority to be found? Naturally, it would be conjured up once again in relation to the questionable character of the theatre audience, as I show in Chapter 4. There is, nevertheless, somewhere else it can be discerned. In fact, nowhere will the structural antagonism, constitutive of the public sphere, become more visible than in the representation of the common rabble who attended the theatre of public executions. Consequently, I shall turn to consider how a theatrocratic alterity – and thus something posited as radically exterior to the public – is discursively constructed through the theatricalised depiction of the mob, which lines the road to Tyburn, in the final section of this chapter. Before then, however, I would like to examine how the internal limits of the public sphere were derived in relation to a controversy over the stage that reached its climax in the satirical attacks launched by Henry Fielding's Great Mogul Company on Walpole's government during the late 1730s, in plays such as *The Historical Register for the Year 1736* (1737), *Eurydice Hiss'd, or, a Word to the Wise* (1737) and *Pasquin* (1736). My objective is not to regurgitate once more the history of a controversy that is already well known (of how the statutory regulation came into being whose purpose was to effectively put an end to political satire on the stage).[3] Rather, it is to show how the stage operated as a discursive limit on what would be construed as the proper form of criticism, and why it came to demarcate

[3] For a comprehensive account of Fielding's part in provoking the parliamentary bill that led to statutory censorship of the stage, see Liesenfeld, *The Licensing Act of 1737*, chapter 5; and for a thorough exposition of political satire, Jean B. Kern's *Dramatic Satire in the Age of Walpole 1720–1750* (Ames: Iowa State University Press, 1976).

the outer perimeter, so to speak, of those agonistic freedoms enjoyed by the eighteenth-century public.

An Agonic Theatre: The Limiting Power of Public Censure

The playhouse bill of 1737 received royal assent on 21 June, imposing statutory regulation on the stage that would endure for two further centuries. Although the act mostly reiterated existing laws – specifically those introduced by Queen Anne threatening actors with penalties aimed at punishing those 'Rogues and Vagabonds who shall be found wandring Begging and Misordering themselves' – its innovation was in its provision for the censorship of plays (1714, 12 Anne, stat.2, c23). Thus it was that any 'new Interlude Tragedy Comedy Opera Play ffarce or other Entertainment of the Stage' would henceforth be 'sent to the Lord Chamberlain of the Kings Household' who would, should he see fit, 'prohibit the acting performing or representing' of it.[4] One inadvertent effect of the licensing act was that it introduced a far more extensive apparatus for the censoring of plays than would be achieved simply through the exercise of arbitrary power by means of the examiner's quill: it induced self-censorship on the part of playwrights, who could ill afford to have their work turned down and so generally eschewed risky and controversial subjects; and it provoked the pre-censorship of the theatre managers, who would have to decide what plays would be agreeable to the Lord Chamberlain's office before submitting them. It was by no means the case that the Licensing Act aimed at suppressing the theatre. Its objective, rather, was to discipline it, to ensure that 'successive governments might be assured of a politically docile stage'.[5] What emerged as a consequence of the act was an increasingly sentimental and moralising theatre – the genteel comedies of Sir Richard Steele or Colley Cibber rather than the acerbic satires of Fielding and Gay.

While the general rationale for the act has been traced back by theatre historians to the Collier Stage controversy, which set the general tenor of the debate,[6] its immediate cause – and indeed primary motivation – lay in the increasingly bitter attacks made by opposition writers on the first

[4] Cited in Liesenfeld, *Licensing Act*, pp. 191–93.

[5] David Thomas, David Carlton, and Anne Etienne, *Theatre Censorship: From Walpole to Wilson*, (Oxford: Oxford University Press, 2007), p. 2. For further discussion, see *The Lord Chamberlain Regrets: A History of British Theatre Censorship*, ed. Dominic Shellard, Steve Nicholson and Miriam Handley (London: British Library, 2004).

[6] See, for instance, Matthew J. Kinservik's account in *Disciplining Satire*.

minister, Sir Robert Walpole, and – to a lesser degree – on the Royal Family, both in the press and in stage satires. Walpole had first come under direct attack from the stage in John Gay's *The Beggar's Opera* in 1728, where (by ingenious association with highway robbery) he was reproached for corruption and bribery. There was certainly a lot of truth in the allegation: even as Walpole presided over a period of relative economic stability, following the turbulent years of crisis caused by the financial crash of 1720, corruption remained endemic.[7] Moreover, there were also many factional political disputes that beset the Hanoverian dynasty, with which Walpole was closely associated, and which began to be mirrored in very public ways through the country's newspapers, journals and theatres. Papers that were opposed to the so-called Robinocracy included the *Craftsman*, the *London Journal* and the *London Evening Post*. The many notable writers who were opposed to Walpole included men such as Gay, Fielding, Swift and Pope. A particularly contentious event – that would inspire Fielding's most excoriating satirical attack on Walpole in *Eurydice Hiss'd* – was the abortive Excise Bill of 1733, which sought to raise an excise tax on the consumption of wine and tobacco. Opposition to the bill was fierce and it was withdrawn after the second reading. Nevertheless, the damage had been done. Two further crises soon followed in the years 1736–37, adding to Walpole's woes. The Gin Act, aimed at curbing the abuse of alcohol among the poor, caused serious outbreaks of rioting in Shoreditch and Spitalfields and provoked a considerable degree of disorder in Edinburgh; while the King's behaviour drew severe criticism, when – during a period of prolonged absence from the country – the Queen appeared (to the public) to have been deserted in favour of the King's German mistress (to compound matters further, the King's son, Frederick, exploiting his father's absence, sided with the opposition against the government).

It was against this torrid state of affairs that theatrical opposition to Walpole began to escalate in the mid-1730s. These attacks mercilessly exploited every opportunity that the situation made available to Walpole's enemies. Above all, lax regulation of the stage, and the apparent inability of the law to deal with the 'illegal' non-patent theatres, saw political satire on the stage reach something of a crescendo and, indeed, a degree of critical intensity that would never again be witnessed on the English stage (notwithstanding an abortive attempt made by Walpole to suppress the non-

7 For further discussion, see Richard Dale, *The First Crash: Lessons from the South Sea Bubble* (Princeton, NJ: Princeton University Press, 2004).

patent theatres in 1735).[8] Of all the theatres that were free from the constraints of Royal prerogative, and which operated with a remarkable degree of impunity, it was the Little Theatre in the Haymarket, where Fielding's Great Mogul Company was based, that provided the main focal point for the most vitriolic criticisms of Walpole's government. In the very year that the playhouse bill was devised and introduced, Fielding had launched a barrage of satirical attacks that employed the stage to devastating effect, '[ridiculing] the vicious and foolish Customs of the Age'.[9] On 9 March, the Little Theatre presented a farce entitled *A Rehearsal of Kings; or, The Projecting Gingerbread Baker, with the unheard of Catastrophe of MacPlunderkan, King of Roguomania, and the ignoble Fall of Baron Tromperland, King of Clouts* – although no extant version of the play survives, the play's title unmistakably announces the two targets of the satire: Walpole, who is characterised as the King of Rogues (a plunderer of the public purse), and King George II, who (renowned for his bad temper) was depicted as the King of Clouts.

It was Fielding's next two plays, however, that ignited the full controversy that is of most concern here: the public dispute over the use of the stage as a means of engaging in the politics of disparagement. On 21 March, Fielding's *Historical Register for the Year 1736* – comprising a series of rather anarchic and loosely related sketches – was performed at the Haymarket Theatre as an afterpiece to Lillo's *Fatal Curiosity*. It proved an immediate success, with the *Daily Advertiser* reporting the following day that it had 'receiv'd … the greatest Applause ever shewn at the Theatre'.[10] Although the play is something of a general satire, lampooning a popular political digest, among other things,[11] it is not difficult to see that its real target was the government. In particular, it had Walpole, with his propensity to offer bribes to members of parliament in an effort to shore up support for government measures, clearly in its sights. The satire on Walpole's corruption is nowhere more overtly

[8] Sir John Barnard's Private Member's Bill, March 1735, which Walpole attempted to co-opt to suppress satiric attacks, failed. The bill had originally aimed only at closing down the non-patent theatres, which were deemed a public nuisance by local residents, and had almost succeeded until Walpole intervened by amending it to include far wider powers of censorship. Barnard had no desire to be associated with the amended act and withdrew the bill (Liesenfeld, *Licensing Act*, pp. 23–54).

[9] Henry Fielding, 'The Historical Register of the Year 1736', in *The Historical Register as It Was Acted at The New Theatre in the Hay-market. To Which Is Added a Very Merry TRAGEDY, Called Eurydice Hiss'd, or, a Word to the Wise* (London, 1744 [1737]), p. 4.

[10] Cited in Liesenfeld, *Licensing Act*, p. 103.

[11] For a detailed analysis of the play, see Thomas Cleary, *Henry Fielding: A Political Writer* (Waterloo: Wilfrid Laurier University Press, 1984), p. 96.

declared than through the character of Quidam, who – in the final act – entices the 'patriots' in the play to dance, knowing that each has a hole in his pocket. Quidam 'intends to make them dance till all the Money is Fall'n through, which he will pick up again'.[12] The play also employs Fielding's novel technique of using the ruse of a rehearsal in order to draw parallels between the management of the theatres and the running of government – thereby convicting both (the second target of the satire is Colley Cibber, who had been made poet laureate in 1730, and who was allied with Walpole). In one of the most savagely satirical passages of the play, 'Sowrwit' interrogates 'Medley', the director of the play that is being rehearsed in *The Historical Register*: 'But what Thread or connexion can you have in this History?' asks Sowrwit. 'For instance, how is your Political connected with your theatrical?' To which Medley responds:

> O very easily – When my Politicks come to a Farce, they very naturally lead me to the Play-House, where, let me tell you, there are some Politicians too, where there is Lying, Flattering, Dissembling, Promising, Deceiving, and Undermining, as well as in any Court in Christendom.[13]

The second play that elicited an enormous amount of public controversy was *Eurydice Hiss'd*, which debuted at the Haymarket Theatre, barely a month after *The Historical Register* had opened, on 13 April. The play satirised attempts made by Walpole to force the excise bill through parliament – a bill that had been 'hissed' out of the Commons.[14] As with *The Historical Register*, the play takes the form of a burlesque on the rehearsing of a fictitious tragedy written by Sowrwit. At the centre of the farce is the attempt of the theatre manager, Pillage, to gerrymander the audience by planting 'friends' among them who are instructed to clap at the first sign of a hiss, thus ensuring – whether they like his farce or not – he will 'fill [his] loaded pockets with their pence'. Only Honestus refuses to be bribed by Pillage, remarking: 'If I approve your Farce, I will applaud it; If not, I'll hiss it, tho' I hiss alone.'[15] Once again, the play effectively deploys a double strategy, condemning politics through the mismanagement of the stage and convicting the improprieties of the stage managers by associating them with the corruptions of government ministers: 'So hangs the Conscience; doubtful to determine, when Honesty pleads here and there a Bribe.'[16]

[12] Fielding, *Historical Register*, p. 32. [13] *Ibid.*, p. 4. [14] Thomas et al., *Theatre Censorship*, p. 33.
[15] Fielding, *Historical Register*, p. 41. [16] *Ibid.*, p. 46.

The Discursive Struggle over the Stage

If this brief account of the historical context of the licensing act is able to stand as representative of what was (above) described as the agonistic character of the public sphere, I would next like to show its pertinence to that 'internal limit' indicated earlier. Previous chapters identified an enduring theme of the discourse on the theatre, which is its tendency to employ different discursive surfaces in order to express moral and governmental concerns over the stage, as well as showing how those concerns were strategically connected to the development of deontic power more generally. The disputes of the 1730s situate the stage of Fielding within the parameters of this same discourse, this same genealogy of government, but in a way not encountered by his predecessors, and which the licensing act would ensure would not be repeated by his successors. Previous playwrights had certainly introduced discursive elements onto the stage in which the moral and social function of the theatre is reflected explicitly in what is said and done on the stage. In Fielding's plays, however, the theatre enters into the space of political commentary to a degree that (with the notable exception of Gay's *The Beggar's Opera*) was quite unheard of in the modern period. No other playwright elicited the same uncompromising response. The reason is simple: with Fielding's political satire the stage will no longer be content to be the pacific object of discourse, but for the first time will function as a kind of irruptive site for a caustic 'counter discourse'.

Or to put it otherwise, for the first time the stage becomes genuinely 'agonic' and outspokenly adversative. It is hardly surprising, therefore, that a political age should produce that 'political drama', which John Loftis once called 'clever rather than profound'.[17] But this is to miss what is profoundly at stake within that drama. Insofar as it constitutes itself as a liberal space for a highly critical commentary on the conduct of contemporary politics it audaciously assumes the equivalence of the liberty of the stage and the liberty of the press. And, indeed, beyond that equivalence, it is vehement in its assertion that liberty corresponds to an unlimited power of criticism, available to anyone capable of entering the agonic space opened up by public censure. In his famous 'Dedication to the Public', prefacing *The Historical Register*, Fielding would respond to his critics with an astonishing degree of defiance: 'If nature hath given me any talents at ridiculing vice and imposture, I shall not be indolent, nor afraid of exerting

[17] John Loftis, *The Politics of Drama in Augustan England* (Oxford: Clarendon Press, 1963), p. 154.

them, while the liberty of the press and stage subsists, that is to say, while we have any liberty left among us.'[18] It is precisely this equivalence of expressive forms, this correlating of the organ of the press and the medium of the stage, this presupposition of an unlimited freedom of speech that will elicit an explosive rejoinder from those who would, contrary to Fielding, deny that the stage possessed any equivalence with the press and who refused to allow it to be the instrument of political discourse. I would like to now consider in detail the main elements of this dispute.

(1) *The case for liberty*. The exercise of freedom presupposes several things but the one thing that it presupposes above all others reveals its affinity with the paradox identified with deontic power in the previous chapter: it is the possibility that freedom will be open to abuse, to misapplication; that freedom provides the opportunity for (and indeed entails the likelihood of) an excessive and insupportable licentiousness. This was one of the arguments deployed in defence of both the privilege of the press and the stage to maintain that unalloyed freedom upon which their existence was said to depend. During the debate on the playhouse bill, which took place in the House of Lords on 2 June after its second reading, the Earl of Chesterfield would give expression to this paradox of freedom in his speech: 'There is such a connexion between licentiousness and liberty, that it is not easy to correct one, without dangerously wounding the other.'[19] The same paradox had been asserted several months earlier in the *Craftsman*, in one of its innumerable attempts to defend the liberty of the stage from those government supporters who wished to suppress it: 'where there is no *Licentiousness*, there can be no *Liberty*.'[20] For this reason those who defended the liberty of the press and the liberty of the stage by no means should be seen to embrace or endorse licentiousness (if by licentiousness one understands acting in flagrant disregard for all rules of propriety in the conduct of public speech). On the contrary, they used it to insist on the reasonableness of the existing law: 'If the stage becomes at any time licentious,' said Chesterfield, 'if a play appears to be a libel upon the government, or upon any particular man, the King's courts are open, the law is sufficient for punishing the offender.'[21]

[18] Henry Fielding, 'Dedication to the Public', in *The Works of Henry Fielding, Esq. with A Life of the Author in Twelve Volumes*, vol. 4 (London: Richards's and Co, 1824 [1737]), p. 11.

[19] Earl of Chesterfield in The Parliamentary Debate on the Playhouse Bill of 1737 in *A collection of the Parliamentary Debates in England from the Year M, DC, LXVIII to the Present Time* (London, 1740) p. 305.

[20] *The Country Journal or the Craftsman*, 25 June 1737; issue 573.

[21] Chesterfield, *Parliamentary Debates*, p. 305.

To tolerate the possibility of licentiousness is not to tolerate licentiousness itself. It is to acknowledge that a certain leniency is necessary in order to preserve the space in which lawful discourse can freely circulate. But it is also to warn that an intolerant law is a law that foregoes all claims to reasonableness; such a law will be defiant of that very necessity upon which liberal society is founded: 'Every *unnecessary* restraint on licentiousness is a fetter upon the legs, is a shackle upon the hands of liberty.'[22] Freedom will come at a price but it is a price worth paying since the cost to a government determined to eradicate all possible licentiousness from society will be far worse. It would have substituted the mere possibility of an intolerable and excessive freedom for the actuality of tyranny that would be far more excessive and intolerable. It is a 'sign of *bad Government*, when any Minister attempts to destroy the *Liberty of the Press*'.[23]

(2) *The case for a liberalised stage*. The accusation of the supposed delinquency of the stage is met with a whole battery of defences. Some of these would draw on standard tropes from the arsenal of pro-theatrical arguments found in past disputes over the stage, while others would be rather more novel, but all were tailored to the specific discursive context of the playhouse bill. What was that discursive context? In the first place, it lay in the representations and perceptions of liberal discourse that maintained a constant vigilance in the face of whatever threatened to curtail the power of the public or destroy those freedoms upon which the very existence of civil society depended.

For this reason, censorship of the stage was seen to amount to an implicit attack on the public itself, and so the concealed aim of the act was the eradication of *all* liberty. This extreme conclusion was reached as the entailment of the argument that the act against the free stage was in reality nothing but a prelude to a far more pernicious design on the part of a government determined to suppress the freedom of the press. This 'most arbitrary restraint on the liberty of the stage', Chesterfield argued, prepares the ground for 'a restraint on the liberty of the press . . . which will be a long stride towards the destruction of liberty itself'.[24] In a short pamphlet published in the run-up to the passage of the act through parliament, *Some Thoughts on the Present State of the Theatres, and the Consequences of an Act to destroy the Liberty of the Stage*, Fielding would also proclaim: 'This I am sure of, There is no Argument for the Liberty of the Press which will not hold in

[22] *Ibid.* Emphasis added. [23] *The Country Journal or the Craftsman*, 9 December 1726, issue 2.
[24] *Ibid.*, p. 303.

all its Force and Strength for the Liberty of the Stage.'[25] For the opposition press, the bill would be taken as evidence of the profoundly unpatriotic drift of the government: 'In short, this Complaint of Licentiousness hath been the constant Plea, in all Countries, and in all Ages for abridging the Liberties of the People.'[26] This frequent refrain of the *Craftsman* – that press (and stage) liberty represents 'that invaluable Privilege of Englishmen and Freemen'[27] – can be found repeated in numerous vindications of the press (and stage) over the previous decade. What, after all, is the freedom of the press – it asked – if not that 'unreserved, discretionary Power for every Man to publish his Thoughts on any Subject, and in any manner, which is not forbidden by the Law of the Land, without his being obliged to apply for a license or Privilege for so doing'? This is liberty exercised in its 'just latitude'.[28]

As a consequence of this, there is a second argument, which might be posed initially in the form of a question: if the stage is to be suppressed (through what is, in effect, a highly partisan abuse of power on the part of the executive) then doesn't this very threat to the liberties of the stage betoken the rise of despotic government? Once again, the context of this defence will be the emergence of liberalism grasped as a mode of governance that is most compatible with the development of civil society – which is to say, an art of government well suited to that society of private individuals whose right to non-interference – to *self-limiting* government, as Foucault puts it – was won through the recognition of the expanding power of private property.[29] Thus there is something of a complex of interconnected issues summoned in justification of the liberty of the stage, incorporating the rights of property owners to be free from molestation by the government, the right of private individuals to the freedom of expression, and, finally, the right of the public as such to censure – or, in other words, to *restrict* – the activities of government. In the first instance, the stage is itself a fundamental means by which the powerful can be brought to account. In his reflections on the consequences of the playhouse bill, Samuel Johnson would ask: 'What is power, but the liberty of acting without being accountable?'[30] The statute, he then went on to propose,

[25] Henry Fielding, *Some Thoughts on the Present State of the Theatres, and the Consequences of an Act to Destroy the Liberty of the Stage* (London, 1737), p. 3.

[26] *The Country Journal or the Craftsman*, 25 June 1737, issue 573.

[27] *The Country Journal or the Craftsman*, 18 January 1735, issue 446.

[28] *The Country Journal or the Craftsman*, 9 December 1726.

[29] Foucault, *Birth of Biopolitics*, p. 20.

[30] Samuel Johnson, 'A Complete Vindication of the Licensers of the Stage from the Malicious and Scandalous Aspersions of Mr. Brook' (1739), reprinted in *Dr. Johnson's Works. Miscellaneous Pieces, the Works of Samuel Johnson, LL.D, in Nine Volumes*, vol. 5 (Oxford: William Pickering, 1825), pp. 335–36.

was designed 'only to bring poets into subjection and dependence, not to encourage good writers, but to discourage all'.[31] Similar concerns over the accountability of the executive no doubt lay behind the reprinting of John Dennis's *The Usefulness of the Stage to Religion, and to Government* in the same year of 1738 (published originally in 1698 under the title: *The Uses of the Stage to the Happiness of Mankind, to Government, and to Religion*). Poor government, wrote Dennis, has its 'source' in the 'perversions and vices of those who Govern' and it is tragedy that reminds those in power of their 'duty', instructing them by its 'sentences and Morals' and by showing them the 'ill and fatal consequences of Irregular Administration'.[32] Now, since it is the business of the stage to 'exhort Men to Piety, and ... persuade them of Justice, and to incline them to Moderation and Temperance',[33] the stage has a key role to play in contributing to a well-governed state.

Fielding would extend the same rationale, the same idea that the stage is an instrument for moral correction, but in order to proclaim the theatre to be the property of the public as such, and thus as falling properly under the public's jurisdiction (rather than that of the government censor). What is the function and purpose of the stage, asks Fielding, given that it 'has always been supported in our politest Times, and by the politest and greatest Men among us'?[34] In the first place, one cannot say that the aims of the stage are contrary to those of a well-ordered state, for not only is the stage an 'Avocation of Evil' in that it provides a distraction from 'worse amusements', but it is also 'perhaps the best Means which can be found for propagating Morality, and infusing Virtue into the Minds of Men'.[35] Of all methods of instruction, the stage proves to be the more powerful since whereas other methods can inculcate virtue only by means of asserting moral precepts, the stage instructs by the power of its example, producing a double-effect that is of great benefit to society. First, it awakens a sense of virtue in the audience, stimulating 'generous Sentiments' in them, but it also evokes the shame of its auditors before the examples of vice and viciousness.

It is not, however, just that private virtues are excited by the example of the stage or that private vices are exposed in their baseness and turpitude. Nor is it simply that the theatre trades in producing affective qualities aimed at producing humility, abasement and mortification in the

[31] *Ibid.*, p. 335.
[32] John Dennis, *The Usefulness of the Stage to Religion, and to Government* (London, 1738), p. 44.
[33] *Ibid.*, p. 3. [34] Fielding, *Some Thoughts*, p. 1. [35] *Ibid.*

audience. For Fielding – more fundamentally – the theatre, through its satire, exposes the defects of (as well as the opprobrious and arrant forms of conduct in) those who hold high office. The stage is the servant of the public, reflecting its concerns, punishing through its satirical cuts those who have transgressed the public trust. Thus it holds the powerful to account. By contrast, what a controlled stage produces are 'castrated' satires that let those selfsame people (those who deserve to be exposed to 'theatrical ridicule') off the hook.[36]

So intense was the fear of tyranny – of a return to despotic government and the vices of absolutism – that some would even ask whether it would be better to suppress the stage entirely rather than risk a censored stage. To understand the nature of the risk, they argued, one need merely look to the experience of recent history, where the censorship of the stage – 'regulation' – should be seen as nothing but a ruse designed by the powerful to place the instrument of the public into the hands of those who would abuse it in order to manipulate the public. The *Craftsman* offered this kind of trenchant critique of the misuses of theatre by arbitrary power when it reminded its readers that 'the Liberty of the Stage was allow'd, when the Liberty of the Press was not [when during] the Reign of King Charles the 2nd . . . the stage was . . . a mere Tool of the Court.'[37] As is well known, it went on to assert, the stage possesses the power to 'delude the people' in 'favour' of despotic authority:

> It hath been strongly urged . . . what a prodigious effect *Theatrical Representations* have upon the minds of the *People*; and there is certainly a good deal of Truth in it. *A great Statesman of Antiquity* used to say, that if He had the Management of the *Stage* intirely in his Hands, He would undertake to govern the world.[38]

A final justification, expressed within this bundle of concerns, sought to draw a parallel between the liberty of the stage and the rights of private ownership. Chesterfield, in particular, would argue that legislation curtailing the activities of the theatres was nothing but a fetter on the rights of individuals to own property: 'it is not only an incroachment upon liberty, but it is likewise an incroachment on property.'[39] There are several reasons for this. First, the freedom to censure governments, whether by means of the stage or the press, is linked to the safeguarding of private property from the reach of arbitrary power. The independent power of the public, after

[36] *Ibid.*, p. 3. [37] *The Country Journal or the Craftsman*, 25 June 1737, issue 573.
[38] *Ibid*; emphasis in original. [39] Chesterfield, *Parliamentary Debates*, p. 315.

all, is necessary for the restraint of court and executive power. Second, and more specifically, Chesterfield asks: who is really going to lose out from the suppression of the stage? The answer is, those entrepreneurs who make their living through the stage: 'These gentlemen,' he pleads, 'who have any such property, are all, I hope, our friends: Do not let us subject them to any unnecessary restraint.' The playhouse bill, in Chesterfield's memorable phrase, amounts to nothing other than a 'tax upon wit'. If the bill is passed, those men who write for the stage – the author-proprietors, as it were – will find their products designated 'prohibited goods' by law. For the author-proprietor, the effect of the bill is that his 'chief and best market will be for ever shut against him'.[40] Implication: the censorship of the stage is an indiscriminate restraint on the market.

(3) *The case against the theatres.* If these arguments in their various ways attempted to make the case for the liberty of the stage, the argument against that liberty took considerable care not to conflate the liberty of the stage with the liberty of the public as such. It was a tactic that was no doubt designed to undercut the central thrust of its opponent's line of attack. This was already perfectly clear in the *Daily Gazetteer*'s criticism of Fielding, published on 7 May – the article that, to all intents and purposes, signalled the beginning of the government's campaign to bring the stage under the statutory regulation of a licenser of plays. The anonymous author, signing off as an 'Adventurer in Politics', begins his argument by conjuring up the purported threat to liberty in general by countering the allegation that the surreptitious aim of any restraint on the stage is the *de facto* restraint of the freedoms of the press. In fact, the two do not correlate at all: the liberty of the press is by no means threatened by the curtailing of the liberty of the stage.

What is more: the liberty of one is guaranteed by the restraint of the other. Nobody denies – or so the Adventurer argued – that every subject is free to speak their mind on any issue of import to the public, either in private or in print, and this is certain proof of that celebrated freedom enjoyed by the English in contrast to their oppressed neighbours in continental Europe. Nevertheless, liberty does not absolve the public of the need to affix the proper limit of free speech or to determine where that limit should lie. With freedoms come responsibilities. For the Adventurer and his supporters, the liberty signified by the freedom of speech could only be exercised properly through the medium of the press – not the medium of the stage: 'I do not mean these Observations against a liberty of

[40] *Ibid.*, p. 316.

publickly reasoning on Affairs, or canvassing a Minister's Conduct, which would look like restraining the Liberty of the Press; but sure no Argument whatever, can be alleged to support the bringing of POLITICKS on the STAGE.'[41] This, he insisted, was no mere apology for the assertion of arbitrary power; conversely, those who held the view that there were no arguments for the restraint of the stage that would not apply equally to the press were gravely mistaken. The stage presented a special case (something that even Fielding appeared to concede when he argued that the theatre requires 'proper Regulation' if it is to be a 'School of Virtue' and that a poorly regulated stage will be a 'perverted' theatre 'turn'd into a Brothel of vice and made the most successful Method of polluting and debauching the Morals of Mankind').[42] So what distinguishes the stage from the printed word? While it is not explicitly stated, nevertheless it is clear that for the Adventurer the stage is distinguished by none other than its capacity to provoke profound affects in the audience; this is what makes it a hazardous power.

In this sense, the stage shares much in common with the pulpit. As the Adventurer pointed out: 'When the *Pulpit* assumed a Right of preaching Politicks to the People, what a confusion was the Nation thrown into!'[43] Just as one must banish politics from the pulpit because of its 'ill effects' on 'government in general', so one must banish politics from the stage – and with Fielding's satires firmly in view, he added: the political stage does nothing but make government appear 'ridiculous to the People'; and its effect is designed for no better end than to stir up 'public resentment'. Fielding is playing a dangerous game:

> Now to insinuate to the *Vulgar*, who must ever be *led*, that *all Government is but a Farce* (*perhaps a damned one too*) is just as bad to Society, as it would be to tell the *People*, that their *Religion* is a *Joke*. There are Things which, from the Good they dispense, ought to be Sacred; such are *Government* and *Religion*. No Society can subsist without 'em: To turn either into Ridicule, is to unloose the fundamental Pillars of Society, and shake it from its *Basis*.[44]

It is the press that will be the permitted organ of criticism, the proper means for holding government to account. Indeed, the article concluded by declaring that if anyone threatened the liberty of the press, it was not those who sought to place the stage under proper regulation, but those – such as Fielding – who insisted on abusing liberty by employing the stage for something for which it was not intended or designed, and whose

[41] *Daily Gazetteer*, 7 May 1737.
[42] Fielding, *Some Thoughts*, p. 2.
[43] *Daily Gazetteer*, 7 May 1737.
[44] *Daily Gazetteer*, 7 May 1737; emphasis in original.

consequences, were it to continue to be tolerated, would be utterly ruinous to the order of the state: to government itself. Liberty, public censure and good government exist in a carefully calibrated set of discursive relationships; the misuse of the stage fundamentally unsettles those relationships and signifies a perverting of the correct and valid use of the theatre:

> To encourage then Politicks on the Stage, is not only unjust in itself . . . but of a most pernicious Tendency to the stage itself, which instead of being a general Mirrour, where the Beauties and Deformities of human Nature are represented Impartially; whence we either *copy* or *reject* as we find our Resemblance *good* or *bad*, because a private Looking-Glass, where Spleen, Resentments, and inconsiderate Levity, displays Objects without any Regard to Truth, Decency, Good Manners or true Judgment.

Aftermath of the Controversy of 1737

With the passage of the Licensing Act through parliament, and with no great public outcry against the statute, it would appear that the kinds of argument advanced by the Adventurer met with general public approval. Without suppressing the theatre, the act achieved its aim of killing off anti-government political satire on the stage. Opposition fears that stage regulation would see the same powers extended over the press proved to be unfounded, even if the press continued to be harried throughout the century through the use of the country's libel laws. What is perhaps more to the point is the broader discursive significance of the act, which corresponded to a more general codification of liberty according to which participation in the public sphere would be conditioned by the imperatives, constraints and obligations of deontic power. At the end of the century that codification was formulated in the most unequivocal and categorical way in the writings of Jeremy Bentham. It is therefore worth considering Bentham's views on the public sphere, however cursorily, insofar as he makes explicit what in effect already tacitly existed in the basic agreement of the aims of the public and the rationality of liberal government.

First, in his reflections on the relation between publicity and justice, Bentham not only sought to tie publicity to the workings of law, but argued that publicity – particularly in the opening up of evidence to the public – was the 'chief instrument of security', without which justice would hardly be conceivable.[45] Two further texts emphasised the

[45] Jeremy Bentham, Chapter 10, 'Of Publicity and Privacy, as applied to Judicature in general, and to the collection of evidence in particular', in *Rationale of Judicial Evidence*, vol. 1 (London, 1823), pp. 511–81.

discursive construction of the public – and indeed constituted the public as the very medium of deontic power. The first was a set of proposals for a constitutional arrangement that, although never utilised, nonetheless stressed the public as a quasi-juridical power: 'Public Opinion,' Bentham wrote, 'may be considered as a system of law, emanating from the body of the people.'[46] That law is embodied in the form of a 'Public Opinion Tribunal' whose task is to provide a check on the 'pernicious exercise of the power of government' and which is a 'beneficial [and] indispensable supplement' in the exercise of good government. The tribunal of public opinion operates wherever the public can be said to congregate or assemble, and where such assemblies can be construed as forming a kind of governmental sub-committee – for instance, '[t]he auditory, at any dramatic entertainment, at which objects of a political or moral nature are brought upon the stage'.[47] Noteworthy here is how the public is cast, first and foremost, in the role of censorious judge – that it thus has an intrinsic governmental character, for Bentham, and that consequently in its role as 'the public' any audience attending (among other things) the theatre already acts as a bona fide censor of plays. In this sense, Bentham simply rendered in formal legalistic terms what Fielding and earlier public sphere liberals had already argued informally: that the tribunal of public opinion exercised its own legitimate authority.

But legitimate in what sense? An answer to this problem can be found in Bentham's posthumously published *Deontology; or, the Science of Morality*. The question Bentham posed in this manuscript is of profound import given the power of the public sphere during the period: if individuals are fundamentally self-regarding and pursue their own self-interest before all other considerations, if they are most concerned with securing their own happiness, then how is morality at all possible?[48] Bentham's answer, in brief, is that individuals will conform to any course of conduct that meets with the approbation of the general public – that is to say, individuals will modify their actions in keeping with the dictates of prudence, knowing that they will always be subject to the 'tribunal' of public opinion:

> Public opinion is made up of individual opinions; and public opinion is that which constitutes the popular or moral sanction. A large quantity of

[46] Jeremy Bentham, *Constitutional Code for the Use of All Nations and Governments Professing Liberal Opinions* (London: Robert Heward, 1830), p. 35.

[47] *Ibid.*, p. 35.

[48] Jeremy Bentham, 'Deontology; or, The Science of Morality: in which the harmony and co-incidence of duty and self-interest, virtue and felicity, prudence and benevolence, are explained and exemplified', in *From MSS. Of Jeremy Bentham*, vol. 1, ed. John Bowring (London: Longman, 1834), p. 18.

> recompense to act upon our hopes, and a large quantity of punishment to influence our fears, are in the hands of popular opinion. Of this influential power, every individual in the community forms a part; and may exercise and apply his portion of reward and punishment.[49]

In other words, it is deontic power that operates as an internal limit on the activities of the eighteenth-century public, and it is 'internal' because it defines wholly and absolutely what the public *is* – a self-limiting force of moral sanction.

Nevertheless, if its mode of conduct, forms of action and even its agonistic freedoms were conditioned by this internal limit, the question remains: what of that *external limit* indicated earlier, and which was designated a theatrocratic supplement? I would now like to consider this external limit, to show how the public sphere was also constituted in relation to a horizon of alterity and to an antagonism that would be fundamental to its identity.

The Excluded Commons: Construction of a Theatrocratic Exterior

Property, Law and the Structural Unity of the Public Sphere

Notwithstanding the threat of censorship, the new publicity managed to open up a field of operations capable of generating new discursivities, at the same time that it enabled new practices of circulation, new flows and forms of exchange, new modes of spectatorship, all of which no doubt helped to stimulate the irrepressibly conflictual disposition of the age. What the agonic public sphere introduced onto the historical stage, thereby, was a new subjective power: that of the public man – convinced of his inalienable rights, as of his right to express his fledgling autonomy by having an opinion on all matters of public interest. It was by constituting himself as a member of the public, in the free exercise of his reason, that private man thus learned to express himself in his political being. In exercising his critical faculties, in learning to discriminate and to pass judgements on matters of taste, in letter writing, in sharing commentatorial opinion, and by engaging in the controversies of the town, the 'public held up a mirror to itself'.[50] By this means, it evolved into the form not only of a critical discourse, but one that was also uniquely self-conscious: 'it was only through the critical absorption of philosophy, literature, and

[49] *Ibid.*, pp. 21–22. [50] Habermas, *Structural Transformation*, p. 43.

art that the public attained enlightenment and realized itself as the latter's living process.'[51] Through critical discourse enlightened opinion discovered its commitment to egalitarianism, principles of liberty, and the liberal right of free expression. Most of all, though, through its capacity to pass critical judgements on anything that came within its purview, civil society realised its neoteric power as a power of censure.

It is through censure – what Fielding called the 'impartial Judgment of the Town'[52] – that the public evolved a parallel and supplementary discourse to the discourse on theatre. In animadverting, moralising, satirising, reproving and disparaging, and in its vindications, abjurations, exculpations, confessions and apologies, what the power of censure produces is one of the supreme discourses of the Enlightenment, that of the cultivation of man, whose themes of taste and genius will reproduce in the secular sphere the same deontic forms of governance that emerged previously in the religious sphere. Both discourses will work in lock-step as counterparts, unifying the public sphere through the coalescing of what would otherwise appear to be a heteromorphic field of dispersion and discordance.

This is not to belie the prevalence of conflict within the public sphere by overestimating this 'unity' and by attributing to the appearance of its discourses an inchoate yet common goal, nor can one find there an as yet imperceptible consensus just waiting to be discovered through the prescience of Enlightenment rationality. It is not the utopian promise of a society founded on reason that ties the public together, nor does the public sphere derive its unifying potential from the practices of deliberation that would append those who participated in it to an impartial search for the common good founded on the sovereignty of universal truth. This is not to say that each of these terms – reason and reasonableness, universality and truth, or validity, detachment and the common good, are not crucial to the formation of the discourses of the Enlightenment. On the contrary, they delineate its rules of formation and permit the ordering and verification of its statements. They allow, above all, the self-assertion of the public as an authority; its construction as a space of 'disinterested' reasons, where opinion submits itself to the assessment of anyone capable of employing their common sense. These statements act as operators within an extensive periphrastic network where criticisms are proposed, reforms recommended, opinions formulated, propositions advanced – all to be confirmed or repudiated through the incessant production of public commentary.

[51] *Ibid.*, p. 42. [52] Fielding, *Historical Register*, p. 47.

Viewed beneath the level of its enunciations, however, what consolidates the public sphere, grasped as planes of interlocking 'rational' practices, is not the discovery of the space of pure reason but the specific hegemonic interests that structure the discursive field and that are ceaselessly at work within it – articulating it as an ensemble of economic relations and cultural affiliations. The rationality of the public sphere operates as a coefficient of expansion for these interests. It multiplies (regardless of the often conflicting goals of its actors) their effects, and the breadth, extent and power of their influence over social reality, which they increasingly dominate. What are these structural interests? They reside primarily in the public's interest in the preservation of property, certainly. But while property entails ownership, what should also be understood here has less to do with a question of proprietorship than the discursive function played by property in consolidating the form of liberal governance. It provides the discourse on social order with a foundation in right and at the same time founds society on the 'natural' order of property. Equally, it grounds possession within a discourse on freedom and liberty, whose enemies will be dispossession by arbitrary power, on the one hand, and criminality, on the other: 'Liberty is the Life and Soul of Englishmen,' as Giles Jacob would write, 'and Property is ever attending on this fair Mistress.'[53] Property, freedom and law are internally enunciated and bound together within the discursive architecture of public order. On this basis, government will be understood as the 'due Administration, Application or Execution of [the] Laws, which the Society has devised for the Security of their several Rights and Properties'. The end of government is nothing more and nothing less than the 'security of Rights and Properties of the Society'.[54]

Correlated with these proprietorial interests are rules determining the legitimation of structures of appropriation as distinguished from illegitimate and criminal possession sanctioned, for instance, through a vast production of juridical discourses around property and law. William Blackstone's monumental *Commentaries on the Laws of England* (1771) is exemplary here, as are the discourses that tie property relations to those that govern the social production of labour and, more generally, to the

[53] Giles Jacob, *Liberty and Property: or, A New Year's Gift for Mr Pope. Being a Concise Treatise on all the Laws, Statutes and Ordinances, Made for the Benefit and Protection of the Subjects of England* (London: J. Baker, 1736), unpaginated.

[54] Thomas Burnett, *An Essay upon Government; or, the Natural Notions of Government, Demonstrated in a Chain of Consequences from the Fundamental Principles of Society* (Dublin and London: T. Warner, 1716), pp. 17–18.

disciplining of labour through the innovations introduced by political economy, labour placed increasingly under the governance of economic rationality in order to increase the productivity of the poor.[55] It is equally discernible in the public interest in morality (key to the establishment of the rules and codes of deontic power) and in 'lawfulness' more generally, whose development, traced so assiduously in Foucault's work, permitted a detailed knowledge of normal conduct and the isolation of behaviours that were pathologised as debased, abnormal and wicked. Its interest is also manifest in the way the century seeks to develop the productive potential of discipline more generally, as a practice of nascent social economy. One finds this already in Fielding's proposal for a County-house of Correction, in his role as magistrate, to be erected in Middlesex, in 1753, designed to house anyone convicted of being a 'Disorderly Person, or a Rogue and Vagabond',[56] such as 'Labourers or Servants ... Who after the Hour of Ten in the Evening shall be found harbouring in any Alehouse or Victuallinghouse'.[57] Such establishments circulate new stratagems aimed at the disciplining of workers and the curbing of idleness. By the end of the century, one has, of course, the elaborate supervisory techniques of Jeremy Bentham's panopticon, targeted at the disorderly and wanton, at criminals and schoolchildren, in order to suppress social deviancy through a system of inspection applied to penitentiary houses, houses of industry, manufactories and so on.[58]

There are, of course, many more instances that could be cited, but the point here is not to enumerate them all. It is simply to indicate that, with the public sphere, grasped as a field of hegemonic relations articulated around a common interest in property, freedom and law, what gradually becomes visible is that 'external limit', against which emerges the problem of governance that so defines the eighteenth-century public. If the eighteenth century is an age in which a general consciousness of the problem of governance emerges, it is because it is an age that felt itself, in large part, to be wholly ungovernable; it is an age that felt itself to be that unhappy society, so disordered by rampant criminality, so bewitched by its genius for corruption and vice, so betrayed by the failures and inadequacies of

55 For a comprehensive treatment of this idea, see Mitchell Dean, *The Constitution of Poverty: Toward a Genealogy of Liberal Governance* (Oxon: Routledge, 1991).

56 Henry Fielding, *A Proposal for Making an Effectual Provision for the Poor* (London: John Smith, 1753), p. 22.

57 *Ibid.*, p. 25.

58 See Jeremy Bentham, *Management of the Poor, or, a Plan, containing the Principles and Construction of an Establishment, in which Persons of Any Description are to be Kept under Supervision* (London, 1796).

government and so ill-served by the disintegrating institution of the magistracy as to be perpetually on the brink of all-out ruination. Hence Jonas Hanway's lamentation, in his famous treatise on police: 'The fact is, that in this land, so justly boasting of freedom, *liberty* is alloyed by *terror*, and the bright enjoyment of property by law, is darkened by rapine. Are the people of any civilised nation upon the earth so subject to be disturbed on highways, and even in their beds, as the *English*; unless we except the outrages sometimes committed by daring violence in *Ireland*?'[59] Martin Madan will go even further, in calling for the brutal suppression of the poor:

> No civilised nation, that I know of, has to lament, as we have, the daily commission of the most dangerous and atrocious crimes, insomuch that we cannot travel the roads, or sleep in our houses, or turn our cattle out into our fields, without the most imminent danger of thieves and robbers. These are increased to such a degree in numbers, as well as audaciousness, that the day is now little less dangerous than the night to travel in; and we are not without fatal instances of the most wanton cruelty and barbarity, exercised on many of those unfortunate persons, who have fallen into the hands of these plunderers of the public.[60]

In short: just as the discourse on cultivation will identify its themes of virtue, etiquette, politeness and civility with the censorious habits cultivated by the public's desire for self-improvement, so the discourse on the theatre – and the wider theatrocratic discourse(s), which I am seeking to trace, and with which it coexists in a nexus of knowledges of deviancy – will find ample motivation in the corresponding concern 'the public' unremittingly expresses, throughout the century, for the corrupted manners and incivility of the lower orders.

Frontiers of Antagonism: Theatrocratic Construction of the Commons

No doubt it will be said that this is something of a commonplace for historians of the period. John Brewer and John Styles argue, for example, that the 'eighteenth-century Englishman's conceptions of government were intimately bound up with their actual experience of the law'[61] – an

[59] Jonas Hanway, *The Citizen's Monitor, Shewing the Necessity of a Salutary Police, Executed by Resolute and Judicious Magistrates* (London: J. Dodsley, 1780), p. iv; emphasis in original

[60] Martin Madan, *Thoughts on Executive Justice, with respect to Our Criminal Law, Particularly on the Circuits* (London: J. Dodsley, 1785), pp. 3–5.

[61] John Brewer and John Styles, 'Introduction', in *An Ungovernable People: The English and Their Law in the Seventeenth and Eighteenth Centuries* (London: Hutchinson, 1983), p. 13.

idea that David Lemmings has expanded on in considerably more detail recently.[62] But perhaps a more significant phenomenon, because more extensive, more insidious even, informed that experience: '[Under] the influence of "public opinion", from the mid-eighteenth century, the criminal law became a positivist instrument in the service of a new ideology about the degeneracy of the common people which amounted to a social pathology of crime.'[63] To say that this new instrument of law will be linked to a social pathology of crime, however, is not to say that the experience of law will be bound entirely by the perception of crime, which flared up occasionally in public concerns over crime, encouraged in print by newspapers such as the *London Journal*.[64] What is important is not the correlation of perceptions of criminality with its actual occurrences, which remain exterior to discourse, and which might permit us to discern the degree to which a public consciousness of crime failed to correspond to its actual frequency; still less is it to show how public perceptions were used and abused in the pursuit of specific ideological agendas. What is of interest, instead, is the way perceptions of criminality take their place and circulate within a network of discursive relations insofar as they enter the field of theatrocratic discourse, the discourses concerned with establishing the reality of disorder, identifying the interests of the public with the consciousness of law and the problem of governance.

What this consciousness of the problem of governance enables thereby is the deployment of a structuring mechanism, a principle of exclusion and division that will operate across the entire surface of the social *topos*. It is the mechanism that permits the partitioning of values by which an anomic exterior, opposed to all that is sociable and lawful, becomes discernible. But it also institutes a twofold division within the community. It produces two communities, in fact, 'consisting', as one author would candidly write, 'of the poor or labouring commonality and the rich part or publick'.[65] This exteriorisation of the poor, with respect to the property-owning public,

62 David Lemmings, *Law and Government in England during the Long Eighteenth Century: From Consent to Command* (Basingstoke: Palgrave Macmillan, 2011), p. 15.

63 *Ibid.*, pp. 106–7.

64 See *ibid.*, p. 86; see also Nicholas Rogers, 'Confronting the Crime Wave: The Debate over Social Reform and Regulation, 1749–1753', in *Stilling the Grumbling Hive: The Response to Social and Economic Problems in England, 1689–1750*, ed. Lee Davison et al. (Stroud: St Martin's Press, 1992), pp. 77–98. Rogers focuses on the crime wave of the early 1750s, following mass demobilisation of the armed forces in 1749: 'Brutalized by war, without jobs and frequently suffering from arrears in pay, these men sometimes resorted to burglary or street or highway robbery to make ends meet, contributing significantly to a soaring rate of prosecuted crime' (p. 78).

65 Anon., Preface to *The Means of Effectually Preventing Theft and Robbery* (London, 1783), unpaginated.

should not be seen as reducing the problem of governance to an act of ideological exclusion; it refers to a structural problem that belongs to the constitution of public discourse. By the same token, lawfulness is irreducible to empirical figures. Thus we misunderstand the emphasis on lawfulness if we imagine that the problem of governance is reducible to the activity of criminals or even to the taxonomic glossology of various categories of offences that it undoubtedly enables. It refers, rather, to a more general condition: to an unsighted line, like the curvature of a horizon, by which the public comes to know itself as that which stands in perpetual relation to something whose very essence is other to it. This structural alterity constitutes a profound evil and ever-present threat to those geometries of reason and order established by discourse: it is ungovernability itself – grasped not simply as the actuality of disorder but as a pure potential for disorder, whose crucible is identified within the indigent and labouring classes.

At the same time, ungovernability belongs to theatrocratic discourse insofar as it constitutes the very limit of order. To say that this limit is unsighted, of course, is not to say that it entirely lacks visibility. On the contrary, it is unsighted precisely because whatever this horizon presents to view falls within the line of sight of theatrocratic discourses. It is an exteriority that is immanent to them, and it is precisely for this reason that it can make felonious, illegitimate and immoral objects available for sight. Moreover, for the eighteenth-century public, it is to be found everywhere but certainly no more so, in a material sense, than in its exposure to the poor: the town's menial workers, its serving men and women, its idling apprentices, and its vagrants and beggars. In short, it is present to the eye of all who have the capacity to perceive the brutish, ill-educated and uncultivated. It is a mode of visibility prepared by the discursive relations established in the formation of the public sphere, which permits us to envisage the underside of enlightenment as the general state of corrupted humanity: 'the idle, vagrant and loose Tribe . . . lost to every valuable Principle, to all Sense and Thought of Obligation and Duty both to God and Man, and scruple no Mischief either with regard to Men's Persons or Properties.'[66]

If the public sphere, then, will have its others, what the figures of the crowd, the mob, the rioters and the common multitude, which feature in

[66] George Ollyffe, *An Essay Humbly Offer'd, for an Act of Parliament to Prevent Capital Crimes, and the Loss of so Many Lives; and to Promote a Desirable Improvement and Blessing in the Nation*, 2nd edition (London: J. Downing, 1731), p. 3.

the descriptions of theatrocratic discourses, represent is not the appearance or self-assertion of a plebeian public sphere, set in opposition to the bourgeois public sphere, but the power of discourse to configure actual sets of bodies and no doubt to configure them as the monstrous reflection of the public's own cultivated gaze: '[It] is a very piercing Lamentation that the inoffensive, wise, and useful part of Mankind, how much soever they are entitled to Protection from illegal Violence and Molestation . . . yet know not whether travelling Abroad, or walking in the Streets, or dealing in their Shops, or resting in their Beds, they may be out of Danger from these Monsters.'[67] What is located in these extreme descriptions are the monstrous figures put into circulation by the discourses of nascent liberal governmentality. They provoke astonishment and dismay, but also a peculiarly affective response, within the bourgeois public sphere. They produce, on the one hand, a censorious contempt for those who should have no place in civilised society, according to the terms of its discourse, while enabling, on the other hand, and as a paradoxical effect, an enormous volume of print to be dedicated to precisely those who have no right to a public existence. Far from repressing theatrocratic phenomena, instead, the eighteenth century publicises them, rendering them visible as an acute condition. It does so feverishly to the extent that those who would wish that it did not exist cannot but conjure the horrible appearance of this loathed 'commonality', this perpetual affront to all those standards of decency and decorum that are constitutive of eighteenth-century public consciousness. It allows the plebeian to take on the form of a vivid and disturbing fact of life.

What should one make of the spectre of the plebeian other – anathema to all men of cultivation and sensibility? I would like to give them their due here by designating them that other, albeit common, 'public' of the eighteenth century. But I also seek to understand the motives lying behind the censorious procedures and disciplinary measures promoted by theatrocratic discourse insofar as they are aimed precisely at the elimination of this common public – either by suppressing or by reforming it; that is to say, by transforming 'plebeian culture' from an inchoative yet threatening presence – a potentially potent social force – into a set of objects that can be determined, corrected and finally dominated. It is precisely the incipient threat of the plebeian other that gives impetus to Ollyffe's proclamation, far from uncommon at the time, that 'it may be highly

[67] *Ibid.*, pp. 4–5.

desirable that there may be some Method taken, as may yet effectually curb such an ungoverned Race'.[68]

The Theatrical Limits of Punitive Power

Nowhere is this common public – criminal, deviant, illegitimate – more visible than on those unofficial days of festival and holiday, when the mob gathers at the scene of execution, which can be found in descriptions of Tyburn. Two remarkable texts are particularly revealing, specifically in terms of showing how discourse employs tropes drawn from the language of the stage: Henry Fielding's *An Enquiry into the Cause of the Late Increase of Robbers*, written in 1751, and Bernard Mandeville's short treatise on penal reform, *An Enquiry into the Causes of the Frequent Executions at Tyburn* (1725), which provides one of the most extravagant descriptions of the mob written during the century. This text, Mandeville concedes, is likely to provoke censure for its graphic detail, among men of 'taste and politeness' – but nevertheless it is, he argues, necessary in order to demonstrate 'what small advantage [executions] are of'[69] to both the condemned and to the 'rest of the spectators, who should be struck with the Awefulness of the Solemnity'.[70] Mandeville's principal target might be called the 'theatrical mismanagement' of public executions. The idea that public execution was, as Frederick Burwick puts it, 'conducted as a theatrical event'[71] is perhaps something of a commonplace today. Likewise, the idea that public execution took a quasi-theatrical form is a recurrent motif in Foucault's *Discipline and Punish*: 'In the ceremonies of the public execution, the main character was the people, whose real and immediate presence was required for the performance.'[72] Indeed, it is precisely because the scaffold is a public stage before which the people are summoned that the spectacle bears all the hallmarks of theatrocratic licence; unsurprising, then, that this spectacle should more often than not undermine the very authority it was meant to endorse, buttress or reproduce: 'In these executions, which ought to show only the terrorizing power of the prince, there was a whole aspect

68 *Ibid.*, p. 5.

69 Bernard Mandeville, *An Enquiry into the Causes of the Frequent Executions at Tyburn: and a Proposal for Some Regulations Concerning Felons in Prison, and the Good Effects to be Expected from Them, to Which Is Added, a Discourse on Transportation, and a Method to Render that Punishment More Effectual* (London: J. Roberts, 1725), p. 5.

70 *Ibid.*

71 Frederick Burwick, *Playing to the Crowd: London Popular Theatre, 1780–1830* (Basingstoke: Palgrave Macmillan, 2011), p. 141.

72 Foucault, *Discipline and Punish*, p. 57.

of the carnival, in which rules were inverted, authority mocked and criminals transformed into heroes. The shame was turned round; the courage, like the tears and cries of the condemned, causes offence only to the law.'[73] But this is to say that public execution, and the kind of public it summoned, belonged to an age that had already rendered the phenomenon peculiarly archaic. It referred to an economy of punishment that will increasingly be seen as obsolete, discredited and barbaric even as it persisted in the form of the century's 'bloody code'.[74] For example, Samuel Romilly will argue in 1786:

> in proportion as these spectacles are frequent, the impression which they make upon the public is faint, the effect of the example is lost, and the blood of many citizens is spilt, without any benefit to mankind. But this is not all; the frequent exhibition of these horrid scenes cannot be indifferent: if they do not reform they must corrupt. The spectators of them become familiarised with bloodshed, and learn to look upon the destruction of a fellow-creature with unfeeling indifference.[75]

It is for this reason that one finds in Mandeville's 'Transactions of Execution Day'[76] the appearance of something oppressive and polluted, but also something whose form and appearance owes everything to the general climate of corruption that permeates the spectacle of execution and that conjures and promotes precisely the kind of deviant and irrational behaviour that must be suppressed insofar as it is intolerable to that newer, 'reasonable' middle-class public, traced by Habermas. It is in the discursive construction of that theatrocratic object par excellence, the mob, that Mandeville finds all the motives for the suppression of this older, philistine and vernacular public; and in this sense he conforms to a general trend, increasingly noticeable over the course of the century, that will lead to the eventual development of governmental and peremptory regulation of this common public through a wholesale reform of the penal system.

It is worth noting, also, that in discourses of reform around the use, purpose, extent, techniques and practice of capital punishment this common public finds itself accompanied by a strange bedfellow: an incompetent if not fundamentally rotten juridical apparatus. Hence to speak of the reform of the judiciary is to speak in every sense of a corollary

73 *Ibid.*, p. 61.

74 For further discussion, see chapter 9 in Vic C. Gatrell, *The Hanging Tree: Execution and the English People 1770–1868* (Oxford: Oxford University Press, 1994).

75 Samuel Romilly, *Observations on a Late Publication Intituled, Thoughts on Executive Justice* (London: Cadell, 1786), pp. 30–31.

76 Mandeville, *Frequent Executions*, p. 5.

discourse to those discourses that call for the suppression of the common public who are convoked by the practices of public execution. Indeed, corruption in existing carceral practices, and among the judiciary more generally, will be a common theme among penal reformers of the eighteenth century. To take just one example, Swift would write, in 1709: 'There is one abuse in this town which wonderfully contributes to the promotion of vice; that such men are often put into the Commission of the peace whose interest it is that virtue should be utterly banished from among us.'[77] Too often the authorities act in collusion with criminals; and, in many respects, it is the authorities themselves who cultivate, foster and sponsor them, to the extent that conspiracy and betrayal inexorably entrap the thief in the law – one of the principal targets of John Gay's satire *The Beggar's Opera*, where thief-takers and corrupt officials such as Peachum and Lockit play both sides of the system, thus profiting, on the one hand, from the proceeds of crime by acting as fences for robbers and highwaymen and, on the other, by cashing in on the rewards arising from their capture, conviction and execution. This will be especially true where, in an age when notoriety entailed celebrity, the felon's name evoked a sense of glamour as was exemplified by the case of Jack Sheppard on whom the character of Macheath would be based:

> It is possible that a dextrous Youth may be esteemed, and be a Favourite to the Superintendant for a great while; but when he grows very notorious, he is hunted like a Deer, and the Premium on his Head betrays him. He may baffle his Prosecutor, find a Flaw of an Evidence, come off once or twice, be reprieved, break Gaol, or be pardoned, the Gallows will be his Portion at last. The Wretch that is train'd up to Stealing, is the Property of the Hangman.[78]

What occurs on the day of execution, nevertheless, is less a matter of official malfeasance than lack of professionalism, a consequence of the sheer incompetence, ill-discipline and no doubt suspect character of the officials involved in the event. It would be reasonable to expect, writes Mandeville, that 'all, who had any Business there, should be grave and

[77] Jonathan Swift quoted in Sir Thomas Skyrme, *History of the Justices of the Peace*, vol. 2: *England 1689–1989* (Chichester: Barry Rose and the Justice of the Peace, 1991), p. 137. Corruption was endemic in the judiciary, and particularly in counties such as Middlesex, where the justices were known as 'trading' or 'basket' justices – an allusion to the common practice of taking bribes. Even as late as 1783, the anonymous author of *The Means of Effectually Preventing Theft and Robbery* would complain: 'our trading justices, who have neither reward nor punishment from the people, pay themselves liberally, in proportion to the trouble they take for themselves, at the ruinous expense of the people' (p. 17).

[78] Mandeville, *Frequent Executions*, p. 17.

serious, and behave themselves, at least, with common Decency, and a Deportment suitable to the Occasion'.[79] What one finds, instead, is as far removed from the scene of sobriety and gravity that Mandeville would like to see as one can get, with 'entoxicating liquors, that are swallow'd in every Part of Newgate'. Consequently, the prison resounds with the sounds of laughter, raillery, belligerence and quarrelling. Particularly shocking to Mandeville is the conduct of the condemned man himself, who is utterly impenitent, 'either drinking madly, or uttering the vilest Ribaldry'.[80] Yet it is from the point of departure onwards, as a 'Torrent of Mob bursts through the Gate', that things deteriorate in a way that most alarms Mandeville. Over the course of the journey from Newgate to Tyburn, it is as if one finds oneself in 'one continual Fair' – a kind of nightmarish 'Jubilee' day for 'Whores and Rogues of the meaner Sort'.[81] Whoever travels this hellish route will keep company with individuals drawn from '[a]mongst the lower Ranks, and working People, the idlest, and such as are most fond of making Holidays, with Prentices and Journeymen to the meanest Trades' – and these are the 'most honourable Part of these floating Multitudes. All the rest', Mandeville pronounces, 'are worse . . . all Thieves and Pickpockets.'[82] What follows is one of the eighteenth century's greatest depictions of the disorderly crowd, comprising a vivid account of the most disreputable classes of the town:

> There the most abandon'd Rakehells may light on Women as Shameless: Here Trollops all in Rags, may pick up Sweethearts of the same Politeness: And there are none so lewd, so vile, or so indigent, of either Sex, but at the Time and Place aforesaid, they may find a Paramour. Where the Crowd is the least, which, among the Itinerants, is no where very thin, the Mob is the rudest; and here, jostling one another, and kicking Dirt about, are the most innocent Pastimes. Now you see a Man, without Provocation, push his companion in the Kennel; and two Minutes after, the Sufferer trip up the other's Heels, and the first Aggressor lies rotting in the more solid Mire.[83]

These tokens and signifiers of the degeneracy of indigence present the reader with an inverted table of values, cast in diametrical opposition to the virtues of politeness, courteousness and civility, by which the eighteenth-century public understood itself. This 'undisciplined Army' whose enemy is 'Cleanliness and good Manners'[84] provides Mandeville's public with a shocking image of this vice-ridden and 'most abominable Rabble'.[85] Its execrable brutality, viciousness and depravity are exacerbated by that great

[79] *Ibid.*, p. 18. [80] *Ibid.*, p 19. [81] *Ibid.*, p 20. [82] *Ibid.* [83] *Ibid.*, pp. 20–21.
[84] *Ibid.*, p. 22. [85] *Ibid.*, p. 23.

infirmity that plagues the lower orders, of endless concern to the reformers of the eighteenth and nineteenth centuries: the poor's prodigious appetite for and consumption of alcohol. Thus the scandalous conduct of the mob will be encouraged and stimulated through the ubiquitous trade in alcohol that can be found along the route:

> Here stands an old Sloven, in a Wig actually putrify'd, squeez'd up in a Corner, and recommends a Dram of it to the Goers-by: There another in Rags, with several Bottles in a Basket, stirs about with it, where the Throng is thinnest, and tears his Throat with crying his Commodity.[86]

These degenerate traders are about as far removed from the decent and reputable bourgeois shopkeepers of the town as one can imagine, as their barely coherent imprecations demonstrate: 'the intelligible sounds that can be heard among them, are Oaths and vile Expressions, with Wishes of Damnation at every other Word, pronounced promiscuously against themselves, or those they speak to.'[87]

There are two further deplorable facts of the occasion that should be observed. The first is the well-known adulation of the mob for the condemned man, who mistake 'Drunkenness for Intrepidity, and a senseless Deportment for Undauntedness';[88] and related to this, second, there is the manner by which the day's hero is presented, swaggering in the cart that will deliver him to the scaffold, acting as a kind of exemplary figure to be emulated, and drawing like a beacon all the 'young Villains, that are proud of being so . . . [tearing] the Cloaths off their Backs, by squeezing and creeping thro' the Legs of Men and Horses, to shake Hands with him'.[89] The final part of the account, however, depicts the *coup de théâtre* of execution as an odious 'scene of confusion [that] grows worse near the gallows'. It is here that the affront to authority and the true inadequacy of this form of punishment is most obvious to Mandeville, as he witnesses the conduct of the crowd and the deplorable scene of disorder and unrest that unfolds around the scaffold:

> [The] violent Efforts of the most sturdy and resolute of the Mob on one Side, and the potent Endeavours of rugged Gaolers and others, to beat them off, on the other; the terrible blows that are struck, the Heads that are Broke, the Pieces of swingeing Sticks, and Blood, that fly about, the Men that are knock'd down and trampled upon, are beyond Imagination; whilst the Dissonance of Voices, and the Variety of Outcries, for different Reasons, that are heard there, together with the Sound of more distant

[86] *Ibid.*, p. 21. [87] *Ibid.*, p. 22. [88] *Ibid.*, p. 6. [89] *Ibid.*, p. 23.

> Noises, make up a Discord not to be parallel'd. If we consider, besides all this, the mean Equipages of the Sheriff's Officers, and the scrubby Horses that compose the Cavalcade, the Irregularity of the March, and the Want of Order among all the Attendants, we shall be forced to confess, that these Processions are very void of that decent Solemnity that would be required to make them awful.[90]

Provoked by the indecency of the crowd and horrified by the degeneracy of these processions, Mandeville's diagnosis (and motivation to reform public execution) becomes explicit: it is not the penalty per se that is wrong, but its dramaturgy. The lesson of the scaffold is illegible; its moral backfires. It does not serve to inculcate in its viewer a temperate sense of sorrow at the lamentable scene to which he or she is witness or bring them to regret the misfortune brought about by a life associated with vice and depravity. The lamentable scene represents the failure of public 'sentiment', when even the 'best dispos'd Spectator seldom can pick out any thing that is edifying or moving'.[91] Worse still, it is a dramaturgy that leads the vulgar to entertain notions of courage, honour and shame that are 'full of dangerous Errors'.[92] For instance, where they take the condemned man's nonchalance before the 'halter' to be a sign of courage, intrepid defiance or perhaps even proof of his gallantry, in reality the bravery they admire is nothing but 'spurious . . . counterfeited, and false at bottom'. The victim merely appears courageous, his daring a superficial consequence of the very thing that belies it – that he has taken 'Refuge in strong liquors'. The reality is he is no more than a 'sham-hero', his pluck and nerve, his insouciance and indifference, little more than a theatrical effect – and the vulgar mob, as is typical of all theatrocratic spectators, demonstrates once again how easily it is duped. They see only what they want to see, only its superficial theatrics, and are consequently incapable of penetrating the spectacle to draw from it a message of any civic worth. Mandeville, however, sees precisely what the crowd is incapable of seeing: that rendered insensible by drink its hero exhibits all the 'courage of a Stone' that 'drops into Eternity . . . without thought'.[93]

This image of the dissolute mob, 'frightful and impertinent', as Mandeville describes them, who swarm around the condemned man – this bleak mass of the lowest of the people, incapable of receiving public instruction or of grasping the moral injunction that the gallows has staged for their benefit, and who seek instead to derive pleasure from this grim theatre of death, would provide the firmest evidence and proof of the dysfunctional

[90] *Ibid.*, p. 24. [91] *Ibid.*, p. 25. [92] *Ibid.*, p. 29. [93] *Ibid.*, p. 35.

nature of the practice of punishing capital offences in public. Far from deterring crime, such practices provided an incitement for the ungovernable elements of society to exercise themselves in the most visible manner. This 'ocular Demonstration' is nothing but a source of encouragement to those 'hardened' 'Profligates that behold them'.[94] Public execution indeed produces a public, but it is in every sense the wrong public, and an enlightened age must not tolerate it.

But what would provide a better model for the dramaturgy of execution – one that would act as a corrective to the spectator, which would not produce an errant and dissolute plebeian 'public' but would ensure that, through the sacrifice of a few of the indigent, the safety of the legitimate public might be assured?[95] To make such sacrifices worthwhile, it is necessary to first attend to the purpose of public execution: 'it is not the Death of those poor Souls that is chiefly aim'd at in Executions, but the Terror we would have it strike in others of the same loose Principles.'[96] If execution is to serve its purpose as deterrence, then it must aim at producing an appropriately affective response in the viewer. The spectacle must be 'awful', for instance; it must 'strike the Hearts of the Beholders' and inspire them with a sense of 'ignominy'. Only then will it deter the 'Rakehells' who 'delight in Mischief'. To accomplish this is to 'render these Tragedies more solemn, and, at the same Time, make room for Spectators of a better sort'.[97] It is to ensure that the spectacle of execution provides no opportunity for the mob to congregate, thus improving the quality of its auditors. Now it is the turn of theatre to rescue execution from the baseness of theatrocratic immoderation and excess, but only if the spectacle of execution should resemble the edifications of tragedy and not the topsy-turvy world of a burlesque.

Mandeville thus imagines a very different kind of performance, a different kind of audience and a very different kind of hero – one designed to ensure that the spectacle will be a civilising one. The victim must be portrayed as a man of misfortune; he is neither a mere criminal nor the crowd's stooge, but a man whose salvation depends wholly on making his contrition visible. To make the condemned contrite is to render the true purpose of the spectacle demonstrable to the commonality. It is to ensure that the corrective lesson of the scaffold will be understood by those at

[94] *Ibid.*, p. 37. [95] *Ibid.*, pp. 36–37.

[96] *Ibid.*, p. 36; and see Sir William Blackstone, for whom the purpose of execution is to set 'a dreadful example to deter others'. William Blackstone, *Commentaries on the Laws of England in Four Books* (New York: W.E. Dean, 1842), p. 14.

[97] Mandeville, *Frequent Executions*, p. 43.

whom it is aimed, those whose predilections tempt them into criminality. Thus the greatest attention must be paid to the conduct of the condemned – transformed by days of seclusion, a meagre diet and hours of contrition spent with a priest – then, finally, the prospect of a miserable death:

> When we had seen an half-starv'd Wretch, that look'd like Death, come shivering from his Prison, and hardly able to speak or stand, get with Difficulty on the slow uncomfortable Carriage; where at first Rumbling of it, he should begin to weep, and as he went, dissolve in Tears, and lose himself in incoherent Lamentations, it would move us to Compassion.[98]

And yet to be moved to compassion at such a wretched spectacle is not the denouement of Mandeville's imaginary scene of execution. Pity and compassion may move the spectator, but they are not in themselves significantly edifying; rather, what he wants is the moment of *anagorisis*, of recognition, and, finally, a communal catharsis: 'But with what Astonishment would it not fill us, to behold the same Creature, near the Fatal Tree, become lively, glow with Zeal, and in Strength of Voice and Action, excel the most vigorous Preachers.'[99] To imagine such a scene is to imagine that it is possible to produce out of the criminal, vulgar and riotous plebeian mob the compliant and suitably pacified public of deontic power. It is to imagine the transformation of the victim of the gallows; converted from depraved felon to man of virtue he becomes a kind of lay preacher. However improbable, such a man will be a wholly reformed character whose 'stupendous' oratory will produce the desired deontic effects; or to put it another way, the condemned man will be the willing instrument of deontic power, and just to the extent that his last words on earth, his own discourse, will 'find uncommon ways to reach the Heart with Violence, and force Repentance on their Hearers'.[100]

Fielding and the Tragic Dramaturgy of the Gallows

Henry Fielding was also profoundly disturbed by the counterfeit morality of public execution. As a sessional magistrate he would produce one of the most influential commentaries on criminal law in the mid-eighteenth century: *An Enquiry into the Cause of the Late Increase of Robbers, &c. with Some Proposals for Remedying This Growing Evil* (1751). Like Mandeville, Fielding was also deeply concerned that the mob was undeterred by public

[98] *Ibid.*, p. 45. [99] *Ibid.*, pp. 45–46 [100] *Ibid.*, p. 46.

execution and that it provided a public stage upon which the prisoner had a final opportunity to immortalise himself through heroic antics and in making defiant speeches. Where execution ought to be the staging of an example, where it should be an 'object of Terror' for the spectators, it tended instead to promote a malicious mythology, spun around the valiant victim of the gallows, and such that the execution of a felon acted as a spur to the criminal classes. Given the frequency of executions, what it threatened was a vicious causality: more people would be attracted by the 'glamour' of crime, resulting in increased criminality and thus a greater frequency of executions:

> No Hero sees Death as an Alternative which may attend his Undertaking with less Terror, nor meets it in the Field with more imaginary Glory ... the Day appointed by Law for the Thief's Shame is the Day of Glory in his own Opinion. His Procession to *Tyburn*, and his last Moments there, are all triumphant; attended with the Compassion of the meek and tender-hearted, and with the Applause, Admiration, and Envy of all the bold and hardened.[101]

As with Mandeville, for Fielding it is the doubtful dramaturgy of public execution that is to blame, dispelling rather than promoting the effects of deterrence. It produces theatrocratic applause when it should 'add the Punishment of Shame to that of Death; in order to make the Example an Object of greater Terror'. The affective power of execution and its lesson are therefore inseparable: if the spectacle of public, state-sanctioned violence does not result in the affective response of a profound shame among those who witness it, then the spectacle of death is without efficacy, reason or purpose. And indeed, '[e]xperience has shown us,' writes Fielding, 'that the Event is directly contrary to this Intention.'[102]

Fielding does not simply follow Mandeville, however, but derives an entirely distinct lesson when applying the knowledge of the theatre to the dramaturgical problem of staging execution. For Fielding, it is not just that it stages the wrong kind of theatrical spectacle; it misunderstands the complex psychological relation that holds between emotional response, affect, instructional intention and theatrical representation. Here Fielding makes two noteworthy observations. First, however one may try, one cannot derive shame from pity – such affective states are incompatible with one another. And because the miserable picture of 'a poor Wretch,

[101] Henry Fielding, *An Enquiry into the Cause of the Late Increase of Robbers, &c. with Some Proposals for Remedying This Growing Evil* (London: A. Millar, 1751), pp. 189–90.
[102] *Ibid.*, p. 191.

bound in a Cart, just on the Verge of Eternity, all pale and trembling' is more likely to provoke pity, public execution cannot produce the effect it seeks, the sense of communal shame, disgrace or humiliation at the prospect of the felon's dishonourable fate. To put the point in rather more theoretical terms: pity cannot 'subjectivate' the viewer; it cannot force (unlike shame) reform in the conduct of the spectator; it cannot compel them into or out of a given behaviour or way of doing something. For a corresponding reason, whenever a 'daring Rogue' seeks glory in a 'heroic' death, again, the idea and effect of shame will be distinctly absent from this image. So in both cases the publicity of violence does not produce the prescribed deontic quality. And yet the point of making punishment public is precisely to induce a collective sense of moral humiliation. It is only shame at the prospect of such an ignominious end that acts as the true deterrent and justifies the penalty through the demonstration of its pedagogical results.

The problem, then, is whether one can achieve this moral end through theatrical means or whether, in order to heighten the efficacy of the pedagogy of execution, it might be better to deny the public the spectacle it craves altogether. The lesson of the theatre, and in particular tragedy, provides an insight into the problem and a plausible solution, for as all poets know, says Fielding:

> Admiration or Pity, or both, are very apt to attend whatever is the Object of Terror in the human mind. This is very useful to the Poet, but very hurtful on the present Occasion to the Politician, whose Art is to be here employed to raise an Object of Terror, and, at the same time, as much as possible, to strip it of all Pity and all Admiration.[103]

Drawing the lesson of the theatrical stage, the only viable conclusion is that the execution of criminals should not be made public at all, but 'be in some degree private'.[104] For just as a murder is made more effective when it occurs 'off-stage' and affects the '[a]udiences with greater Terror than if it was acted before their Eyes' – so executions would be all the more powerful were they to take place behind closed doors: 'If Executions therefore were so contrived, that few could be present at them, they would be much more shocking and terrible to the Crowd without Doors than at present, as well as much more dreadful to the Criminals themselves.'[105]

For this reason, to increase the affective power of the lesson, one must deprive the theatre of punishment of its spectacular form. To be sure, it

[103] *Ibid.*, p. 192. [104] *Ibid.*, p. 193. [105] *Ibid.*, p. 194.

will take a further century of argument, and the Capital Punishment Amendment Act of 1868, to finally abolish the spectacle of public execution. Still, what Fielding anticipates, in envisaging the end of the 'Holiday at Tyburn', will correspond, eventually, to the emergence of the idea of the cold, one might say 'anti-theatrical', and ceremonial dramaturgy that characterises the disciplinary apparatus of the modern state. A profound shift can thus be discerned here: away from a general regime of spectacular terror towards the idea that the mob, comprising a brutish commonality, must be subject to systems of deontic exclusion and correction. Only insofar as one can inculcate, whether by pedagogical or disciplinary means, a general sense of public morality, transforming the habits and behaviours of the indigent and labouring classes, will law and the practices of governance result in an order of prevention consistent with the age of civility. Thus a new spirit of reform is mobilised by the bourgeois public sphere at this point. At the same time, it reveals its basic inconsistency, for the external limit constituted by the discursive imaginary of the bourgeois public sphere is precisely a *structural* – that is to say, *necessary* – limit in relation to which its own identity becomes decipherable; it is therefore a limit that cannot be surpassed or overcome without provoking the dissolution of that identity. It is a structural limit that is revealed precisely through the prejudices of the public. Thus the movement for reforming plebeian tastes, behaviours and dispositions, through a range of governmental techniques, can be accomplished only through the suppression of every opportunity whereby an autonomous plebeian culture might assert itself. Government circumscribes its spaces of appearance ever more vigorously from this point on, directing its interpositions at all the sites where the poor might assemble or become visible – the theatres, fairs and, of course, the festival that is execution day. Fielding provides a succinct summary of the basic direction of travel that will determine the course of reform from this point on, as well as the underlying prejudice of emergent liberal governmentality when he asserts that nothing will be resolved until one can 'put a Stop to the Luxury of the Lower People, to force the Poor to Industry'.[106] What he reveals in saying this is nothing other than the illiberal underside of the liberal public sphere.

106 *Ibid.*

CHAPTER 4

The Beggar's Opera *and the Criminal 'Picturesque'*

Introduction

The previous chapter showed how a governmental consciousness came to define the permissible space of critical discourse during the eighteenth century. It is hardly surprising to discover that it thoroughly permeates attitudes towards the stage, too; that it exerted a considerable influence over practices such as emergent theatre criticism or practices of spectatorship; that it navigated the stage ever more firmly by the compass of deontic power, thereby expanding its pervasive hegemony; and that it transformed the theatre gradually but inexorably into a space for practising techniques of control over the social body. For this governmental consciousness, the theatre is profoundly problematic, then; but it is not necessarily intractably so. On the contrary, theatre presents an opportunity to promote deontic governance, and just to the extent that it is considered, not simply as a diversion but as a school. In fact, it would be naïve to imagine that for such a consciousness the stage can ever be seen as a merely innocent amusement. Even the most harmless entertainment secretes within its depictions a lesson for the audience. However covertly, inadvertently or indirectly, the stage instructs. Two plays will serve here to exemplify, in the acutest way possible, this problem of the pedagogical efficacy of the stage – John Gay's *The Beggar's Opera* (1728) and George Lillo's *The London Merchant, or The History of George Barnwell* (1731). If these plays stand out over the century as two of the most influential (and widely performed) plays on the London stage, their respective influence was nevertheless felt in radically distinct ways. And, of course, crucially, that influence would be amplified by the way each play entered into the discursive positioning of the theatre. Indeed, it is no coincidence that both plays were frequently cited alongside one another throughout the century in discussions of the governance of the stage.

In *The Apprentice's Vade Mecum*, for example, Samuel Richardson urged the prohibiting of theatre to any young man bound apprentice to a trade. This quintessential Platonic fear, that the young are essentially vulnerable to the corrupting influence of the stage, would lead him to lament the immense popularity of plays such as *The Beggar's Opera*:

> Genteel comedy ... has long left the Stage, as well as the nobler Tragic Muse: And all our late Heroes and Heroines of the Drama, have been fetch'd from *Newgate* and *Bridewell* ... now [we have] the horrid Pantomime and wicked Dumb Shew, the infamous Harlequin Mimicry, introduc'd for nothing but to teach how to cozen, cheat, deceive, and cuckold; together with the wretched Group of Rogues, form'd from the characters of *Shepherd, Jonathan Wild, Blueskin* ... [acted] not for the sake of Poetical Justice, in their *Execution*, but to divert the Audience by their *Tricks* and *Escapes* ... [These characters are the] edifying subjects [that have delighted] crouded Audiences [and] Disgrac[ed] both of the British Taste and Stage.[1]

There is, however, one exception in Richardson's view of the corrupted world of the theatre with its 'crouded audiences' – and one play that is condoned:

> I know but of one Instance ... where the Stage has condescended to make itself useful to the City-Youth, by dreadful Example of the Artifices of a Lewd Woman, and the seduction of an unwary young Man ... I mean the play of *George Barnwell* ... [a play of] good Moral and Design.[2]

What distinguishes these two plays and how they shed further light on the discourse on the theatre will be the principal concern in the following two case histories. In the present chapter, I examine reaction to *The Beggar's Opera* insofar as it corroborates what had long been asserted within the discourse on the theatre: that in valorising those who ought not to be valorised, the stage is essentially criminal. What should be immediately noted is that if *The Beggar's Opera* embodies a crisis for the discourse on theatre, it does so not by diminishing but precisely by intensifying the pedagogical efficacy of the stage, grasped as a satirical and moralistic form. The problem with the *Opera* is not that it is ineffective but that it is too effective. It is too efficient at providing its auditors with a lesson. Unhappily for the *Opera*, it is the wrong lesson. There is, consequently, something hapless in the play: its deontic effects are inverted or, perhaps more

[1] Samuel Richardson, *The Apprentice's Vade Mecum: or, Young Man's Pocket-Companion*, the Augustan Reprint Society, Publication Numbers 169–70, William Andrews Clark Memorial Library (Los Angeles: University of California, 1975 [London, 1734]), pp. 12–13; emphasis in original.

[2] Richardson, *Apprentice's Vade Mecum*, p. 16.

accurately, deflected – away from the deontic message and the idea that the stage ought to promote the civic good – towards something evil, or at least wildly inappropriate and threatening, which the satire substitutes for the scene of instruction. What it confirms through this inversion is the inappropriateness of the stage as a pedagogical tool. As one commentator would write, Gay's 'admirable satire' had originally intended to 'lash the vices of the Great', but it produced 'in its event, very great and manifest injury to the publick'.[3]

George Lillo's *The London Merchant*, by contrast, will be lauded as the most celebrated example of the kind of theatre that a thoroughgoing reform of the stage would attempt to produce. Whereas in *The Beggar's Opera*, whose message is criminally misdirected, the example is of the failure of public deontology, *The London Merchant* represents an exemplary use of the stage – and a theatre whose message is wholly subordinated to the moral precepts it advocates. What *The London Merchant* sought to prove is that the stage can indeed be a scene of instruction. What it endorses is the idea that the theatre must not simply entertain, but must also 'condescend', to use Richardson's term, to be socially useful. Its legitimacy derives not just from the immense rigour with which it embraces this undertaking but from the discursive alignment of the stage with two expedients advantageous to society. First, by demonstrating that a socially useful stage is conceivable only insofar as the theatre is able to be an adequate vehicle for the promotion of deontic power, it uses the example of the stage, not just to punish deviant forms of behaviour but to verify 'correct' (socially virtuous) forms of conduct, as staged by the deontic message of the play. Furthermore, in offering a positive model of good and suitable conduct, it serves a second function or use: that of persuading its auditors that the precepts of virtuous conduct correlate with the economic norms required to ensure the good governance of commercial society. In Lillo's hands, the theatre becomes several things: a demonstration of theatre as a legitimate laboratory of reform, a therapeutic intervention or experiment, a preventative lesson whose effect is to vitiate vice before it takes hold, a non-punitive mode of correcting delinquent behaviours, and a dramatic representation of the table of values, derived from the new political economy, to be instilled in its auditors.

I begin my analysis by first examining the discursive crisis engendered by the appearance of *The Beggar's Opera*. In the following chapter, I turn to consider the case for a reformed or deontic stage, surveying the more

[3] *Morning Chronicle and London Advertiser*, 20 September 1773, issue 1349.

general deontic codifications advocated by theatrical reformers, as they came to be expressed during the century.

The Criminal Lesson of *The Beggar's Opera*

The Beggar's Opera belongs to a cycle of plays made popular in the first decades of the eighteenth century that traded in the 'criminal picturesque'.[4] This is the 'Newgate pastoral', a name first suggested by Jonathan Swift,[5] which included the *Opera*'s forerunners: John Thurmond's wordless pantomime, *Harlequin Sheppard*, for which Gay had provided the prisoner's song 'Newgate's Garland' and which was staged in 1724, barely two weeks after the execution of Jack Sheppard (the petty thief who would provide inspiration for the character of Macheath);[6] and Christopher Bullock's earlier comic farce, *A Woman's Revenge: or, A Match in Newgate*, produced at Lincoln's-Inn-Fields in 1715 and whose satirical side-swipes at the 'Corruption of the Age' no doubt helped inspire Gay's own efforts. Certainly, the sentiments in *A Woman's Revenge* might have come straight out of the pages of the *Opera* – as the roguish Vizard says, in a manner befitting Macheath's own gang of thieves: 'few Men, indeed, suffer for Dishonesty, but for Poverty, many. The greatest Part of Mankind being Rogues within, or without the Law, so that little Thieves are hang'd for the Security of great ones.'[7] Nevertheless, there the resemblance with Gay's opera begins – and ends. Notwithstanding Padwell's claim that 'Mr Gay stole [*The Beggar's Opera*]

[4] This term may strike the reader as somewhat anachronistic – the picturesque wasn't common currency in Britain until later in the century, although it appears in the 1750s (and dates back to the previous century in France – the first known English usage is around 1700 or so). However, to speak of the 'criminal picturesque' is to capture the subversive spirit of Gay's play – and by the late 1700s we are safely in the domain of the picturesque, with William Gilpin's aesthetic theory of the picturesque emerging in the late 1760s.

[5] Swift had proposed the idea that Gay might write a 'Newgate Pastoral' in a letter to Alexander Pope – proclaiming that the 'pastoral ridicule is not exhausted' – a reference to Gay's earlier burlesque of the 'sentimental pastorals' then very much in vogue, the 'Shepherd's Week', published in 1714. See Swift to Pope, 30 August 1716, published in *The Works of Alexander Pope*, vol. VII (London: John Murray, 1871), p. 17.

[6] The Newgate 'garland' is a reference to the widely held but erroneous belief that the thief-taker Jonathan Wild's 'Throat was cut from Ear to Ear' by Blueskin (one of Sheppard's associates) during his trial at the Old Bailey; *Harlequin Sheppard* (London: J. Roberts and A. Dodd, 1724), p. 16. For a historical account of Gay's participation in *Harlequin Sheppard*, see Calhoun Winton, *John Gay and the London Theatre* (Lexington: University Press of Kentucky, 1993).

[7] Christopher Bullock, *Woman's Revenge: or, a Match in Newgate. A Comedy. As it is acted at the Royal Theatre in Lincoln's-Inn-Fields. The Second Edition. To Which Is Added, a Complete Key to The Beggar's Opera, by Peter Padwell of Padington, Esq;*. (London: J. Roberts, 1728), p. 4. A later play in the 'Newgate' cycle is *The Prisoner's Opera*, attributed to Edward Ward and performed in 1731.

from Mr. Bullock, who only borrowed it from Mr. Marston' (*A Woman's Revenge* is a rewriting of Marston's *The Dutch Courtesan* of 1605), not only does Bullock's farce contain no music or songs; it is, at best – and to borrow a distinction made by Jean B. Kern – only occasionally satiric and can by no means be called a satire.[8] Moreover, as Kern argues, while 'comedy works toward a resolution; satire does not'.[9] On the contrary, its aim is 'to expose by the use of irony, grotesque fantasy, wit and ridicule the folly of man'.[10] It is specifically insofar as the *Opera* combines satirical criticism *with* the criminal picturesque, however, that it came to uniquely embody the worst excesses of the eighteenth-century stage. In order to comprehend the discursive and governmental significance of *The Beggar's Opera*, I will examine a cluster of issues drawn from the two major controversies that erupt around the play, albeit from disputes separated by fifty years: the controversy of 1728, sparked by the play's first performance at the Theatre Royal, Lincoln's-Inn-Fields, and later, the reactivation of this controversy in the 1770s, which came to a head in the quarrel between David Garrick, who wanted to stage the *Opera*, and the magistrate Sir John Fielding, who had intervened to prevent him from doing so.

To begin the analysis, consider for a moment the idea that the *Opera* commits a 'manifest injury' to the public, for what could be worse than the idea that an 'admirable satire', written with all the right motives in mind, might afflict the public with such poisonous consequences, in other words, that the pedagogical effects of the stage are far from being determined by the moral intentions and values of the playwright? How can the best motives produce the worst results? What is encountered in *The Beggar's Opera*, perhaps more than any play of the eighteenth century, makes explicit this discursive problem, since the *Opera* hits upon that equivocal limit where criticism, in the form of dramatic satire, threatens to work against the very interests it was meant to serve – that is to say, those interests of the public, as surveyed in the previous chapter, clustered around a nexus of liberal ideals incorporating the freedom of speech, the right to private ownership and protection under the rule of law. This limit signals a contradiction that emerges as a direct effect of the rules of formation of the public sphere, insofar as criticism is predicated on the discursive construction of freedom. The controversy surrounding Gay's ballad opera is, in many respects, explicitly provoked by the way it brings to the fore this

[8] Kern, *Dramatic Satire in the Age of Walpole, 1720–1750*, p. 5. [9] *Ibid.*, p. 146. [10] *Ibid.*, p. 143.

contradiction internal to satirical criticism, which becomes both a means and an obstacle to the realisation of that freedom. The problem is twofold: give too much space to the attacks of the critic, that censor of public morals, and no man will be free to act for fear of provoking public censure; curtail the freedom of the individual to act as public censor, and succumb to the heavy and oppressive hand of the government.

And yet it is not the oppressions and curtailments of the despotic prince, the repressive state or the authoritarian politician that finally determine the nature of the threat contained in the century's most popular play. The far greater threat to the public contained in the *Opera* adverts to the sense of theatrocratic licence that an unregulated stage threatens to unleash, and which, like a Trojan horse, this immensely popular comic opera bears within it. For its critics, and particularly for those towards the end of the century, what the play demonstrates is precisely the reasons why restrictions must be placed upon freedom – at least when it comes to the theatre. It establishes beyond all doubt that the freedom to censure does not come at any price; that, on the contrary, freedom entails a degree of domination in virtue of the greater necessity demanded by the public for order and law. For this reason, the problems raised by Gay's satirical comedy are manifold and complex: discerning the effective limits of criticism, addressing the scope and purpose of dramatic representation, promoting the necessity of poetic justice, as well as addressing the question of how to ensure that satire produces the right deontic effects and does not provoke a far greater magnitude of disorder than it was meant to punish. I will address each of these *seriatim*.

(1) *The existential question over the role and limits of criticism on stage.* How is one to permit criticism, thus ensuring the space of hard-won freedoms essential to the existence of the public, yet at the same time ensuring the coherence and general order of society that are associated with good and virtuous governance? How does a censorious age prevent itself from being undermined by the disorders that satirical criticism might provoke if permitted to appear on the stage? And is it not the case that disorder is precisely the risk authority runs whenever it permits 'open' criticism? In this context, *The Beggar's Opera* flirts dangerously with the critical distinction, already identified by John Dennis, in his essay of 1704, on dramatic criticism – that there is a fine line between a libel and a lampoon, and that while one may be useful for ridiculing errant passions and minor vices, the other is wholly destructive.[11] To be sure, Gay's satiric

[11] John Dennis, *The Grounds of Criticism in Poetry* (London, 1704), p. 2. To be sure, Dennis was just one voice among many engaged in the development of critique and commentary – the development

pen is adept at sidestepping the charge of seditious libel, and indeed the *Opera* is far less explicit in its attack on political targets, compared with Fielding's austere satires on corrupt electioneering practices a decade later.[12] Nevertheless, the satirical attack of the *Opera* openly targets the policy of the Whig government and the figure of Walpole in particular, who is depicted in various guises.[13] Walpole is cast, first, as a dishonest and corrupt official, who acts as a fence for London's criminal underclass ('And the Statesman, because he's so great Thinks his trade as honest as mine' – as Peachum sings); at the same time Peachum, and by analogy Walpole, is depicted as a treacherous villain, prepared to betray his friends for private gain or personal advantage. Thus Peachum remarks in his dispute with Lockit: 'like Great Statesmen, we encourage those who betray their friends' (II.x). Perhaps most egregious of all to Walpole's supporters is the way in which Gay depicts the first minister through the figure of Captain Macheath – the leader of a gang of thieves.[14] This comparison would elicit particularly partisan praise from Gay's friend Swift, who, in defending the play, proclaimed it an 'excellent moral performance':

> In this happy Performance, all the Characters are just, and none of them carried beyond Nature, or hardly beyond Practice. It discovers the whole System of that Common-wealth, or that *Imperium* in *Imperio* of iniquity, established among us, by which neither our lives, nor our Properties are secure, or even in our own houses.

But it is not hard to see this line of defence as disingenuous. Swift does not take the play to be a grave warning to the public over the threat of criminality to the security of their property. Nor is it plausible that he

of criticism is far from homogenous or straightforward. Dennis, of course, is mercilessly satirised by Gay's friend Alexander Pope in his *The Dunciad*, published in the same year as *The Beggar's Opera*. However, as I suggested in the previous chapter, the public sphere embodies precisely this kind of agonistic struggle during the period – with all its contradictions – expressed particularly through literary rivalries and controversies.

12 Gay's play has much more of a broad censorship of human vices than Fielding's plays, together with elements of the 'bread and circus' tradition that made the *Opera* so popular; but it is precisely these elements that become so problematic in the 1770s, when Fielding's plays were by then disregarded, their topicality having been exhausted by the passage of time.

13 A well-known story that circulated following the first performance of the play – attended by Walpole himself – is summed up in Swift's letter to Gay, later that year: 'We hear a million stories about the Opera, of the applause of the song *That was level'd at me*, when two great Ministers were in a box together, and all the world staring at them' (letter Dr Swift to Mr Gay, Dublin, 27 November 1727, pp. 105–9, published in *The Works of Alexander Pope, Esq., in Verse and Prose, in 10 Volumes*, vol. 9 (London: Strahan and Preston, 1806)). Walpole's discomfort and private grievance against Gay would lead eventually to the suppression of Gay's sequel to *The Beggar's Opera*, *Polly*, in 1729.

14 Captain Macheath is 'drawn to Asperse somebody in Authority . . . the Head of a Gang of Robbers'; *Country Journal or the Craftsman*, 17 February 1728, issue 85.

sees this comedy of grotesque characters as a sincere attempt at depicting the 'miserable lives, and the constant Fate of those abandoned wretches' who appear in the play. What it really does is take political criticism to the stage – and this is where Swift's interest in the piece lies – in its satirical exposure of the political vices of the 'present age . . . [where] the Author takes occasion of comparing these *common Robbers* to *Robbers of the Publick*; and their several Stratagems of betraying, condemning, and hanging each other, to the several Arts of *Politicians* in Times of Corruption'.[15]

It is precisely this comparison, which the play invites, that constitutes the nub of the controversy. But also, in a sense, it is in relation to the general satirical orientation of the play that one can best understand in what sense satirical criticism encounters its social limit. Beyond its personal attack on Walpole, the *Opera* satirised the vices of the age – an age precisely benighted by official corruption; and it is this fact that provides, no doubt, an explanation as to why it was greeted with 'more than ordinary Applause'[16] by its audience. And yet a satire that criticises a political culture in general is likely to offend everyone – something Gay had already anticipated in the *Opera* itself:

> When you censure the Age,
> Be cautious and Sage,
> Lest the Courtiers offended should be;
> If you mention Vice or Bribe,
> 'Tis so pat to all the Tribe,
> Each cries, that was levell'd at me.

If the comparison is questionable – intolerable even – to those concerned with the problem of governance it is because the question that is really asked is this: what is the ultimate effect of this kind of satirical identification? What happens when 'things of the greatest Importance [are] turned to Ridicule'?

This is the question posed by Walpole's supporters in the *Country Journal*. In the 'burlesquing' of the coronation; the mockery of 'Nobles, Prelates, the Judges and Magistrates' by 'Harlequin and his Associates'; the 'traducing' of honourable politicians, now the 'subject of Mirth and Derision to crowded and clapping Audiences', *The Beggar's Opera* 'is the most venomous allegorical libel against the [government]'. What satire does, inadvertently perhaps, is criticise not just the faction in power, or

[15] Jonathan Swift in *Mist's Weekly Journal*, 6 July 1728, issue 168.
[16] *Mist's Weekly Journal*, 23 March 1728, issue 153.

impugn government ministers. It undermines the basis of the very possibility of governance by undermining the natural order of social distinction upon which it is based. If one wishes to know the principle by which Gay's satire works, it is that of equalising those who are (by breeding and social status) unequal:

> [The] very *Title* of this Piece and the *principal Character*, which is that of a *Highwayman*, sufficiently discover the mischievous Design of it, since by his Character every Body will understand *One*, who makes his Business arbitrarily to *levy* and collect Money on the People for his *own Use*, and of which he always dreads to give *any Account* – Is not this squinting with a Vengeance and wounding *Persons in Authority* through the sides of a *common Malefactor*?

It is precisely through the satirical strategy of criticism by analogy – 'innuendo', as the author of this piece puts it – that all are made equivalent. The greatest part of mankind is levelled with the meanest. If the play is correct in its attack, then the question arises: are not all lords the same as highwaymen in making poor husbands for their wives; will it not be said that a statesman is bad if not worse than the corrupt Peacham, that courtiers are less honest than highwaymen since 'every Courtier is corrupted either with Vice or a Bribe, or with both' – and does this equating of the highest with the lowest not promote a 'general libel on Men of all Professions, even the most sacred'?

But what is perhaps most treacherous of all about this play is that in its pretence to serve the public, it undermines the very freedom that makes public censure viable – its criticism is biased. For this reason, the author argues, while he does not wish to see the 'Liberty of the stage intirely abolished', it should at least 'restrain' itself from permitting such 'licentious invectives' and making the stage the medium of intolerance:

> [For] if they continue to be allowed, the *Theatre* will become the *Censor* of the Age, and no Man, even of the *first Quality* or *Distinction*, will be at Liberty to follow his *Pleasures*, *Inclinations* or *Interest* (which is certainly the *Birthright* of every *Free Briton*) without Danger of becoming the May-game of the whole Town.[17]

The 'danger' spoken of here by no means refers to a merely imagined menace or to the inflated hyperbole of oppositional commentary – exaggeration aimed at scare-mongering. It is to be understood as something rooted very much in the specific experience of theatre audiences at the

[17] *Country Journal or the Craftsman*, 17 February 1728, issue 85; emphasis in original.

time, with their peculiar demographics. This was a period that had, since the 1690s, seen the rapid 'democratisation of the theatre', as Jim Davis puts it.[18] And with the immense popularity of the *Opera* in particular (Gay had astutely adapted his songs to fit instantly recognisable melodies), its audience would have been viewed very much as the embodiment of the 'town'.

John O'Brien has observed that terms such as 'nation', 'public' and 'town' are 'in part fictional, imaginary constructs, summoned into being through their repeated articulation, but lacking easily comprehended form'.[19] Nevertheless, it was the theatre that provided the locus in which such imagined entities were made visible, materialising these abstract publics in the concrete and tangible form of the audience. Later in the century, the actor Theophilius Cibber would explicitly invoke this notion that the town is somehow found embodied in the material reality of the theatre audience: 'I think, the Town may be supposed to include all Degrees of Persons, from the highest Nobleman, to the lowly Artizan &c. who, in their different Stations, are Encouragers of dramatic Performances: – Thus all Persons who pay for their Places, whether Noble, Gentle, or Simple, who fill the Boxes, Pit, and Galleries, in a theatrical Sense, form the Town, as K—g, L-rds, and Commons . . . [making] that great Body, the nation.'[20] From the footmen and servants in the galleries to the aristocrats in their boxes, the audience described a vector through which all social classes passed. Quite literally, the whole 'world' came to view the *Opera* – not just the 'fleering Coxcombs' in the pit, but clergy, too – according to Swift's account:

> All *Ranks*, *Parties* and *Denominations* of Men . . . crowding to see [Gay's] Opera . . . even *Ministers* of State, whom he is thought to have most offended . . . appearing frequently at the *Theatre*, from a Consciousness of their own Innocence, and to convince the World how unjust a Parallel, *Malice, Envy* and *Disaffection to the Government have made.*[21]

The problem was that the *Opera*'s audience also embodied something rather less palatable – at least to anyone inclined to share Addison's vision of an ideal of genteel spectatorship or who imagined the theatre as a space of intellectual absorption in which the audience is composed of 'thinking

[18] Jim Davis, 'Spectatorship', in *Cambridge Companion to British Theatre 1730–1830*, ed. Jane Moody and Daniel O'Quinn (Cambridge: Cambridge University Press, 2007), pp. 57–69 (p. 57).

[19] John O'Brien, *Harlequin Britain: Pantomime and Entertainment, 1690–1760* (Baltimore, MD: John Hopkins University Press, 2004), p. 69.

[20] Cited in *ibid.* [21] Jonathan Swift in *The Intelligencer*, No. 3, 1729, p. 22; emphasis in original.

statues' and in which the very act of spectating would be commensurate with the government of one's passions and the regulation of otherwise wayward desires.[22] This image would seem far removed from that immense gathering of people who congregated before Gay's stage, and which rendered fully visible the entire social sphere of the town. Not that it is possible to say exactly what occurred during the performances, other than that the crowd is reported to have responded with great enthusiasm to the play. The point, even so, is that such a crowd would inevitably have embodied the social antagonisms of the day. In an etching that depicts a performance of *The Beggar's Opera*, Hogarth represents the figure of 'harmony' fleeing its stage in search of the Italian opera that it burlesqued, implying that what Gay's opera produced was cacophony – musical as well as social, as is symbolised by the musicians playing a ragbag of instruments (mouth harp and bagpipes) and the actor playing Macheath, who is depicted as a braying ass.[23] As O'Brien remarks, the theatre or playhouse 'served as a site within which relations between classes were made visible, and violations of norms of deference and behaviour became particularly clear'.[24] A play that explicitly exploited distinctions between social classes, by 'levelling' all distinction in order to score its satirical points, no doubt also encouraged certain elements of the crowd to express their insubordination vocally – something that would have been viewed with alarm by the politer part of the audience.

There is one final problem associated with the bias of the critical stage. This problem must be discerned through an extrapolation that moves beyond the explicit problems associated with satirical plays, such as *The Beggar's Opera* and the theatre of Fielding, so as to implicate the general condition of theatrical representation in an age of criticism. In a censorious age, the undesirable critical effects of theatre explode their confines in genre, particularly when criticism of authority can and will be read into *any* performance, regardless of the original intention of the playwright – as one critic would write:

> The great Rock to be avoided . . . is any Reflection upon Ministers of State . . . The Characters of Richard the Third, Macbeth, Bajazet, and many

22 See O'Brien, *Harlequin Britain*, pp. 72–85.

23 See also Hogarth's cartoon 'Rich's Glory', which depicts John Rich, the theatre manager at Lincoln's Inn Fields who was made immensely wealthy with the success of *The Beggar's Opera* and who subsequently moved to the newly built Covent Garden Theatre which the success of the play allowed for – it is the procession to the new theatre in Covent Garden that Hogarth satirises in his cartoon, capturing a sense of 'invasion'.

24 See O'Brien, *Harlequin Britain*, p. 67.

> other Wicked Princes have long been represented on the Stage, without being interpreted into libellous Parallels, or giving any Offence. But as soon as a wicked, corrupt Minister is exposed, his Character is immediately apply'd, and the Secular Arm is call'd upon to punish the audacious transgressor. For this Reason, I would have it establish'd as an eternal Rule, that no Character, of this Sort, should be ever suffer'd to appear on the Stage . . . the Characters of Ministers, however, wicked, ought always be inviolable.[25]

(2) *The regulatory question over the proper scope and purpose of satire and the problem of governing dramatic representation.* What *The Beggar's Opera* exemplifies can be posed more broadly as the question of whether satire should be permitted on the stage at all. There are several reasons why the stage is not a suitable medium for satirical attack, if by satire one means a punitive form of criticism that operates in a highly abrasive, agonic mode, employing the method of public ridicule to punish its targets.

Matthew Kinservik draws a useful distinction between punitive and 'sentimental' satire. Where the former targets the conduct of government, institutions and public figures, the latter, according to Kinservik, shifts the object of satirical criticism away from politics towards domestic morality. For Kinservik, the aim of this domestic form of satire is not to punish so much as to discipline. It is to render satire 'deontic'.[26] Indeed, as Kinservik argues, the principal consequence, if not ambition, of the Licensing Act of 1737, motivated in no small part by *The Beggar's Opera*, will be to recalibrate the use of satire on the stage. Its aim is not primarily to censor (in the sense of repress) the stage but to force it back to disciplinary or 'moral' satire, to 'encourage the production and consumption of "acceptable" [forms of criticism]'.[27] It becomes pertinent, nonetheless, to ask why theatrical satire was seen to be 'morally dubious', as Kinservik puts it. The answer, however, cannot be simply that 'stage plays were widely regarded as potentially dangerous forms of expression that could corrupt as easily as they could edify'[28] – albeit that is certainly true. They were seen to be dangerous because of the peculiar capriciousness of the stage and the way it was thought to rely upon an all-too-human fallibility that would degrade its spectators' capacity to reason. In this sense the irrational effects of the

[25] *Country Journal or the Craftsman*, 8 March 1729, issue 140.

[26] For Kinservik's account of the shift towards punitive satire and *The Beggar's Opera*, see Kinservik, *Disciplining Satire*, pp. 55–94.

[27] *Ibid.*, p. 10 – 'the licensing Act was designed to achieve its censorial goals by training playwrights how to produce unobjectionable texts, not by punishing them for producing objectionable ones' (p. 11).

[28] *Ibid.*, p. 23.

stage will always override the intended rational effects of satire as imagined by men such as Pope. And the reason for this is that the efficacy of the stage lies in stirring up the spectator's passions – at least this was the belief of many during a period in which 'the discourse of sensibility powerfully shaped [audience] responses to performance', and where both men and women would openly engage in public expressions of emotion.[29]

John Dennis would put it this way: 'The great Disorders of the world are caus'd by great Passions, and one punish'd by Tragedy. The little Passions cause little Disquiets, and make us uneasie to ourselves and one another, and they are expos'd by Comedy.'[30] While it is true that good poetry employs righteous passions in order to punish errant passions, to instruct both by example and by effect, it must also aim at the 'satisfaction of the whole man together' – his reason as well as his passion.[31] But it is precisely because it is so poorly equipped to combine reason and passion in the right measure that the stage becomes such a dubious vehicle for punitive satire. Later in the century, Corbyn Morris would write that the stage was 'not fairly addressed to the Judgement, but to the Sight and the Passions' of spectators. And because of the stage's reliance on the affective power of spectacle, legislation that regulates the theatre is justified, just as for an inverse reason it would be indefensible to regulate satire in print. In contrast to the written word, which provides its readers with a non-spectacular form of criticism designed for private or sequestered consumption, the stage in its affective immediacy does not appeal to reason, so much as bypasses it altogether. Morris thus concludes that 'this prudent Restraint of the Profligacy of the Stage [is possible] without any Encroachment upon the Liberty of Printing'.[32] Regulation of the stage is perfectly consistent with the non-regulation of the press. Certainly, the aim of satire is 'corrective'; but it must also, as John Brown was to write, 'calm the wild Disorders of the Heart', not work to stir them up:

> It is certain that Opinions are no less liable to Ridicule than Actions. And it is not less certain that the Way of Ridicule cannot determine the Propriety or Impropriety of the one, more than the Truth or Falsehood of the other; because the same Passion of Contempt is equally engaged in both cases, and

[29] Davis, *Spectatorship*, p. 59.

[30] John Dennis, *The Advancement and Reformation of Modern Poetry: A Critical Discourse* (London: Rich. Parker, 1701), p. 55.

[31] *Ibid.*, p. 169.

[32] Corbyn Morris, *An Essay towards Fixing the True Standards of Wit, Raillery, Satire and Ridicule* (London: J. Roberts, 1744), p. xi.

> therefore ... Reason only can examine the circumstances of the Action or Opinion, and thus fix the Passion on its proper Objects.[33]

It is this 'passion of contempt' that is dangerously magnified and inflamed when punitive satire is placed upon the stage.

But there is also a more general point to be made here. In placing a critical emphasis on the role of reason, what is also revealed by these kinds of statement testifies to a more general tendency within the criticism of the age – also of considerable import and consequence: it represents the reassertion of reason as a means of preventing the delinquency of the stage. As a consequence, the regulatory question posed to satire will ultimately be answerable only by means of a rationally justified form of criticism, not by brute regulation, administered by means of the statute book (although the government's approach in 1737 was ruthlessly effective). To put the same point in a slightly different way: diagnosing and correcting the ailments of excessive criticism on the stage will be the responsibility of a new kind of man: the 'dramatic critic' – a man of discernment and taste deemed qualified in adjudging poetic production and applying the generic rules of critical discourse to its specific instances. This was, to be sure, the age of the gentleman amateur rather than the professional critic. Indeed, the very designation 'critic' must be seen as referring to a permeable category of public activity during the period and not to a specialised occupation (only with the closing decades of the century did theatrical criticism and the role of the theatre critic begin to be professionalised, with theatre criticism becoming a regular and fixed feature of newspapers and journals).[34] But what, then – if not professionalism – qualifies the critic, at this point? He must be a man of 'genius, taste, and learning', in Pope's words, someone who belongs to a certain stratum of society – a man of cultivation, capable of engaging in public discourse, capable of deftly navigating the turbulent and intensely politic world of public opinion.[35] (No doubt this general sense of criticism – of being able to critically comment on, if not actually

[33] John Brown, *An Essay on Satire* (London: R. Dodsley, 1749), p. 32.

[34] Gray points to the period 1770–80 when 'theatrical criticism at last arrives at a respectable position in English journalism' and adds that by 'the end of the period hardly one of the larger newspapers failed to carry paragraphs on the performance, and even in more or less responsible manner to criticize them'. Charles Harold Gray, *Theatrical Criticism in London to 1795* (New York: Columbia University Press, 1931), p. 191.

[35] Alexander Pope, *An Essay on Criticism* (London: W. Lewis, 1711), p. 6. Note also Pope's admonishment to the amateur critic, remarking, in his well-known phrase, 'A little Learning is a dang'rous Thing' (p. 14).

incorporate, the stage as a complete entity – was made possible by actual material circumstances, with only two licensed theatres, standing within a stone's throw of each other, surrounded by the dwellings of artists, scholars and politicians.)

Along with the dramatic critic, whose concern is with the propriety or otherwise of the dramatic text, the period also sees the emergence of another type of critic: the 'theatrical critic', to employ Charles Harold Gray's distinction. The theatrical critic is a man whose 'task requires a good deal more than a capacity to judge with knowledge and taste the art of writing. It requires a sensitiveness to the complementary arts of acting, painting, architecture, music and dancing.'[36] Thus the eighteenth century witnesses an extraordinary explosion of criticism directed at both theatrical and dramatic form. Still, despite the distinction, both types of criticism share certain common precepts, expectations and 'rules' that were to guide the critic's assessment of the productions of the stage from whatever point of view he wrote. These rules derived from the literary criticism of the previous century: from men such as Thomas Rymer, whose *Tragedies of the Past Age*, influenced by Horace and published towards the end of the seventeenth century, provided a ready-made set of prescriptive maxims for the newly emerging arts of theatrical and dramatic criticism.[37] To give an example whose pertinence to the present discussion of *The Beggar's Opera* is obvious: 'The Malefactor of Tragedy must be a better sort of Malefactor then those that live in the present Age. For an obdurate and impenitent Malefactor can neither move compassion nor terror; nor be of any imaginable use in *Tragedy*'[38] (clearly not a hero such as Macheath, then – the kind of dangerous libertine drawn from the *demi-monde* of London's criminal underbelly). Although there were certainly disagreements over the correct interpretation of these rules and maxims – and different ways in which they were applied – nevertheless, when viewed in terms of their general discursive function, theatrical and dramatic criticism must both be understood as belonging to the same space of critical judgement, justified by appeal to reason and exercised over what was to be presented on the stage: 'in the contrivance and *oeconomy* of a Play, reason is always principally to be consulted. Those who object against reason, are the

[36] Gray, *Theatrical Criticism*, p. 2.

[37] This is not to say that everyone accepted these rules – Pope certainly did not and publicly scorned critics such as Dennis who spoke authoritatively of 'principles' or the 'Laws o' the stage' only to – in his view – misapply them. See Pope, *Essay on Criticism*, p. 17.

[38] Thomas Rymer, *The Tragedies of the Last Age. Consider'd and Examin'd by the Practice of the Ancients and by the Common Sense of all Ages in a Letter to Fleetwood Shepheard, Esq.*, part 1, 2nd edition (London, 1692), p. 36.

Fanaticks in Poetry, and never to be sav'd by their good works.'[39] In the exercising of critical judgement, theatrical and dramatic forms of criticism represent a key expansion of theatre's governance during the period. It evolves as a discursive system of checks and controls that are to be applied to the signifying mechanisms of the stage – theatrical criticism will be just as prescriptive, in its own way, as the dramatic criticism that dominated the playwright's text.[40]

It is for this reason that the problem of satirical criticism, of punitive satire, insofar as it occurs on the stage, will be best answered by the selfsame critical tendency that the eighteenth century itself unleashed with the birth of the critic, who appears at its commencement and increasingly populates its newspapers, magazines and theatrical periodicals. As the century proceeds, satire in poetry and dramatic performance will increasingly be answerable to a meta-critical theatrical discourse that will specify what is obligatory, necessary and universal in dramatic construction, and tasteful, appropriate and decorous in its performance. Criticism proclaims, as Gray was to put it, 'the "rules" of the drama, which critics held up to dramatists for their guidance',[41] prescribing how characters must act, speak and appear on stage. For this reason, to the extent that critical discourse proposes to judge the conduct of the drama according to its conformity or lack of conformity to such doctrinal precepts, it establishes and promotes a set of deontic codes for the stage – most notably, with the doctrine of poetic justice – and provides dramatic and theatrical criticism with an inherently 'moral' outlook. Once applied to the use of satire on stage, the aim of critical discourse (unlike censorship) will be to govern the satirical genius from within, as if correcting the very space of criticism so as to better regulate its effects. In this way, Charles Abbott sought to show how one can both preserve the autonomy of poetry, as the freedom to censure, reprove and criticise, and, at the same time, obviate the abuses of punitive satire. The 'liberty of censure', he wrote, is essential to the 'spirit of

39 *Ibid.*, p. 8.

40 To be sure the theatre was also pretty good at holding its own against these implicit rules of theatre governance – one reason perhaps why formal legislation had to be passed. Satire was getting audiences and those audiences may well have laughed heartily at the very assertion of such 'rules', particularly in the highly ironic speech that Fielding gives to Medley in addressing Lord Dapper: 'They are such men as your lordship who must reform the age. If persons of your exquisite and refined taste will give a sanction to politer entertainments, the town will soon be ashamed of laughing at what they do now.' Act 1, Scene 1, 'The Historical Register for the Year 1736', in *The Works of Henry Fielding complete in One Volume with Memoir of the Author by Thomas Roscoe* (London: Henry G. Bohn, 1853), p. 1051. I am grateful to Simon Shepherd for directing me towards this line.

41 Gray, *Theatrical Criticism*, p. 6.

equality'[42] just as the 'freedom of Political Satire [is] connected with the establishment of general liberty'.[43] Nevertheless, the abuses of satire are to be guarded against, and in the case of political satire – such as can be found in *The Beggar's Opera* – it is well known that it can spread falsehood and sedition, undermine authority through ridicule and pernicious attack, or embitter and sow discord: 'By the improper exercise of Satire; individuals have sometimes been exposed to undeserved contempt; nations have been inspired with unjustifiable animosity; immoral sentiments have been infused; and false taste has received encouragement and support.'[44]

(3) *The pedagogical question of whether dramatic and 'punitive' satire is a corrective promoting order or the cause of greater disorder.* The question here might be phrased as follows: what effect does an unregulated satire such as *The Beggar's Opera* have on its auditors? At this point I turn to the reception of the play in the late eighteenth century, when the controversy over *The Beggar's Opera* was about to break out once again. It is important to take note of the changed circumstance of the period, which would have a significant influence over how the play was perceived. It was a period that witnessed a growing mobilisation of new and volatile social forces – not least under Wilkes's 'national cause of Liberty'[45] – and which would soon give rise to the disturbances of the 1780s. In light of the turbulence of the period, it is hardly surprising to observe that the answer to this question of the pedagogical influence of forms of punitive satire and its social effects had – within the discourse on theatre – already been decided: punitive satire destroys society, undermining the principles of order to the extent that it turns the public in favour of what it should spurn and abhor. An intensity of critical debate now focuses on the issue of what effect the *Opera*'s satirical criticism has on society as such:

> [If] satire is exercised to lessen the deformity of vice; and if genius is directed to the destruction of society, then wit, satire, and genius, become dangerous, in proportion as they render us enamoured of what we should despise, and the possessor is criminal, in the same proportion, for destroying, as he has the power to improve the principles of the public.[46]

[42] Charles Abbott, *An Essay on the Use and Abuse of Satire* (London, 1786), p. 4. [43] *Ibid.*, p. 5.

[44] *Ibid.*, p. 15.

[45] John Wilkes, *English Liberty: Being a Collection of Interesting Tracts from the Year 1762–1769, Containing the Private Correspondence, Public Letters, Speeches, and Addresses, of John Wilkes, Esq.* (London: T. Baldwin, 1769), p. 156.

[46] Crito, 'Criticism on the Beggar's Opera', *Hibernian Magazine, or, Compendium of Entertaining Knowledge* (1771, November), 518–19.

If criminality is here imputed to the very form of satire, it is because *The Beggar's Opera* is seen to openly promote it. There is nothing particularly novel in this viewpoint. One of the first attacks on the *Opera* protested that 'our Streets [have been filled] with Robbers and Foot pads, who have swarmed in this Town ever since that mischievous Piece was first exhibited on the Stage'.[47] And Daniel Defoe had complained that *The Beggar's Opera* was 'the bane and ruin of our lower Class of People'.[48] What is perhaps noteworthy, however, is the far subtler but more profound problematic it contains. Far from being corrective, satire tends to be ethically indecipherable. This is especially true where a 'corrupt' audience is taking such clear pleasure in it: its message cannot be assimilated to one, single moral perspective; its lesson is therefore open to a radical inversion of the avowed aim and ambition of the satirist. And so the conclusion is reached that one cannot rely on the pedagogical intention of censure – at least insofar as it is meant to correct vices by shaming those drawn to them or by making them contemptible to the audience. On the contrary, it is necessary to always err on the side of caution.

Advocacy of caution and restraint is the explicit emphasis of a piece published in 1776, *On the Moral Tendency of the Beggar's Opera*. The issue for this commentator is that too few of the play's spectators are capable of adequately distinguishing 'the vices from the virtues' of the play, since in the *Opera* the shades of good and evil, vice and virtue are 'so artfully and insensibly blended, that the nicest eye alone is incapable of ascertaining the bounds of either'. Given the remarkable portrait of the highway robber Macheath, it 'is more probable that the audience will be displeased with specious virtues, because they are united with witty vices, or dazzled with the glare of wit, generosity, and courage [and so] receive the whole character without examination'. It is precisely because Macheath possesses qualities audiences admire, precisely because they recognise his 'intrepidity' and his 'generosity', that they respond to Macheath's example with a degree of admiration – and it is precisely for these reasons, too, that his example is all the 'more dangerous'.

For this reason, also, much – too much, perhaps – will be demanded of the audience who attend *The Beggar's Opera*: if the audience lack the appropriate degree of moral scrupulousness, and if their taste is not already tutored by a highly refined sense of discernment and probity, then the play

[47] *Country Journal or the Craftsman*, 2 March 1728, issue 87.

[48] Daniel Defoe, *Second Thoughts Are Best: or, a Further Improvement of a Late Scheme to Prevent Street Robberies* (London: W. Meadows, 1729), p. 5.

cannot be called an 'innocent representation'. In truth, the writer goes on to remark, there will always be two audiences for this kind of satire; two ways of experiencing the Opera and thus two lessons to be drawn from it – both, alas, working in diametrical opposition to one another. For the cultivated, for those in the 'upper galleries', who have a 'taste for philosophy', the work is received as a 'clear perception of ridicule and a cultivated and uncorrupted moral sense'. But this will not be the case for the lesser audience in the pit, whose tastes are rather more vulgar, and whose capacity to reason is weakened by their penchant for immoral pleasures and by their inherent dishonesty:

> [If] a great part of every audience be composed of uneducated and unprincipled spectators, whose minds, prone to the commission of crimes, are continually inflamed by those objects of gratification with which every large city abounds; of men whom vigilance of magistrates, the dreadful spectacle of public executions, are scarcely sufficient to restrain; how must shall we lament the misapplication of genius in Mr. Gay, who has heightened every temptation to vice, and softened all the terrors of punishment?

If *The Beggar's Opera* exemplifies all the best qualities of satire, it also promotes the worst, becoming by definition the most abusive satire of all. It would be prudent therefore to be sceptical with regard to the efficacy of satire in its prevention of official corruption and punishment of vice, just as no one can be complacent when it comes to the play's promotion of perfidy and crime given that there are those in the audience who are already predisposed to a life of vice in virtue of their innate criminal tendencies: 'it cannot be doubted, that numberless deluded wretches have proposed Macheath as their example, and endeavoured to harden themselves against an ignominious death by a repetition of his songs.'[49]

Sir John Hawkins would go even further, issuing a stark warning about the 'dangerous tendency' of *The Beggar's Opera*, observing that it was the public's irresponsibility in first countenancing the play that was to blame for the injury it had caused to society. The specific consequence of that injury was equally instructive insofar as the public inadvertently provided a theatrical context that would act as a focal point for that spirit of resentment against government that stirred dangerously within the 'people':

> The malevolence of the people, and the resentment which they had been taught to entertain against that conduct of administration, which they were

[49] 'On the Moral Tendency of the Beggar's Opera', *Sentimental Magazine*, (1776, February), 60.

equally unqualified to approve or condemn, were amply gratified by the representation of it; but the public were little aware of the injury they were doing society, by giving countenance to an entertainment, which has been productive of more mischief than anyone believed at the time; for, not to mention that the tendency of it, by inculcating that persons in authority are actuated by the same motives as thieves and robbers is, to destroy all confidence in ministers, and respect for magistrates, and to lessen that reverence which, even in the worst state of government, is due to the law and to public authority.[50]

Fear of the 'inverted' pedagogy of the satirical *Opera*, which threatened to undermine the power and authority of the magistracy, had no doubt played its part in Sir John Fielding's application to the theatre managers to have the play suppressed 'on account of the increasing number of rogues, which . . . proceeds from that Opera being so often performed today'.[51] Garrick had planned to perform the *Opera* at the theatre in Drury Lane on 18 September 1772, but buckled under Fielding's request that he 'desist'.[52] Of course, whether or not there is any substance to the allegations that the *Opera* incited criminal goings-on remains moot, although *The Beggar's Opera* is cited in at least one reported crime in the *Middlesex Journal*, in 1773, which describes an armed robbery in Lincoln's-Inn-Fields, involving the theft of a coat: 'The fellow was not under the least timidity, but, while he was pulling off the [gentleman's] coat, repeated the words in the Beggar's Opera, A lawyer's is an honest employment, so is mine.'[53]

The veracity of such reports and the factuality of the supposed effects of the *Opera* in inspiring increased crime are not, however, the point here. Nor is it a question of relating such reports and fears to a histrionic culture of fear generated by the century's notorious crime waves. The point, rather, is to understand that what is revealed with this inverted pedagogy is the great ambivalence with which the stage was treated insofar as, through the example of *The Beggar's Opera*, it brings to the fore the contradictions inherent in the discursive fabric of eighteenth-century governance. Those contradictions are by no means concealed or hidden

[50] John Hawkins, 'On the Dangerous Tendency of the Beggar's Opera', *Universal Magazine of Knowledge and Pleasure*, 60 (1777, January), 47. Note here the distinctions that Hawkins mobilises: public-people-society-public authority (government). The public is now grasped explicitly in opposition to society – the social totality; it is but one part of society, representative of propertied interests, confronted by another part – the ignorant people.

[51] *General Evening Post*, 8–10 October 1772, issue 6084.

[52] For reports on the exchange, see *Morning Chronicle and London Advertiser*, 20 September 1773, issue 1349, and *London Chronicle or Universal Evening Post*, 14 September 1773, issue 2616.

[53] *Middlesex Journal or Universal Evening Post*, 21–23 January 1773, issue 596.

from thc (property-owning) public – indeed, they are public knowledge – but that does not mean that they should be publicised to the commonality, and that is the problem that comes with staging the *Opera*. A way of grasping the dilemma of the *Opera* is to see that its satire presents itself, however unintentionally, as a discourse of truth that is quite at odds with the accepted precepts of law and justice. It is for this reason that it contradicts the social and economic order that makes bourgeois hegemony over the public sphere precisely 'bourgeois', i.e., oriented by laws ensuring the privileges of private property. If it is 'theatrocratic', it is because – in its satiric inversions – it promotes a different idea of economic justice, a different idea of poetic justice and, finally, a different social ordering – one that is 'very ill calculated to mend the morals of the common people, who are pleased to find all ranks and degrees, the highest and most respectful characters brought down to a level with themselves'.[54] These contradictions are most starkly revealed in two of the play's most infamous sequences.

The first is the notorious opening scene of the second act, described as the 'Thief's Creed and Common-Prayer-book' by the *Morning Chronicle*, in which Macheath's gang engage in a discourse about their profession: 'Why are the laws levell'd at us? Are we more dishonest than the rest of Mankind? What we win, Gentlemen, is our own by the Law of Arms, and the Right of Conquest.' And at the end of the scene, one gets what amounts to a kind of thieves' manifesto, which verges on the assertion of a revolutionary credo:

> We are for a Just Partition of the World, for every Man hath a Right to enjoy Life.
>
> We retrench the superfluity of Mankind. The World is avaricious, and I hate Avarice. A covetous Fellow, like a Jack-daw, steals what he was never made to enjoy, for the sake of hiding it. These are the Robbers of Mankind, for Money was made for the Free-hearted and Generous, and where is the injury of taking from another, what he hath not the Heart to make use of?[55]

The second moment of notoriety comes at the end of the play with the last-minute reprieve of Macheath just as he is due to be hanged. The 'Beggar/Author' of the play tells the audience: 'I was for doing strict

[54] *Morning Chronicle and London Advertiser*, 20 September 1773, issue 1349.

[55] Gay, *The Beggar's Opera*, pp. 21–22. The notion of the 'free-hearted' is an obvious example of the slipperiness of satire: an apparently ethical value within which resides the implication that there is no respect for private property (sexual 'generosity' was a trope of the Restoration stage). Here Gay is playing a game with the posturing of the moralised theatre of the 1690s and after.

poetical Justice – Macheath is to be hang'd' – but then a player intercedes: 'Why then, Friends, this is a down-right deep Tragedy. The Catastrophe is manifestly wrong, for an Opera must end happily.' It is not just, of course, that the rules of genre conflict with those of poetic justice; that comic opera cannot end in this kind of calamity. Rather, the failure of the play to deliver poetic justice betrays the deeper indiscernibility of the play's satire and the peculiar undecidability of its message. In projecting an alternative notion of poetic justice it cannot but help imply an alternative notion of justice.

This will be the fundamental discursive, ethical and political crisis that the play engenders for the public, leading one critic to make explicit in the most remarkably candid manner the extent to which this kind of satire creates a doubling of critical discourse – one that serves to destabilise or undercut the values of moralising censure. But it also produces an entirely distinct set of unintended effects, effects that imply a fundamental recodification of the social terrain itself. Thus what is made explicit here is that, however unpremeditated, *The Beggar's Opera* becomes a means of conveying to the public an alternative and very 'dangerous' truth about itself:

> tho' I evidently see the falsehood of these levelling principles, and tho' I doubt not but any Gentleman, of either House of Parliament, could with as much ease refute such impertinent sophistry . . . yet I humbly apprehend there may be some danger in publicly displaying these doctrines to the vulgar.

Although an educated public possessing a 'truly philosophical spirit' penetrates beyond the surface of things and 'sees that the good of millions is justly sacrificed to the ease and convenience of a few beings of superior merit and dignity', nevertheless, one cannot conceal the fact that for this to be possible 'a thousand wretches drudge, starve, and shiver to supply the banquet which Lordship daily lavishes on pimps and parasites . . . that a thousand cottages must fall, before the great man's hounds and horses are properly accommodated'.

These lines are written not by a partisan of the play; on the contrary, they are written as a sardonic warning against the play's performance, insofar as it must be grasped not simply as a satire on the corruptions of Walpole's government, whose topicality was in any case by now several decades out of date, but precisely as a discourse of truth. What is this truth if it is not a truth that is implacably opposed to theatrocratic discourse? And for this reason it is a truth that will always tempt those for whom 'discourse', with its deontic and disciplinary effects, will be seen as oppressive. Will the play not be understood, then, as a kind of 'counter-discourse'? This is what the author of this text understands well enough, since if *The Beggar's Opera* appeals to the misguided part of the audience, it is because of 'some inconveniences which the gross of mankind . . . is doomed to suffer, and suffering well sometimes mistake for injustice'. And he continues, by enumerating some uncomfortable facts: 'such are, a youth of toil, an old age of disease and want; the sight of a naked, and a starving family, and the insults not only of the rich, but of all those pampered slaves, who swell the retinue, and imitate the vices of their masters.' These are 'truths' that need to be concealed from the commonality for the sake of maintaining public order; just as, conversely – and precisely because the play is a discourse of truth – they provide every reason in the world why it must not be staged, for fear of what it might inspire:

> There may come a time when the voice of misery shall be louder than that of the habitual obedience they have imbibed; and when the passions shall obscure their prospect of that glorious system of subordination, in which it is by law established, that the poor shall resign all the advantages of life, to the rich, in return for the trouble the rich sustains in governing, punishing and eternizing this righteous distribution of things; it should not, therefore, seem prudent to direct the attention of the indigent to such enquiries as may render them impatient of their present situation. The populace is an ungovernable testy beast . . . there have been times, when the indigent multitude . . . hath unanimously burst its shackles, and swept its tyrants from the earth.[56]

Conclusion: Towards a Reformed Macheath?

The eighteenth-century theatre was, then – as I hope this chapter has gone some way to show – assimilated into that space of permissible criticism opened up by the developing governmental rationality of the age. I have tried, also, to highlight the mechanisms by which this occurred, showing that it was not dependent on top-down, prescriptive government, taking the form of official censorship, but rather, occurred through the localisation of the effects of deontic power, working through the obsessions and fears that animated the public sphere. That Gay's stage constituted a particularly volatile locus for this process, I think, is obvious and has everything to do with the way in which it concentrated those agonistic forces unleashed by the public sphere in the most extraordinarily intense

[56] *Morning Chronicle and London Advertiser*, 5 October 1773, issue 1363.

manner. By the same token, it would be entirely wrong to reduce what is at stake in the discourses circulated around *The Beggar's Opera* to the idea that it did so merely because it focused concerns, among some contemporaries, over how the stage might have acted as an incitement to criminality; that certain members of the audience – the uneducated and poor, who are always hostile to authority and animated by a spirit of resentment – preferred to read the play as an indictment of government in general, to suit their own reprehensible ends, rather than as targeted criticisms aimed at legitimate objects of satirical attack, and whose actual purpose was to punish corruption. Indeed, what I hope to have revealed through this case history are two things. The first is the way in which those concerns were effectively mobilised so as to impose more firmly that internal limit on the function of the stage – discussed in Chapter 3 – by producing theatre as a space of moral but not political censure. Second, I have sought to show that, in order to accomplish this task, the discourse on theatre necessarily drew on the 'anti-theatrocratic prejudice' in forcefully asserting that external limit by which it could demarcate that which is to be excluded and prohibited from the theatre. That this occurred primarily through a deontic imaginary that viewed the spectatorial practices associated with the commonality, upon which it projected itself, as grotesque, ghastly or monstrous, is beside the point. Both tendencies work on the stage in order to draw the discursive space of the theatre into the space demarcated by government so as to better determine its effects, producing appropriate or correct behaviours and developing a set of subsidiary techniques for circumscribing the forms of speech the theatre is able to produce – speech whose legitimacy is either confirmed through criticism or condemned by it as aberrant and as something to be curbed or deprecated. What one thereby witnesses during this period is a considerable narrowing of the scope of what can be said and shown in the theatre; but also what begins to emerge is a conspicuous sense of what theatre should – and will – become under a regime of deontic power. For not only must it not challenge government or the symbols of its authority, it must also be able to actively promote its purposes and ends. It is not simply a matter of ensuring the 'prudent restraint on the profligacy of the stage', then, but of recasting the theatre as an instrument of reform.

The Beggar's Opera will itself show how this is possible, for there is a postscript – a coda of sorts – to the controversy unleashed by that charming brigand Macheath, which comes in the form of a final question that is raised over the play and which provides a convenient point of transition from the problem of the criminal stage to that of the reformed stage. It is a question of whether one might not in fact retrieve a moral lesson from *The Beggar's Opera* after all so that, in diametrical opposition to the play's first appearance, what is to be presented will stand as a kind of antidote – a corrective to the accursed and immoral stage of the satirist. What is asked can be posed as follows: what would it take to transform *The Beggar's Opera* such that it offers the discourse on theatre with a practical model for a reformed stage, a deontic and pedagogical model of the theatre? Would not a wholly reformed *Opera* amount to a reformation of the stage itself? Furthermore, if the *Opera* could be reformed, would this not provide the firmest demonstration of the victory of virtue over vice? The traditional enemies of the stage would be reconciled with this detested school for scandal by the most extraordinary means: through the purification, distillation and sanitisation of this most extreme, vilified and abhorred instance of theatre's corruption. That was the question posed in 1818, in a curious text published in *Blackwood's Edinburgh Magazine* – 'Proposed Reform of the Beggar's Opera'.

What is offered to the public is nothing less than a plan, presented in summary form, to obtain an 'expurgated' – otherwise put, decontaminated – version of the play. Immediately, one understands that by these means a reformed stage will not simply be one that has been purified of its unpalatable elements. On the contrary, it is a theatre that seeks to actively purify its auditors by employing those selfsame elements against themselves. It is a theatre that uses vice as a pedagogical measure – and in fact this adjustment, this alignment of the text of the *Opera* with the aims of deontic pedagogy, achieved by applying the principles of the moral corrective to the dramaturgy of the play, is precisely what distinguishes the new *Beggar's Opera* from the old; for while the punitive satire of the first *Opera* aims to punish its victims, it makes no pretence whatsoever of teaching its audience anything at all. Stripped of its satire, the school for scandal is transformed into a school for the promotion of virtuous conduct, in which reforms can now be expounded and preached. The cost of such an endeavour, however, will be obvious to all, since what one understands, in the final analysis, is that a pedagogical model ineradicably – and indeed purposefully – weakens the stage, and not least because it ensures the subjugation of the passions that lend it its force to the ultimate authority of moral reason. The consequence: a reformed theatre becomes all but in name a suppressed theatre. This will be the price the theatre will pay for substituting moral for punitive satire. The price extracted by the demands of moral governance, and paid by the theatre, will be examined in greater detail in the following chapter. But for now it suffices to simply note, in conclusion, the effect governmentality will have on *The Beggar's Opera* once applied to the play itself.

The first victim will be the play's protagonist, who will no longer be the roguish but likable Captain Macheath, but, instead, a young gentleman, Sir George Woodberry, who could not be further from Gay's original anti-hero. Sir George is described as a man 'of a very considerable property in the West of England, a member of Parliament, and of the Society for the Suppression of Vice, adorned with the most elegant and refined manners, and endowed with a true and lively sense of religion'. Meeting Polly Peachum by chance at a staging post, and 'enamoured by the beauties of her mind', he immediately falls in love with her. On proposing marriage to her, however, he encounters an unexpected obstacle: she refuses to offer her consent – not because she does not love him, but because she is secretly ashamed of her 'profligate parents'. Sir George quickly divines her true motives and embarks on a plan to rescue her 'from a situation so revolting to female purity, and so dangerous to those principles of piety which … had been instilled into her by the precepts and example of a respectable maiden aunt, now deceased'. An opportunity soon presents itself to Sir George when he is held up by 'Captain Ruffian' (Macheath) – a common or garden highwayman – whom he manages to overpower and capture. A deal is struck: Sir George will release the thief on condition he instructs him in all the 'mysteries of his profession' – for Sir George's plan is to pass himself off as Macheath, and thus gain access to Polly via her father, Peachum.

Suitably disguised, Sir George gains the confidence of Polly's father; but Polly, who remains a virtuous and pious character, thinking he is a common robber, resists him. Further tests of Polly's rectitude ensue, as Sir George enlists the help of several characters, adapted from the original play: Lockit – now the 'well-intentioned and pious, keeper at Newgate' – and a group of 'upper girls' who replace the play's original prostitutes – 'those poor deluded wretches who, in the old opera, used to offer so much licentious amusement to the galleries; but who, by this ingenious contrivance, are converted into a vehicle for so much pious and grateful reflection'. The action unfolds, then, according to the 'strict propriety of the principal characters' – and, to underscore the deontic and pedagogical justification for the sordid milieu of the story, Macheath is permitted only insofar as he serves a 'particular purpose' – namely, to enable Sir George to 'assume a temporary disguise of iniquity' in order to rescue Polly. The play reaches its new conclusion and a satisfactory ending for all concerned. Sir George wins Polly's heart, once he discloses his true identity, and she, in having passed various tests, demonstrates (with her 'virtuous obstinacy') that she is worthy of marrying him. Peachum repents and is reformed; Filch – a young rogue enlisted by Sir George to assist him – is also reformed after demonstrating his 'sincere repentance' and receiving a Bible from 'the British and Foreign Bible Society, of which [Sir George] has been a most worthy member'; while, finally, Lockit's faith in his mission is restored and – with a reinvigorated sense of duty – he promises to 'continue to contribute to the reform of prisoners committed to his charge'.[57]

[57] 'Proposed Reform of the Beggar's Opera', *Blackwoods Edinburgh Magazine*, 3 (1818, August), 575–76.

CHAPTER 5

The Deontic Stage in the Eighteenth Century
George Lillo's The London Merchant

Introduction

The theatre of the eighteenth century, far from being subjected to discourses of exclusion or to the prejudices of virulent anti-theatricalism, found itself instead increasingly absorbed by discourse into the emergent rationality of modern deontic government. It is in this context – of a theatre wholly absorbed by deontic power, actively encouraging reform in the conduct of its audience – that *The London Merchant* takes on its full significance. And it is in this sense, also, that the play, perhaps uniquely in the history of the theatre, confronted head-on the following critical problem: how can an irrevocable weakening of the affective power of the stage produce 'good' theatre, rather than bad theatre – a theatre subdued by banal moralism or dull proselytism? This question is by no means resolvable by showing the equivocal nature of the terms 'good' and 'bad', as though it were simply a matter of substituting aesthetic for moral evaluations of the theatre. On the contrary, to understand the reforming zeal of the deontic governance of the stage during this period is to understand how the age sought to circumscribe and overcome a basic contradiction. This contradiction was well known in the eighteenth century. It is concisely expressed in a remark by Rousseau, found in his *Letter to Monsieur D'Alembert on the Theatre*, translated into English (and published) in 1767,[1] in which he observes that moral failings

> are so inherent to our theatre that, in wanting to remove them, it is disfigured. Our contemporary authors, guided by the best of intentions, write more refined plays. But what happens then? They are no longer really comic and produce no effect. They are very instructive, if you please; but they are even more boring. One might as well go to a sermon.[2]

[1] Originally translated under the title *An Epistle to M. d'Alembert . . . on the Project of Establishing a Playhouse in Geneva* (London, 1767).

[2] Rousseau, *Politics and the Arts*, pp. 46–7.

In what way is a reformed stage able to advance the aims of deontic government while retaining, at the same time, the power of the theatrical example? How can there be a genuinely moral lesson delivered on the stage that is efficacious and so does not become tedious to the audience? Lying behind this question is the conundrum of how to redirect the dangerous facility of the stage, its exceptional power to disturb the passions of the audience, so as to produce an unequivocal deontic message – precisely what *The Beggar's Opera* had failed to do. It is this dilemma that motivates Rousseau's famous scepticism about the use of the stage as an instrument of deontic government: 'is it not ridiculous to pretend that the motions of the heart can be governed, after the event, by the precepts of reason?'[3] Responding to the sceptical challenge requires showing how it is possible to irrevocably weaken the hold of dangerous passions at the same time as deploying them on the stage in order to procure the most affective and morally persuasive outcome. The one play that attempted to address this question by understanding itself, explicitly, as an experiment in how theatre might be made to fit a deontic model of government was George Lillo's domestic tragedy *The London Merchant.*

Deontology and the Reforming Theatre of George Lillo

So successful was the experiment deemed that even Rousseau would extol its virtues, proclaiming that *The London Merchant* was an 'admirable play the moral of which is more to the point than that of any French play I know'.[4] Lillo's answer to those who, along with Rousseau, would 'deny the Lawfulness of the Stage'[5] is as radical as it is unique: one must turn to the most honourable of all theatrical genres – tragedy – to 'engage all the Faculties and Powers of the Soul in the Cause of Virtue'.[6] But one must first recalibrate its effects in order to take account of the specific target of the deontic message – in this case, the apprentices of London. To do so, one must overcome the 'Aristotelian' dogma that tragedy has a 'proper' subject; that only noble subjects can procure and safeguard the virtuous sentimental effects of tragic action. In practice, one must reject the idea that importance and weight are bestowed upon the drama only through the elevation of its characters. Lillo poses this astonishing challenge to one

[3] *Ibid.*, p. 51. [4] *Ibid.*, p. 56 n.

[5] George Lillo, *The London Merchant; or, The History of George Barnwell. As It Is Acted at the Theatre-Royal in Drury Lane* (London: J. Gray, 1731), p. viii.

[6] *Ibid.*, p. vi.

of the most firmly held convictions of the theatre in the preface to his play, asking: does tragedy lose its 'dignity' when it is 'accommodated to the Circumstances of the Generality of Mankind'? Where previously tragedy provided a moral lesson only to the elite, by representing the hubris of nobles and kings, in *The London Merchant*, the moral will be aimed at the common apprentice. For this reason, the unlikely hero of Lillo's tragedy – George Barnwell (apprenticed to the eponymous London merchant of the play's title) – will be of no higher standing than the play's average audience member. And its story will be uniquely calculated to maximise its effect on them.

The story of the play concerns the corruption of an innocent youth who falls under the malignant influence of Sarah Millwood – a 'woman without virtue . . . capable of any Action' (I.iii.6) who is described by her own maid as a 'bird of prey' (I.vii.12). Barnwell is blinded by 'youth and innocence' to Millwood's inimical and sanguineous scheming – after all, 'having never injured a woman', the last thing he expects is to be injured by one himself (I.iii.7). The artless and naïve youth is immediately and impossibly besotted with Millwood, while she quickly sets about '[stifling] his Conscience' and '[wheedling] him out of his Virtue of Obedience' (I.v.11). The desire that Barnwell stirs in Millwood is of quite a different order from that of selfless love – as her servant Blunt remarks, 'so does the Smoothness and Plumpness of a Partridge move a mighty Desire in the Hawk to be the Destruction of it' (I.vii.12). An easy target for Millwood's 'disgraceful' designs, Barnwell is soon persuaded to rob his master, Thorowgood, in order to fund her lascivious and decadent lifestyle. Things deteriorate rapidly, however, as Barnwell begins to experience the alienating and character-altering effects of his own dishonesty and bad conscience. Gripped by remorse, shame and self-contempt, he is no longer able to face his kindly master, whom he has betrayed, or his good friend and fellow apprentice Trueman, and flees his apprenticeship. Unable to steal from his master, his relationship with Millwood becomes untenable. To exacerbate his problems, Barnwell is incapable of releasing himself from Millwood's siren-like influence and must find another solution or risk losing her for good. With grim inexorability, he agrees to murder his wealthy uncle with the aim of robbing him. It is only after having carried out the brutal attack on his uncle, and in being confronted with the sheer depravity and horror of the act, that Barnwell finally comes to his senses – of course far too late to escape justice at the end of a rope. The play ends with the execution of the thoroughly contrite and pious Barnwell, and the unrepentant but now deranged Millwood.

There is a shrewd calculation behind Lillo's reasoning and choice of subject matter here – one that explicitly assimilates the dramatic action of the play to the instrumental aims of a wider governmentality, recalling its central problem is the supervision of population: '[tragedy is] truly august,' argues Lillo – not because of its nobility, but 'in Proportion to the Extent of its Influences, and the Numbers that are properly affected by it. As it is more truly great to be the Instrument of the Good to many, who stand in need of our Assistance, than to a very small Part of that Number.'[7] The target of the play will be a class of workers (apprentices) and the vices to which they are prone. More broadly viewed, what the play asserts is the idea that if one seeks to abrogate vice, the best way to do so is to dramatise it. Permitting vice its latitude on the stage is to expose it in all its contumacy, disobedience and insubordination. When Lillo speaks of the lawfulness of the stage, it is not simply to proclaim that the stage can be made permissible under the law, but that its lawfulness is vouchsafed to the extent that it becomes an instrument of law – an extension of law.

I shall return to examine the play in greater detail later, but before doing so I would first like to examine the wider discursive context of the play. The initial aim of the chapter is to decipher the specific governmental imperatives and forms of deontic power that circulate within the play in order then to show how an instrumentalised tragedy, producing a deontic stage, was able to be calibrated with an emerging governmentality applied to work. Both trajectories of my argument – the production of a deontic stage and those of the moral coercions applied to regulate the behaviour of labour – converge on what I call, borrowing from Eve Sedgwick, the 'homosocial covenant' that will be central to the particular form of moral self-governance that the play advocates, and whose contradictions and caprices the play will be seen to embody.

Recreation, Luxury and the 'Theatrocratic' Effects of the Market

First: what are the principal imperatives for government if it wishes to exert an influence over the behaviour of workers, to render more efficient the reproduction of social labour? During the eighteenth century, this question was understood particularly in relation to the specific problem of how one might discipline the productive forces within the social body through the attempt to regulate recreational time. Fielding's *An Enquiry into the Causes of the Late Increase of Robbers* provides a useful starting point for

[7] *Ibid.*, p. iv.

understanding these concerns, since in this text he attempts to cast light on that neglected constituency of government most in need of governmental attention and supervision – the lower orders, the 'ignoble' part of the population. The diseases of the working part of the community, he writes, will eventually spread to the 'whole body' of the polity. The 'law of the Kingdom' – the legislature and judiciary, and those authorities charged with municipal administration – are therefore advised to take note of the 'Customs, Manners and Habits of the People'.[8] When a regime of government works as it should, the political body, like the 'animal Oeconomy', with which it is compared, becomes a 'well-tuned' instrument – and what results is a constitution that combines the proper dispositions of all the elements of the political body. But for this very reason, because it is a body, says Fielding, 'Disorder of any Part will, in its Consequence, affect the whole.'[9] Also, the general political economy is always susceptible to two things that should be of ongoing concern to government: the depredations and iniquities of the social sphere, but also its vices and moral deformities. Unfortunately, where government is most needed, Fielding argues, it is also most lacking, which is precisely in the regulating of the habits, morals and customs of the commonality.

But there is a second general point that he makes, which is of crucial import to the argument. One must take into account, he says, that there has been a wholesale transformation of the 'estate of the commonality', which has seen its fortunes rise, just as it has, correlatively, slowly but surely enabled it to shake off its vassalage and 'become more and more independent'.[10] Where this transformation is most visible – where the greatest change can be perceived in the 'Manners, Customs and Habits of the People, more specifically the lower sort' – is through the development of recreation. This transformation is traced through a series of negative effects: 'The Narrowness of their Fortunes,' he writes, 'is changed into Wealth; the simplicity of their Manners into Craft; their Frugality into Luxury; their Humility into Pride, and their Subjection into Equality.'[11] Fielding's conclusions share more than a passing resemblance with Rousseau's analysis of the effects of luxury on the work force in the *Letter to Monsieur d'Alembert*, in which 'a prosperous people . . . which owes its well-being to industry, exchanging reality for appearance, ruins itself at the very moment it wants to shine.'[12] What both analyses identify is a new source of theatrocratic threat – one that will also be identified later in the

[8] Fielding, *Late Increase of Robbers*, p. xii. [9] *Ibid.*, p. xii. [10] *Ibid.* [11] *Ibid.*, p. xiii.
[12] Rousseau, *Politics and the Arts*, p. 64.

century by Adam Smith, who advocated 'private frugality and good conduct of individuals'[13] to counter it: they are threats that circulate within and are inspired by the development of the capitalist market.

To be sure, where Rousseau is sceptical about the benefits of commerce, Fielding is rather more sanguine: the generation of increased wealth leads to significant improvements in the arts and sciences, and increases the comforts of all. It is not a question of simply lamenting the introduction of luxury caused by increased wealth and trade. Fielding has little patience with this kind of view, for how – he asks – can one have trade and riches if one is to put into effect sumptuary laws that would banish luxury? In contrast to Rousseau, the problem is addressed by Fielding in a way that explicitly takes into account the emergent dynamics of class. The real issue will be whether one can have trade, with all the luxury it produces, and with its cultural and social benefits, and at the same time prevent the market from producing theatrocratic effects in certain parts of the populace. This is one of the most fundamental and pressing problems for government, and is distilled in summary form in Fielding's question: 'How far is it the Business of the Politician to interfere in the Case of Luxury?'[14]

In fact, the problem that Fielding identifies has to do with a singular contradiction introduced into the polity with the development of modern forms of commerce. Commerce brings two powers into conflict with one another: on the one hand, there is civil power – the authority of the state, its law and its government, whose object is to ensure 'good order'; while, on the other hand, there is the 'power of the purse', represented by the circulation of money and its increased availability and disposability. The specifically governmental problem with money is that it induces a change in the conduct of the people. What results is a contradiction and a problem for government since the rebellious nature inculcated in personal forms of conduct – the effect on the manners and morals of the people by their exposure to the money form – undermines the voluntary submission of the people to civil power: 'Self-opinion, Arrogance, Insolence, and Impatience of Rule, are its most inseparable Companions.'[15] To fully grasp this as a social and economic predicament, however, one must also take into account the differential of social class: the problem is not the effect of luxury on those who are rich (for whom luxury is at worst a moral and not

[13] Adam Smith, *An Inquiry into the Nature and Causes of the Wealth of Nations*, abridged (Indianapolis: Hackett, 1993 [1776]), p. 80.

[14] Fielding, *Late Increase of Robbers*, p. xxv. [15] *Ibid.*, p. xii.

a 'political Evil'). Indeed, if luxury could be 'confined to the Palace of the Great', then no wicked consequences would ensue. The problem is that the market has a democratising effect insofar as it sparks a desire for consumption in *all* classes as each order of society seeks to emulate the lifestyle, aspirations and tastes of the one above it. While it cannot be said that there is 'democratic access to luxury', there is nevertheless a democratisation of the vices inspired in coveting it. If the higher orders enjoy the privileges of luxury produced by trade, then its mischievous effects reach down to the 'very Dregs of the People'; and where 'this Vice descends downwards to the Tradesman, the Mechanic, and the Labourer' it is 'certain to engender many political mischiefs'.[16]

The issue of how one prevents the contagion, inspired by the effects of the market – how one stops the democratisation of desire – is more difficult to determine or resolve. For Fielding, it must begin, as it does for Rousseau, in understanding luxury first and foremost as spectacle ('appearance') and in then determining the effects of spectacle on the productive part of the population. Luxury arises 'where every Sense and Appetite . . . are fed and delighted; where the Eyes are feasted with Show and the Ears with Music, and where Gluttony and Drunkenness are allowed by every Kind of Dainty'. The problem with spectacle is twofold: the masquerade, the ridotto, the play, oratorios and the opera – all of these induce theatrocratic desires in the common audience participant: a desire for *more* than they can have or afford. Worse still: the very moment desire implants a taste for luxury in the worker it has already taught them the vice of idleness. After all, to attend the theatre *takes* time – *takes it away*, that is, from the time a worker can spend in productive employment. The economic consequences are obvious: 'Idleness . . . adds greatly to the Debtor's side in the Account.'[17] The effects of spectacular consumption on the 'thoughtless and tasteless rabble' will have not just moral but financial implications – although, of course, both are mutually implicated in the workings of deontic power: 'If a Computation was made of the Money expended in these Temples of Idleness by the Artificer, the Handicraft, the Apprentice, and even the common Labourer,' Fielding remarks, 'the sum would appear excessive.'[18]

In order to prevent the mischief, it is necessary to remove its cause, and that entails preventing the worker from entering the very space of the spectacle – the theatre. Fielding's proposal is simple: to raise prices for admission to plays and other forms of spectacular entertainment – to put

[16] *Ibid.*, pp. 7–8. [17] *Ibid.*, p. 16. [18] *Ibid.*, p. 15.

them firmly beyond the economic reach of the average worker; but he also suggests the need to determine the appropriate forms and uses of recreational time that are necessary for 'Relaxation from Labour'.[19] Entertainment is not to be forbidden, but diversions for workers should be regulated by the state and placed under the limitation of law, restricting them to amusements that befit the 'necessary Temperament of Labour'.[20]

This is not to prohibit the spectacle generated by the capitalist market, obviously, or to covertly argue for the suppression of the theatre. It is to simply limit access to the (theatrical) market to those who can afford it:

> But while I am recommending some Restraint of this Branch of Luxury, which surely appears to be necessary, I would be understood to aim at the Retrenchment only, not at the Extirpation of Diversion; nay, and in this Restraint, I confine myself entirely to the lower Order of People. Pleasure always hath been, and always will be, the principal Business of Persons of Fashion and Fortune . . .[21]

And he goes on to assert the economic benefits of regulated luxury to society more generally:

> In Diversion, as in many other Particulars, the upper Part of Life is distinguished from the Lower. Let the Great therefore answer for the Employment of their Time, to themselves, or to their Spiritual Governors. The Society will receive some temporal Advantage from their Luxury. The more Toys which Children of all Ages consume, the brisker will be the Circulation of Money, and the greater the Increase in Trade.[22]

Employment of Time and the Practices of Temporal 'Self-Government'

The need to regulate productive time has a particular bearing on those forms of deontic governance that were directed towards workers and specifically at apprentices.[23] The apprenticeship system originated in the Elizabethan period where it emerged as a means to regulate previously unregulated tradesmen and professions. With the introduction of the Elizabethan statute, the law prohibited the practice of any trade, art or profession unless a seven-year apprenticeship had been served. The

[19] *Ibid.*, p. 14. [20] *Ibid.*, p. 13. [21] *Ibid.*, p. 17. [22] *Ibid.*, p. 18.

[23] In a lecture course on what he then termed the 'punitive society', Foucault spoke of the 'sequestration of time', proclaiming: 'Now, all this, which appears in the literature of the time as an apprenticeship in moral qualities, actually signifies the integration of the worker's life into the time of production, on the one hand, and the time of saving, on the other.' Michel Foucault, *The Punitive Society, Lectures at the Collège de France, 1972–1973*, trans. Graham Burchell (Basingstoke: Palgrave Macmillan, 2015), p. 211.

contractual and economic nature of apprenticeships required apprentices, young men and women under the age of twenty-one, to freely assent to their indenture. Typically, apprentices, once contracted, were legally bound to their master for a term of seven years, with the payment of a stamp duty on binding providing legal proof of contract, along with various forms of legal redress available to the master, including the threat of imprisonment for any apprentice who breached that contract. There was also a class of apprentices who were rather less 'free' in giving their assent: those who found themselves indentured through the Parishes, since the statute gave legal authority to Church wardens and overseers of the poor to compel the children of the poor into apprenticeships. The apprenticeship system also gave rise to a set of legal rights and obligations. For the master, it was the 'right to the labour of his apprentice during the whole term of his apprenticeship' (and the obligation of the apprentice to provide it).[24] It was the right of requisition of whatever the apprentice acquires while serving his or her apprenticeship, so that whatever the apprentice 'possesses' is the lawful property of the master.[25] It was the right to correct and punish the apprentice for any infractions of his obligations and for any unseemly or untoward behaviour. And finally, for the apprentice, it was the right to receive a proper education or training in a specified trade, art or profession, and the obligation of the master to provide him with one, under the terms of the indenture.

But an apprenticeship was by no means simply a means of learning a particular trade, art or profession.[26] It also provided training in the proper conduct of life for a 'man of business': 'Let every apprentice consider, that this is the time not only of learning a trade, but of fixing his character for honesty, sobriety, and prudence.'[27] In Fielding's terms, it was training in the 'necessary temperament of labour'. During the eighteenth century, a number of conduct books were produced that were designed to assist the

[24] J.B. Bird, *The Laws Respecting Masters and Servants; Articled Clerks, Apprentices, Journeymen and Manufacturers* (London: W. Clarke and Son, 1795), p. 32.

[25] *Ibid.*, p. 33.

[26] See George Kearsley, *Kearsley's Table of Trades, for the Assistance of Parents and Guardians, and for the Benefit of those Young Men, Who Wish to Prosper in the World, and Become Respectable Members of Society* (London, 1787). Possible trades for apprentices were numerous, encompassing anything from public notary to pin maker, a house painter to exchange broker, an undertaker to surgeon. Economic context of families was a key determining factor in the kinds of apprenticeships made available. Equally important was educational opportunity; as Kearsley writes: 'if his friends are not in circumstances to give him so liberal an education; or if he does not appear to have that refined and elegant taste which ought to distinguish an architect, the youth may yet make a great figure as a mason, a bricklayer, or a carpenter' (p. 29).

[27] *Ibid.*, p. 43.

apprentice in acquiring that temperament, that sense of duty, diligence and obligation: to help him learn, in short, how to practise and master the art of government over the self. Often these books were purchased for the young apprentice by their master – texts such as Richardson's *The Apprentice's Vade Mecum*, Sir John Barnard's *A Present for an Apprentice* (1743), or Jonas Hanway's *Moral and Religious Instruction, Intended for Apprentices and also for Parish Poor* (1767). In addition to the conduct books it was not uncommon for preachers to offer advice on the proper conduct of apprentices in their sermons, such as John Waugh's *The Duty of Apprentices and Other Servants* (1713). The apprentice was not simply governed by statute – by a legal-contractual apparatus; he was also, and more fundamentally, governed by a quite different understanding of what an apprentice was and ought to be, as based on the deontic construction of the apprentice's character.

To begin to understand that character one must start with an analysis of the weaknesses of youth. To understand what measures must be taken, it is important for the deontologist to know that any youth is prone to irrational behaviours, is under the sway of simple and untutored sentiment; and that, in the age of youth, reason is weak and dangerously underdeveloped. It is a 'season' of 'temptation' where the 'passions of nature encrease with rapid force [and] the mind is daily opening to new sentiments, and a larger expansion of idea'.[28] It is because the passions of the young are 'violent and impetuous'[29] that youth is thought particularly susceptible to the 'contagion of corrupt examples'.[30] And it is for this reason that youth require mentorship: a critical friend, able to warn the unwary and unsuspecting of the innumerable dangers and temptations to which they will be prey, of those forces that are as 'malicious' as they are 'cunning'. What youth lack is prudence and good judgement born of experience. Thus the precepts of practical reason need to be inculcated in the young so that they might successfully navigate the 'affairs of the world'.[31] This is the function of the conduct book – it is written from the perspective of a critical companion 'who has an affectionate concern for your welfare . . . [and who] will endeavour to lead you in the right way, and to arm you against temptation'.[32]

[28] R.L., *The Apprentice's Companion; or, Advice to a Boy, upon Being Bound Apprentice; and for His Conduct During His Apprenticeship* (London: W. Button, 1795), p. 6.

[29] John Fawcett, *Advice to Youth; or, the Advantages of Early Piety. Designed for the Use of Schools, as well as Young Apprentices and Servants, and the British Youth in General: To Draw the Attention to Matters of the Greatest Importance in Early Life*, 2nd edition (London and Leeds: G. Wright and Son, 1780), p. iv.

[30] *Ibid.*, p. xii. [31] R.L., *Apprentice's Companion*, p. 10. [32] *Ibid.*

Just as in earlier texts that aimed at instructing those charged with the performance of domestic duties, now the same deontic techniques were applied in order to teach the young apprentice how 'properly to conduct' himself in the world of business, commerce and work; but also those techniques were modified to account for the specific context of youth – to be practised as a different kind of relation of self to self, requiring a different kind of vigilance over the self. Less explicitly confessional, they employed what might be called a 'mnemonic' technology of the subject. Because the particular fallibility of youth was thought to be self-forgetfulness, they employed techniques that aimed to bring the subject of deontic governance back to themselves, through acts of self-recollection or in remembrance of obligations. Its lessons were taught through imperatives such as: remember what God is, what man is, what one's duty is – to oneself and to one's master.[33] But as with all deontic technologies of the self, they were techniques that sought to isolate the conduct of the individual, that attempted to inculcate good conduct through instruction in the precepts of virtue and the norms of society. And while their aim was not punitive, they did make use of the idea of future punishment in the afterlife for temporal sins as a corrective to inspire obedience and self-discipline. This 'corrective' threat (remember 'His eye is upon us tho' we are forgetful of him')[34] played first on the subject's fear, the self's most intimate fear for itself, employing a kind of inchoate understanding of the function of the Freudian super-ego; but principally it also invoked the affective dimension of the person's conscience, in seeking to inspire in the deontic subject a sense of shame, mobilising it as a force of self-restraint. Most of all, what was fundamental to all of these techniques was that for the apprentice – as for all workers – the government of the self was to be understood, in practical terms, as the government of one's time: 'youthful time' should not be squandered was the basic idea.[35] In this sense, deontic power was assimilated in the conduct of individuals in the form of a temporal art of self-government. There were two aspects to this notion of the government of (one's) time.

[33] *Ibid.*, p. 12.

[34] *Ibid.*, p. 13. Jonas Hanway makes explicit the secular utility of religion to government when he writes: 'Statesmen, in the process of time, have been obliged to confess, that the great mass of government could not be moved in its proper orb, merely by the force of the civil magistrate . . . therefore it has been necessary to influence the minds of a people by motives of fear in respect to an invisible power above.' Jonas Hanway, *Moral and Religious Instructions, Intended for Apprentices, and also for Parish Poor; with Prayers from the Liturgy, and Others, Adapted to Private Use* (London: J. Rivington, 1767), p. xx.

[35] R.L., *Apprentice's Companion*, p. 20.

In the first place, the time that the apprentice could call his own, in any 'lawful' sense, belonged to him only periodically in the time given over to recreational activities. But it was precisely in 'those Hours of Recreation [that the apprentice] will be most in danger'.[36] It is a danger that can be expressed as a relational nexus of problems, risks and threats: given that a man's recreational choices very much determine his character, poor decisions over how he spends his recreational hours will inevitably begin to influence his overall attitudes and temperament, and ultimately the performance of his duties. For this reason, the apprentice is warned to choose his companions with care: To a great extent one's character is formed by the temperament of one's associates. It is impossible, for example, for a man to preserve his integrity if he associates with 'Abandon'd and Licentious' types.[37] It is inevitable that 'low, sordid, ignorant, vulgar spirits, would debase you to their own level'.[38] One should also avoid excessive drinking, gaming, the company of women – one should avoid consorting with female servants, for instance – or keeping company with less diligent 'fellow-apprentices'.[39] One should – indeed one must – avoid 'unnecessary' recreations that not just are bad economically, since they are costly, but also tend to corrupt one's character. Of particular danger is the theatre: above all, 'never be prevail'd upon to set your foot behind the Scenes at a Play-house; the Creatures there, being but so many Birds of Prey.'[40] The apprentice must steer clear of the 'society of Sensual, or designing Men'.[41] This nexus of dangers, then, around which the temporal art of self-government will be formulated, constitute – as Foucault once observed – a 'certain number of points in existence, which are, generally, the body, sexuality, and relationships between individuals'.[42]

The delimitation of illegitimate uses of time thus provided all the reasons why apprentices should avoid theatres, masquerades, gaming houses or visiting prostitutes. Aside from the immorality inherent in these activities, they inculcated all the vices that undermine that diligence, duty and sense of industriousness upon which the good character of the apprentice is to be formed. But they were also illegal in a stricter sense because such entertainments necessarily contravened the fundamental bond established by apprenticeship – that is to say, the master's right to the labour of the apprentice:

36 Sir John Barnard, *A Present for an Apprentice: or a Sure Guide to Gain Both Esteem and Estate. With Rules for Conduct to His Master, and in the World* (London: William Innes, 1743), p. 21.
37 *Ibid.*, p. 22. 38 *Ibid.*, p. 26. 39 *Ibid.*, p. 31. 40 *Ibid.*, p. 34. 41 *Ibid.*, p. 22.
42 Foucault, *Punitive Society*, p. 212.

> You are not . . . at liberty to dispose that Time and Labour, as you please, which in Truth is not yours but your Master's, by his Purchase, and by your promise and Engagement; and to waste or detain what is thus agreed for, is a Defrauding them of what is their due.[43]

In the *Apprentice's Vade Mecum*, Richardson insisted in the most unequivocal terms on the necessity of respecting the proper governance of one's time: 'an Apprentice has no Time that he can properly call his own, but is accountable to his Master for every Hour.'[44] He must therefore avoid any activity that involves the 'loss of his Master's Time, and a Neglect of his Business'.[45] To do otherwise amounted to a kind of 'robbery', where the 'master [was] defrauded of his Apprentice's Time, and of his Application to his Business'. It was, wrote Richardson, robbery of the 'worst sort' in which there would be two victims. First, the master would be the victim because he would be robbed of his 'interest'; and second, the apprentice would be the victim, because he would be robbed of his 'morals'. It was because of this that the apprentice should on no account 'haunt Play-Houses'.[46] The theft of time – its diversion from its use in honest employment, in 'industry and Oeconomy' – was easily explained when one compared, as Richardson did, the contracted hours of employment with the average times of theatrical performances: 'The play generally begins about Six in the Evening, and the Usual Time of an Apprentice's Business holds him . . . till Eight or Nine',[47] which demonstrates that the 'Hours of a Play-house . . . must undoubtedly interfere with the Hours of such Persons of Business'.[48]

But what constituted a 'positive' use of one's recreational time? The second aspect of temporal self-government embraced a fundamental 'Maxim of Life' for the apprentice and the future man of business: 'use Oeconomy in the husbanding of Time.'[49] Free time was to be used for one purpose only: the cultivation of the self, the improvement of the self. It was not, naturally, that the apprentice should eschew all recreational activity – the 'Bow of Life must not be kept continually Bent'.[50] But he must spend

[43] John Waugh, *The Duty of Apprentices and Other Servants. A Sermon Preach'd at the Parish Church of St. Bridget, alias Bride, August 24th, 1713. Being the Festival of St. Bartholomew* (London: G. Strahan, 1713), p. 19.

[44] Richardson, *Vade Mecum*, p. 7. [45] *Ibid.*, p. 8. [46] *Ibid.*, p. 9. [47] *Ibid.*, p. 15.

[48] *Ibid.*, p. 16. Others would go so far as to attempt to monetise the loss sustained to the country's economy by the presence of theatres. The writer of an anonymous letter to the Right Honourable Sir Richard Brocas, the Lord Mayor of London, in 1730, would calculate a sum of £300,000 – 'by the loss that is sustained in the Work and Labour of the Artificers, and other Spectators'. Anon., *A Letter to the Right Honourable Sir Richard Brocas, Lord Mayor of London. By a Citizen* (London, 1730), p. 21.

[49] Barnard, *Present for an Apprentice*, p. 49. [50] *Ibid.*, p. 21.

his spare time nurturing the best qualities in himself and perfecting the outward manners appropriate to the best society: he must cultivate 'Prudence, Address, Decorum, Correctness of Speech, Elevation of Mind and Delicacy of Manners.'[51] These could be learnt in pursuing recreations that were both economical and left no remorse afterwards: 'Reading, [enjoying] fresh air, good weather, fine Landscapes, and the Beauties of Nature'.[52] He should choose books as his companions – not, needless to say, mere amusements and trifles such as romances, poetry or plays, which 'distract the Mind with wrangling, Altercations, or Controversy', but books on history, morals, law and 'authentick Tracts on the *British Constitution*'.[53] The apprentice, the future man of business, might – depending on his trade and the status it afforded him – one day be an eminent citizen. And even if he did not become the Lord Mayor of London, as Hogarth's industrious apprentice would, he would nevertheless be entitled to vote – hence the need to vigorously promote all the best qualities of the self: one must incorporate into one's very being the sanctified behaviours and forms of seriousness and learning, betterment and refinement, that are required if one is to be eligible for participation in public life.[54]

Daniel Defoe was particularly concerned to warn of the dangers of underestimating the seriousness with which the government of time should be taken: 'The purposes, for which time is given, and life bestow'd, are very momentous; no time is given useless, and for nothing; time is no more to be unemploy'd, than it is to be ill employ'd.'[55] In Defoe, there are three fundamental legitimate uses of time for a man of business: the time spent on the 'necessities of life', such as eating and sleeping or recovering from illness, the time spent in observing religious duties, and the time dedicated to the duties of one's business and calling.[56] What this brings into view is a question that was even more pertinent for Defoe: whether there was such a thing at all as an 'innocent' pastime for a man of business. Clearly, there were the 'criminal' 'pleasures and diversions' found in the theatre that 'necessarily interfere with, and interrupt' a man's obligations and duties.[57] But it was not simply that entertainments were intrinsically

[51] *Ibid.*, p. 26. [52] *Ibid.*, p. 33. [53] *Ibid.*, p. 32.

[54] *Ibid.*, p. 73. See also Hogarth's engravings, 'Industry and Idleness', printed in 1747, thought to be inspired in part by *The London Merchant*, which depicts the fate of two apprentices. The idle apprentice, like Barnwell, consorts with prostitutes and turns to crime, ending up at Tyburn; while the good, 'industrious' apprentice not only marries his master's daughter but grows into a rich citizen and eventually becomes the Lord Mayor of London.

[55] Daniel Defoe, *The Complete English Tradesman, in Familiar Letters: Directing Him in all the Several Parts and Progressions of Trade*, 2nd edition (London: Charles Rivington, 1727).

[56] *Ibid.*, p. 50. [57] *Ibid.*, p. 98.

corrupt; and – as he would argue – it is the easiest thing in the world to be deceived into thinking that it is simply a matter of dividing inherently corrupt pastimes from innocent diversions, where nothing could be further from the truth:

> [The] innocence lies here, not in the nature of the Thing, not in the diversion or pleasure that is taken, but in the Time it takes; for if the man spends the Time in it which should be spent in his shop or warehouse, and his business suffers by his absence, as it must do, if the absence is long at a time, or often practiced; the Diversion so taken becomes criminal to him, tho' the same diversion might be innocent in another.[58]

The extent of the vigilance required in the task of temporal self-governance will be wholly dependent on what one does. For anyone involved in trade, business and labour – in short, for any worker – 'pleasure is *a thief* to business'.[59]

The Deontic Codification of *The London Merchant*

It is not difficult to show that Lillo's play belongs to this extended discourse on the government of work and leisure time. *The London Merchant* promotes in dramatic form the same deontic message conveyed in the conduct books of the period. But its novelty also resides in the fact that it endeavoured to make concrete that frequent assertion found within the discourse on the theatre – namely, that moral precepts are best taught through dramatic exemplification. And it is for this reason that the play was held in such high esteem. What *The London Merchant* demonstrates is 'the great Influence of Stage Effect over the Passions' – the use of the stage as a tool for 'improving' the 'morals' and 'mending' the heart.[60] On the eve of its opening performance, on 21 June 1731, the *Daily Post* would announce, rather presciently, that *The London Merchant* 'is as moving a Story in Private Life as ever was touch'd by the Stage Writers; that the Moral drawn from thence is as fine a Lesson to Youth as can be form'd by Dramatic Representation'.[61] It was an almost universally held view of the play. Not only would the play 'continue to be acted with great Applause'[62] throughout its first run, it soon attracted the attention of Queen Caroline,

[58] *Ibid.*, p. 101. [59] *Ibid.*, p. 102.

[60] Anon., *Lillo's Admirable Tragedy of George Barnwell: Or, The London Apprentice. Since the First Institution of the Theatre to the Present Day, No Dramatic Piece Has Been of More Service to Society Than This Admirable Tragedy, and If to Point Out the Allurements of Vice, as a Warning for Unthinking Youth to Avoid the Snares of Debauchery* (London, 1790).

[61] *Daily Post*, 21 June 1731, issue 3668. [62] *Daily Post*, 5 July 1731, issue 3680.

who sent for a manuscript of the play. The royal family attended a performance at the Theatre Royal in October 1731, along with a 'great Concourse of Nobility'[63] – and there are further reports that it was performed by the King's Company of Comedians at Hampton Court Palace.[64] Throughout the century the same fulsome assessment of Lillo's tragedy was endlessly repeated: never was a play so 'well calculated to do Good';[65] 'No Dramatic Piece has been of more service to society than this admirable Tragedy';[66] 'No Dramatic Tale was ever better told . . .'.[67] The reason is simple and has to do with the explicitness with which the deontic message of the play was received and understood: 'the guarding of Youth from the Snares and Temptations of Vice, was a Design worthy of a new Legislator in the Drama . . . the Tragedy of George Barnwell had done more service to Society than Half the Plays that ever were acted.' The deontic message of the play explicitly declares the same principle of industriousness and the proper governance of time that can be found in conduct books when Trueman proclaims: 'Business [is] the Youth's best Preservative from ill, as Idleness his worst of snares' (II.ii.17). Needless to say, the play won the approval of 'many eminent Merchants of the City of London'[68] – hardly surprising given its subject matter; and it is well known that it became that 'periodical admonition to apprentices'[69] performed during the holiday season to the City's youth during the eighteenth and well into the nineteenth century.

That the play garnered more or less unanimous support and praise from the establishment provides no confirmation, of course, that it had any particular effect in its specifically avowed aim of persuading the City youth to embrace the ethic of the mercantile concept of work – particularly for such a notoriously exuberant constituency as the class of apprentices – but that is perhaps beside the point.[70] What is significant is the extent to which

63 *London Evening Post*, 28 October 1731, issue 611.
64 *London Evening Post*, 5 October 1731.
65 *Public Advertiser*, 28 September 1765, issue 9644.
66 Anon., *Lillo's Admirable Tragedy*, 1790.
67 *St James Chronicle or the British Evening Post*, 27 November–1 December 1774, issue 2153.
68 *Daily Post*, 12 October 1731, issue 3765.
69 *Morning Post*, 9 April 1822, issue 15933.
70 There is, however, an interesting 'legend' that was born with a later performance of the play, occurring in 1752, which has various iterations. According to one version of the story, which was frequently printed as part of the playbill, a doctor treating a young man for a fever concluded that his illness was the result of some mental distress. When the young man – an apprentice to a merchant – was pressed, he confessed that he had embezzled £200 from his master, but 'going two or three nights before to Drury Lane Theatre, to see Ross and Mrs. Pritchard, in their characters of George Barnwell and Millwood, he was so forcibly struck, that he had not enjoyed a moment's peace since, and wished to die, to avoid the shame he saw hanging over him' (in *The Mirror of Taste and Dramatic Censor*, vol. 2 (London, 1810), p. 416). In another version of the story, the apprentice becomes a reformed gentleman, and even rewards the actor, Mr Ross, with a yearly stipend of £100

Lillo was able to align the stage with the discursive aims of deontic government – specifically through the codification of the action of the plot and through its use as a vehicle for disseminating a series of deontic messages.

There are, broadly speaking, four domains of deontic codification in the play. In the first place, it acts as a vehicle for extolling the virtues of 'honest' trade. In particular, it explicitly promotes the values of mercantile capitalism as a set of specifically moral and thus desirable values to which the young man of business should aspire. In this sense, the play is designed to present its apprentice auditor not just with a set of moral precepts in which the character of the good and diligent apprentice is to be grounded, but with a practical demonstration of fundamental bourgeois ideals as embodied by the character of Thorowgood.

Second, the play contrasts two forms of economy: it promotes a virtuous economics identified with the mercantile trade of Thorowgood, while disparaging, at the same time, an immoral and criminal set of investments – a 'libertine' economics – identified in the play with Millwood. The immediate historical circumstances of the play bear some mention here, as writers such as Catherine Ingrassia have pointed out: the play must be understood against the backdrop of the catastrophic events surrounding the South Sea Bubble and the economic crash that followed when it burst. Ingrassia identifies two sets of economic relationships around which the action of the play is constructed.[71] First, there are the highly precarious forms of speculative trading – the 'speculative investment' that Barnwell makes in Millwood; and, second, there is the dependable world of mercantile capitalism, grounded in the exchange of fungibles and secured by what Ingrassia, following Eve Sedgwick, calls the 'male homosociality' of the patriarchal order. Importantly, each of these two forms of economic practice is explicitly associated in the play with forms of sexuality – opening up sexual practices to the scrutiny of governmentality, by distinguishing conducts that are provident from those that are improvident.

A third set of deontic codes can be found in the way the play depicts the vices of unwary youth. Through the entrapment of Barnwell, and his tragic

for having saved him, writing in a note to the actor: 'He who is indebted to your admirable representation of George Barnwell for more than life, for his redeemed honour and credit, begs your acceptance of the inclosed', in James Plumtre, *The English Drama Purified: Being a Specimen of Select Plays, in Which all Passages That Have Appeared to the Editor to Be Objectionable in Point of Morality, Are Omitted or Altered, with Prefaces and Notes*, ed. Plumtre (Cambridge: F. Hodson, 1812), p. 177.

[71] Catherine Ingrassia, 'Money and Sexuality in the Enlightenment: George Lillo's *The London Merchant*', *Historical Reflections/Réflexions Historiques*, 31:1 (2005), 93–116.

fate, the play acts as a discourse on love and desire, advocating homosociality as the means to guard against the corruptions of the market ('when every Passion with Lawless Anarchy prevail'd').[72] In other words, the play contrasts two things: first, the stable, asexual, homosocial world of the good apprentice, Trueman, whose love for Barnwell promotes the 'Platonic' ideal of sentimental love and 'tender' friendship, which is the source of mutuality, reliability and trust within trading relations; and second, the erotically charged love that is exemplified in Barnwell's desire – impossible to satiate or fulfil – to possess Millwood. One is a form of love that remains under the tutelage of reason and is commutative and transparent; the other is a concept of love that is irrational and opaque – concealing (as Millwood does from Barnwell) its underlying motivations.

There is, finally, a fourth domain of deontic codification: the play's characterisation of Millwood as embodying the evils of the market for those incapable of escaping its seductions and allurements. But there is also something else in the characterisation of Millwood that requires specific attention, since she remains, as Lisa A. Freeman shrewdly observes, 'unassimilated' within the moral message of the play.[73] Two things arise here: first, that this unassimilated remainder has much to do with the way Lillo employs Millwood to extend the deontic message of the play through a general 'satirical' attack on the corruptions of the age; and, second, that precisely insofar as Millwood is permitted to become the vehicle for this satire, her effect on the play is to introduce a profound ambiguity into it that will, not unlike the effect of introducing the criminal picturesque into *The Beggar's Opera*, undermine the very deontic message the play purports to endorse.

I would like to examine each of these four points in some detail.

(1) *Mercantile capitalism and a new table of values.* It is telling, given the politics of the play, that Lillo dedicated it to Sir John Eyles, who had – in addition to being a member of parliament – recently been elected a sub-governor of the South Sea Company. Eyles became a director of the joint-stock company following the financial crash of 1720, for which its corrupt trading practices had been largely held responsible.[74] Presumably, Eyles

[72] Lillo, *Barnwell*, p. 34.

[73] Lisa Freeman, *Character's Theatre: Genre and Identity on the Eighteenth-Century English Stage* (Philadelphia: University of Pennsylvania Press, 2002), p. 116.

[74] Edward Pearce writes: 'Eyles was a paid-up Walpole man, entitled to the full Walpole cover. He had been entrusted with running the residual South Sea Company after the crash and spoke for its interests in the Commons'. Edward Pearce, *The Great Man: Sir Robert Walpole: Scoundrel, Genius and Britain's First Prime Minister* (London: Random House, 2007), p. 293.

was to help stabilise the company during a period of great economic anxiety and national indebtedness;[75] this at least seems to have been the view held by Lillo: 'The Proprietors in the South-Sea Company . . . gave the greatest Proof of their Confidence, in your Capacity and Probity of their Company, at a Time when their Affairs were in the utmost Confusion, and their Properties in the greatest Danger.'[76] Setting apart the intrigues and conspiracies surrounding the South Sea Company in the years of the crash, it is important to understand the dedication specifically in terms of the way it serves to position the play according to the order of a certain kind of economic discourse. In the first instance, the choice of dedicatee – as is typical during the period – assumes a particular discursive function: Eyles, a man held in great esteem, who enjoys the love of his fellow citizens and is an alderman and Member of Parliament, provides the text of the play with a form of vouchsafement and authorisation. He authorises it *as* discourse. Given Lillo's avowed aim to render the stage 'lawful', the endorsement of a man of standing and probity is clearly significant. As such, Eyles's dedication can be viewed as equivalent to a speech act that validates the text for performance.

In this way, the function of the dedicatee is to act as counter-signer to Lillo's own signatory gesture ('I am, Sir, Your most obedient humble Servant, George Lillo'), conferring upon it a status and authority it could not possess in itself. On the other hand, there is a further complexity circulating within the economy of discursive authorisation, with the introduction of the viewpoint of an additional guarantor, suggesting that Eyles's own authority needed to be verified – accounted for. And indeed Lillo makes it quite plain to his readers that Eyles's authority is verifiable. He has the endorsement of the South Sea Company proprietors, who include a number of people 'considerable for their Rank, Fortune, and Understanding, as any in the Kingdom'. But it is perhaps the *context* of Lillo's choice in Eyles, during the period following the financial crash, that is most relevant in terms of understanding the discursive function of this signatory statement. A dedication is more than an act of alliance-building, in which the author seeks the protection of a powerful benefactor; it is an act that permits an implicit discursive correlation, where the deontic message of the play is aligned with a more general political aspiration. In

[75] 'The company was . . . destined to become the vehicle for what has been variously described as the greatest speculation, the biggest scam and the most extreme example of manic investor behaviour in English financial history' (Dale, *Lessons from the South Sea Bubble*, p. 40).

[76] Lillo, *Barnwell*, p. ix.

the aftermath of the South Sea Bubble, it seeks to establish a new table of values for trading companies and to identify the values of good and virtuous government ('lawfulness' as the foundation of propitious economic activity) as being specifically mercantile.

There are two scenes in the play where these values are explicitly declared. The first is the opening scene, which depicts an exchange between the merchant, Thorowgood, and his apprentice, Trueman, who arrives bearing a letter to his master from Genoa. (Significantly, the play is set during another period of crisis – the Elizabethan conflagration with Spain.) What is discovered from the letter is that Thorowgood, along with other city merchants, has interceded on behalf of his country to thwart a loan agreement between Spain and the Genoese, frustrating the invasion plans of the 'revengeful Spaniard' by persuading the Genoese not to invest in the planned armada. The play thus commences with a powerful image of the merchant-as-patriot: Thorowgood is the very embodiment of 'pure religion, liberty, and law'. An 'honest Merchant', he says (counselling Trueman), has two basic duties: to 'contribute [when necessary] to the Safety of their Country' and always to its 'happiness' (I.i.2). In recalling these duties, Trueman will not only understand the 'Dignity of [the merchant's] Profession' but will be able to resist the temptations of 'Vice and Meanness'. The character of the merchant must always be dependable, and Thorowgood is nothing if not an exemplar of the honest, patriotic man of business, who pursues trade not out of self-interest or improvidential *amour propre* but as a service to his country. If these qualities of honesty, patriotism and disinterestedness begin to articulate the table of desirable values for the new political economy, it is in Trueman's response to Thorowgood that the deontic message of the play is first articulated, foreshadowing – at the same time – the tragedy to come: 'Shou'd Barnwell, or I, who have the Benefit of your Example, by our ill Conduct bring any Imputation on that honourable Name, we must be left without excuse' (I.i.2). The apprentice must always remember that his conduct will reflect – for better or worse – on the character, reputation and honour of his master.

The second scene, which opens act III, has Thorowgood instructing Trueman on the 'Method of Merchandize' (III.i.28). Mercantile trade is not only a means of becoming wealthy – although there is nothing inherently dishonourable in being prosperous – it is a promoter of the values of cosmopolitan enlightenment: trade has 'promoted Humanity'; it encourages 'intercourse between Nations'; it has allowed men to overcome differences in 'Situation, Customs and Religion'; it has promoted 'Arts, Industry, Peace and Plenty'; above all, it 'diffuse[s] mutual Love from Pole to Pole'. These are the 'Advantages of honest Traffic' – a discourse invoked to legitimate trading empires. According to Thorowgood, while trading might be understood as the efficient cause of the merchant's wealth, it is not his ultimate goal or purpose. To see why this is necessarily the case, one must acquire a 'scientific' understanding of trade that will demonstrate that its precepts are 'founded in Reason and the Nature of Things' rather than in irrational human passions. In other words, grasped in the cosmopolitan terms advocated by Thorowgood, mercantilism reveals its inherent teleology; and if its *telos* is adhered to and respected by the merchant, it confers upon him a great amount of moral excellence. It is in this regard that Thorowgood's advice to Trueman should be taken: 'Method in business is the surest Guide' (III.i.29). What is that method? Thorowgood paints it in providentialist terms: 'It is the industrious Merchant's Business to collect the various Blessings of each Soil and Climate, and, with the Product of the whole, to enrich his native country.' The benefit of trade, however, is not solely a matter of national interest, because trade will 'improve Mankind by Love and Friendship' (III.i.28). Thorowgood has the plight of 'uncivilised' non-European peoples in mind when he argues that trade will 'tame the fierce, and polish the most savage' (Lillo neglects the trafficking of African slaves in which the South Sea Company was rather notoriously implicated). In fact, Thorowgood insists on the cosmopolitan ideals underpinning mercantile trade and acquisition: it does not expropriate goods from those with whom it trades, since they give the merchant with their 'own consent' what appears to them as a useless 'superfluity' and receive in return the benefits of enlightenment: 'giving them,' as he puts it, 'what, from their Ignorance in manual Arts, their situation or some other Accident they stand in need of'.

(2) *Mercantile and libertine forms of (economic) life*. Towards the end of the play, Thorowgood offers a comparative assessment of his own character (as a virtuous man of business) and Millwood's rather less scrupulous methods in conducting her affairs. Notably, he frames the comparison in normative terms but also tacitly invokes the language of economic discourse: 'my Credit,' he says, 'is superior to thy Malice' (IV.xvi.49). In this short statement, one understands immediately the set of correlations by which forms of economic and market activity can be arranged according to a certain logic and ordered by a system of deontic qualifications into what might be called 'economic forms of life'. Throughout the play these will be conceived as either lawful or unlawful; as productive and rooted in the security of honest trade or as unstable, insecure and finally ruinous; as virtuous in their ultimate effects or as morally reprehensible, not to say

criminal, in their consequences. And as forms of life – as expressing economic life choices – they are also articulated in terms of the conflicting forms of sexual conduct that motivate the play's antagonisms.

On the one hand, Barnwell represents the type of 'irrational' speculator who is 'defined by his overwhelming desires for money, personal profit or sexual conquest'[77] – that is to say, by a set of economic choices that are emblematised through his relationship with Millwood. Millwood, on the other hand – part libertine, part prostitute – exemplifies the risk of engaging in highly precarious forms of speculative investment. As Ingrassia points out, Millwood represents a form of investment that belongs entirely to the order of the imaginary, and thus to the disorders of theatrocratic desire that the imaginary investment inspires in its victim. Her particular genius is to maintain the passionate, obsessive and immoderate investment Barnwell makes in her by incrementally raising the stakes – and the degree of his risk and exposure – while at the same time intensifying the hypothetical returns on that investment. As Lucy wryly observes, thus 'one vice as naturally begets another' (II.xii.26).

It is an economy founded on two things. First, it is founded on the powerful affects that incapacitate the speculative investor's ability to make reasoned or prudent judgements. Reducing him instead to a kind of feverish state of slavery, these intensely affective relations induce a debilitating crisis in the investor's psyche, which result directly from the passionate attachment he has made in his investment. This is symptomatic of the 'effeminating' effects of libertine economics. Hence Barnwell's disintegrating resolve that he can name but do little to prevent: 'Will nothing but my utter Ruin content you?' (II.ix.21). The reason, I would suggest, is that the scene of imaginary enjoyment, to which Barnwell endlessly returns – and in which he stages the fantasy of finally possessing Millwood – will always diffuse whatever agonies of remorse follow as a consequence of the failure of that desire. It is an investment that will never yield a return but will consign him to endlessly repeat the cycle of compulsive pleasure followed by 'Confusion, Horror, and Remorse' (II.xiv.27).

Second, it is an economy founded on the necessity that defines Millwood's own situation as a woman operating within an exclusively male market, in which she is compelled to earn her income by trading in 'luxury' (and indeed luxury of dubious legitimacy). Millwood says in a rather bitter exchange with Lucy that her 'Wit and Beauty' have made her a 'Wretch' and continue to do so (I.iii.6) – exploited by men, who

[77] Ingrassia, 'Money and Sexuality', p. 97.

have stolen her innocence, her only recourse is to exploit in return. In Gail Kathleen Hart's eloquent formulation, 'Here, predation renders the prey predatory.'[78] Millwood understands all too well that she must become that 'imaginary being' of male fantasy in order to 'further her own financial ends'.[79] Forced to trade in desire, she keeps a 'House of Entertainment' (II.xii.26). Thus Millwood, inevitably, occupies an adversarial position within the play. However, it is in respect of the position she occupies within the market that the deontic function she performs for Lillo is ultimately revealed. It is not just that Millwood acts as the representative for imprudent speculative investment; she is more explicitly inscribed into the play as the object that incites a desire for criminal consumption in Barnwell. She represents a semi-illicit and highly toxic commodity. In this context, Millwood embodies the theatrocratic threat contained in the market itself; and the risk to the speculative consumer of this doubtful commodity is that it is always purchased, not on the basis of credit so much as the assumption of debt. It leads to bad credit, in other words, because Millwood represents a luxury commodity that soon outstrips the capacity of the purchaser to pay for it, leading to ever-increasing liability and, in the case of Barnwell, criminality and, eventually, death.

It is against this libertine form of economic life, which is ruinous because morally bankrupting, that the play proposes an alternative mode of economic life that appears in the form of 'a near-monastic homosociality'.[80] Male homosocial relations are so defined, of course, because – for the most part – they exclude women from participating in them. That mercantilism embraces male homosociality as a form of economic life is a direct consequence of the correlation of patriarchal discourses and practices of government during the period. It is not that women play no economic or social function within these relations, however – Eve Sedgwick has demonstrated how they employ women 'as exchangeable, perhaps symbolic, property for the primary purpose of cementing the bonds of men with men'.[81] In *The London Merchant*, this function is nowhere more visible than in the figure of Thorowgood's daughter – Maria – who provides a virtuous counterpoint to Millwood's dissolution and decadence. Where Millwood threatens to disrupt the circuitry of patriarchal power

78 Gail Kathleen Hart, *Tragedy in Paradise: Family and Gender Politics in German Bourgeois Tragedy 1750–1850* (Columbia, SC: Camden House, 1996), p. 33.

79 *Ibid.*, p. 34. 80 *Ibid.*, p. 33.

81 Eve Sedgwick, *Between Men: English Literature and Male Homosocial Desire* (New York: Columbia University Press, 1985), p. 25.

and government – literally coming between Barnwell and his fellow apprentice and master, breaking the homology upon which patriarchal relations are founded by introducing the heterogeneity of sexual difference, which inevitably corrupts them – Maria acts to suture the homosocial order, to reassert its authority.

In fact, when she acts, it is in an effort to reaffirm the order of symbolic exchange, to try to reverse and neutralise the powerful effects of the imaginary, linked as it is to the disorders of the fetishised commodity – she applies, in effect, her considerable symbolic capital to the situation in order to restore to the afflicted world of economic capital the scrupulousness and integrity it has forfeited through Barnwell's imprudent actions. What Maria does, in other words, is to ratify mercantilism's image of respectability, honour, virtue and competence – and to stabilise the moral order upon which the market is properly founded. When, as occurs later in the play, she discovers that Barnwell has embezzled funds from her father, she thinks only of restoring Barnwell to the symbolic order, even if that means concealing 'this unhappy Mismanagement from [her] Father' (III.iii.31) by surreptitiously replacing the embezzled sum with her own money. Maria's action is presented as a wholly selfless one – as an attempt 'to save from Shame, one whom we hope may yet return to Virtue, to Heaven' – something she is prepared to do even at the risk of 'sullying' her own 'fame', should her action ever become public knowledge (III.iii.32).

(3) *The discourses of 'love' and 'desire'*. Barnwell's eventual return to the 'homosocial fold' occurs at the end of the play just prior to his execution.[82] Although his reinstatement cannot save him from the penalty demanded by law, he is nevertheless saved in a more profoundly moral (and, importantly, governmental) sense. Barnwell is saved not simply because he professes sincere contrition and remorse for his crimes, engaging in 'Severe Reflections, Penitence and Tears' (V.ii.57), but rather because, having established the prodigal apprentice's religious salvation, the way is now cleared for a reconciliation with his fellow apprentice Trueman – crucially, Barnwell's first offence was a 'Breach of Friendship' (V.v.60). What is at stake in the reunion of Barnwell and Trueman, which takes place in the gloomy and melancholic surroundings of the condemned man's cell, is nothing less than the restoration of Barnwell to the ethical order from which – as his present circumstances testify – he has so fatally fallen. Not only does the play reach its emotional climax in the scene between the two men, but it does so precisely because Barnwell's ethical restitution takes the

[82] Freeman, *Genre and Identity*, p. 121.

immediate form of a purgative act in which the love of the two apprentices is reaffirmed as an 'Intercourse of Woe' (V.v.61). It is through his reintegration into the practices of homosocial love that Barnwell is reinserted into the symbolic order and reminded of the 'virtues' of honesty and mutuality that once defined him. Where Barnwell despairs that he is not fit for Trueman's 'honest Arms, and faithful Bosom', Trueman answers with a demonstration of his 'tender friendship' for the wretched Barnwell, in which the ideals of homosocial love are represented as an act of selfless compassion and unbounded solicitude: 'Thy Miseries cannot lay thee so low, but Love will find thee . . . Upon this rugged Couch then let us lie, for well it suits our most deplorable Condition . . . Our mutual Groans shall echo to each other thro' the dreary Vault.' Once in Trueman's arms, Barnwell finds, for the first time in the play, 'Sure Peace and Comfort . . . [and] the Work of Heaven, who, having before spoke Peace and Pardon to me, now send thee to confirm it' (V.v.60).

While it is tempting to view the scene as expressing a suppressed homosexual conflict within the homosocial order,[83] it is more important to understand its fundamental deontic function within the play. The principal point here is this: homosocial relations are advocated by deontic power as a corrective to the corruptions of the market. Just as the threat is personified in the figure of Millwood, Trueman represents the remedy – the paradigm of virtuous sentimental attachment, in which 'friendly counsel' (II.ii.15) can be promoted, and which is the best way of preserving oneself from the market's sordid temptations: 'O had you trusted me when first the Fair Seducer tempted you, all might have been prevented' (V. v.60). The homosociality of *The London Merchant* is precisely what the play prescribes as the curative to the affective disorders of youth – which is to say, to the disorders of 'love' – and is fundamental to the deontic message of the play. It is precisely because deontic order underpins homosocial relations that the profoundly intense affective relations re-established between Barnwell and Trueman, grounding the play emotionally, are permitted. The homosociality of the play does not advocate asceticism. Rather, it seeks a legitimate degree of physical intercourse and affection between men, expressive of that permissible feeling that saves Barnwell from Millwood and from the decadence that she epitomises.

[83] Hart is no doubt right to say that Barnwell and Trueman's 'homosocial extravagances are rendered legitimate by Maria's [sudden] presence [in the scene], which enables the apprentices' copulation. It also draws a line between heterosexuality and the realm of ecstatic male friendship' (Hart, *Tragedy in Paradise*, p. 30).

And yet the play acknowledges that there is also something self-contradictory in the struggle that marks the moral trajectory involved in establishing and preserving the homosocial order. The problem that confronts Barnwell is that the dichotomy that is staged between desire and duty, and through which the opposition between virtue and vice is inscribed into the play's discourse on love, can only appear as wholly intolerable to him. In an early scene, Thorowgood, sensing Barnwell's distraction, attempts to offer him solace through the homilies of paternal advice; but when Barnwell attempts to confess his misdeeds – the only point in the play at which he might have been saved – Thorowgood throws him off his stride by blithely pardoning him without wishing to hear what it is that Barnwell has done. Thorowgood's advice might be good, but such precepts can only strike Barnwell as platitudinous: 'be on your Guard in this gay thoughtless Season of your Life ... when the Sense of Pleasure's quick, and Passion high, and voluptuous Appetite's raging and fierce demand the strongest Curb' (II.iv.19). Although the deontic message is expressly asserted here – 'When Vice becomes habitual, the very Power of leaving it is lost' (II.iv.19) – there is little Barnwell can do about it, and when Thorowgood departs, he leaves his apprentice distracted and despairing. Maria seems to understand this dilemma better than her father when she reflects on 'the Wretch, who combats Love with Duty ... [whose] Mind, weaken'd and dissolved by the soft Passion, feeble and hopeless opposes its own Desires' (III.ii.29). It is not that Barnwell does not know and fully understand at a rational level what is happening to him; on the contrary, it is precisely because he retains his lucidity and his reason that he is tormented by the fact that reason remains powerless in the face of the tumultuous vicissitudes of desire: 'I wou'd not. – yet I must on ...' (I.viii.13).

The person who understands this dialectic of love and desire most of all is the person who mercilessly exploits it to her own advantage. What Millwood understands is that both the Merchant's discourse on cosmopolitan love, in which the love of one's fellow man signifies the greatest virtue in one's conduct, and Trueman's discourse on homosocial devotion and solicitude are impotent in the face of those passions that define the state of youth. Millwood inspires in Barnwell something far more powerful than the gentle oaths practised by the homosocial covenant; she instils in him 'desires [he] never knew before' (I.v.10). Millwood's 'scheme of government' is utterly intemperate and, at one point, likened to the Spanish conquest of the 'New World' – 'I would have my Conquests compleat' (I.iii.6); she knows precisely how to put Barnwell on the 'Rack of wild

Desire' (I.viii13). As he will later complain, she has 'got such firm Possession of my Heart, and governs there with such despotick Sway' (III.v.37). The effect on Barnwell is nothing less than the global disordering of the constitution of the self. Where once 'Never had Youth a higher Sense of Virtue . . . an open, generous, manliness of Temper; his Manners easy, unaffected and engaging (III.iii.30)', now 'Various Passions tore his very Soul . . .':

> in Anguish [he] threw his Eyes towards Heaven, and then as often bent their Beams on her; then wept and groan'd, and beat his Breast; at length, with Horror, not to be express'd, he cry'd, Thou curs'd Fair! Have I not given dreadful Proofs of Love! What drew me from my Youthful Innocence, to stain my then unspotted Soul, but Love?

(4) *Discourse's unassimilated supplement.* The virtues of self-governance and the conduct of the apprentice may well lie at the heart of the play's message; nevertheless, it also stages – albeit involuntarily – the 'unassimilated supplement' that belongs to every order of discourse. It is inassimilable because what is signified in the supplement must be disavowed by the order of discourse as its ownmost impossibility and as the unthinkable catastrophe unleashed by disordered speech. Supplementarity nonetheless appears in *The London Merchant* in the form of an accusation, made by Millwood, which she levels at the entire homosocial order: 'Men, however generous or sincere to one another, are all selfish Hypocrites in their Affairs with us' (I.iii.6). As Stephanie Barbé Hammer writes:

> Millwood observes that while male society has established a code of virtuous behaviour that governs men's actions with each other, all men unthinkingly violate this code in their assessment and treatment of women [who] are valued only as unessential extensions of male desire.[84]

But this does not quite bring into view the radical nature of the threat posed by the supplement – that its demand is a *theatrocratic* demand and not an additional message that is seeded into the play by Lillo. When Lillo has Millwood assert – in the extraordinary confrontation with Thorowgood, who visits her in her cell – 'Women are your universal Prey' (IV.xviii.54), he is hardly advocating the overthrow of homosocial relations. Quite the contrary, Millwood's attack is deployed, as noted earlier, for 'satirical' purposes: it aims to punish the general corruption that follows from hypocritical practices in order to correct them. When, in the previous

[84] Stephanie Barbé Hammer, *The Sublime Crime: Fascination, Failure, and Form in Literature of the Enlightenment* (Edwardsville: Southern Illinois University, 1994), p. 31.

scene, Trueman attacks Millwood's character, calling her an 'impious Wretch', Millwood responds by laying the blame firmly at the feet of 'your barbarous Sex, who robb'd me of [the perfections of mind and body]'. If Millwood's crimes represent the excesses of the market, those excesses are the product of men's vices. Whatever else Millwood may be, she is above all the product of her treatment by men – and not, as Trueman would have it, the worst of men, but men of 'all Degrees and all Professions . . . all were alike Wicked to the utmost of their Power' (IV. xvi.52). Who, she asks, taught her 'pride, contention, avarice, cruelty and revenge' – the priesthood; who taught her how to falsely accuse others of crimes that belong to her alone, but the corrupt magistrates – the very men who cover their own scandalous and dishonest activities by ensuring that there is no one who does not fall under suspicion. The true levellers of distinction, she contends, are the 'venal Magistrates . . . with them not to be guilty, is the worst of Crimes; and large Fees privately paid, is every needful Virtue' (IV.xvi.53).

It is in her response to Thorowgood, however, that Millwood's defiance is granted an astonishing degree of licence – astonishing because, unlike the scene with Trueman, it meets with no rebuttal or refutation: 'I hate you all, I know you, and expect no Mercy; nay, I ask for none; I have done nothing that I am sorry for; I follow'd my Inclinations, and that the best of you does every Day' (IV.xviii.53). With this speech, Lillo gives Millwood the freedom to launch what is effectively an unreserved polemic against the combined hypocrisy of men, law and religion:

> I am not fool enough to be an Atheist, tho' I have known enough of Men's Hypocrisy to make a thousand simple Women so. Whatever Religion is in it self, as practis'd by Mankind, it has caus'd the Evils, you say, it was design'd to cure. War, Plague, and Famine, has not destroy'd so many of the human Race, as this pretended Piety has done; and with such barbarous Cruelty, as if the only Way to honour Heaven, were to turn the present World to Hell. (IV.xviii.54)

It is an attack that ends, remarkably enough, with Thorowgood not only persuaded by Millwood, but obliged to verify her speech: 'Truth is truth, tho' from an Enemy, and spoke in Malice. You bloody, blind, and superstitious Bigots, how will you answer this?'

It is Millwood's speech that contains that excess of meaning – that discursive supplement – which proclaims the moment when the discourse of 'lawfulness' – indeed, the very order of discourse – is compelled to confront what it had hitherto excluded as a possibility: that its own axiological order does everything but speak in the name of 'truth'. Suddenly, all that had the appearance of solidity becomes insecure and doubtful; even the law, embodied in the figure of Thorowgood, who is confronted with an unassailable accusation, is rendered momentarily supine. This is because what breaks free from Lillo's text is the truth it permits to escape in the attempt to deride the corruptions of the age. No doubt the merchant's position, aligned as it is with an emergent liberalism, has some responsibility to bear for this eccentric outcome. It is not that Thorowgood is tolerant of Millwood's native savagery, but rather that, despite himself, he is momentarily allied with her in refusing a platform to religious bigots. After all, what Thorowgood rejects – in agreeing with Millwood – is what must, from a liberal perspective, be viewed as an improper cure to the ailments of youth (Lillo's likely target is the resurgent puritanism of the period). The merchant, then, playing the part of the doctor, lets the poison out through the very act of countenancing its vituperative presence in the truth that Millwood proclaims as her affliction. And it is for this very reason that – just as was the case with *The Beggar's Opera* – counter-discursive 'truth' threatens to break loose from its confinement in discourse at this point in the play. Millwood's envenomed monstration has, I think, the implicit potential at least for this kind of corrosive effect on the putatively cathartic and purgative ambition of the play, with its attempt to disinfect the stage of its corruptions by rendering it useful to government.

This is also the reason why the eighteenth century's most thoroughgoing attempt to reform the stage would be itself finally subject to the logic of expurgation, no doubt in an attempt to correct what in Lillo's theatre once more becomes recrudescent. Republished in 1812, in a volume of plays edited by James Plumtre, *The London Merchant* would undergo a series of modifications – the removal of a line here, a seemingly inconsequential inflection added there. However, two rather significant interventions occur in the text. The first effectively cauterises Millwood's satirical attack, so that where, before, Thorowgood conceded to Millwood a 'discourse of truth', in the expurgated version he refutes each charge in turn. When Millwood, for example, says, 'I know you, and I hate you all', Thorowgood now reasserts the patriarchal authority he had previously surrendered: 'I say, woman, this is false!'[85] And where, in the original play, Lillo had permitted Millwood's critique of the magistracy, in Plumtre's amended version Thorowgood

[85] James Plumtre/George Lillo, 'The London Merchant', in *The English Drama Purified*, p. 230.

silences Millwood, asserting, rather intolerantly: 'I can no longer bear this insidious mixture of falsehood with truth.' What is precisely 'purified' in this moment is, of course, the very act of verification that allowed Millwood's invective to escape the stage in order to accuse the world beyond it. Plumtre thus takes exceptional care to excise Thorowgood's line, 'You bloody, blind, and superstitious Bigots, how will you answer this?'

Plumtre's second significant addition is to place the scene of execution on stage, including a gallows and ladder (a scene initially written by Lillo but on the advice of friends omitted from the original production of the play). The reason he does this is clear enough: it is to rectify the possibility that the audience will misinterpret the message contained in the dramatisation. This effort of deontic power to complete or accomplish a total circumlocution of the message no doubt has the effect of rendering the play laborious – but it is also to render acceptable two things. First, it presents, indisputably, Barnwell as that reformed character of deontic power who – facing death – is able to face down his fear, in order to proclaim, with his last words, the lessons of public deontology – 'How humble and compos'd young Barnwell seems!' Millwood, by contrast, is presented as a wretched figure – described as 'wild, ruffled with passion, confounded and amaz'd'.[86] At the foot of the gallows, Barnwell commands Millwood: 'Oh, bend your stubborn knees, and harder heart, humbly to deprecate the wrath divine!' Millwood remains defiant, but – in this version – it is out of fear of the punishment that awaits her in the afterlife: 'I cannot repent, nor ask to be forgiven.' Here is the logic of deontic power played out to its inevitable conclusion: Millwood refuses to repent; Barnwell insists she must: 'add not to your vast account despair; a sin more injurious to Heaven, than all you've yet committed.' Barnwell begins to pray, prompting Millwood to observe that he is already 'ascending' to heaven; he has shown contrition and will be the beneficiary of divine mercy. For Millwood, however, even if she were capable of praying, she would find the gates of heaven 'shut with adamantine bars to her prayers'. Barnwell's last words proclaim the message of Christian forgiveness: she will 'find mercy where she least expects it', but it is a message for the audience, not Millwood.

On the other hand, the lesson of Millwood is clear: 'The impenitent alone die unforgiven.'[87]

[86] *Ibid.*, p. 248. [87] *Ibid.*, p. 241.

Conclusion: The Lawfulness of the Stage

In this chapter I have set out to show how, in Lillo's tragedy, the stage is entirely adapted to exhibit the scene of deontic instruction. But it would be quite wrong to understand the play thereby as presenting its spectators with a mere parable, just as it would be quite misleading to view *The London Merchant* as an attempt to sermonise its auditors through theatrical means. Its aim was rather more precise, more tangible, more focused: it was to discipline the audience, and to do so by generating the maximum degree of affective power capable of being produced by theatrical performance, so as to direct it against the very passions that the stage typically stirs in those who are exposed to it. For this reason, Lillo's experiment is not to be understood as a question of whether or not one can reform the stage. Rather, it set itself the more ambitious task of resolving a problem for which the theatre was thought to be particularly ill-equipped: whether or not, in being reformed, the stage can become the instrument of reform. Lillo sought to answer that question with a resounding affirmation of the moral power of the stage; in doing so, he thereby discovered, perhaps for the first time, a 'theatre of reform'. The specific governmental ambition of Lillo's theatre of reform was nothing other than the disciplining of untutored passions, but it also had a subtler aspiration, of course: to encourage, persuade – perhaps incite – the spectator to adopt a different conduct of life. In this sense, it would be incorrect to say that Lillo's stage merely moralised its audience. On the contrary, it provided the spectator with a set of precepts to be picked up, adopted, implemented, so as to establish a different way of conducting oneself in the face of the expanding reach of the market, of particular import during a period that saw the emergence (and dangers) of recreational time. In other words, if it had a 'lesson' for its spectator, it was rather more practical in orientation, but also shrewder in the way it profiled and then targeted its audience, since what it sought to inculcate in those apprentices to whom it addressed itself was a different way of practising the 'husbanding' of time. In this way it belonged to the wider governmental discourse with which I began this chapter, whose objective was to guide those entering the labour market into embracing the practice of deontic governance over oneself (and, as Lillo's play discloses, specifically by embracing the homosocial covenant).

That it is a matter of profound indifference to this argument whether or not the theatre of reform actually realised its intended effect on its audience should, I think, be self-evident: not only would it be quite impossible to prove such a supposition, but, more important, it would be to misunderstand what was actually verified with the appearance of this play, first, through its discursive positioning and, second, through the extraordinary manner in which it delivered the stage to the educative vision of government. In terms of what it verified, I would suggest that its fundamental significance should be located in the way that it demonstrated the capacity of the theatre to act as a means of promoting deontic power, and not simply as being subdued by it. In short, it demonstrated the 'lawfulness of the stage', thereby realising an ambition that had grown out of the moral turn taken by the theatre at the start of the eighteenth century. But also, in the sense that it can be seen to belong to a discursive event – that extended well into the next century – Lillo's domestic tragedy might be said to have a broader significance and a wider, more diffuse influence: it can be seen as a distant precursor to the 'moral reform drama' that emerged a century or so later;[88] but also, perhaps, it stands as the harbinger of the 'moral' spirit of the melodrama that, by the end of the eighteenth century, and at the cusp of the nineteenth, had seized so profoundly, indeed so resolutely, the theatrical imagination – that is, the way theatre was to be imagined. It thereby belongs to that long trajectory of discourse that would produce the kind of theatre Peter Brooks once described 'not only [as] . . . moralistic drama but the drama of morality'.[89] In so doing, however, it also affirmed the power of deontic government before which the bourgeois stage would prostrate itself.

[88] For an informed discussion of the 'moral reform drama', see John W. Frick, '"Not from the Drowsy Pulpit!": The Moral Reform Melodrama on the Nineteenth-Century Stage', in *Theatre Symposium*, vol. 15: *Theatre and Moral Order* (Tuscaloosa: University of Alabama Press, 2007), pp. 41–51.

[89] Peter Brooks, *The Melodramatic Imagination: Balzac, Henry James, Melodrama, and the Mode of Excess* (New Haven, CT: Yale University Press, 1995), p. 20.

PART III

Theatre in the Age of Reform

CHAPTER 6

The Governmentalisation of the Stage

Introduction

The previous three chapters examined how the government of the theatre came to be dominated by an idea of deontic power that assimilated the stage to the precepts of moral governance. To that end, regulatory matters devolved to practices of licensing and censorship, whether provided for by the state in the form of the theatrical licensor's office, whose task was to expurgate texts of any material deemed to be injurious to the public good, or to the more dispersed form of the public itself, conceived as an extra-juridical moral authority. Even so, by the end of the eighteenth century, there was a subtle but discernible change in the discourse on the theatre – one that shifted, however fractionally or marginally, its centre of gravity, and shifted it just enough to eclipse the hard-won moral certainties attached to the claims of deontic power. The pressures that led to this transformation were complex, and I will not deal with them here, but I would like to mark the point at which that transformation reached a threshold of visibility.

On 1 April 1795, John Thelwall, the radical reformer, journalist and member of the London Correspondence Society, delivered a public lecture entitled 'On the Political Prostitution of the Public Theatres'. While Thelwall's treatment of the stage was essentially consistent with the deontic view of the theatre, there was one notable difference. For Thelwall, it was just because the subject of theatre was moral that the stage must be considered political; and whereas, over the course of the eighteenth century, the effort had been to guard theatre against politics, by entrusting it to the safe-keeping of deontic power, Thelwall's argument now began to displace the locus of the discourse on theatre that had led to the establishment of this fundamental principle of theatrical governance – that the stage should be apolitical. Politics, he argued, necessarily belong to the stage and for no other reason than that the theatres were 'connected, in a considerable degree, with the morals, the manners and interests of society'.[1]

It is precisely because theatre is moral, for Thelwall, that it is political. When one considers that both theatre and politics share the common 'stem ... of all morals, of all manners, of everything that can affect the interest, the good conduct and happiness of society', then no great difference exists between theatre and government. But for the same reason, it is their very proximity that leads to a critical problem. If 'our very amusements are intimately connected with the political system: and ... if our grand political system is corrupt, that corruption will flow through every little meandering rivulet which should water even the pleasure-grounds of private recreation'.[2]

Taking the decline of the theatre as a kind of epiphenomenon, how might one read off the symptoms displayed on the theatrical body, the disease of a corrupted system of government? This is Thelwall's basic question. And if the theatre at the dawn of the nineteenth century really is symptomatic of the disease of political corruption, then what is the specific aetiology of this disease, its material cause? These things need to be established if one is to begin the task of curing the ailments of the stage. To establish the symptoms of corruption, Thelwall draws a simple analogy with the decline of the Roman stage, which – as is common knowledge – deteriorated into 'one monstrous puppet-show of splendid exhibitions, in which the mind had no share'.[3] Likewise, the modern theatre is also in danger of becoming a circus: a mere tool of distraction to its audience, instead of the instrument of critical edification for which it was originally intended. Nevertheless, the disfigurements of the stage present merely the outward signs of a more profound malady, and so for this reason it is important not to confuse symptom with cause, the boorish and indecorous tomfoolery found on the stage for the hidden source of the canker. The root of the problem in fact lies, for Thelwall, with the system of theatrical governance. Specifically, it was the system of monopoly under which theatres at the time operated that was to blame; the system according to which only two theatres in London – Drury Lane and Covent Garden – were able, under the authority of the Lord Chamberlain, to perform dramatic works. What the monopoly system produced was a fundamental

[1] John Thelwall, 'On the Political Prostitution of the Public Theatres, Part 1. With a Digression on the Character and Fate of Socrates', in *The Tribune, a Periodical Publication, Consisting Chiefly of the Political Lectures of J. Thelwall, Volume III* (London, 1795), pp. 279–98 (p. 279).

[2] *Ibid.*, p. 280. [3] *Ibid.*, p. 281.

abuse: 'Can it be conceived that any three or four men can have a right to purchase, or that any set of men can have a right to sell the exclusive privilege of amusing and instructing the public?' Indeed, what was monopoly if not, in itself, the surest sign of the corruptions of a debased state run on the basis of preferment and patronage, for the benefit of the few and to the detriment of the many?

> This monopoly is equally insulting to the town and oppressive to genius. It infects the morality and justice of the whole country. It has the power of confining any species of instruction and amusement within a narrow compass. It has the power also of dictating the particular sentiments to be uttered, the opinions that are to be propagated, and the factions, however despicable, to which all talents are to be prostituted. Thus we see dramatic energy, whether among writers or performers, dwindle away.[4]

The search for a remedy to this intolerable situation, which only commences here, nevertheless initiates the beginnings of a fundamental discursive displacement that will have profound consequences for the way theatre will be governed. What has shifted in the discourse on the theatre is not its preoccupation with the reform of the stage, any more than it signals the unravelling of the basically deontic mentality of reformers. All the same, the axis of discourse from this point onwards begins to revolve, and quite profoundly so, away from its preoccupation with the stage and its representations, the objects of moral governance, so as to discover a different entity altogether. Now, it will be nothing less than government itself that is to be reformed: that 'system by which the theatres are at this time so considerably shackled'.[5] Government, in other words, will be brought into question, challenged, defied, resisted and repelled – all in the name of preserving the 'national drama' from its corruptions. In this sense, the theatre will play its role in the great social reform movements of the nineteenth century. And what will eventually emerge, albeit gradually and painfully throughout the protracted disputes of the nineteenth century, will be the governmental apparatus that dominates the theatre in the modern era.

It is with a view to tracing the provenance of this apparatus, this new attribution of governmentality to the stage, that the final section of this book is primarily concerned. In one sense, I am tempted to say that what is at stake here is nothing less than the emancipation of the stage from government; and at the same time – as I suggest by the end of the

[4] *Ibid.*, p. 283. [5] *Ibid.*, p. 285.

study – this liberated theatre will have gained its autonomy only insofar as the autonomy of the stage is made possible by the mentality of government. By the close of the nineteenth century the mentality of government will be wholly entrenched, having entirely captured the stage. Increasingly, theatre will be set free from government, breaking the chains of its vassalage, yet everywhere more bound by that comprehensive apparatus of governance that the theatre itself has become. There is thus an omnipotence of government at the end of the century such that its mentality reaches a point of maximal saturation, such that it can be found everywhere, from the great purpose of the stage, viewed as the cultural vessel for the 'national drama', down to all the trivial, daily rituals of accounting and management – of health and safety and so on – that attach to the economic administration of the theatre. And there is a new autonomy for the stage, albeit one that is limited and circumscribed – a measurable increase in freedom, in other words, that should be understood as the paradoxical product of theatre's governmentalisation.

In order to assay the historical emergence of this apparatus of theatrical government, this chapter will examine three key moments in its development, where in each case the question of the 'theatrical franchise' provided the principal impetus behind the demands of theatrical reformers: (1) the so-called Old Price Riots of 1809, (2) the debates that were concluded in the discussions of the parliamentary Select Committee of 1832 and (3) the peculiar rehashing of those debates in the context of the Select Committee of 1866. In a sense, what each of these disputes of the nineteenth-century stage sought to address might well be seen in relation to the question John Stuart Mill was to ask of government more generally: what are the 'limits of the province of government . . . the question, to what objects governmental intervention in the affairs of society may or should extend, over and above those which necessarily appertain to it?'[6]

A Night at the Riot

The doors were to open at 5.30 on the evening of 18 September 1809, unveiling the New Theatre Royal to London's theatregoers. There had been favourable previews of the building in the press a few days earlier, but aside from a handful of journalists, the public had yet to catch sight of the ornamentations and splendid gildings that embellished it: the ceiling

[6] John Stuart Mill, *Principles of Political Economy with Some of Their Applications to Social Philosophy, in Two Volumes*, vol. 2 (Boston, 1848), p. 512.

painted to resemble a cupola, the panels decorated with golden wreaths and honeysuckle; the expansive auditorium – almost circular in form – unusual for the period and reminiscent of the old Elizabethan playhouse.

As the event drew nearer, John Philip Kemble, the theatre's manager, no doubt set aside whatever residual apprehensions he might have had (was it all an immense folly?), indulging that comfortable sense of self-satisfaction that to the eyes of less sanguine souls can appear as perilously hubristic. It is likely that he envisaged the opening night as a great personal triumph that would be part vindication (the building had almost ruined him financially) and part emancipation from the burden of mounting expectations. Kemble could be forgiven for feeling confident that the public would view his extraordinary achievement as he did – with a sense of pride and as the expression of a prodigious patriotic spirit. After all, exactly one year earlier, charred ruins had smouldered where the theatre once stood, streaks of watery ash had stained the streets, and an acrid smoke, lit by embers, had hung heavily in the air around Covent Garden; worse still, more than thirty people had perished in the conflagration. If a new theatre was to arise like a phoenix from the ashes of the old, Kemble made sure that it would do so as a magnificent symbol of British cultural power – as the playbill asserted: it would be 'an ornament to the Metropolis of the British Empire'. How did Kemble imagine the crowd would receive him as he stepped onto the stage that first night to make his occasional address? Perhaps he imagined them greeting him with an ovation, perhaps he had already calculated how long he would permit their applause to fill the cavernous space before silencing it with an appreciative gesture that signalled his desire to speak to them. They would be awestruck at the theatre's architectural grandeur – no theatre was bigger than this; they would marvel at the elegance of its design – its 'purity of taste and classical splendour and magnificence ... in modern times, without equal';[7] and they would comprehend that its allusions to the Temple of Minerva, whose portico, Doric columns and entablature it borrowed, were designed to flatter them. What the building embodied in architectural form was nothing less than an aspiration: that the visitor treat this building not as a theatre but as a temple to the 'national drama' that it housed.

But in the event, none of this came to pass.

Instead, Kemble's appearance on stage that night inspired neither adoration nor gratitude but the last and greatest revolt of the English

[7] *The Monthly Mirror: Reflecting Men and Manners. With Strictures on the Epitome, the Stage, Vol. VI* (London, 18 September 1809), p. 169.

audience – the last great display, in fact, of theatrocratic disorder witnessed in the British theatre, and the first great consumer protest of the modern era. Never before had the phrase 'all hell broke loose' been more aptly descriptive of events – at least if the following eyewitness is to believed: 'all the demons, inhabitants of that abode of the damned, best describe the audience that filled the new theatre that night.'[8]

In actual fact, Kemble knew that trouble was brewing. The playbill for the opening performance of *Macbeth* reveals as much with its unusual appeal begging the understanding of London's 'enlightened and liberal public'. What motivated Kemble to take such an extraordinary measure came down to the cost of rebuilding the theatre, which – for the period – had been exorbitant. The total came in at a staggering £150,000 – three times greater than the average cost of building a theatre at the time. Kemble thus sought compensation for the vast outlay by increasing the price of admission: boxes would rise from six to seven shillings; admission to the pit would be four shillings – a rise of sixpence; the lower and upper galleries would remain at the old price. Knowing that the move would prove controversial (ticket prices had been remarkably stable over preceding years), Kemble sought to defuse any trouble by forewarning the public. It was for this reason that the playbill published, along with the new prices, Kemble's justification for the rise, several days before the opening of the theatre.

While the bill conceded the extravagant cost of the building, it also argued that it was a worthwhile expenditure, and indeed a necessary one, 'in order to render the Theatre worthy of British Spectators, and of the Genius of their native Poets'. Unfortunately for Kemble, neither the public nor the press saw it that way – instead they took it as a provocation. On 11 September, *The Times* declared that public opinion would not tolerate such an imposition, and promised to interrogate the issue in greater detail, which it duly did, two days later in an extensive report (a further report appeared three days before the theatre was due to open). To what extent these reports incited the events that followed is difficult to say – they certainly captured a sense of seething public resentment. The theatre was to provide the public with 'legitimate dramas', *The Times* argued, not to 'suffer actors to wear upon their backs the profits of the night, to gratify private vanity'. And, in a more ominous assertion, which proved prophetic, it added: 'A crowd of venal applauders may be purchased, Police Officers may be planted in every part of the house to thwart discontent,

[8] *Ibid.*, p. 170.

and Bow-Street is at hand' – but still the public will make its displeasure known.[9]

And so it did. The story bristled on the pages of the city's newspapers the morning after opening night. Even as they paid for their seats, *The Times* reported, the discontent of the crowd was palpable; and if on entering the theatre the playgoers were momentarily 'silenced by the beauty of the spectacle they beheld' they soon regained their voices, drowning out the orchestra when it came time to sing the national anthem. But that was nothing as compared with the immense uproar that greeted Kemble when he took to the stage to begin his opening address before the night's production of *Macbeth*. Nothing could be heard of Kemble, although his lips could be seen mouthing words, giving him the disconcerting appearance of a ventriloquist's puppet. As the play began, the audience appeared to settle into a begrudging silence, but not for long. When Kemble reappeared in the title role the protests began again, and continued unabated throughout the performances of *Macbeth* and the musical farce, *The Quaker* – also on the bill – that followed. Of the plays,

> not a single word of either was heard by the most acute listener in the house: hisses, groans, yells, screeches, barks, coughs, shouts, cries of 'Off! Lower the prices! Six shillings! Pickpockets! Imposition! Cut-purse!' &c. &c. served to vary, but nothing could add to, the clamour of the house, which was painfully kept up whenever there was a single performer on the stage, but which was the highest when Mr. KEMBLE was there.[10]

Not only did this extraordinary scene announce the beginnings of what came to be known as the Old Price Riots but the conflict that erupted that night would continue – intensifying even – over the succeeding sixty-six days, until eventually a bruised and battered Kemble, acquiescing to all the demands of the rioters, finally conceded defeat. This made the Riots, as has been pointed out by Marc Baer, 'the longest-running disturbance in the history of theatre in Britain'.[11] It is not, however, its longevity that is of concern here; nor am I primarily interested in the remarkable tactics the 'OPers' employed to disrupt the workings of Kemble's theatre – what one contemporary aptly described as 'vocal and instrumental warfare',[12] a reference to the OPers' use of rattles, whistles, songs, imprecations and even (if Joseph Grimaldi is to be believed) squealing pigs in pursuit of their

[9] *The Times*, 13 September, part 1, 1809. [10] *The Times*, 19 September 1809.

[11] Marc Baer, *Theatre and Disorder in Late Georgian London* (Oxford: Clarendon Press, 1992), p. 2.

[12] *Caledonian Mercury*, Edinburgh, 9 October 1809, issue 13698.

strategy of 'noise and discordance'.[13] What is of interest, rather, is what those events signify when all the noise, bluster and commotion are set to one side. What stimulates that display of popular dissent is not just the rise in prices but the underlying problem that those rises have made discernible. Jane Moody, in her study of London's illegitimate theatres, comes close to grasping this when she argues that the 'events at Covent Garden drew popular attention . . . to the hidden relationships between the patent institution and the state'.[14] But I would suggest nuancing this insight, since what it specifically revealed was the hidden relationship of the patent system to government; and it is precisely this sudden visibility of the system of government over the theatrical franchise that enabled the OPers to convert, so persuasively and so incisively, Kemble's price rises into the sign of economic corruption: 'The question is not whether we will consent to pay sixpence or a shilling more for our admission; that to most of us is no object; but whether you will sanction the project of the managers to realize for ever an additional profit of fifteen per cent upon their capital.'[15]

The Extraordinary Monopolising Patent

In order to more fully understand how the price rises came to stand as a sign of economic injustice, I would like to return to the report published in *The Times* on 13 September. It is noteworthy that *The Times* did not deny that the proprietors of Covent Garden had the right to raise their prices; what concerned them was that this 'right' was the product or gift of an 'extraordinary monopolizing patent'. The provenance of that patent was old indeed: granted to William Davenant in 1662 by Charles II 'in perpetuity', the theatre had operated under its terms ever since. Drury Lane's patent – the Killigrew patent – established a somewhat different arrangement for that theatre, which required renewal once every twenty years. The patent system nevertheless gave both theatres sole authority to produce plays in London, prohibiting all other theatres in the city from staging the 'legitimate drama'. It is important, however, to grasp the nuances of the situation in relation to the patent system. The patents had many enemies – not just among the managers of the minor theatres but, one must suspect, within the Lord Chamberlain's office

[13] Joseph Grimaldi, *Memoires of Joseph Grimaldi*, vols. 1–4 (London, 1838), p. 80.

[14] Jane Moody, *Illegitimate Theatres in London, 1770–1840* (Cambridge: Cambridge University Press, 2000), p. 62.

[15] *Covent Garden Theatre!! Remarks on the Cause of the Dispute*, 1809, cited in Baer, *Theatre and Disorder in Late Georgian London*, pp. 83–84.

itself – despite the apparent support and protection it offered them. The inconsistency with which the Lord Chamberlain treated the minors led to many more theatres being opened illicitly, or else being granted licences to stage at the very least 'musical dramatic entertainments and ballets of action' – such as Arnold's theatre at the Lyceum in 1809; two years earlier, Scott had been given a licence for the Sans Pareil and Astley a licence for the Olympic theatre to perform burletta, pantomime and musical entertainments.[16] The Lord Chamberlain, the Earl of Dartmouth, had also been persuaded by Henry Grenville of the need to license an English Opera House – and so a degree of ambivalence, if not quite outright opposition to the patent system, permeated the entire system. Nevertheless, the system held firm – at least in principle.

And what that system gave rise to, according to its critics, were the abusive effects of monopoly. Moreover, in 1809 those effects were severely exacerbated because the only rival to Covent Garden – the Drury Lane theatre – had burnt down earlier that year, leaving Kemble's new theatre as the only provider of the legitimate drama in London. As *The Times* asserted, the absolute monopoly he enjoyed led to the disadvantaging of the theatre-going public – the inevitable outcome of any monopoly. Worse yet: the proprietors of the theatre, it proclaimed, who are the 'sole remaining possessors of the power of affording dramatic entertainments . . . act with a spirit as illiberal as it is rapacious, in taking undue advantage of the public propensity'.[17]

But in what way is the use of the word 'monopoly' to be deciphered in this context, and specifically how should it be understood in relation to its extensive employment by those who sought to dismantle the patent privileges of the theatre in the first part of the century? It is tempting to argue, as Tracy C. Davis has done, that the situation of the patent theatres cannot be understood in terms of monopoly for the obvious reason that both houses, promoting the same commodity, were in competition with one another – the exception to this, of course, being 1809, when by dint of circumstance Kemble presided over, however momentarily, an actual monopoly. Notwithstanding this fact, what one encounters during this period, writes Davis, is better described as a cartel system.[18] While I agree with Davis that in strict terms the situation of the London stage bears a

[16] 'The Metropolitan Theatres: A Chronological History of Their Origin and Progress', *The New Monthly Magazine*, 1833, part III, London, p. 264.

[17] *The Times*, 13 September 1809.

[18] Tracy C. Davis, *The Economics of the British Stage, 1800–1914* (Cambridge: Cambridge University Press, 2000), p. 20.

closer resemblance to oligopoly than to monopoly, I do not think that the debate that sprang up around the patentees (castigating them for exemplifying the excesses of monopoly) can be explained simply as a misnomer. To be sure, no comprehensive theory of monopoly was available at the time; nevertheless, the negative effects of monopoly were well known (and indeed, as Davis acknowledges, they were to become ever more visible over the ensuing years with the imposition of the Corn Laws by the government in 1815). What I suggest, as an alternative way of understanding this problem, is that the accusation of 'monopolising', within the discourse on the theatre (particularly as it was being rearticulated during the first part of the nineteenth century), provided reformers with a powerful and palpably effective means of attacking the patent system as such. Indeed, the key tactic of the 'reform' movement, when it came to the theatre, was to ensure this discursive identification of the words 'patent' and 'monopoly' such that they became virtual synonyms in the mind of the public. For that consciousness, the word 'monopoly' becomes code for an illiberal system of government. Moreover, it provides a shorthand that connotes an entire discursive declension, one whose ultimate objective is the deconsecrating of the privileged ground afforded to (the) government in matters of theatrical governance.

All the same, the criticism that the patent system was nothing other than an illiberal monopoly must seem, if not entirely opaque, then certainly puzzling from the perspective of a twenty-first-century observer for whom economic liberalism with its 'free market' nostrums – however much one disapproves of them – appears to be the only game in town. As the eighteenth century gave way to the nineteenth, however, the question of liberalism had by no means been resolved; on the contrary, it was fiercely debated, and specifically in relation to the project of economic and political reform. For economic liberals and radical reformers, monopoly signified both excessive government interference in the market and, more fundamentally, an excess of government. The intervention of public authority in the sphere of the economy (which must remain unadulterated and immune from regulatory meddling) could only result in a distortion of prices. Adam Smith had already warned, twenty years earlier in *The Wealth of Nations*, of the detrimental effects of the 'regulations of police' on the market; that whenever government intrudes in economy the result will be the perversion of the 'natural price' of the commodity – that is to say, the tendency of monopoly is to keep 'the market price of particular commodities above the natural price'. And endorsing the benefits of laissez-faire economics over monopoly, he declared: 'The price of monopoly is upon every occasion the highest which can be got. The natural price, or the price of free competition, on the contrary, is the lowest which can be taken.'[19]

The primary indicator of the illiberal nature of monopoly, then, lies in its opposition to free competition. But it produces other profound consequences: in rigging the market, monopoly falsifies and distorts its basic instrument: prices. It has, as Foucault says, 'a disturbing effect inasmuch as it acts on prices . . . that is to say, on the regulatory mechanism of the economy'.[20] The monopolistic power is also subject to a paradoxical effect, as Kemble was to discover to his cost: one way or another, the monopoly price must find, if not the 'natural price' for the commodity in question, then at least a reasonable 'market price'. In other words, as an economic mechanism, even in the absence of competition prices predictably behave as if there were competition. The consequence of failing to respect this tendency of prices is that the inflated monopoly price will quickly become untenable; it will be seen as intolerable and as an abuse of monopoly rights – a second, and more profound, demonstration of its illiberality.

It is for this reason that prices – the key term in the disturbances of 1809 – act as indicators or the objective signs of economic injustice in relation to which the malfunctions of the market are gauged. According to Smith the natural price of a commodity is arrived at through the combination of the costs involved in producing it – rent, wages and the outlays associated with bringing the commodity to market (for instance, the costs of scenery, costumes, rehearsals, advertising and so on). Where all of these are paid at their 'natural rates', this produces, says Smith, the 'natural price' at which commodities are sold: 'The commodity is then sold precisely for what it is worth, or for what it really costs the person who brings it to market.'[21] Importantly for Smith, natural rates of wages and profit and the 'natural price' of commodities are ensured so long as 'there is perfect liberty', in other words, trade without 'police' interference. However, there are times when the natural price of the commodity may not correspond to its market price, since the latter is determined in part by demand and in part by the laws of supply in relation to demand. Where there is greater supply than demand, then the market price will sink below the natural price. Where supply and demand are equally balanced, then the market price falls more or less in line with the natural prices. Thus the active and determining agent here will be 'effectual demand', and its degree in relation to the supply or availability of the commodity on the market. But at the

[19] Smith, *Wealth of Nations*, p. 28.
[20] Foucault, *Birth of Biopolitics*, p. 136.
[21] Smith, *Wealth of Nations*, p. 24.

same time this produces an interesting tension, placing a different type of 'competition' at the very heart of the capitalist market: it establishes competing interests, not between sellers, but between seller and consumer. For the former, their interest lies in ensuring the supply of the commodity never exceeds the effectual demand; while for the latter, their interest lies in ensuring that the supply of a commodity does not fall short of that demand. It is here, in the dynamic of competition between the interests of sellers and consumers, that the problem of the injustices of the patent system begins to fully emerge, for when supply falls short of effectual demand, the price of the commodity will invariably rise above its natural rate.

Now, under 'normal' circumstances, the dynamics of the market tend towards equilibrium, ensuring that supply meets demand, and it is for this reason that Smith says the natural price is the 'central price' around which commodities tend to gravitate: the central price reveals the propensity of the open, free and competitive market towards price stability, of supply adjusted to effectual demand. The problem, though, was that the patent system and the context of monopoly enjoyed by the theatre in Covent Garden were anything but 'normal' in 1809. On the contrary, they led to a pressing problem – one that demanded a resolution: that the patent system of theatrical government provoked a perpetual supply-and-demand crisis. It was this problem that was starkly exposed by Kemble's gambit of raising the price of admission to the new theatre; and it was this same problem that would lay bare the liabilities and limitations of the patent system over the ensuing thirty years. But it was also here that those advocating liberal reform of the theatre, by 'throwing open' the theatrical franchise, confronted a peculiar contradiction – a contradiction, or ambiguity, that becomes intelligible once one understands that, behind the problem of demand, is the problem of population. If there was an increased demand for the theatre, in other words, it was because there was a rapidly increasing population in London. For the monopolists, this led to the obvious problem of how to maintain a system that took no account of shifting demographics; for the liberal reformers, by contrast, it led to a different problem: how far to extend the theatrical franchise?

This is not to claim that, in 1809, the crisis Kemble provoked was explicitly understood or experienced in this sense. Attention was directed explicitly on Kemble's attempt to increase profits by inflating receipts, along with the variety of other demands made on him by the OPers, beyond a return to the 'old prices'. Most significant among these, they called for the removal of private boxes from the theatre – Kemble had added private subscription boxes that encroached on the space once reserved for less affluent playgoers, prompting *The Times* to remark: 'it was a cunning trick not to raise the price of the galleries; and at the same time to contract their space.'[22] They also demanded the dismissal of foreign actors – notably the Italian opera star Catalini, who had been lured to the theatre by Kemble with the promise of a vast salary. The OPers objected to the 'corruption' of English values and tastes, and voiced their preference for home-grown talent over imported performers. Still, what lay behind all of these issues and demands recurred inevitably to the problem of statutory monopoly, as if each represented a token of that government-granted exclusive privilege and its corrupting effects on the theatre. The hiring of Catalini, after all, was an expensive vanity project of the management. There is, however, one final aspect of the controversy that I would like to mention, since it anticipated a key argument in the later reform debate over the stage: the patent system, insofar as it enabled monopoly, had become self-corrupting – as the *Morning Chronicle* maintained:

> A patent is granted by his Majesty, in right of his prerogative, to secure to his people a rational Entertainment at a reasonable rate, and if that patent should either be not used at all, or should be abused, his Majesty would be advised by the proper officer to correct the evil, either by making new grants, or by opening the way, under certain regulations, to all who might chuse to embark their capital, time, and taste, in the speculation.[23]

Although the paper does not explicitly call for an end of the patent system, it does specify that the kind of monopoly intended through the granting of a royal patent is utterly distinct from capitalist monopoly. It is not meant to be a *commercial* monopoly that benefits the proprietors at the expense of the public. The question remains, all the same, whether the economics of privilege – of a stagnating monopoly – are now too firmly entrenched, and should that prove to be the case, then it 'shall be infinitely better . . . to see the monopoly laid open, by a universal conviction of the benefits that would arise from competition'. For this reason, the paper makes the following prediction: that Kemble's 'present ill-advised proceeding . . . will terminate in emancipating both the Public and the Performers from the caprice of exclusive establishments'.

The Road to Emancipation: 1832–1843

During the period of the Great Reform Act in the early 1830s, the condition of the theatres was chaotic, to say the least. First, absolutely

[22] *The Times*, 13 September 1809. [23] *Morning Chronicle*, 19 September 1809, issue 12592.

nothing had been resolved: the patent theatres continued to stand as anachronistic symbols of the 'old corruption' – of aristocratic privilege, parasitism and patronage – and of those 'exclusive establishments' protected by a 'capricious' law that still remained very much in force. All the same, not only were the patent theatres seen as a symbolic impediment to reform, and consequently as an obstacle on the path to economic and social progress that had to be removed, but their very existence now proved culturally toxic. For the reformers, these vast shrines to monopoly power were merely elegant carapaces that concealed a multitude of ugly vices and venalities, characteristic of a tainted political system. Nowhere else was this toxicity more evident than in their being held responsible for the 'decline of the Drama'. Salvation lay not in reforming the large houses but in legalising the minor houses, where the smaller stages and auditoria better suited the performance of dramatic works. For that reason, what aggravated matters further were the attempts made by the patent theatres to use existing laws to suppress the so-called illegitimate and 'minor' theatres of which many had sprung up across London's boroughs. These theatres endlessly tested the law by transgressing their limited remit: prohibited from performing dramatic works, they did so anyway, however 'unlawfully' – each risking prosecution in staging the drama without the protection afforded by a government licence. Theatres such as the Royal Coburg, modelled on the Paris Boulevard theatres and managed by George Davidge, were frequently subject to prosecutions and injunctions for trying to stage the 'serious' drama, as were theatrical venues such as the Olympic and Sans Pareil theatres – just some of the many 'minor' theatres that served the rapidly expanding neighbourhoods and suburbs of London. To confuse an already complicated situation further, the large patent theatres had themselves begun to emulate the smaller illegitimate theatres: seeking commercial advantage in exploiting the fluctuating popular tastes of the period, they began to cater to the public's desire for novelty amusements and spectacular attractions. Thus, elements of the repertoire would frequently be found interspersed with orientalist fantasies – entertainments such as 'Hyder Ali, or the Lions of Mysore', for example, appeared on the playbill in November 1831 along with *Macbeth* at the Theatre Royal, Drury Lane.[24] Inevitably, this blurring of 'high' and 'low'

[24] Jacky Bratton, whose work on the period I am indebted to here, writes: 'Drury Lane is obviously, from the evidence of such bills as this, locked in a hegemonic struggle between art and entertainment' (p. 44); chapter 3 provides a thorough analysis of the conflict between the patents and minor theatres in London. Jacky Bratton, *New Readings in Theatre History* (Cambridge: Cambridge University Press, 2003), pp. 36–66.

culture, appealing to a wide variety of audiences and demographic constituencies, led to accusations that the patent theatres had degenerated into mere menageries. Hence the decline of the drama could be mapped as a set of discursive relations forming a nexus of equivalential effects, influences and causal derivations: the corrupting patent system, the vicious and unjust use of the legal apparatus employed in suppressing the minor theatres, the rise of populist dispositions as mirrored in the increasing demand for theatricalised spectacle, the deteriorating taste of the public and ensuing loss of the principles of cultivation and civility, and so on. The role played by the patents in provoking such a byzantine state of affairs is tersely captured in summary form in the following passage, taken from the *Theatrical Pocket Magazine*, published in 1825 – although the sentiments reflected here were by now utterly commonplace:

> It has been complained by the patentees of the larger Theatres, that the minor Theatres are permitted to infringe upon their exclusive privileges, by performing the legitimate drama. The complaint is groundless; it is the patent theatres that have first disgraced themselves by condescending to imitate the performances of the minor theatres, by introducing on their boards, the senseless mummeries and spectacles that were formerly confined to the shows of Bartholomew fair, and the very lowest of the minor theatres. Having once stepped down from their lofty bulwarks which formerly secured them from all the attacks of their pigmy rivals, the spell was broken which marked the distinction between their performances, and those of the minor theatres, which they were mean enough to infringe upon. They set the fashion for these degenerate species of entertainment, the public caught the infection, and tragedy and comedy were neglected for melodrama and burlesque. Mark the consequence; the minor theatres now finding themselves on a more level footing with the patentees, took advantage of their position, improved their performances, and, as they offered them at a lower rate than their rivals, they drew away the audiences which formerly patronized the regular drama, but who now were not clever enough to distinguish proportionable superiority in the performances of the larger houses, to compensate their higher prices of admission.[25]

The arguments in favour of continuing the monopolising patent system had been rendered insupportable, then, if by nothing else than the facts on the ground: it was the patents themselves that had 'levelled' the field in 'condescending' to flatter lower and subordinate tastes. No longer could the patent managers claim, therefore, to be the guardians of the prestigious

[25] Anon., 'The Decline of the Drama, Considered', *The Drama or, Theatrical Pocket Magazine*, October 1825, 2, British Periodicals, pp. 40–41.

national drama. Nevertheless, the old accord was about to be challenged, and decisively so, by a series of events whose ramifications would eventually define and shape the future of the stage and precisely because they redefined the terms of its governance for good.

Seizing the historical moment, the radicals moved quickly to organise opposition to the patents. The events of 1832 commenced with a public meeting held on 3 January at the Freemason's Tavern on Queen's Street. The meeting was well attended by authors, actors and managers, as well as by public officials and sympathetic members of parliament. Proceedings began in lively fashion with uncompromising criticism of the patent managers who had attempted to use their 'prescriptive rights and their privileges to shut out their fellow citizens from the exercise of THEIR rights' – a speech that drew loud cheers of support; as did proclamations that denounced the 'tyranny' of monopoly.[26] Those proclamations, hyperbolic perhaps, nevertheless struck a deep chord with all those present in that crammed room: a few weeks earlier, solicitors acting on behalf of the two patent theatres had threatened legal action against the New Strand Subscription Theatre, and, in reaction, a committee of like-minded theatre reformers had set about devising a petition to send to parliament calling for the 'opening up' of the theatre franchise in London to free trade.[27] Thomas Serle, an actor and dramatist associated with the Royal Coburg, presented the assembly with a draft copy of the petition, arguing that the cause of the minor theatres was synonymous with the cause of the drama. The problem of the deterioration of dramatic literature, he said to his attentive listeners, could not be attributed to the failure of the authorities to enforce the 'present system', as the patent managers maintained. Rather, the 'present system' *was* the problem. The progress of the drama depended on its being 'free and unfettered', while under monopoly it was diminished and 'languishe[d]' in 'bondage'. The public wanted 'competition' to 'cater for its amusement', and for this reason, the petition demanded that parliament repeal the theatre act of 1737 (10th Geo. II), which would effectively end the monopoly of the patents.

But how far should the petition go? This question was debated in relation to an amendment to the petition proposed by Eugene Macarthy of the Dublin Theatre: 'that the patentees of Covent-Garden and Drury Lane Theatres have totally neglected to comply with, or conform to, the conditions upon which alone their patents were originally granted'. They

[26] Reported in the *Morning Chronicle*, 4 January 1832.
[27] For further discussion, see Jacky Bratton, *New Readings*, p. 71.

should thus be 'revoked', argued Macarthy, although the amendment was eventually voted down for being unnecessarily provocative. Davidge argued, for instance, that it was not necessary to get rid of the patent, only to open up the licensing system to the minors, which would produce the same effect. Nevertheless, Macarthy's speech undeniably caught the radical mood of the room. But it also did more than that: it articulated the key principles of theatrical reform as a *radical* agenda. In fact, he alleged, 'every condition named in the letters patent has been completely violated'. Moreover, the 'odious system of exclusive privilege [had] destroyed the very principle it was intended to support' – to 'cultivate and improve' the dramatic literature of the country. In betraying that basic principle, inevitably the patent system betrayed all others that followed from it: to establish through the people's exposure to the drama 'good manners and discipline among our loving subjects in all stations and ranks of men', to support the objectives of 'religion' and 'virtue', to build theatres suitable for the purpose of representing the drama – these must all be considered the founding principles of the patent that were now under threat of extinction. Was it not the principles themselves that counted, and not the patent system itself? This was Macarthy's central point. Indeed, only 'fair and honourable competition', Macarthy proclaimed (prompting 'loud and tumultuous plaudits'), could reverse the 'paralysis' inflicted upon the drama by the despotic patent system.

A second public meeting was held on 24 February in the City of London Tavern. This time it would be chaired by Bulwer Lytton. Not only was Lytton a member of parliament and a political radical, he was also a dramatist who enthusiastically advocated for reform of the laws relating to dramatic copyright. This meant that he was well placed to lead the movement for the opening up of the theatrical franchise. As chair, it was Lytton who spoke first, announcing the objective: to consider 'the propriety of petitioning Parliament for the removal of all such laws as restrict the free performance of the Drama at the Minor Theatres'.[28] Once again, the principal issue is one of monopoly, which is an impediment to trade. Indeed, as Lytton pointed out, there are no longer monopolies in trade, in the sale and distribution of corn, or even in the 'exercise [of] the political franchise' – a reference to the Reform Bill that was passing through parliament; nor is there a monopoly in knowledge – a reference perhaps to educational reforms. Why, then, asked Lytton, is there still a monopoly in theatre? The question was by no means posed in a rhetorical manner,

[28] *Morning Chronicle*, 25 February 1832.

and the reformers knew precisely what it meant to answer it: monopoly is to be understood not merely in economic terms but in relation to the broader political aims animating the reform agenda – and indeed the fundamental aim of consolidating the emerging liberal governmentality with its core themes of openness, freedom, fairness and 'justice'. But these very principles also, paradoxically, represented the rocks upon which the reform of the theatre franchise might be wrecked. The open market provided the means of distributing rational amusements, to be sure; but left to itself, the market provided no means of guaranteeing that *what* it circulated *would* be 'rational'. This led to the great caveat and indeed compromise of the reform movement: open competition must be encouraged, and the minor theatres should be permitted to 'furnish the public with rational amusement'. In this sense government must not interfere by placing restrictions on the market; and yet this market freedom was not unbounded, for while it was to promote an unrestricted trade in dramatic representation, it did so 'excepting only in the preservation of public morality and decorum'. Government should not inhibit 'full and free competition', but it must possess the necessary means of intervening whenever the market produced commodities that might pervert or degrade the morals of the consumer (or audience). This view was reiterated at the third and final public meeting, held on the 22 March, with the addition of the resolution to the petition that there should be no 'restriction in the performance of domestic entertainments, except for the preservation of morality and decorum'.[29]

Turning now to the pamphlet published alongside the petition, it is quite clear that resolving the problem of the governance of the stage in the context of a free market required a clear answer to Mill's question, addressed to liberal governmentality, of the limits and relative extent of government powers. On the one hand, it is the absolute 'duty and interest of government to promote a free and rigorous Drama'.[30] On the other, it is necessary to show that competition is of benefit to 'society' insofar as it is consistent with a 'well-regulated Drama'.[31] There are several aspects to this argument. First, it is necessary to recognise the effect that dramatic performance has on its audience: a '[d]rama operates most directly on society'. Its effect – ideally deontic, of course – is to sway the 'generality' by

[29] *Morning Chronicle*, 23 March 1832.

[30] *Major and Minor Theatres, a Concise View of the Question, as Regards the Public, the Patentees, and the Profession, with Remarks on the Decline of the Drama and the Means of Its Restoration. To Which Is Added the Petition Now Lying for Signature. By One of the Public* (London, 1832), p. 4.

[31] *Ibid.*, p. 5.

its example, hence the benefit of the drama to a 'crowded and complicated society'.[32]

Second, to ensure this benign effect, it is obligatory to assimilate the 'drama' to governmental discourse, in other words, to constitute the drama discursively in terms that are consonant with the deontic aims of government itself. For this reason, how the drama is defined and how it is performed will determine whether or not it is consistent with those aims. As the pamphlet makes clear, the drama is fundamentally a moral object, and its performance must respect that fact, thus:

> A fine play, with reverence be it spoken, is but a sermon or moral discourse, given with all the advantage of elocution and action, and of course must be so much the more impressive as it has at its command so many aids to attract the attention and enforce its precepts.[33]

To view the drama, in this way, as a deontic and therefore discursive object, is to understand it, in its representative function, as nothing other than a pure transcendental, as an abstract and formal designation. What it signifies is as open, pallid and empty as the word 'morality' itself, and it is from this emptiness that it derives all its prescriptive force. Thus, regardless of the fact that nobody can quite say *what* the drama is – a persistent theme in the debates over the reform of the theatre – nevertheless, it is always against the formal openness of the drama that both plays and performance must be equally adjudged, either as adequate to it, in the case of the actor's performance, or representative of it, in the case of plays. As a signifier of the discourse of 'good governance', the drama provides assurance that the theatre belongs to the 'great net of the law'.[34] Indeed, '[t]he high drama is the natural ally of the law – that is of just law – as all arts and inventions are, that promote morality and intellectual power.'[35]

The emphasis placed on the intellectual power of the drama, here, provides the key that unlocks the third part of the argument. In whatever way one construes it, in practice the drama is essentially exemplified by literary theatre. The movement, instigated by the radical reformers, in other words, is towards a theatre that will be resolutely cerebral and non-spectacular in form. Even if the ascription of a deontic function to the theatre hearkens back to the days of Lillo's theatre and a drama capable of 'purifying the passions', it also foreshadows the development of a new kind of theatre: an 'intellectual and sober' theatre that will be realised most explicitly towards the end of the century, with playwrights such as Shaw

[32] *Ibid.*, p. 6. [33] *Ibid.*, pp. 5–6. [34] *Ibid.*, p. 18. [35] *Ibid.*

and Wilde, in the 'drama of ideas'.[36] This will be a theatre that will be wholly liberated from the corruptions of common tastes, from all vulgarity and uncouthness associated with the populism embraced by the patent theatres. But for such a theatre to exist the stage must first be liberated from the turpitude and improbity of the patentees as the following question makes clear: 'are the proprietors of these two exclusive monopolizing theatres desirous or capable of delighting or drawing audiences of the reasonable and cultivated?'[37] If they are incapable of doing so, then it is because they do not seek to 'foster in any manner the mental part of the Drama'.[38] The crisis of the drama is mirrored, inversely, by the tawdriness of the spectacle that the monopoly theatres are now only fit to display: the patents have 'formed their stages for tiger hunts and dioramas'.[39] This shift to spectacle signifies that the theatre has – quite literally – been overrun by common life and that these theatres now pander only to the 'coarse, the silly, and the uncultivated' – those who 'cannot be delighted with the same mental amusements as the refined, the intellectual, and the cultivated'.[40] The logic of monopoly refers – and this is the fundamental point – to a cynical form of government, whose primary doctrine is that 'the lower orders of society must be degraded in order to be governed'.[41] In other words, the very form and system of government itself has a foreseeable power of influence over the drama, and the laws that regulate the theatre by means of monopoly privilege and which, correlatively, empower all other theatres to perform only 'Tom Foolery-Farce-Sing Song-Dancing-and Dumb Show' represent nothing other than an 'admirable contrivance for the degradation of society'.[42] This is why the reform of the stage entails nothing less than the reform of government itself – the final step of the argument:

> If it is the duty of a legislature to regard the interests of a society – to endeavour to humanize those whom they govern – if it is more easy to rule justly a reasonable and reasoning people, than a headstrong and unthinking one . . . it is certainly incumbent on the legislature to encourage a reasonable Drama.[43]

To encourage a reasonable drama is to reverse the logic of degradation – but how? The answer to this question seems almost too easy: 'a perfect freedom of capital is all that is required to give us, in every grade of society, and in every class of taste, a drama that could affect and benefit all

[36] *Ibid.*, p. 7. [37] *Ibid.*, p. 6. [38] *Ibid.* [39] *Ibid.*, p. 16. [40] *Ibid.* p. 12. [41] *Ibid.*, p. 17.
[42] *Ibid.*, p. 15. [43] *Ibid.*, p. 17.

parties.'[44] Nevertheless, since it has been demonstrated that monopoly induces the degradation of the stage, which is wholly inconsistent with 'the intellect and morality of the age',[45] one must start from the diametrically opposing presupposition. One must assume that a laissez-faire economy is consistent with morality. In supposing a 'clear stage and fair play', the application of laissez-faire as a means of governing the theatre will produce – through the power of competition – the reformation that is desired and for no other reason than that it clears the space so that this discursive figure, 'the Drama', may dominate the stage. Insofar as this reformation of the government of the theatre preserves the stage for the drama, that is all that is required to ensure that theatre and government are harmonised; it matters little how many theatres there are, as long as each maintains fidelity to this basic understanding. In other words, if one understands laissez-faire, applied to the apparatus of the theatre, as 'Capital directed by intelligence',[46] then the free market in theatrical entertainment is indeed consistent with the aims of morality. Left to its own devices, the market will produce what governmental intrusion has failed to produce – rational entertainment for an enlightened public.

The Report of the Select Committee on Dramatic Literature, 1832

The House of Commons debated the petition against the monopolising of the drama at a sitting on 31 May. Lytton rose to 'move for a Select Committee for the purpose of inquiring into the State of the Laws affecting Dramatic Literature, and the Performance of the Drama'.[47] His speech to the House reiterated the now well-rehearsed arguments for liberalising the law governing theatres in the name of preserving the 'dignity of the National Drama'. Proclaiming the need to extend the theatrical franchise beyond the patents to include the minors, he reassured the members assembled there that these theatres were very far from what they perhaps imagined, not the 'scene of very disorderly and improper exhibitions' but, owing to the 'good taste and civilisation of the age', establishments of the 'most decorous and orderly description'. There was now no reason to support their suppression, while there were, by contrast, very many reasons to undo the patent monopoly that had seen the large houses deteriorate into mere circuses populated by jugglers, fire-eaters, sword-swallowers, wild beasts and harlequins – evidence that the 'dignity of the drama has not been preserved, and the object of these patents has

[44] *Ibid.*, p. 18. [45] *Ibid.*, p. 19. [46] *Ibid.* [47] *Morning Chronicle*, 1 June 1832.

not been fulfilled'. Objections to Lytton's proposal were fairly muted. The principal fear was that an extension of the theatrical franchise might possibly result in similar spectacles spreading across the city ('we should have lions and leopards in Lambeth and camels and camelopards in all parts of the town'), but these were absurd complaints. The House granted Lytton a select committee, agreeing that its aim would be to examine the principal issues and put 'the police of theatres on a consistent and intelligible basis'.

The emancipation of the theatres seemed within reach, and Lytton wasted no time. In little over two months, the Select Committee on Dramatic Literature had published its report, along with the minutes of evidence collected over twelve days of hearings. The printed document, 250 pages long, reproduced the testimony of a number of witnesses who had been examined between 13 June and the final session, which was held on 12 July. It included men such as the respected theatre historian John Payne Collier, theatrical managers from both major and minor theatres – Charles Kemble and George Davidge – and also political radicals – among them, the playwright Douglas Jerrold and journalist Francis Place. The report itself proposed a number of key reforms affecting the governance of the stage. Each reform was carefully calibrated to add redress to the report's narrative of decline – but specifically in two key areas: first, in the standard and quality of plays, and second, in the decline of the 'taste' of the theatre-going public. In the first place, then, existing law had, according to the report, failed to protect literary talent and the commercial interests of any theatre willing to invest in new dramatic works. In fact, this had been a longstanding complaint of Lytton's, that playwrights had no protection under the law for their work. Lytton had already published on the subject in the *New Monthly Magazine* earlier that year, pronouncing that the 'extinction of the English Drama' was caused by the 'unparalleled injustice of the law relative to dramatic copyright'. The problem Lytton had identified was that once an author published a play they automatically ceded all rights to its performance to any theatre wishing to stage it – thus the writer lost 'control over [the play's] representation on the stage',[48] and any theatre that had invested in the play was exposed to its immediate piracy by any other theatre wishing to cash in on its success. Whenever a play did become successful – as Jerrold, drawing on his own experiences as a dramatist, was to testify – it was immediately restaged in any number of other theatres,

[48] Bulwer Lytton, 'The State of the Drama', *New Monthly Magazine and Literary Journal*, 34 (London, 1832), 131–35, (p. 131).

with no remuneration to the writer or recompense to the original producers of the play. It was this issue that the report addressed in arguing for a change in the law on dramatic copyright that would henceforth require the formal consent of an author before any work could be performed.

The second major recommendation attacked the problem of licensing along with a cluster of associated issues. By the 1830s, the system by which theatres were licensed – that is to say, the buildings themselves rather than the licensing or 'censoring' of plays, which was something separate – had become vastly complicated and more or less unworkable: the report responded to the demand for much-needed clarity in this area. It reasoned that all theatres in the metropolis should fall under one statutory licensing authority, whereas – as things stood – they fell under two: either the Lord Chamberlain, for theatres located in the borough of Westminster (and in any borough housing a Royal residence), or the jurisdiction of local magistrates, who were responsible for licensing theatre buildings in all other boroughs. The complexity of the situation is revealed in the minutes of the report through the testimony of Thomas Baucott Mash, Comptroller under the Lord Chamberlain. Patiently and meticulously he explained to the committee the anomalies of the present system: that the Lord Chamberlain licensed the patent theatres, which fell within the 'liberties of Westminster', but that the minor theatres, not falling within the City of Westminster, did not come under the jurisdiction of the Lord Chamberlain but under the jurisdiction of the Secretary of State for the Home Department. On the other hand, the Lord Chamberlain had jurisdiction over the entirety of the country in deciding what plays might be performed. Thus, when viewed as a censor, he could be said to possess an authority that was ubiquitous; but regarded as a licensor of theatres, his was only a minor and restricted power. To complicate matters further, the Act governing the licensing of the theatres was an Act of parliament; and yet the Lord Chamberlain derived his authority not from parliament but from the court. But perhaps most significantly – on the question as to whether or not the patent theatres derived any 'rights' from this Act, that is, a right to monopolise the performance of the drama – Mash responded, on the contrary, 'refusal is discretionary'; indeed, 'it is no right at all, it is merely [a matter of] custom.'[49] Collier's testimony would later reaffirm the point: the power of the Lord Chamberlain was merely 'permissive'.[50] And

[49] *Report from the Select Committee on Dramatic Literature with Minutes of Evidence: Ordered by the House of Commons, to be Printed, 2nd August, 1832* (London, 1832), p. 14.
[50] *Ibid.*, p. 23.

when it came to the question of rights, he located right elsewhere – not with the patents but with the public. The public, he said, had 'a right to obtain their amusements as cheaply as they [could], provided care [was] taken that those amusements [were] innocent'.[51]

Nevertheless, the fundamental recommendation of the report, setting aside the need to clarify the licensing of theatres, was for the opening up of the theatres to the wider market. In the interests of nurturing the 'legitimate Drama', the report contended, there needed to be 'a fair competition in its Representation'.[52] However, advocating the opening up of the theatrical franchise to the minor theatres, under the 'general advantages of competition', meant not only that the report thereby located economic reasoning at the heart of the governmental interest, but also, correlatively, that it compelled government to acknowledge the facticity of the situation: that a growing population also belonged essentially to the field of economic activity and that it was therefore the responsibility of government to nurture and encourage its participation in the drama. How? By 'letting things be' – by means of laissez-faire: theatres were for the 'amusement of the Public', and it was the public who should determine the number of theatres, while 'the Chamberlain should be bound to comply with the Public wish'.[53] As Collier argued during the hearings, 'I think the great evil has always been that instead of *multiplying* theatres in proportion to the increase of population, the proprietors have *enlarged* theatres in proportion to the increase of population.'[54] The result, as was now painfully obvious to all, was far from satisfactory. Ignoring a basic economic fact threatened to render the situation absurd, since it was clear that, when the population grew, so the market must expand to meet the increased demand. The key absurdity in laws regulating the stage was that they were based on past historical circumstances and did not take into account the facts of the demographic explosion that the 1830s were experiencing: 'London and its vicinity,' he argued, 'have increased in population, perhaps to four or five times its amount in the reign of Charles II [and yet] there are no more theatres now than there were then.'[55] And he added, the 'population of London exceeds that of Paris by about one-third', yet it had fewer theatres.[56]

Unsurprisingly, Kemble – defending the monopoly – disputed the point, saying, '[p]opulation and theatrical population are very distinct things,'[57] but Collier had already addressed the issue, observing: 'While

[51] *Ibid.*, p. 24. [52] *Ibid.*, p. 4. [53] *Ibid.* [54] *Ibid.* [55] *Ibid.*, p. 25. [56] *Ibid.*, p. 26.
[57] *Ibid.*, p. 43.

there are a great number of habitual play-goers still in London . . . there would be a great many more if they had theatres of a proper size, with a sufficient variety of good actors, and sufficient encouragement for good plays.'[58] Davidge pressed the point home: it was unfair, he argued, that the law should take no account of fluctuations in population; rather, the law governing the number of theatres should make allowances for further increases in population.[59] Population, then, stood as an unassailable fact that no system or perception could dispute; it gave credence to the demands of the free marketers by grounding their claims in a positivity few could quibble with. Necessity had provided its advocates with an unassailable rationale for extending the theatrical franchise. Confronted with the rise in population, the ambiguities in existing legislation concerning the regulation of the theatres were revealed. But, perhaps more important than this, the question of population also exposed the law to a fundamental contradiction. That contradiction was demonstrated through a further related fact that was palpable to anyone who cared to look: the increase in demand for the theatre was being met by the minor or illegitimate theatres – their very success proved the point. That the minors had to act outside the law in giving the public what it wanted was precisely what was contradictory and unsustainable in the relation of government to theatre. Again, Collier put his finger on the problem:

> My opinion is that the public interest is superior to any private consideration and if the minor theatres tend to make the drama a better school of morals and conduct, no private interest ought to stand in the way of that advantage.[60]

In other words, the contradiction that had emerged existed between two sets of interests: the private interests invested in the patent theatres, which sought to maintain the status quo – its shareholders, investors and so on – and the interests of the public as represented by the managers of the minors. As the proprietor of the Covent Garden theatre, John Forbes, was to be asked by Lytton: 'You think your patent rights are of more consequence than the amusement of the public?'[61] Private right against public interest – this, fundamentally, was what was at stake, while addressing that conflict meant nothing less than the wholesale reform of the entire theatrical apparatus, with the weight of the argument now entirely on the side of the reformers. If the entertainment of the public took priority, as it should, then the theatrical apparatus must be secured *for* that public. Only

[58] *Ibid.*, p. 27. [59] *Ibid.*, p. 83. [60] *Ibid.*, p. 25. [61] *Ibid.*, p. 98.

through the liberalisation of the market would the public obtain the entertainment it deserved – only with the arrival of competition. This is what the enfranchisement of the minor theatres meant.

Establishing the Limits of the Theatrical Franchise

It would, however, take a further ten years for the full recommendations of the 1832 Select Committee to be realised. The Bill on the Regulation of the Theatres, encountering the opposition of peers in the Lords, narrowly failed to make it onto the statute books in 1833 – although legislation on dramatic copyright did succeed. Only with the passing of the Theatre Regulation Act of 1843 (6 & 7 Vict. c.lxviii), dismissing forever all patent monopoly rights, were the ambitions of the free marketers finally achieved – although by 1833 the 'illegitimacy of the illegitimate' theatres, as Jane Moody puts it, had already 'begun to disappear'.[62] The sweet taste of success savoured by the triumphant managers of the minor theatres and their supporters was, however, about to sour. The reason for this was to do with a problem that those arguing for extending the theatrical franchise had, to this point, failed to address: how far, exactly, should enfranchisement extend? To be sure, in 1832, the issue was rather inchoate for the theatres; but from the middle of the century circumstances began to change, and by the 1860s the issues that dogged nineteenth-century reformers more generally and that were crystallised in Disraeli's 'Working Class Question' could no longer be ignored by the proprietors of the theatres – major or minor.[63] What had changed in terms of their situation? It was simply the emergence and rapid growth of a new form of entertainment, one that catered to lower-middle-class and working-class audiences: the music hall. To provide a sense of the scale of that growth, the Middlesex Bench of Magistrates alone issued 291 licences for music performances in 1865 and 60 for music and dancing, whereas 20 years earlier they issued only 67 licences in total. By 1866, no one knew exactly how many music halls were operating in London and its environs.

But the sheer number of music halls was not the problem. Originating as dancing saloons attached to public houses, pleasure gardens and concert halls, as well as song and supper clubs, the music halls had, in the latter half

[62] Moody, *Illegitimate Theatres in London, 1770–1840*, p. 47.

[63] Benjamin Disraeli in a letter to John Bright wrote: 'The Working Class Question is the real question, and that is the thing that demands to be settled.' Cited in Philip Corrigan and Derek Sayer, *The Great Arch: English State Formation as Cultural Revolution* (Oxford: Blackwell, 1985), p. 114.

of the century, slowly but surely strayed onto the territory claimed by the theatres, with inevitable consequences. The first prosecution brought against a music hall was an action against the proprietor of Canterbury Hall for performing a pantomime – considered a 'stage play'. It resulted in a fine, but also, more important, it realised the suspicions and fears of the theatre managers that the music halls were intent on encroaching on their commercial terrain in staging theatrical performances, even though they were prohibited from doing so by the 1843 Act just as the minors had been, long before them, by the 1737 Act. The problem was compounded by the fact that the Act was poorly written and highly ambiguous: 6 and 7 Victoria did not define what a 'stage play' was – whether it should include opera, operetta, burlesque, or other forms of performance. A bill had been drawn up in 1860 to resolve the matter, but for one reason or another it was never introduced to parliament. The issue festered, as prosecutions mounted and the canker of litigations spread, until finally a petition signed by a number of dramatists was submitted to parliament calling for an amendment to the law and a further liberalisation of the theatres so as to include the music halls. Just as the minors once sought equal rights with the patent theatres to perform the drama, so now the music halls were engaged in a similar struggle to obtain the same privilege of staging plays. The petition resulted in the forming of a new Select Committee, which was convened in 1866, with the following aim:

> Our great objective is to ascertain whether the theatres and music and dancing places can be so licensed and brought under control, that they may amuse the public without conducing to immorality . . . If [the music halls] were brought under the management of some competent authority [they might] exist to the extent that they do now, and contribute to the public amusement, without interfering more with the morals of the people than the ordinary theatres do.[64]

What the 1866 Select Committee ran up against, however, was remarkably staunch opposition from the theatre establishment and – with the inversion of the arguments of 1832 – a spectacular piece of hypocrisy. Theatre managers of all persuasions closed ranks: there could be no accommodating the wishes of the music hall proprietors, no extension of the franchise, and for the simple reason that music halls and theatres were distinct in

[64] 'Reports from the Select Committee on Theatrical Licenses and Regulations; together with the Procedures of the Committee, Minutes of Evidence, and Appendix' in *Reports from Committees: Eleven Volumes; Theatrical Licenses and Regulations; Trade in Animals, Session 1 February–10 August, 1866,* Vol. 16 (London, 1866), p. 92.

kind, not in degree. To argue otherwise, they declared, would be detrimental to the drama; and it would be to render *indistinct* the very difference separating the business of theatres from the business of the music halls. These were arguments not for laissez-faire but for 'restricted' competition – and behind them, of course, lay the language of 'distinction'.

'Restricting' Competition: The Select Committee of 1866

As it happens, it was one of the key recommendations of the Committee that music halls should be permitted to stage theatrical presentations; and yet no new legislation emerged as a consequence of 1866. The status quo held sway. The importance of the Committee must therefore be determined not in relation to what transpired from its extensive examination of the issues, so much as from what failed to transpire. The question that arises at this point, then, is: exactly what lay behind this curb on the activities of the music halls, and what does the testimony of the Committee reveal in terms of better understanding the limits and restraints that prevented any further extension of the theatrical franchise?

To answer these questions is to go to the heart of the debates of 1866 and to the three fundamental issues that they addressed: first, the defining of what a music hall is, and in what way it is to be differentiated from the theatre proper; second, the determining of the nature of its audiences, and their basic tastes and disposition; and third, allocating a form of entertainment that (given an understanding of the previous two points) is proper and fitting. From these, a number of questions arise, such as: how does one determine the function and purpose of a building, and what forms of inspection are necessary to ensure public safety – providing, for example, security against fire hazards, adequate ventilation, or facility of ingress and egress? How does one bring the music halls under proper control of government – for instance, how does one adequately censor and police the activities of the music halls? And how does one ensure orderliness while at the same time respecting the different temperaments of audiences and their differing investments in forms of entertainment? I shall address these issues in the remaining part of this and in the concluding chapter by drawing on the testimony presented to the Select Committee. I begin my analysis by looking at the problem of how to classify the essential character and defining features of the music hall.

There is an easy, brute, but nonetheless effective way of deciding the basic difference between theatres and music halls. Simply put: 'In one the dramatic element is the chief object, and in the other the drinking is the chief object.'[65] This understanding was already operative in the 1860s. The benefit of such a distinction was that – superficially at least – it bypassed the intractable problem of how to distinguish between venues by starting with forms of performance. Applications of music hall proprietors to obtain licences to perform plays – as Mr Strange, the manager of the Alhambra had attempted – met with refusal simply on the grounds that no smoking or drinking should take place in the auditorium and that refreshments should be taken either at the back of the pit or elsewhere in the building. The committees of 1832, 1853 and 1854 had all recommended that smoking and drinking should be prohibited in the audience part of the theatre, while all agreed that the aim of public houses and music halls – their principal trade and purpose – was the sale of alcohol. In this regard it is very easy to say what differentiates a theatre from a music hall – no ethereal conjecture or abstract speculation on the nature of the drama is needed, only a cursory glance at the purpose behind the trade. The object of the theatre is to provide 'intellectual entertainment', while the object of the publican is to 'sell his spirits'. Consequently, entertaining the people is, for the music hall proprietor, a 'subordinate thing'.[66] To license a music hall *as* a music hall is already therefore to enact a certain form of *de facto* restriction: to prohibit and proscribe certain forms of performance, while to regard other kinds of entertainment as being fitting and proper given the aims of such establishments. It is not because they are inherently execrable that they are distinguishable from theatres but because the purpose of the music hall is really the trade in alcohol. To take this approach to the problem is to get around the ambiguities that arise whenever one asks the question: 'Where does one draw the line between what should constitute a "theatre" and what should not?' The answer, as inelegant as it may be, is best understood in practical terms: 'it is difficult to draw the line, but practically it should be carried out.'[67]

This did not prevent people from trying, nevertheless, to determine the difference under the principled terms of the law – but inevitably the attempt to define what was meant by 'stage play', given the looseness of 6 and 7 Victoria, tended to the same absolutist and rather unhelpful conclusion: more or less anything placed on the stage could be interpreted as a 'dramatic representation'. For example, dramatic representation is present whenever someone is dressed in costume, engaged in dialogue or in making a speech, no matter how banal, or wherever scenery is present.

[65] *Ibid.*, p. 3. [66] *Ibid.*, p. 25. [67] *Ibid.*, p. 37.

Even in apparently ambiguous cases such as ballet it would depend on whether or not it could be considered a 'ballet d'action' – a ballet that 'told a story' as opposed to meaningless 'dancing about'. In the former case, the ballet is a dramatic presentation, and suitable only for theatres; in the case of the latter, it is the standard fare of the music hall. Evidently, there are marginal cases: a dancer in 'character', wearing traditional costume, as could be found in a Spanish dance, might not be considered 'dramatic',[68] although even this might be seen as problematic, depending on how stringently one applied the law: there must be '[n]othing scenic; nothing theatrical'; no 'dressing or decoration'.[69]

It is to avoid such reductive generalities that places of entertainment are better distinguished not by what they exhibit but more fundamentally in terms of what they are designed for; and, once again, the 'chief attraction' of the music halls is not the performance, it is 'what is drunk'.[70] Only on this basis can the extent and remit of different kinds of establishment be determined, as well as what ought to and ought not to occur within them. Indeed, nothing more is needed than to ask: 'what is the objection to watching a play while eating or drinking?' since the answer will furnish the essential criterion around which a differentiation can be made: 'it is very sensual.' In other words, one form, the music hall, is sensual; while the other, the theatre, is intellectual. It is for this reason that the two forms of entertainment cannot be conflated without producing catastrophic results. To pit the theatres against sensuality would do two things. In the first place, it would put them in a very 'unfair position', forcing them to compete with audiences whose preference is not for 'intellectual entertainment' but for 'tobacco and spirits'. But more important, to introduce the drama into the music hall would be to 'vulgarise and injure the drama'. This is why extending the theatrical franchise is not in the 'interests of the pure drama'.[71] Given that the principal purpose of the theatre is the 'education of the people', there can be only one consequence that follows from the insertion of stage plays into the quite alien environment of the music hall. It will 'degrade' the drama:[72]

> The audience go to the theatre for a specific thing: for an intellectual not a sensual enjoyment; you cannot carry on the two together; you might reduce the intellectual enjoyment to a level which addresses itself to the eye or the ear, and that can be enjoyed at the same time as smoking, eating, and drinking; but if you want to enjoy a purely intellectual entertainment, such

[68] *Ibid.*, p. 42. [69] *Ibid.*, p. 72. [70] *Ibid.*, p. 121. [71] *Ibid.*, p. 122. [72] *Ibid.*, p. 7.

> as the drama, the concentration of the mind required for it to be enjoyed thoroughly is such that it is impossible to combine the two together.[73]

This basic criterion, then, is what permits the separation that effectively governs the two forms of entertainment as essentially oppositional. Audiences that attend music halls are different from those that attend theatres; they are different 'publics'. One public is drawn by market factors, by what is popular, what is immediately pleasurable and gratifying, or what is fashionable. It produces entertainment that is entirely driven by the vagaries of 'supply and demand'. The other public is convoked by something else – not by market forces but by something that altogether transcends the market and that lays claim to a certain autonomy with respect to the market, with its logics of supply and demand: 'I look on the drama as a matter of high art, and I think its development is a great benefit to the public, lifting them far above the usual routine of their lives.'[74]

Distinction in kind must also be taken, therefore, as the essential criterion when considering the merits of extending the theatrical franchise. This is not to say that one should not work to improve 'the people's tastes [which] should be raised . . . instead of listening to trash'.[75] But it is also to acknowledge that whenever one performs the legitimate drama, one cannot have drinking and smoking without dissipating its intended effects. In many respects, this is because the conditions of spectatorship determine the purpose and use of buildings. The conditions for auditing a play are determined by the ideals of the drama – in providing intellectual entertainment for the public; and for that reason smoking, eating, drinking or dancing cannot be located within the auditorium. On the other hand, if the performance of music and song is understood for what it is – a pretext for drinking, smoking and dancing – then one cannot say that any establishment providing this kind of entertainment is a theatre.

But of course nothing is more revealing than this association of the music hall with forms of sensuality and of the theatre with a form that is essentially ideative – and this is the fundamental point. What this attitude confirms is nothing less than that the theatre has been *displaced* as the privileged term in the old theatrocratic discourse of the stage. In terms of the discourse on theatre, I would suggest, it is now no longer the theatre that constitutes a predicament for government, it is the music hall. Meanwhile, as a correlative effect, the key differential, isolated in the criterion that separates theatre from the music hall, can easily be distilled

[73] *Ibid.*, p. 145. [74] *Ibid.*, p. 108. [75] *Ibid.*, p. 52.

into the particularities of class division. Thus, if one asks why the production of the 'more intellectual drama' should prohibit tables in the auditorium, and why there should be a clear distinction between places licensed to perform the legitimate drama and those 'inferior places' and the kinds of entertainment suited to them, then: 'It comes to this, that it is the class of people appealed to which makes the difference.'[76] After all, 'it is degrading to act before such a class of people as prefer drinking and smoking to the intellectual amusement of the drama'.[77]

A further set of governmental problems are amplified by this recognition that different classes possess different dispositions and tastes. First, one must accept the irrevocable and permanent nature of differences founded on the social partitioning of classes: 'What a cultivated audience might reject as vulgar, a vulgar audience might fail to appreciate, and reject as dull ... – The same amusement would not suit all classes.'[78] To argue otherwise would be to impose a levelling of taste – one of the 'evils' identified with extending the theatrical franchise to the music halls: 'you must either bring down the performances of the higher classes ... to a low level, or else have them of such a character that the less educated people would not appreciate them.'[79] This invokes one of the fundamental controversies of the period: should the market be determined by the tastes and dispositions of the audience and thus according to predilections conditioned by class, or should it seek to improve what is lower, by exposing it to more elevated forms of entertainment? To seek to cultivate the lower classes by subjecting them to the drama is not without its consequences, however, and the social benefits of cultivation will take a toll on the drama itself, which 'in all its forms, has equally gone down'. The reason is that the 'lower classes cannot rise, but we can stoop; that is, the lower classes cannot at once rise to a high standard of the drama, but we can stoop and raise them gradually'.[80]

Others asked, would it not be better for 'second rate folks', the 'class who frequent the music halls', to 'hear two scenes of a good play than none at all'? Would it not be the case that 'some people's minds may be the better for a little training'? The answer is no, not if that means placing the drama in a music hall. After all, how can one improve the minds of those 'trained on gin, beer, and tobacco; it is casting pearls before swine'.[81] The problem here is exactly a 'theatrocratic' problem in the Platonic sense. The actor is very much determined by the public to which he or she performs;

[76] *Ibid.*, p. 54. [77] *Ibid.*, p. 109. [78] *Ibid.*, p. 28. [79] *Ibid.* [80] *Ibid.*, p. 150.
[81] *Ibid.*, p. 119.

it is their 'taste that guides the actor', and it is well known that the audiences at the music halls have had a corrupting influence on nascent artistry and talent – another reason to resist further liberalisation. Already music halls are threatening to destroy the 'art of acting'. For any performer acting in a music hall, 'their style is vitiated by the very applause which they receive from the class of persons they act to'.[82] This is the applause of those who are not fit to judge, and while it may indeed flatter the performer, flattery from such an audience is quite fraudulent: it leads only to self-deception and a corruption of whatever talent they may naturally possess. This is what it means to say that 'taste produces the actor'.[83]

It is therefore all too easy to say that the 'aim should be to elevate the lower mind to the level of the higher',[84] but how realistic is such an aim? What if the 'lower mind refuses elevation' – refuses to be cultivated? On the other hand, to balance 'competition' against 'public morality' is to see that the need to cultivate is more pressing, and one should not assume that the 'common people' have no taste for 'refined speech' or a preference for 'buffoonery'. It is a fact that the 'humbler classes of the community' enjoy classical music, and the government might look to the example of France, where such amusements are provided by the state to the people; in England, as long as the people have to pay for it themselves, 'the labouring classes' will not be able to afford it.[85] What the debate discloses here are the contradictory impulses of laissez-faire and the insistence of Mill's problem of the extent and limits of governmental intervention in the market. Left to itself, the market does not improve tastes or lead to cultivation – at least when this principle is applied to the lower classes. Rather, it exacerbates existing problems by indulging base dispositions and flattering incontinent and untutored tastes. And yet one cannot entirely govern taste, which is swayed by the powerful effects of fashion. The law must be adaptable, then, to such swings and shifts, whims and caprices. For example, where once it would have been impossible to envisage drinking beer and smoking in an auditorium, it is now 'very much in accordance with the growing taste of the lower classes, and [government] must, to some extent, yield to that taste'.[86] There must be strategic and tactical flexibility in practices of supervising forms of entertainment, while by the same token some recognition that certain forms of performance are clearly insufferable – in particular, the taste of the working classes for 'Ethiopian entertainments'[87] or 'minstrelsy'. So, the natural disposition of the music hall audience

[82] *Ibid.*, p. 106. [83] *Ibid.*, p. 119. [84] *Ibid.*, p. 28. [85] *Ibid.* [86] *Ibid.*, p. 38.
[87] *Ibid.*, p. 97.

presents a double dilemma for government. On the one hand, it is the duty of the executive to improve the tastes of the working classes – to cultivate taste *in* them: 'It is in the power of the Executive to make the people better.'[88] On the other hand, there is a limit as to what can be done – and extending the theatrical franchise, thus corrupting the drama, marks precisely where that limit lies: 'it is not as if the music hall theatre would be under the restraint of anything like taste; the entertainment would be in the hands of men who have no taste whatever, except for filling their pockets.'[89]

In the end, however, there is a more fundamental governmental logic at work that circumvents such obdurate disputes; it is a logic that supposes that, even in the worst places of public entertainment, a calculus of the 'lesser of the two evils' is necessarily in play, ultimately determining governmental pragmatism. This logic reveals itself in arguments such as those of the Middlesex magistrate Henry Pownall, who testified that the 'great improvement' in the streets at night can be directly attributed 'to the increase of these places of public entertainment . . . though they have their evils, and very great evils, they have their benefits too'.[90] Here one understands perfectly clearly that if one cannot improve the people, one can at least 'withdraw' them from the streets 'and concentrate them'. This logic of concentration is wholly consistent with the logic of police, then – if not with the higher aims and ideals of deontic governance. At the same time, that logic translates, in practical terms, and with a certain degree of inexorability, into the perpetual necessity of increased surveillance. It intensifies suspicion and circumspection on the part of the authorities, since it also entails that places such as music halls must be viewed as concentrations of vice. This is not to say that licences should be withheld from music halls because, without them, 'worse consequences might ensue'.[91] But it does disclose that – at least when it came to the discursive alignment of music halls with governmentality – a fundamental 'theatrocratic prejudice' remained in force, even if by now that same prejudice, insofar as it had once characterised the theatres, was more or less obsolete.

How does that prejudice express itself? It identifies the theatrocratic disorders of immorality and vice with what is *unseen*: 'It is after 11 o'clock at night when spirits are served to greater profusion, and when those private rooms are used, that the mischief occurs.' Indeed, for the kind of 'theatrocratic imaginary' that symbolic power conjures up in order to

88 *Ibid.*, p. 201. 89 *Ibid.*, p. 174. 90 *Ibid.*, p. 28. 91 *Ibid.*, p. 24.

constitute its own rationality, however prurient it may be, the insuperable fact of vice requires no evidence, as one key exchange made plain:

> You have never seen this immorality, have you?
> No; but one does not want to taste poison to know that it exists in a chemist's shop.[92]

What does such an assertion amount to other than the following avowal: that if vice is an inviolable fact requiring no evidence, it is because it exists simply in virtue of the fact that common life exists – as the ceaseless presence of the necessity for government.

Conclusion: Discourse and *Dispositif*

If this chapter describes, as I hope it has done, the historical unfolding of that discursive context through which theatre's 'governmentalisation' occurred in the nineteenth century, I hope it is also clear that what I have presented is not simply a 'descriptive' history. For at stake within this history is a profound genealogical transformation in the way in which the stage was to be governed later; and this transformation, in turn, should be seen to correspond to the extraordinary advance of governmental practices more generally during the century. What the period witnessed was the great progress of the 'liberal mode of government' with its commitment to laissez-faire economics, combined with a massive expansion of state administration over the social terrain; and it is the influence of the latter, I think, that can be identified within the problem of establishing the limits of theatre's enfranchisement. What results, for the theatres, is the need to establish barriers that will not only preserve a space for the emergence of the 'national drama' but that will also create a space in which an 'intellectual' drama might flourish. Thus, in the complexity of the debates surveyed above and the extraordinary thoroughness with which they were conducted, in the factionalisms they nurtured and fostered, in the schisms and contradictions they produced, and in the way they threw up problems that seemed to be impenetrable, not to say irresolvable, to those charged with bringing the theatres under a rational 'system of police', what this chapter has identified is simply the vast and expanding surface that comprised the discourse on the theatre in the nineteenth century. But that discourse is also to be understood more specifically as a 'plane of

[92] *Ibid.*, p. 23.

emergence' for the *practice* of the government of the theatre. Thus, finally, what it produces is nothing other than the theatre *dispositif* of the modern age, which emerges within the folds and reverberating chambers of discourse, in those rarefied and recondite spaces in which discourse seems to speak interminably and repetitively to itself.

CHAPTER 7

The Theatre Dispositif *of the Late Nineteenth Century*

Introduction

Throughout this book, I have sought to describe a discourse on the theatre that began to emerge in the early modern period and whose aim was nothing less than to bring the stage within the orbit and sphere of influence of government. I have argued that to elaborate on the discourse on theatre is to understand the word 'discourse' in a specific terminological sense but, more important, perhaps, that contrary to the view of some commentators, discourse is misunderstood if reduced to the notion of a 'text'. Rather, discourse and practices are intimately articulated together in the form of a nexus of discursive relations oriented by social practices whose pragmatic aim is to shape and determine what counts as social reality. The specificity and locality of those practices, applied to theatre, I have suggested, can be mapped following methodological hints first elaborated by Foucault. Hence, mine has been an attempt at a genealogical endeavour aiming to show the formation of a discourse on the stage or, rather, to trace the lineaments of a discursive event whose insuperable effects on the growth of theatre can be found dispersed over a great period of time, drawing the theatre, in the process, into a great number of often contradictory spaces of knowledge. Occupying the 'centre' of that systemic event, I have argued, were the unfolding logics and the problematic of government. As such, I have shown how theatre was thought in relation to governmental discourses, whether in the domain of law and criminal justice or in relation to economics and the genealogy of political economy. I have tried to describe how the discourse on theatre drew from the critical indignation of religious commentary a sense of moral purpose for the stage, and how that purpose, in turn, came to be echoed, recursively, in theatre, through poetics and criticism. In short, I have tried to show the extent to which the mentality of government (not to be confused with government in the narrow sense of the body of a political executive) has influenced the development of the European stage. For this reason, I have taken the discourse on the theatre to constitute statements issued in relation to the practices of the theatre, at specific places and times, in order to influence and reform those practices in one way or another. I have sought also to show how the theatre itself has thus learned, over this long history, to bear the inscriptions of its discourse, or at least to show how it has been shaped and reshaped by it. I have shown that it was, at times, compelled to do so by law; that occasionally it attempted to resist or corrupt or modify governmental prescriptions – to circumvent them and defy them. But more often than not, indeed for the most part, this history shows that theatre willingly conceded and adapted itself to the imperatives of government. The discourse on the theatre thus becomes theatre's discourse to the extent that the theatre slowly but surely conformed to the objectives and necessities of government, even that it became its willing accomplice, providing a space for its enunciations.

I have not attempted to rewrite the history of the theatre as though it had not been written a thousand times before. Nor have I tried to seek out untold novelties or to approach that history from one ingenious angle or another in order to prise free from its grip some remarkable and glittering treasure or collocation of facts, however fascinating they may be. Nor for that matter have I attempted to liberate from the archive, and the glacial pall it casts upon the shadowy events of history, the repertoire of forgotten or neglected but still vital practices. Such approaches are essential, of course, but they do not describe what I have done. My own approach has been simply to examine what are, when all is said and done, well-known moments in the history of the London stage, and to do so with a view to elaborating the enunciative space that constitutes the topos of that discourse flowing through them, to show that while it is a space that is not concealed, nor is it entirely self-evident, since it is a space defined less by the needs of the theatre and rather more by the demands made on the theatre by government. In particular, I have made every effort to indicate the extent to which both pro- and anti-theatrical statements occupy the same space of discourse. One set of statements articulates the discursive conditions necessary in granting the appearance of the theatre as a legitimate object habituated to the requirements of a well-governed state; the other articulates what is to be denied in the theatre, given the discursive field established by government. It specifies what is illegitimate about the stage. Thus the discourse on theatre grows out of differential and contradictory positions, which appear, nevertheless, to belong to the same discursive formation.

Throughout this book, I have been guided by certain assumptions that I have wished to dispel, or at least complicate, in order to show that the notion of an 'anti-theatrical prejudice' does not fully capture the nature of the prejudice that most certainly provides a motive for the emergence and development of the discourse on the theatre. I have argued that this prejudice does not set discourse against theatre per se; that it does not oppose it on the basis of sheer principle alone; and that the specific problems discourse has had with forms of theatricality owe more to the influence theatre supposedly has on the behaviour of those who are already of concern to government than to the existential threat some claim to have derived from the putatively 'queasy' effect theatrical performance has on our general sense of being. I have argued for an alternative view: that this prejudice is better grasped as a prejudice against common life, which circulates in both pro- and anti-theatrical statements. It is a prejudice that has a long history: it can be traced throughout the scholastic period; it inflects the neo-stoic revival; it owes much to the attitudes promoted by the early Church; it can be discerned in the elevated rhetoric of Roman orators as much as in the 'plain speaking' of English puritans. But it achieves its first and most comprehensive treatment at the hands of Plato, with his notion of theatrocracy. For that reason, I designated this prejudice an 'anti-theatrocratic prejudice', and the discourse on the theatre, insofar as it embodies that prejudice, a 'theatrocratic discourse'. As I demonstrated in the first chapter, this discourse, at least in its properly modern and systemic form, emerged with the arrival of the theatres during the Renaissance, which quickly became the locus for discourses on multitude, responding to the rapid emergence of an urban population in cities such as London. It is in this sense that I have taken the discourse on theatre to articulate a specific problem for government that emerged only at the dawn of modernity, and which thus requires that one distinguish between earlier forms of anti-theatrical statement and those that began to materialise during the late Renaissance.

Establishing the modernity of this discourse, my aim was to derive its principal object of enunciation, albeit understanding that object to be constituted within the imaginary dimension of discourse that provides symbolic power with a suitable degree of motivation for its effective exercise. That power is ultimately what accounts for the emergence of modern forms of government, originating in reason of state and the contortions in governmental knowledge unleashed by Machiavelli, the development and growth of mercantilism, and finally through its consolidation with the arrival of political economy and liberalism in the eighteenth century. What that power attempted to discipline were objects and practices immanent to forms of common life. It sought to curtail its pleasures, to suppress its vivacity, to rid it of every sign of carefreeness – or of the 'idleness' that revealed its inherent corruption, shame and mortification. It subjected common life to the diagnoses of governmental knowledge, which found it to be weak and infirm and contemptible. It thus imposed upon it regimes of great austerity, exposed it to sumptuary laws and strived to discipline it by depriving it of all luxury, prohibiting the slightest superfluity or indulgence or excess. It evolved techniques designed to retrain its inclinations and redirect its proclivities, with the sole purpose of adapting it to an ascetic and penurious existence, as befits the character and conduct of honest labour. It tried thus to convince the 'productive' part of the population that only a life devoted to authentic frugality was a life worthy of salvation – hence one sees the reason why the theatre, constituting an object of decadence, was of immense concern to government.

But the same discourse on the theatre also produced a different set of calculations; it arrived at diverse, apparently contradictory, conclusions. It did not banish the theatre outright, but wished only to reform it; it did not suppress the theatre, but only suppressed aspects of it; it did not run in fear of theatre's effects, but sought to exploit them, and did so by assimilating into the very fabric and materiality of the stage a novel form of power that would purge it of its corruption. I have designated this power 'deontic power' – extending Foucault's notion of pastoral power in order to define the specifically moral and social orientation of governmental practices. Thus understood, theatre reformers employed deontic power in order to reform the stage, but also – in satisfying themselves that a deontic stage could exist – they then used the theatre for the sake of reforming its audience. Deontic power rehabilitated the theatre or, better still, reclaimed it from the Platonic insipidities with which it was for so long associated. It is a moot point, of course, whether in the process of reforming its audience, the deontic theatre also 'cleansed' it of those it placed beyond the pale. At any rate, it made the theatre more suitable to certain sensibilities and interests. And it is in light of this deontic aspect of the story that I would say that, increasingly, the history of the modern theatre – at least Western theatre – is dominated not by a Platonic hatred of the stage but by that essentially Platonic vision of the theatre that Martin Puchner identifies with the 'theatre of ideas'. I do not agree, however, that the nature of that influence has been quite as benign as he has suggested, although, as I shall come to remark later, the theatre of ideas opens up the possibility for the kind of autonomous stage that we are used to experiencing today. There was always going to be a high cost, however, for that right to autonomy. Indeed, theatre's freedom from government invites the question, or so it seemed to me when I began this book, of who exactly would be compelled to pay the price for that autonomy? Here my argument was influenced by reading the work of David Wiles, marking, nonetheless, the substantial difference between us: I hold no idealised conception of an autonomous public sphere, however tacitly expressed, that might be recuperated by the theatre. Theatre's autonomy is of a different order from the critical reason Wiles attributes to the stage insofar as it might provide the locus for a revitalised public sphere. For me, there is no autonomy that exists in the sense of a free, uninhibited critical reason that is not always already bound to the social contradictions that, through its very participation in agonistic struggle, begot it in the first place. As my chapters on the context of eighteenth-century theatre attempt to show, the form of agonistic struggle constitutive of the bourgeois public sphere should alert us to the inconsistency of reason when it comes to matters of underlying proprietorial interests. Nor, for that matter, should that contradiction blind us to the structural and necessary limits that operate both internally and externally in order to secure the identity of the 'critical' public itself – for such a public, it is essential that a rational public sphere must nevertheless govern what can and cannot be said within the space of tolerance that it claims to originate, and that governing that space by imposing limited membership, forms of exclusion, prohibiting certain places of speech and forbidding certain modes of utterance, particularly the utterances of the plebeian, is the price it pays for its limited autonomy. In this sense, a public sphere is not without a sense of entitlement, but the point that matters most is: a critical public sphere seldom if ever opposes itself to government; at best it holds government to account, although only in relation to the interests that are invested in it.

Nevertheless, it would be an error to insist that all that emerges from this history can be reduced to the negative effects of hegemonic struggle insofar as it has produced the 'embourgeoisment' of the stage; just as the aim of this book would be misconstrued if it led to the trivial conclusion: 'The theatre is dead, long live the theatre!' Rather, my aim has been to show how governmental discourses shaped the practices of the stage, by intercepting theatre's capacity to produce certain effects. To that end, I would like to turn now to two ways in which those ends attained a 'positive' outcome. The first task is to provide a sense of that comprehensive apparatus of theatrical governance that emerges out of this history, indicated in the previous chapter, and whose basic shape can be discerned towards the end of the nineteenth century; and the second is to understand how that apparatus – having finally secured a space of autonomy for the theatre – then made possible the theatre of the modern age.

The Theatre Apparatus at the Close of the Nineteenth Century

What I present here admittedly can do little more than indicate that vast and complex system forming the apparatus that would govern the theatre from the end of the nineteenth century into the twentieth century and, indeed, down to the present day. One might get a sense of the complexity at stake in such an endeavour simply by recalling Foucault's description of what he calls (using a word that is, strictly speaking, untranslatable) a 'dispositif'. A *dispositif* (or 'apparatus'), he says, is a 'thoroughly heterogeneous ensemble' comprising 'discourses, institutions, architectural forms, regulatory decisions, laws, administrative measures, scientific statements, philosophical, moral and philanthropic propositions'.[1] But it is perhaps better to understand it in terms of what it does. Thus an apparatus can also be defined instrumentally: it is a 'process of functional overdetermination'[2] – meaning, an apparatus is not a fixed thing; there is no point at which it is complete. Equally, it cannot be reduced to one single aim. Rather, it incorporates a range of goals, interests, applications and objectives – some compatible, others antagonistic – in a 'perpetual process of *strategic elaboration*'.[3] An apparatus, in other words, is provisional, responsive to the effects it produces, even if it cannot anticipate or mitigate those effects entirely. In this sense, it can be elaborated only saccadically – in fragments, emerging at points of pressure that alight on a tangled network of possibilities. From the outside, it appears as a web of planned contingencies; from the inside, as a series of necessary and purposeful relations established to manage often contradictory impulses, motives and needs. It is an articulatory machine of governance, as productive as it is prohibitive. This is something that becomes clear in relation to theatre particularly around the period of the 1866 Select Committee. Indeed, it is in respect of that committee that one can really begin to see the extent of the apparatus that had begun to emerge at that time.

[1] Michel Foucault, 'The Confession of the Flesh', in *Power/Knowledge, Selected Interviews and Other Writings 1972–1977*, ed. and trans. Colin Gordon (Essex: Longman, 1980), p. 194.
[2] *Ibid.*, p. 195. [3] *Ibid.*

And, in fact, what is increasingly apparent – markedly so – is the way in which the theatre *dispositif* found its locus in relation to the theatre building itself, according to which specific regulatory regimes needed to be devised and implemented. It was this problem of the theatre building that the 1866 Committee made explicitly visible for the first time, at least in any comprehensive form. For that reason, the discussion that follows will circulate primarily around the consolidation of the government of building-based theatres. It was during this period that the building-based theatre attained its privileged position with the systematisation of the governing apparatus of the theatre, while earlier practices, once centred on actor-led companies, declined or were at least absorbed into its fabric.

Recall, first, that for the 1866 Committee, as I established in the previous chapter, the theatre building was to be defined by the mode of entertainment it housed. From this fundamental decision, a range of consequences would follow. In the first place, having understood that the aims of theatrical entertainment must be oriented to the edification of the audience, then it became possible to specify the ideal conditions of reception for enhancing intellectual attention (for instance, that to appreciate the drama one must exclude smoking and drinking). Thus the theatre was defined relationally in contradistinction to a music hall, as 'a place where there is scenery and performance in costume, and so on, and where there is no drinking, and it is under proper censorship'.[4] In this way the *dispositif* defined, specified, limited and justified what was permissible in terms of theatre's architectural practices. In so doing it inevitably provided nominations that determined the use to which buildings could be put and even how they should be designed. It ascertained what was specific to a theatre building and what was not. It introduced taxonomies of performance into nomenclatures of architectural practice, along with regulatory designations and technical vocabularies – partly for the purpose of identifying infractions, but principally to demarcate what was deemed most appropriate, given a particular theatrical need. Thus, in seeking to determine what was or was not permissible within the music hall, governmental logic began with a fairly basic but nevertheless necessary proposition: 'one must clearly define what [the music halls and by implication the theatres] should be permitted to act [and] under what proper regulations.'[5] In the case of the music halls, this led to the insight that while burletta, ballet and vaudeville might be 'compatible with the conditions of the place', tragedy and comedy were not, with the audience 'fluctuating and moving about at

[4] Report, 1866, p. 132 [5] *Ibid.*, p. 271.

times'.[6] One type of building therefore assumed the constant free movement of people, and a space of circulation; the other – the theatre proper – demanded a sedentary space of concentrated audition. But it was not just in relation to these kinds of assumptions regarding the proper use of theatre buildings that the *dispositif* was revealed or produced. More signally important was what those assumptions disclosed – namely, that the conditions of spectatorship acted as the determining norm. The central aim of the theatre *dispositif* was to establish the norms of reception and to regulate practices in relation to them. It was on this basis that specific forms of entertainment entered into the rationality of government via the classification of buildings. It was also on the basis of this normative, classificatory rationality that the regulatory apparatus revealed its essentially relational structure, and that, specifically, it operated in relations established between the different institutional sites of government – between the executive, the office of the licensor, the judiciary, the police and municipal authorities. This was seen clearly in disputes that had to be adjudicated by the courts in relation to those perennial problems that practices, in their vagueness and ambiguity, threw up from time to time around the licensing of the drama, as was evident in those interminable attempts at litigation by theatre managers who alleged violations by the music hall proprietors, or in the numerous appeals to the court of common pleas by disgruntled music hall managers, seeking to overturn prosecutions – a frequent occurrence of the late 1800s. Instituting a system for the identification of perversions of architectural nomenclature, courts provided a system of legal redress; but the *dispositif* remained always pragmatic, strategic. Where prosecution and litigation failed to resolve a specific need, the problem was referred back to executive authority, hence the number of Select Committees with their evidentiary protocols, testimonies, expert witnesses, cross-examinations, findings, recommendations, compromises and concessions. The 1892 Select Committee, for example, would return to the perennial problem of unlicensed theatrical performances in music halls, left unresolved in 1866, suggesting that theatrical sketches should be permitted, on the proviso that they lasted no more than forty minutes, required no more than six performers on the stage, and imposed an interval of thirty minutes between sketches. Thus it ensured no 'connected plot' could be established between isolated sketches (although no legislation followed from this recommendation, the theatres and music halls entering into the arrangement on a voluntary basis in 1896).

[6] *Ibid.*

It was not just that the *dispositif* that emerged in the latter half of the nineteenth century came to prescribe theatre's architectural practices; it also necessitated a rational system of inspection and superintendence. It gave birth thereby to a coordinated system of licensing regulation, policing, sanction and compliance. Indeed, one of the key problems the 1866 Select Committee set out to resolve was the anomaly of the so-called double jurisdiction that caused so much confusion in London, with its two separate licensing authorities: the licensing of theatre buildings coming under the authority of the Lord Chamberlain, and the music halls falling under the jurisdiction of local magistrates. What resulted were inconsistent inspection practices, leading at times to conflicts of jurisdiction. In 1857 the Alhambra music hall, for example, was simultaneously granted and denied a licence, when the Lord Chamberlain's surveyor found its galleries unsafe, whereas the magistrates, without so much as entering the building, had agreed to a licence. This chaotic and decentralised administrative system had emerged over a number of years, through haphazard legislation, and the Committee sought to remedy it. A single authority, it argued, would 'secure more uniformity of system'.[7]

The Influence of Municipal Authority: Improving the Licensing Regime

Essentially, the situation came down to the question of how to resolve certain systemic problems; of guaranteeing adequate superintendence, thus improving regulatory vigilance; and of preventing (and punishing) non-compliance through increased legal powers, motivated by genuine concerns over matters of health and public safety.[8] Thus a key recommendation of the 1866 Committee was that, in order to be granted a licence, it would become compulsory for all theatres and music halls to pass 'the inspection and survey'[9] to be carried out by someone qualified to do so, preferably an architect. The inspectorate of theatres and other places of entertainment would be specifically charged with maintaining standards of safety and the preservation of public health. Government, in the guise of the licensing authority, would henceforth assume responsibility for

[7] *Ibid.*, p. 19.

[8] For a comprehensive survey of the health and safety issues that beset nineteenth-century theatre – particularly regarding the frequency of fires but also the risk of epidemic, associated with the theory of miasma (airborne contagion falsely attributed as the cause of cholera during the period) – see Davis, *Economics of the British Stage*, pp. 94–114.

[9] Report, 1866, p. iii.

devising appropriate regulations, determining standards and formulating criteria that were to be met, as well as carrying out regular inspections to ensure 'the safety and accommodation of the public'.[10] What made this possible in practice was the wider historical context and, specifically, a significant development in local government organisation that saw the rapid expansion of civic government in London, granting extensive devolved powers to municipal authorities.

For the government of theatre buildings, the key event occurred in 1878 when the Metropolis Management and Buildings Acts Amendment Act transferred power from the Justices of the Peace and Lord Chamberlain to the Metropolitan Board of Works, 'providing for the structural supervision of Theatres and Music halls' within London; all were subject from this moment on to annual inspections administered by a centralised local authority.[11] The Local Government Act of 1888 would extend these powers to the new county councils throughout the country, although many county councils delegated licensing powers back to the magistrates. Nevertheless, a comprehensive system of governance had begun to emerge with the consequence that – in London at least – no new theatre or music hall could be licensed without first having been issued with a certificate from the Board. The Board itself, responsible for the municipal government of London as a whole, delegated the task of issuing certificates to a special committee, the Building Acts Committee, charged with examining new applications for theatre buildings, who would then make their recommendation, along with the advice of the superintending architect. For a building to be issued a certificate, not only did it need to have its plans approved, but the building itself would then need to be built and surveyed to ensure it complied with all structural requirements. The new protocol insisted: no certification can be issued 'until the Theatre or Music Hall has been completed in accordance with the requirements of the Board'.[12]

The first theatre to undergo this new system of inspection and licensing, with its multiple layers of scrutiny, its committees, its surveys and reports, and what no doubt felt like (at least for proprietors) the interminable duration of governmental processes, was Richard D'Oyly Carte's proposed new theatre in Beaufort-buildings, on the Strand – the Savoy Theatre. His experience is instructive in terms of revealing the multiple strata of

[10] *Ibid.*

[11] Minutes of Proceedings of the Metropolitan Board of Works, 11 January 1878, in Metropolitan Board of Works, January–June 1878, p. 35.

[12] Minutes of Proceedings of the Metropolitan Board of Works, 2 May 1878, in Metropolitan Board of Works, January–June 1879, p. 242.

governance that now applied to the licensing of theatre buildings, its layers of scrutiny, oversight, examination and appraisal. An application for the new theatre was submitted to the Board by the theatre's architect, Walter Emden, on 5 March 1880. The Board, receiving the application, referred it along with the report by the superintending architect to the Building Acts Committee, which rejected it on 19 March on the grounds that it failed to comply with the new safety regulations and contravened by-laws. An amended plan for the building was drafted and resubmitted to the Board, which once again referred it to the Building Acts Committee for its consideration. Although the committee now approved the theatre, issuing a conditional certificate on 23 April, still the tortuous process of licensing the building was far from over; an amendment to the vote meant the application was referred for further scrutiny to the Works and General Purposes Committee, with complaints that the approaches to the theatre were 'insufficient', while the members of the Building Acts Committee resolved to view the site of the theatre for themselves. Meanwhile, the Strand District Board of Works – whose jurisdiction was rather obscure, as D'Oyly Carte later pointed out in a letter to *The Times* – having been sent the 'block plans' for the building, interceded with an objection: a letter from their clerk, dated 19 April, proclaimed 'that they considered the scheme would lead to the public convenience being greatly and injuriously interfered with, and that they disapproved of the proposal'.[13] The letter was forwarded to the Works and General Purposes Committee for further deliberation, although deliberation was delayed by an adjournment. Even after the application was officially approved by the Board, which occurred on 4 June, scrutiny continued until the following November[14] – all of this going to show that, while it exasperated the proprietors (D'Oyly Carte complained bitterly in his letter to *The Times*: 'I am struggling in the meshes of red tape'),[15] the system now in operation, with its orderliness, regularity and insistence on method, protocol and procedure was a far cry from the erratic and unreliable regulation of buildings that dominated the first half of the century. With these administrative developments, then, not only was the health and safety of the public more thoroughly assured, with the hazards of fire mitigated by a system of compliance and prevention (the Board was empowered to issue notices for improvements, threatening legal

[13] Minutes of Proceedings of the Metropolitan Board of Works, 30 April 1880, in Metropolitan Board of Works, January–June 1880, p. 610.

[14] Minutes of Proceedings of the Metropolitan Board of Works, 5 November 1880, in Metropolitan Board of Works, July–December 1880, p. 616.

[15] Richard D'Oyly Carte, 'Building Difficulties', *The Times*, 22 May 1880, issue 29888.

action for non-compliance); but also, as a consequence, the theatres were now, more than at any other time in their history, under a rigorous system of inspection – one that enabled government to fully determine what the theatres were permitted to do, and how and where they were permitted to do it.

A further consolidation of governmental powers occurred when the Metropolitan Board of Works was replaced, in 1889, by the London County Council, who assumed responsibility for licence applications in the form of the new Theatre and Music Halls Committee. The committee drew up comprehensive guidelines for the 'regulation of the manner of dealing with applications'. Of particular import was the requirement that all applications to the Committee be made public and visible through issuing a notification of intent to apply, for instance, through notices advertised in 'daily newspapers circulating generally throughout the country'.[16] Once notification had been given, the Clerk of the Council would then

> send a copy of the list of applications arranged in alphabetical order of parishes and a copy of these orders to every Member of the Council. He shall also send copies to the Clerks of the Peace, to the Clerks to [*sic*] the Justices in the several Petty Sessional Divisions, to the Commissioner of Police, to the Superintendent of each Division of the Police in the County, and to the Excise Office, with an inquiry whether any and what complaints as to any of the applications or the licensed premises have been made.[17]

Needless to say, where objections or complaints arose, the committee would take them into consideration. And in cases where objections did arise, a system for adjudicating them, modelled on court proceedings, was devised: 'every applicant for a license and every person objecting to the granting thereof . . . shall be each heard either personally or by his counsel, and shall be entitled to call witnesses.'[18] Two grounds were provided for refusing a licence: the first was the failure to meet structural requirements – a failure to comply; and the second was through a provision covering complaints of possible or actual nuisance, as occurred when the Pied Bull on Holloway Road was refused a music licence due to the opposition of local tradespeople, shopkeepers and residents: 'serious annoyance would be

[16] Report of the Theatres and Music Halls Committee, 24 June 1889, in London County Council Minutes of Proceedings of the Council, January–December 1889, p. 512.

[17] *Ibid.*, p. 511.

[18] Report of the Theatres and Music Halls Committee, 24 June 1889, in London County Council Minutes of Proceedings of the Council, January–December 1889, p. 513.

caused to the neighbourhood, owing to large numbers of persons separating when the entertainments were over at a late hour of the night.'[19]

It was not that the Licensing Committee of the London County Council merely dealt with matters relating solely to structural issues concerned with fire hazards, irregular building practices, health and safety, nuisance and so on – since implicit in the licensing of buildings was the intended *use* of buildings. Thus the committee also policed the strict distinctions that prescribed certain classes of entertainment given the prevailing norms, outlined earlier, that governed theatre's architectural practices. The Royal Park Hall in Camden Town fell afoul of this kind of precise classificatory distinction when it applied to the council for a certificate to license the building for the performance of dramatic works: the application was rejected on the grounds that the 'building was not considered suitable for the performance of stage-plays'.[20]

Disciplining Buildings: Social Conduct, Police and Audiences

Thus far I have indicated the role of government as it emerged in relation to the inspection of theatres: that 'the public security should be well cared for'.[21] All of this would have a profound influence on how theatre practices would be thought in relation to the buildings that housed them. James George Buckle's *Theatre Construction and Maintenance*, published in 1888, is exemplary in this regard, providing comprehensive proposals for ensuring the safety of all visitors to the theatre, even recommending that the pit should be located beneath ground level, for the ingenious reason that in the event of a fire, people would be less likely to fall ascending a staircase than descending one.

The governance of buildings was not, however, simply a matter of ensuring the safety of theatre construction – preventing fires and so on. There was also the important matter of the social conduct of audiences and the role that architecture played in modifying that conduct. Directing conduct was already implicit in Buckle's recommendations for ensuring comfortable seating in all parts of the house – even in the gallery: 'Discomfort in the gallery will create disturbance, and consequent

[19] Report of the Theatres and Music Halls Committee, 18 October 1889, in London County Council Minutes of Proceedings of the Council, January–December 1889, p. 806.

[20] LCC/PC/ENT/2/2 – Theatres and Music Halls, Licensing Sessions, Printed Papers, 1894–97, p. 17.

[21] Report, 1866, p. 76.

annoyance to the whole house.'[22] Insofar as conduct is always conditioned by social relations, with their inherent antagonisms, what is made visible here is the way in which class divisions were conspicuously inscribed into the very design of the theatre building. To be sure, the fact that theatre-building was to accommodate the problematic of class distinctions was nothing new; the practice had already been established as early as the first decade of the century. The playbill for the opening of the new theatre in Covent Garden, in 1809, provided discrete instructions to its audience on how they should divide and segregate into isolable groups, identified by economic status, according to the entrances they used. Entrants to the pit, for example, were to use the Bedford Avenue ingress on the piazza or the entrance in the Bow Street arcade. More affluent visitors would use the 'grand entrance to the boxes' that opened onto a vast staircase, feeding a capacious saloon; while those inhabiting the more exclusive boxes, purchased through private subscription, were provided with a private entrance and staircase – each box equipped with its own private antechamber. Benjamin Wyatt employed the same logic of segregation when he designed the new theatre building in Drury Lane, proclaiming that among the standard design problems of audition and vision, the architect should also build with a view to guaranteeing 'decorum', understood in terms of the social separation of classes:

> Among the principal objects which call for reform, in the Theatres in London, none appears to be much more important, than that of protecting the more rational and respectable class of spectators from those nuisances to which they have hitherto been exposed, by being obliged to pass through lobbies, rooms, and avenues, crowded with the most disreputable members of the community, and subject to scenes of the most disgusting indecency.[23]

Wyatt acknowledged that while the 'exclusion of any particular class of people . . . would be utterly impracticable', nevertheless, in designing 'separate' spaces suited to different class dispositions he constructed his building so that there would be few opportunities for different classes to intermingle. Wyatt also innovated in another way, designing the theatre to ensure that 'no gloomy recess [might] favour the riotous or improper proceedings of disorderly persons; everyone will be brought in full view of the house, and within the light of the chandeliers'.[24] Thus the very

[22] James George Buckle, *Theatre Construction and Maintenance* (London, 1888), p. 25.

[23] Benjamin Wyatt, 'Observations on the Principles of the Design for the New Theatre Now Building in Drury-Lane', *Court and Fashionable Magazine*, 5 (1812, January), 9–14, (p. 13).

[24] *Ibid.*, p. 13.

architecture of the building was designed to inhibit, as he put it, 'noisy and licentious conduct'.

But as it transpired, Wyatt's contention proved false. There was a way to resolve the problem of how to exclude an entire class from the theatre – as became apparent in the 1880s. One theatre that stood out above all others for the absolute priority it gave to the question of manipulating audience demographics was Bancroft's theatre at the Haymarket. On becoming the licensee of the theatre, Bancroft immediately began refurbishments, stripping out the interior of the original theatre, which dated back to 1821, until all that remained were its bare walls. When the new theatre opened on 31 January 1880, it was thus utterly transformed; but importantly, it also introduced a range of startling innovations. As is well known, it erected around the proscenium a vast and rather elaborately gilded frame, removed the footlights from the front of the stage, and relocated the orchestra beneath it, out of sight of the audience. In this way it instituted what would become the orthodoxy of the bourgeois stage, ensuring that the events it presented would unfold as though occurring in a world that existed in parallel with the one inhabited by the audience, yet somehow ontologically distinct from them. But Bancroft's theatre also innovated in a way that was rather more uncompromising when it came to the question of how to improve the 'quality' of the theatre's clientele. What it did was to utterly transform the traditional social distribution of the audience in British theatres, as the *Morning Post* observed only days after the theatre had opened:

> Superb in decoration and luxurious in appointment, the house has an aspect of courtly grandeur, but you look in vain for the 'people' as distinguished from the more refined classes. It may be compared to a Parliament without a House of Commons. The reason is that the pit, that place where beats the heart of the house . . . has been altogether banished.[25]

What Bancroft and Phipps, the architect who had redesigned the theatre for him, had done was abolish the pit in order to replace it with high-priced seating, upholstered in expensive crimson velvet. Bancroft had justified this 'improvement' by protesting, at the time, that he could not 'afford' the pit, but this explanation was only partly convincing. A few years later, the journal *The British Architect* was rather more candid in declaring what had really been at stake in the reconstruction of the Haymarket theatre: Phipps had redesigned the theatre specifically to

[25] *Morning Post*, 2 February 1880.

'meet the demands of the class of performance given at this house and the class of people frequenting it'.[26] But it also observed that while Bancroft's decision had proved right, commercially speaking – given the increasing wealth of the West End – the same innovation could not be made by theatres such as the Olympic, or the Grand Theatre in Islington, without being financially ruinous for them. In effect, the theatres could now be demarcated by London's differential demographics, which they reflected, conditioned by the vast economic disparities in wealth and the relative poverty of its boroughs. Such social and economic conditions were increasingly reflected in the pricing of seats. Theatres such as the Surrey Theatre, located on Blackfriars Road in Lambeth, could hardly afford to charge West End prices, for this was an area that, according to Charles Booth's remarkable map describing the distribution of wealth and poverty in London, was populated in large part by residents classified as either 'vicious, semi-criminal' or in 'chronic want'. The West End theatres, meanwhile, were able to charge considerably more, drawing on a 'well-to-do' clientele.[27]

There was a further problem the Select Committee of 1866 rendered vivid, which was the problem of policing the theatres. Once again, this touched on the practical complications arising with the system of double jurisdiction: should the same police measures be applied to the music halls as were applied to the theatres, or should they be treated as separate cases? The immediate problem was that existing legislation provided 'no legal authority under which the police can take direct proceedings against unlicensed houses'.[28] The problem was redolent of the complex issues that derived from the decision to prohibit music halls from staging dramatic works. Since music halls were not entitled to perform the drama, they had no need of the licensor of plays, and that meant, in effect, they were free of the censor. One of the issues that consequently arose for the committee was whether or not music halls should come under the same 'prohibitory powers' as the theatres; indeed, how could they not if they were permitted to stage dramatic works? It was also asked, for that matter, why censorship should not be extended to cover the songs performed by the music halls, some of which contained highly questionable material. The issues here were never really resolved – primarily for pragmatic reasons.[29] But it also

[26] *The British Architect*, March 1892, p. 227.

[27] Charles Booth, *Booth's Maps of London Poverty, East and West 1889* (Old House Books, 2013).

[28] Report, 1866, p. iv.

[29] A further complication here is that the music halls, but not the theatres, fell under the Disorderly Houses Act, 25 George II, Chapter 36, 1751. The act remained in force into the twentieth century

explains, in part, the reluctance of the authorities to permit dramatic works in the music halls: it would have placed too great a burden on the examiner of plays, the task being both expensive and onerous. Still, the question remained: how did one ensure any 'security for morality and propriety of conduct' in the music halls?[30] The answer to that question also went some way to explaining why the executive favoured the status quo, and why no parliamentary legislation resulted from the 1866 Select Committee. There was little appetite for placing the music halls and theatres on the same footing, setting aside the fact that it would be almost 'impossible to enact adequate superintendence of every concert-room and music-hall in London at the same time'. Instead, ordinary police regulations were thought sufficient to maintain an appropriate level of public order, 'to keep all those places within the limits of respectable conduct'.[31] Thus, given the costs involved, the complexity of superintendence, not to say anything about the controversy involved in resolving the issue of double jurisdiction in placing the theatres and music halls on the same legislative footing, it is unsurprising that matters were left to resolve themselves, not by wholesale reform, but in piecemeal fashion.

But the debates of the committee also reflected the overwhelming discrepancy that existed in social attitudes in terms of the way in which theatre buildings were valued as opposed to those buildings that housed the music halls. It was an attitude that provided further justification for maintaining the separation of jurisdictions: whereas public houses and music halls were considered 'low' in significance, the theatres, by contrast, represented 'public buildings of great importance'.[32] The latter, after all, were licensed by the Lord Chamberlain, and his mandate could not be underestimated. It went a 'great way to keep [the theatres] in order'.[33] Little wonder the theatre managers saw the Chamberlain's licence and even his censorial powers in preferential terms. The more important the public building, after all, the more prestigious the amusement it housed; and the higher the level of protection it required, the more that superintendence and oversight needed to devolve to the appropriate authority. In other words, the theatres, coming under the jurisdiction of the Lord Chamberlain, derived their status and prestige from his office. Not only

and covered – as was remarked during the Select Committee of 1909 – the 'multitude of places of entertainment, which it impolitely describes as being for the lower sort of people, as a great cause of thefts and robberies . . .' *Report from the Joint Select Committee of the House of Lords and the House of Commons on the Stage Plays (Censorship)* – Ordered by the House of Commons, to be printed, 2 November 1909, p. 4.

30 Report, 1866, p. 7. 31 *Ibid.*, p. 8. 32 *Ibid.*, p. 24. 33 *Ibid.*, p. 24.

was it unnecessary to extend that authority to cover the music halls, it was hardly desirable to do so.

Establishments that provided entertainment to the lower orders required, by contrast, a different kind of supervision. Not only must a 'lower class of entertainment' be kept distinct from the higher class of amusements provided by theatres, it required a different form of superintendence; what it required was a practice of tactical supervision. An example of the extent of the tactical supervision of music halls by police can be found in the minutes of the proceedings that occurred following the Alhambra's application for a renewal of its licence in 1896. An objection had been raised – as was quite typical during the period – by the Social Purity Branch of the National Vigilance Association: 'that the drinking bars and promenades are permitted to be largely and habitually used as a resort of common prostitutes for the purposes of prostitution and immoral bargaining, and that excessive drinking, indecent conversation, and disorderly conduct takes place there'.[34] What is instructive is how the theatre's manager, Douglas Cox, responded to these allegations by outlining in great detail the extent of police surveillance in his theatre. Those 'exercising supervision' over the house included the manager, his assistants and janitors as well as the 'constables of the Metropolitan police – amounting to twenty nine [people] in all'.[35] Police were placed in different positions in the building: 'there is one man immediately at the bottom of the stairs, two at the top of the stairs, and two men furthermore on the promenade itself . . . there are men placed in different positions so that there is always a man in view of any portion of the audience.' And for this reason, he added, there is a 'very close supervision upon the conduct of all the persons there'.[36] Moreover, the women on the promenade could not be 'common prostitutes' for the following reason: 'we have a man down at the bottom who is an old constable, and who knows most of the common prostitutes.'[37] Indeed, he concluded, there was a policeman at the entrance 'who had instructions to refuse admittance to persons who are known to walk the streets'.[38]

What this reveals is precisely a form of supervision based on intelligence, provided by informants, the magistrates and the police, with their local knowledge, their familiarity with the audience and its weaknesses, and their acquaintance with 'ne'er-do-wells' and prostitutes. The Report of the

[34] Session of the Licensing Committee, 18 October 1894, in Theatres and Music Halls Licensing Sessions, Printed Papers, 1894–97, LCC/PC/ENT/2/2.

[35] *Ibid.*, p. 110. [36] *Ibid.*, p. 111. [37] *Ibid.*, p. 112. [38] *Ibid.*, p. 113.

Theatre and Music Halls Committee, on 24 July 1889, explicitly remarked on the desirability of

> placing before the Licensing Committee such information as may be in the possession of the Police, with respect to the various premises sought to be licensed for music or music and dancing. The members of the force have frequently been able to give valuable evidence to the justices as to the personal character of applicants for licenses, and also as to the manner in which their houses are conducted, and have been in the habit of attending the sessions for this purpose.[39]

What is revealed, then, in these examples is the way in which the police apparatus was wholly calculated to oversee a specific 'class of the community'. It was for this reason that the supervision of music halls was necessarily tactical, determined as it was by the problem of security, as the Middlesex magistrate Henry Pownall would assert in his testimony to the 1866 Select Committee: 'In a great measure those laws are framed to fence [the audience] round with security, so that they shall not be improperly drawn into temptation.'[40] In a sense, what was really under inspection in the music halls – and this was something that fundamentally differentiated them from the theatres – was not what occurred on the stage; it was what happened in the auditorium. This was the principal concern of the authorities. Sir Richard Mayne, Chief Commissioner of the Metropolitan Police, saw no reason to conceal this fact from the committee when he declared: 'The inspection of the police is rather an inspection of the audiences than of the pieces that are performed.' The police were concerned with 'indecencies and improprieties' in the crowd of onlookers; they focused on what was 'disorderly in the behaviour of the audience' – for instance, 'uproarious hooting', 'derisive applause', 'misdemeanours' and 'conspiracies'. Thus, it was the 'conduct of the people' and not the indiscretions on the stage that defined the policing of the music halls and the kinds of surveillance it required.[41]

It is for this reason, I think, that, finally, one can say the theatre *dispositif* of the late nineteenth century produced a machine whose cogs, gears and wheels – however cumbrous they appeared to be from a certain point of view – were nonetheless scrupulously coordinated to ensure a singular result: the transformation of the multiple and differentiated sites of theatrical production into a bifurcated space of distinction. In this way, the general tendency of the government of the stage was by now turned quite

[39] Report of the Theatre and Music Halls Committee, London County Council, 24 July 1889, p. 664.
[40] Report, 1866, p. 26 [41] *Ibid.*, p. 39.

fundamentally towards the regulation of an entire social milieu, whose limits and frontiers were established by the preconceptions of discourse, and whose effect on practices was to fix them in their proper locality – thus stabilising whatever potentially transgressive effects might be released by the forms of exchange previously associated with theatrical commerce. This tendency of government towards the polarisation of the social terrain was summarised in a rather sardonic question put by the committee to the Assistant Judge for Middlesex, William Henny Bodkin, when he was asked: '[Is it] your opinion that the poorer class of people should have one class of men to license entertainments for them, and that the richer class should have the Lord Chamberlain to licence entertainments for them?'[42] The question may as well have been rhetorical: what it acknowledged was nothing less than the underlying prejudice of governmental discourse; but it also contained that long-sought-after recognition – that the legitimate theatre had earned the 'right', so to speak, to be treated quite differently from common forms of entertainment. What the governmentalisation of the stage produces, in other words, is the idea that the legitimate theatre in London had at last earned the right to a certain kind of autonomy *from* government – a right that, as the century drew to an end, it would begin to assert in a quite remarkable way.

From Theatre's *Dispositif* to the Autonomy of the Stage

There can be little doubting, or so claimed a group of dramatic authors as the new century began to encroach on the old, that theatre's autonomy from government was the prerequisite for an intellectual, rigorous and, above all, serious drama. And yet this by no means entailed the abandonment of the stage by government or the dismantling of its *dispositif*, any more than it envisaged the return of the stage to a state of immoderation, licentiousness or unbridled vulgarity – to a theatrocratic state of savagery. On the contrary, theatre's autonomy from government could be secured only by means of government, and only insofar as theatre accepted and embraced its fundamental responsibility *to* government. It is to this suggestion, paradoxical as it may seem, that I would like to turn in concluding this book, for the twentieth century, in its tumultuous incipiency, brought this idea – that of the rights of an autonomous stage – to a level of critical visibility that quite frankly blindsided the old discursive order. And it did so by means of a bold demand that rejected outright what

[42] *Ibid.*, p. 72.

had hitherto dominated the discourse on the theatre – indeed, that had hitherto dominated the theatre over the previous two centuries. It was a demand that quite literally stood that discourse on its head. This is not to say that what occurred in the closing decade of the nineteenth and inaugural decade of the twentieth century brought to an end the controversies over the government of the stage; but it is to say that a Rubicon was decisively crossed from which there would be no turning back. Discourse itself was breached – not by another discourse, however, and not by a 'counter-discourse', but by an implacably executed discursive manoeuvre that occupied the very terrain of the governmental discourse on the stage by specifically targeting its deontic logic along with its emblematic figure, 'the censor'.

This demand would be fuelled in no small part by the phenomenon of Ibsenism that arrived in London in the 1880s – although Ibsen merely provided the accelerant that ignited the flames of a new theatrical revolt against the Lord Chamberlain's office. In his fiercely argued essay of 1886, *The Censorship of the Stage*, William Archer pronounced – as Shaw would also do elsewhere – that the problem of theatre governance, far from being resolved by the censor's office, was actually exacerbated by it. Censorship, in fact, was directly responsible for a crisis of morality in the theatre. This was because what censorship repressed was not immorality, which in any case it failed to understand, but the kind of theatre Archer wanted to see: a theatre 'better qualified to grapple with ethical questions'.[43] For Archer, the problem could never be resolved by a government fixated on producing a deontic stage; it required a government capable of accepting an *immoral* theatre, understanding that here, in Archer's words,

> there is a distinction to be drawn between the different senses in which the word 'immorality' is commonly used. It is applied on the one hand to indecency, obscenity, pruriency, and on the other to any form of thought or action, however conscientious, earnest, and high-principled, which transgresses the conventional rules of social decorum . . . Vulgar sensualism, and devotion to ideals more advanced than those of the crowd, are in popular parlance alike immoral. Now the policy of good government, if good government had in reality anything to do with the matter, would clearly be to repress the former and to give the latter as much currency as popular prejudice would allow.[44]

[43] William Archer, 'The Censorship of the Stage', in *About the Theatre: Essays and Studies* (London: T. Fisher Unwin, 1886), p. 164.

[44] *Ibid.*, pp. 163–64.

Thus there was an immorality that should be viewed as the theatre's highest achievement; and there was the old immorality to be guarded against and shunned, associated with the theatrocratic conduct of the vulgar. It was the same argument Shaw would use a few years later in his defence of Ibsen: 'The statement that Ibsen's plays have an immoral tendency is, in the sense in which it is used, quite true. Immorality does not necessarily imply mischievous conduct: it implies conduct, mischievous or not, which does not conform to current ideals.'[45] These arguments, rehearsed over a number of years, would be used to devastating effect by Shaw in 1909 when he appeared before the Joint Select Committee of the House of Lords and the House of Commons, which had been assembled to examine the question of stage censorship. During the hearings of 1892, only one witness – William Archer – had spoken against the censorship, but by 1909 the issue was no longer so clear-cut, with the majority of dramatic authors demanding an end to government interference. It was only the theatre managers who wanted to retain governmental control over plays – primarily due to the fear that they would be subject to *ex post facto* prosecutions of performances, as they put it, should *a priori* censorship of plays be abandoned. It would, they argued – and, as it turns out, rather persuasively – be financially ruinous for them to see plays banned, after having already invested in the full costs of production. The situation presented the committee, then, with something of a dilemma, conceding, as it did on the one hand, the wishes of the managers and public to maintain censorship, lest it lead to a 'gradual demoralisation of the stage',[46] while on the other hand recognising that official control 'conventionalises the stage', hampering a critically engaged drama, capable of examining contemporary life and 'customary ideas'.[47] The committee arrived at an outcome that favoured the managers: 'We conclude that the producers of plays should have access, prior to their production, to a public authority which should be empowered to license plays as suitable for performance.'[48] But it also acknowledged the validity of the objection to the censor, agreeing with Shaw and Archer that the 'conventional standards of the day' were 'not absolute' and that the theatre, which was 'attracting writers of intellect' and was intent on producing 'sincere and serious dramas, critical of existing conventions', was, if not exactly suppressed, certainly 'hampered' by the existence of censorship.[49]

[45] George Bernard Shaw, *The Quintessence of Ibsenism* (London: Walter Scott, 1891), p. 129.
[46] Report, 1909, p. xxvi. [47] *Ibid.*, p. xxv. [48] *Ibid.*, p. xxvi. [49] *Ibid.*, p. xxvii.

The inevitable reassertion of the status quo infuriated Shaw, who would later write that the case against censorship was 'overwhelming'; yet while the committee was 'unanimous as to the necessity of reforming the censorship ... unfortunately, the majority attached to this unanimity the usual condition that nothing should be done to disturb the existing state of things'.[50] Despite admitting the failings of censorship, government opted to sit on its hands – as Shaw complained: 'Everything is to be changed and nothing is to be changed.'[51] But this is to underestimate the subtle impact Shaw's appearance before the Select Committee would have. Actually, he had caused a degree of controversy that helped publicise his cause – publicity gifted to him in no small part by the committee itself when they deemed inadmissible as evidence a written memorandum that Shaw had prepared for them, despite the precedent of Henry Irving, who had successfully submitted a written statement during the proceedings of 1892.[52] Shaw later reflected: 'As far as I can guess, [what] happened was that some timid or unawakened member of the Committee read my statement and was frightened or scandalized out of his wits by it.'[53] At any rate, as a consequence of its notoriety, the suppressed statement was immediately publicised and disseminated to the public beyond the committee room. Shaw himself published a summary of it in *The Times* the following day, before republishing the document in its entirety as part of the preface to *The Shewing-Up of Blanco Posnet* later that year. And what the statement articulated – as did Shaw's testimony to the startled committee members who heard him speak (since they could hardly deny him that right, having invited him) – was nothing less than the intellectual case for the development of a fully autonomous theatre. Even if the censorship continued, as it would do, well into the twentieth century (abolition came with the passing of the Theatres Act of 1968), it could do so only on the basis of ever-increasing anachronism; and what rendered it anachronistic was that, from that point on, the theatre and its 'purpose' would be divorced from the principle of deontic governance to which it had for so long been shackled.

This is what the suppressed statement argued: not that the theatre should be exempt from law, but that it should be released from the deontic mentality of government. There are in fact broadly three lines of argument pursued by Shaw here. In the first instance, the problem was

[50] George Bernard Shaw, 'Preface to *The Shewing-Up of Blanco Posnet*', in *Prefaces by Bernard Shaw* (London: Constable and Company, 1934 [1909]), p. 399.

[51] *Ibid.* [52] Report, 1909, p. 47. [53] Shaw, *Prefaces*, p. 404.

not so much government but the managers. Why, he asked, did the managers of theatres 'love censorship'? The reason was really quite practical: the manager was not a man who was 'expert in politics, religion, art, literature, philosophy, or law' – he was a 'man of business'. As such, he was something of a philistine. Consequently, most managers were unable to judge if a 'play [was] safe from prosecution or not'. On the other hand, every manager knew that to produce a play was to accept legal responsibility for it, 'as if he had written it himself'. Which is why the manager of the theatre would always reject the *ex post facto* solution to censorship: 'His sole refuge is the opinion of the Examiner of plays, his sole protection the license of the Lord Chamberlain.' The censor's refusal to issue a play with a licence did not harm the manager since he was always able to produce a different play. It was only the dramatic author who suffered. And when a play was issued with a licence, then the manager had all the insurance from prosecution he needed – for the Lord Chamberlain's licence 'place[d] him above the law'; it provided him with *de facto* immunity from prosecution.[54] But Shaw countered: inasmuch as it conferred a special privilege on the plays it licensed, censorship worked against the very principle of sound government it professed to embody. Why should the theatre be subject to special privileges when all other art forms and even the newspapers were treated as equal *under* the law? This was Shaw's question and, behind it, his core argument: that the theatre would be better governed without censorship, since in removing the Lord Chamberlain's protection (for managers) every play and production would be rendered equally liable under the law:

> The abolition of the censorship does not involve the abolition of the magistrate and of the whole civil and criminal code. On the contrary, it would make the theatres more effectually subject to them than it is at present; for once a play now runs the gauntlet of the censorship, it is practically placed above the law.[55]

Freedom from censorship would not produce anarchy, as most feared; nor would it result in a wholly unregulated stage or a return to theatrocratic disorder – quite the opposite. Here Shaw's argument drew out the full lesson of the paradox of government, mentioned earlier. To render the stage autonomous from government was to ensure not less but, rather, more appropriate government: 'It must not be concluded that the uncompromising abolition of all censorship involves the abandonment of all

[54] *Ibid.*, p. 401. [55] *Ibid.*, p. 413.

control and regulation of theatres.'[56] In this sense, the theatre *dispositif*, as it developed in the latter part of the nineteenth century, did so as something quite distinct from the form of theatre government based on the censorship of plays. Even if it could (and did) work in conjunction with that older system, whose origins dated as far back as the Master of the Revels, it did not need to. And indeed, in Shaw's terms, the new system was far more effective in its administration of the social dimension of the theatre. After all, as Shaw pointed out, it was not censorship that preserved the legitimate theatre from corruption, and not least because censorship was quite incapable of preventing the social ills that brought the theatres into disrepute, such as prostitution and so on. (Had not Macready already laid the groundwork for this new system when he drove prostitution from his theatre?) It was only with the development of a comprehensive system for the licensing of theatres – only with the development of the theatre *dispositif*, in other words – that one might find a 'better means ... for securing the orderly conduct of houses of public entertainment, dramatic or other'.[57] No manager would dare risk his licence by allowing his house to fall into disrepute, given that licences would be reviewed on an annual basis.

There was a second line of argument, however, and this was that censorship, even on its own limited terms, did not work. It did not produce the effects it claimed to produce; it did not produce, as it were, a 'deontic' stage. On the contrary, it had 'sanctioned and protected the very worst practicable examples of the kind of play it professed to extirpate'.[58] The Achilles heel of censorship was found by looking not at the 'fine plays it has suppressed, but [at] the abominable plays it has licensed'.[59] This was the true nature of the paradox that arose from the deontic governance of the stage: the censorship did not inhibit theatrocratic corruption; it first encouraged it and then – by the very means provided by government – validated it. Where once it was the player who pandered to the base inclinations of the crowd, it was now government itself that sought the 'support of the mob – that is, of the unreasoning, unorganized, uninstructed mass of popular sentiment'. This was the flawed logic of government, which rendered the mob 'indispensable to the censorship as it exists today in England'.[60]

Denouncing the perverse effects of the Examiner's power, Shaw remarked, in conclusion:

[56] *Ibid.*, p. 422. [57] *Ibid.*, p. 423. [58] *Ibid.*, p. 403. [59] *Ibid.*, p. 404. [60] *Ibid.*, p. 417.

> The Lord Chamberlain dare not, in short, attempt to exclude from the stage the tragedies of murder and lust, or the forces of mendacity, adultery, and dissolute gaiety in which vulgar people delight. But when these same vulgar people are threatened with an unpopular play in which dissoluteness is shewn to be no laughing matter, it is prohibited at once amid the vulgar applause, the net result being that vice is made delightful and virtue banned by the very institution which is supported on the understanding that it produces exactly the opposite result.[61]

To bring an end to censorship, then, is to make possible a theatre that will not only be free from government interference – it will also, for Shaw, be free from the influence of popular taste, with all its stupidity, coarseness and venality. An autonomous stage is thus a 'free stage' in these two related senses: it is free from government intrusion (because) it is free from the corrupting influence of common life and the crudeness of common tastes.

But free for what, exactly? This question leads to the third and most important part of Shaw's argument, which is that it will be free to develop an *immoral* theatre – that is to say, a theatre that is no longer constrained to reproduce the precepts of deontic power, a theatre that is no longer required to preach its lesson to the audience, a theatre, in short, that will be free to openly practise its heresy in critically departing from the false wisdom of social convention. Shaw is remarkably insistent on this point: 'I am not an ordinary playwright in general practice. I am a specialist in immoral and heretical plays. My reputation has been gained by my persistent struggle to force the public to reconsider its morals.'[62] To understand this new 'heresy' of the stage – this freedom from orthodoxy – is to begin to understand the nature of the break announced by Shaw with the previous regime of theatre governance. This, I suggest, is Shaw's fundamental challenge, not just to the power of censorship but to the entire deontic orientation that had dominated the governance of the stage since the eighteenth century.

As with Archer, for Shaw, key to this is to understand the true nature of immorality:

> Whatever is contrary to established manners and customs is immoral. An act or doctrine is not necessarily a sinful one: on the contrary, every advance in thought and conduct is by definition immoral until it has converted the majority. For this reason it is of enormous importance that immorality should be protected jealously against the attacks of those who have no

[61] *Ibid.*, p. 418. [62] *Ibid.*, pp. 408–9.

> standard except the standard of custom, and who regard any attack on custom – that is, on morals – as an attack on society, on religion, and on virtue.[63]

It is here that Shaw's objection to the censor becomes fully visible. The objective of the censor is to protect morality. But what, after all, asks Shaw, does it mean to 'protect' morality? To begin to understand how Shaw answers this question, one must first understand that the aim of censorship is at one with the wider governmentality: it is to impose upon the 'great mass of persons who are incapable of original ethical judgement' the forms of conventional conduct that society requires of them if it is to cohere. For Shaw, there is nothing intrinsically wrong about this requirement, of course – indeed, a form of deontic governmentality is needed so as to provide, for those who would otherwise be 'quite lost', the 'leading-strings devised by lawgivers, philosophers, prophets and poets for their guidance'.[64] But this is to concede that the acceptable standards of social conduct among the wider population are seldom if ever grounded upon individual acts of conscience. Rather, their conduct is governed through publicly instilled morality, by an insistence on convention and custom, without which society could not function. And yet by the same token, no society can progress if it is wholly dominated by such forces – and this is where the problem with theatre censorship arises for Shaw. All great advances, whether in scientific knowledge or in social progress, arise not from conformity to convention, through which society stagnates, but from heretical acts that defy the existing social mores and moral codes established by deontic power. Heresy is not in and of itself an evil; it designates the very space of progress and its principal mechanism, making possible the 'march of enlightenment'.[65] It signifies the necessity for a discursive space uninhibited by government and dedicated to genuinely critical endeavour. This is the space of autonomy that the censorship of the stage suppresses – and along with it the very possibility of engendering a new theatre and an enlightened stage.

For this is what the new theatre will be – the theatre of Shaw's future: it will be a critical theatre that demands for itself the right to challenge and disturb existing custom. This does not mean it will produce plays that cheaply offend the public by egregiously transgressing the laws of the land, producing blasphemies and libels with impunity (indeed, in stark contrast to the theatre under censorship, the new system of governance – as Shaw

[63] *Ibid.*, p. 409. [64] *Ibid.* [65] *Ibid.*

envisions it – will not exempt the stage from law).[66] No, these – says Shaw, in his testimony to the committee – will be plays that are 'conscientiously immoral'.[67] To be conscientiously immoral is to adopt a higher ethical standpoint that understands morality as purely conventional, as something that can thus, within certain limits, be defied. Immorality then becomes the name under which an emancipated theatre operates, a theatre that is no longer the place in which social conduct is merely reaffirmed unquestioningly. It is a theatre that consequently derives its authority not from its mission as an instrument of deontic power but from the critical attitude that now animates it. Such a theatre will no longer be a school for morals; instead, the lessons of the stage will henceforth teach its audience to question those norms of conduct that they have taken for granted: it will teach its auditors to become critics of the conventions by which they have hitherto allowed themselves to be governed.

And yet what of government itself, should such an independent theatre actually exist? Must the role of government recede entirely from all interference or engagement with the stage? Must it have no interest in what the stage is or does? Not so, proclaims Shaw. It is possible, after all, to imagine a different role for government and to conceive a different way for the stage to be governed. For this one must be alert to the fact that it is not immorality, but *morality*, that requires 'restraint' – just as democratic excess, and the blight of theatrocracy with which it is associated, must be continually resisted and repelled to ensure theatre's new-found autonomy. Government's new role must be grasped in relation to this double insight. Only then will the proper role of government vis-à-vis the theatre be established; and then, only on the basis of a fundamental precondition, which asserts that the entire logic of censorship – and along with it, of the old governmentality – is finally to be reversed. Then – and only then – will it be understood that it is 'immorality, not morality, that needs protection'.[68] Thus the 'deontic' stage will be eclipsed, finally, by a theatre that proclaims immorality to be the highest ideal or virtue worthy of the modern drama.

Conclusion

To be sure, the struggle for an autonomous stage continued to define much of the course of theatrical history during the twentieth century in Britain. While the complexity of that struggle – its advances and its

66 Shaw argued before the Select Committee of 1909: 'I may offend against the law, and I am responsible for what I do; but I am responsible to the law and not to . . . the Lord Chamberlain [and his Examiner].' Report, 1909, p. 48.

67 *Ibid.* 68 Shaw, *Prefaces*, p. 409.

setbacks, its causes célèbres, its sacrifices and its martyrs, as well as its ultimate victory – merits more discussion than I have space for here, that an autonomous theatre came into existence is a matter of fact and of historical record. More difficult to discern, I think, is what that autonomy signifies – understanding autonomy, as I have done in this study, in relation to the way in which the stage came under the influence of modern forms of government from which it was then compelled to liberate itself. That goal of autonomy was accomplished with the passing of the Theatres Act of 1968, which repealed the Theatres Act of 1843, signifying the end of the powers of censorship invested by royal prerogative in the Lord Chamberlain's office. No longer would the theatre be required to submit to the demands of deontic governmentality; no longer would it either be subject to coercive constraints, designed to suppress tendencies deemed to encourage the 'demoralisation' of the audience, or demonstrate to a censorious public that it had become an instrument for the reformation of the manners and morals of the people to whom it was addressed. Still, if the Act, proclaiming that no licensing authority would henceforth have the power 'to impose any term, condition or restriction as to the nature of the plays which may be performed under the license', succeeded in liberating the theatres from legal censorship, it by no means disentangled theatre from its entanglement with government.[69] As I have suggested in this chapter, theatre's autonomy was won only insofar as it came under the aegis of the theatre *dispositif*, grasped as an alternative mode of theatre governance. What this study has sought to show is the long and complex history that first made that alternative possible, of how theatre came to occupy a space whose intellectual freedoms, whose cultural exclusivity and whose critical formation required that it expel once and for all the 'old corruption' that had tainted its reputation, within the discourse on theatre, for so long. This recurrent motif of 'the lawfulness of the stage', which, as I have suggested, should be understood in terms of an 'anti-theatrocratic prejudice', fully permeates the intellectual privilege of the modern theatre. It is a privilege in the strict sense that it could be granted only at the expense of the social reification of the stage. It is for this reason that although the autonomous stage was able to establish a remarkable critical relation to the social world, for the first time in its history, without fear of government interference, it could do so only by opening up an immeasurable distance that would permanently separate it from the interests of common life. It is a distance that today's theatre is still struggling to traverse.

[69] www.legislation.gov.uk/ukpga/1968/54/section/1.

Works Consulted

Abbott, Charles, *An Essay on the Use and Abuse of Satire* (London, 1786).

Anthony, Sister Rose, *The Jeremy Collier Stage Controversy, 1698–1723* (New York: Benjamin Blom, 1966 [1937]).

Archer, William, *About the Theatre: Essays and Studies* (London: T. Fisher Unwin, 1886).

Bacon, Francis, *The Works of Francis Bacon*, vol. 2 (London, 1740).

Essays Moral, Economical and Political (London: T Payne, 1800).

The Works of Francis Bacon, vol. 4 (London, 1815 [1620]).

Baer, Marc, *Theatre and Disorder in Late Georgian London* (Oxford: Clarendon Press, 1992).

Barish, Jonas, *The Anti-theatrical Prejudice* (Berkeley: University of California Press, 1981).

Barnard, Sir John, *A Present for an Apprentice: Or a Sure Guide to Gain Both Esteem and Estate: With Rules for Conduct to His Master, and in the World* (London: William Innes, 1743).

Baxter, Richard, *A Christian Directory*, vol. 2 (London: R. White, 1673).

The Practical Works of Richard Baxter in Four Volumes, vol. 1 (London: Arthur Hall, 1847).

The Reformed Pastor (London, 1888 [1655]).

Bentham, Jeremy, *Management of the Poor, or, a Plan, Containing the Principles and Construction of an Establishment, in Which Persons of Any Description Are to Be Kept under Supervision* (London, 1796).

Rationale of Judicial Evidence, vol. 1 (London, 1823).

Constitutional Code for the Use of All Nations and Governments Professing Liberal Opinions (London: Robert Heward, 1830).

From Mss. of Jeremy Bentham, vol. 1, ed. John Bowring (London: Longman, 1834).

Bird, J.B., *The Laws Respecting Masters and Servants; Articled Clerks, Apprentices, Journeymen and Manufacturers* (London: W. Clarke and Son, 1795).

Blackmore, Sir Richard, *A Satyr against Wit* (London, 1697).

Blackstone, Sir William, *Commentaries on the Laws of England in Four Books* (New York: W.E. Dean, 1842).

Blencowe, Claire, *Biopolitical Experience: Foucault, Power and Positive Critique* (Basingstoke: Palgrave Macmillan, 2012).

Bodin, Jean, *On Sovereignty*, trans. Julian H. Franklin (Cambridge: Cambridge University Press, 1992).
Boltanski, Luc, and Laurent Thévenot, 'The Sociology of Critical Capacity', *European Journal of Social Theory*, **2**:3 (1999), 359–77.
Booth, Charles, *Booth's Maps of London Poverty, East and West 1889* (Old House Books, 2013).
Botero, Giovanni, *A Treatise Concerning the Causes of the Magnificencie and Greatness of Cities*, trans. Robert Peterson (London, 1606).
Reason of State, trans. P.J. Waley and D.P. Waley (London: Routledge & Kegan Paul, 1956).
Bradbrook, Muriel Clara, *The Rise of the Common Player: A Study of Actor and Society in Shakespeare's England* (London: Chatto & Windus, 1962).
Brathwaite, Richard, *The English Gentlewoman* (London: B. Alsop & T. Favvcet, 1631).
Bratton, Jacky, *New Readings in Theatre History* (Cambridge: Cambridge University Press, 2003).
Brewer, John, and John Styles, *An Ungovernable People: The English and Their Law in the Seventeenth and Eighteenth Centuries* (London: Hutchinson, 1983).
Brooks, Peter, *The Melodramatic Imagination: Balzac, Henry James, Melodrama, and the Mode of Excess* (New Haven, CT: Yale University Press, 1995).
Brown, John, *An Essay on Satire* (London: R. Dodsley, 1749).
Buckle, James George, *Theatre Construction and Maintenance* (London, 1888).
Bullock, Christopher, *Woman's Revenge: or, a match in Newgate. A comedy. As it is acted at the Royal Theatre in Lincoln's-Inn-Fields. The Second Edition. To which is added, a compleat key to The beggar's opera, by Peter Padwell of Padington, Esq;*. (London: J. Roberts, 1728)
Bunyan, John, *Christian Behaviour* (London, 1674).
Burnett, Thomas, *An Essay upon Government; or, the Natural Notions of Government, Demonstrated in a Chain of Consequences from the Fundamental Principles of Society* (Dublin and London: T. Warner, 1716).
Burwick, Frederick, *Playing to the Crowd: London Popular Theatre, 1780–1830* (Basingstoke: Palgrave Macmillan, 2011).
Calvin, John, *Institutes of Christian Religion*, trans. Thomas Norton (London, 1561).
Carlson, Marvin, *Theories of the Theatre: A Historical and Critical Survey, from the Greeks to the Present* (Ithaca, NY: Cornell University Press, 1993).
Cassirer, Ernst, *The Myth of the State*, trans. Charles W. Hendel (New Haven, CT: Yale University Press, 1974 [1946]).
Chambers, Edmund K., *The Elizabethan Stage*, vol. 4 (London: Clarendon Press, 1923).
Chesterfield, Earl, *A Collection of the Parliamentary Debates in England from the Year M, DC, LXVIII to the Present Time* (London, 1740).
Christian, Lynda G. *Theatrum Mundi: The History of an Idea* (Harvard Dissertations in Comparative Literature) (New York: Garland, 1987).
Cleary, Thomas, *Henry Fielding: A Political Writer* (Waterloo: Wilfrid Laurier University Press, 1984).

Collier, Jeremy, *A Short View of the Immorality and Profaneness of the English Stage* (London: S. Keble, 1698).
A Defense of the Short View of the Profaneness and Immorality of the English Stage (London: S. Keble, 1699).
Essays upon Several Moral Subjects, Part III (London: George Strahan, 1720).
Cook, Anne J., *The Privileged Playgoers of Shakespeare's London* (Princeton, NJ: Princeton University Press, 1992).
Cordner, Michael, 'Marriage Comedy after the 1688 Revolution: Southerne to Vanbrugh', *Modern Language Review*, **85**:2 (1990, April), 273–89.
Corrigan, Philip, and Derek Sayer, *The Great Arch, English State Formation as Cultural Revolution* (Oxford: Blackwell, 1985).
Critchley, Simon, and Jamieson Webster, *Stay Illusion! The Hamlet Doctrine* (New York: Pantheon, 2013).
Curtius, Ernst, *European Literature and the Latin Middle Ages* (Princeton, NJ: Princeton University Press, 1990).
Dale, Richard, *The First Crash: Lessons from the South Sea Bubble* (Princeton, NJ: Princeton University Press, 2004).
Davis, Jim, 'Spectatorship', in *Cambridge Companion to British Theatre 1730–1830*, ed. Jane Moody and Daniel O'Quinn (Cambridge: Cambridge University Press, 2007), pp. 57–69.
Davis, Tracy C., *The Economics of the British Stage, 1800–1914* (Cambridge: Cambridge University Press, 2000).
Dean, Mitchell, *The Constitution of Poverty: Toward a Genealogy of Liberal Governance* (Oxon: Routledge, 1991).
Governmentality, Power and Rule in Modern Society (London: Sage, 2010).
Defoe, Daniel, *The Complete English Tradesman, in Familiar Letters: Directing Him in all the Several Parts and Progressions of Trade*, 2nd edition (London: Charles Rivington, 1727).
Second Thoughts Are Best: or, a Further Improvement of a Late Scheme to Prevent Street Robberies (London: W. Meadows, 1729).
Dekker, Thomas, *The Gull's Hornbook, or Fashions to Please All Sorts of Gulls* (London: J.M. Gutch, 1609).
Dennis, John, *The Advancement and Reformation of Modern Poetry: A Critical Discourse* (London: Rich. Parker, 1701).
The Grounds of Criticism in Poetry (London, 1704).
The Usefulness of the Stage to Religion, and to Government (London, 1738).
Dollimore, Jonathan, *Radical Tragedy, Religion, Ideology and Power in the Drama of Shakespeare and His Contemporaries* (Basingstoke: Palgrave Macmillan, 2010).
Ellezweiz, Sarah, 'The Faith of Unbelief', *Journal of British Studies*, **44**:1 (2005), 27–45.
Elyot, Thomas, *The Book Named the Govenour* (London: John Hernaman and Ridgeway and Sons, 1834 [1564]).
Evans, G. Blakemore, ed., *Attitudes Toward the Drama in Elizabethan-Jacobean England: The Theatre in Its Time*, (New York: New Amsterdam Books, 1990).

Fawcett, John, *Advice to Youth; or, the Advantages of Early Piety. Designed for the Use of Schools, as well as Young Apprentices and Servants, and the British Youth in General: To Draw the Attention to Matters of the Greatest Importance in Early Life*, 2nd edition (London and Leeds: G. Wright and Son, 1780).

Fielding, Henry, *Some Thoughts on the Present State of the Theatres, and the Consequences of an Act to Destroy the Liberty of the Stage* (London, 1737).

The Historical Register as It Was Acted at the New Theatre in the Hay-market. To Which Is Added a Very Merry TRAGEDY, called Eurydice Hiss'd, or, A Word to the Wise (London, 1744 [1737]).

An Enquiry into the Cause of the Late Increase of Robbers, &c. with Some Proposals for Remedying This Growing Evil (London: A. Millar, 1751).

A Proposal for Making an Effectual Provision for the Poor (London: John Smith, 1753).

The Works of Henry Fielding, Esq. with A Life of the Author in Twelve Volumes, vol. 4 (London: Richards's and Co, 1824 (1737)).

Fletcher, Anthony, and John Stevenson, *Order and Disorder in Early Modern England* (London: Cambridge University Press, 1985).

Foucault, Michel, *The Archaeology of Knowledge*, trans. A.M. Sheridan Smith (New York: Pantheon, 1972).

'The Confession of the Flesh', in *Power/Knowledge, Selected Interviews and Other Writings 1972–1977*, ed. and trans. Colin Gordon (Essex: Longman, 1980).

Discipline and Punish, the Birth of the Prison, trans. Alan Sheridan (London: Penguin, 1991).

Power, Essential Works of Foucault 1954–1984, vol. 3, ed. James B. Faubion (New York: New Press, 2000).

Abnormal, Lectures at the Collège de France, 1974–1975, trans. Graham Burchell (New York: Picador, 2003).

The Birth of Biopolitics, Lectures at the Collège de France, 1978–1979, trans. G. Burchell (New York: Palgrave Macmillan, 2008).

Security, Territory, Population, Lectures at the Collège de France, 1977–1978, trans. G. Burchell (New York: Palgrave Macmillan, 2009).

Lectures on the Will to Know, Lectures at the Collège de France, 1970–1971 and Oedipal Knowledge, trans. Graham Burchell (Basingstoke: Palgrave Macmillan, 2013).

The Punitive Society, Lectures at the Collège de France, 1972–1973, trans. Graham Burchell (Basingstoke: Palgrave Macmillan, 2015).

Freeman, Lisa A., *Character's Theatre: Genre and Identity on the Eighteenth-Century English Stage* (Philadelphia: University of Pennsylvania Press, 2002).

'Jeremy Collier and the Politics of Theatrical Representation', in *Players, Playwrights, Playhouses: Investigating Performance, 1660-1800*, ed. Michael Cordner and Peter Holland (New York: Palgrave Macmillan, 2007), pp. 135–51.

Frick, John W., '"Not from the Drowsy Pulpit!": The Moral Reform Melodrama on the Nineteenth-Century Stage', in *Theatre Symposium: Theatre and Moral Order*, vol. 15 (Tuscaloosa: University of Alabama Press, 2007).

Gatrell, Vic C., *The Hanging Tree, Execution and the English People 1770–1868* (Oxford: Oxford University Press, 1994).

Gouge, William, *Of Domesticall Duties* (London: George Miller, 1622).

Gray, Charles Harold, *Theatrical Criticism in London to 1795* (New York: Columbia University Press, 1931).

Grigg, D.B., *Population Growth and Agrarian Change: An Historical Perspective* (Cambridge: Cambridge University Press, 1980).

Grimaldi, Joseph, *Memoires of Joseph Grimaldi*, vols. 1–4 (London, 1838).

Gurr, Andrew, *Playgoing in Shakespeare's London* (Cambridge: Cambridge University Press, 2004).

Habermas, Jürgen, *The Structural Transformation of the Public Sphere*, trans. Thomas Burger (Cambridge: Polity Press, 2008 [1962]).

Legitimation Crisis, trans. T. McCarthy (London: Heinemann, 1976).

Hammer, Stephanie Barbé, *The Sublime Crime: Fascination, Failure, and Form in Literature of the Enlightenment* (Edwardsville: Southern Illinois University, 1994).

Hanway, Jonas, *Moral and Religious Instructions, Intended for Apprentices, and also for Parish Poor; with Prayers from the Liturgy, and Others, Adapted to Private Use* (London: J. Rivington, 1767).

The Citizen's Monitor, Shewing the Necessity of a Salutary Police, Executed by Resolute and Judicious Magistrates (London: J. Dodsley, 1780).

Hart, Gail Kathleen, *Tragedy in Paradise: Family and Gender Politics in German Bourgeois Tragedy 1750–1850* (Columbia, SC: Camden House, 1996).

Heinemann, Margot, *Puritanism and Theatre, Thomas Middleton and Opposition Drama under the Early Stuarts* (Cambridge: Cambridge University Press, 1982).

Heywood, Thomas, *An Apology for Actors* (London: Garland, 1973 [1612]).

Hobbes, Thomas, *On the Citizen*, ed. Richard Truck and Michael Silverthorne (Cambridge: Cambridge University Press, 2010).

Houston, Robert Allan, *The Population History of Britain and Ireland 1550–1750* (Cambridge: Cambridge University Press, 1995).

Ibbett, Katherine, *The Style of the State in French Theatre 1630–1660: Neoclassicism and Government* (Farnham: Ashgate, 2009).

Ingrassia, Catherine, 'Money and Sexuality in the Enlightenment: George Lillo's *The London Merchant*', *Historical Reflections/Réflexions Historiques*, **31**:1 (2005), 93–116.

Jacob, Giles, *Liberty and Property: or, A New Year's Gift for Mr Pope. Being a Concise Treatise on all the Laws, Statutes and Ordinances, made for the Benefit and Protection of the Subjects of England* (London: J. Baker, 1736).

Johnson, Samuel, *Dr. Johnson's Works. Miscellaneous Pieces, the Works of Samuel Johnson, LL.D, in Nine Volumes*, vol. 5 (Oxford: William Pickering, 1825 [1739]).

Jonson, Ben, *The Works of Ben Jonson, in Nine Volumes*, vol. 2, ed. W. Gifford (London: W. Bulmer and Co, 1816).

Kearsley, George, *Kearsley's Table of Trades, for the Assistance of Parents and Guardians, and for the Benefit of those Young Men, Who Wish to Prosper in the World, and Become Respectable Members of Society* (London, 1787).

Kelleher, Joe, *Theatre and Politics* (Basingstoke: Palgrave Macmillan, 2009).
Kern, Jean B., *Dramatic Satire in the Age of Walpole, 1720–1750* (Ames: Iowa State University Press, 1976).
Kinservik, Matthew J., *Disciplining Satire: The Censorship of Satiric Comedy on the Eighteenth Century London Stage* (Lewisburg, PA: Bucknell University Press, 2002).
Leggatt, Alexander, *Jacobean Public Theatre* (London: Routledge, 1992).
Lemmings, David, *Law and Government in England during the Long Eighteenth Century: From Consent to Command* (Basingstoke: Palgrave Macmillan, 2011).
Liesenfeld, Vincent J., *The Licensing Act of 1737* (Madison: University of Wisconsin Press, 1984).
Lillo, George, *The London Merchant; or, the History of George Barnwell. As It Is Acted at the Theatre-Royal in Drury Lane* (London: J. Gray, 1731).
Lipsius, Justus, *Sixe Bookes of Politickes or Civil Doctrine*, trans. William Jones (London: William Ponsonby, 1594).
Locke, John, *The Reasonableness of Christianity: As Delivered in the Scriptures* (London: Awnsham and John Churchill, 1696).
The Lord Chamberlain Regrets: A History of British Theatre Censorship, ed. Dominic Shellard, Steve Nicholson and Miriam Handley (London: British Library, 2004).
Loftis, John, *The Politics of Drama in Augustan England* (Oxford: Clarendon Press, 1963).
Madan, Martin, *Thoughts on Executive Justice, with Respect to our Criminal Law, Particularly on the Circuits* (London: J. Dodsley, 1785).
Malcolm, Noel, *Reason of State, Propaganda, and the Thirty Years' War* (Oxford: Oxford University Press, 2010).
Mandeville, Bernard, *An Enquiry into the Causes of the Frequent Executions at Tyburn: And a Proposal for Some Regulations Concerning Felons in Prison, and the Good Effects to Be Expected from them, to Which Is Added, a Discourse on Transportation, and a Method to Render that Punishment More Effectual* (London: J. Roberts, 1725).
Manning, Gillian, 'Rochester's Satyr Against Reason and Mankind and Contemporary Relgious Debate', *Seventeenth Century*, **8.1** (1993), 99–121.
Markham, Gervase, *The English Housewife; Containing the Inward and Outward Virtues Which Ought to Be in a Complete Woman* (London, 1675).
Mill, John Stuart, *Principles of Political Economy with Some of their Applications to Social Philosophy, in Two Volumes*, vol. 2 (Boston, 1848).
Utilitarianism (London: John W. Parker, 1864).
Montrose, Louis, *The Purpose of Playing, Shakespeare and the Cultural Politics of Elizabethan Theatre* (Chicago, IL: University of Chicago Press, 1996)
Moody, Jane, *Illegitimate Theatres in London, 1770–1840* (Cambridge: Cambridge University Press, 2000).
Morris, Corbyn, *An Essay Towards Fixing the True Standards of Wit, Raillery, Satire and Ridicule* (London: J. Roberts, 1744).
Norden, John, *A Christian Familiar Comfort* (London, 1596).

Norton, Frances, *The Applause of Virtue, Consisting of Several Divine and Moral Essays Towards the Obtaining of True Virtue* (London: James Graves, 1705).

Novak, Maximillian E., 'Margery Pinchwife's "London Disease": Restoration Comedy and the Libertine Offensive of the 1670s', *Studies in the Literary Imagination*, **10**:1 (1977, spring), 1–23.

O'Brien, John, *Harlequin Britain: Pantomime and Entertainment, 1690–1760* (Baltimore, MD: Johns Hopkins University Press, 2004).

Ollyffe, George, *An Essay Humbly Offer'd, for an Act of Parliament to Prevent Capital Crimes, and the Loss of so Many Lives; and to Promote a Desirable Improvement and Blessing in the Nation*, 2nd edition (London: J. Downing, 1731).

Pearce, Edward, *The Great Man: Sir Robert Walpole: Scoundrel, Genius and Britain's First Prime Minister* (London: Random House, 2007).

Pincus, Steven, *1688: The First Modern Revolution* (New Haven, CT: Yale University Press, 2009).

Plato, *Plato: Complete Works*, trans. Trevor J. Saunders (Indianapolis, IN: Hackett, 1997).

Plumtre, James, and Georges Lillo, 'The London Merchant', in *The English Drama Purified: Being a Specimen of Select Plays, in Which All Passages that Have Appeared to the Editor to Be Objectionable in Point of Morality, Are Omitted or Altered, with Prefaces and Notes*, ed. Plumtre (Cambridge: F. Hodson, 1812).

Pope, Alexander, *An Essay on Criticism* (London: R. Dodsley, 1711).

The Works of Alexander Pope, Esq., in Verse and Prose, in 10 Volumes, vol. 9 (London: Strahan and Preston, 1806).

The Works of Alexander Pope, vol. 7 (London: John Murray, 1871).

Prince, Michael, *Philosophical Dialogue in the British Enlightenment: Theology, Aesthetics, and the Novel* (Cambridge: University of Cambridge Press, 1996).

Prynne, William, *Histrio-Mastix: The Player's Scourge, or Actor's Tragedy* (London: Edward Allde, Augustine Mathewes, Thomas Cotes adn William Iones, 1633).

Puchner, Martin, *The Drama of Ideas: Platonic Provocations in Theatre and Philosophy* (New York: Oxford University Press, 2010).

R.L., *The Apprentice's Companion; or, Advice to a Boy, upon Being Bound Apprentice; and for His Conduct during His Apprenticeship* (London: W. Button, 1795).

Rancière, Jacques, *The Philosopher and His Poor*, ed. Andrew Parker, trans. John Drury, Corinne Oster, and Andrew Parker (Durham, NC: Duke University Press, 2003).

Read, Alan, *Theatre, Intimacy and Engagement: The Last Human Venue* (Basingstoke: Palgrave Macmillan, 2009).

Reynell, Edward, *An Advice against Libertinism* (London: Roper, 1659).

Richardson, Samuel, *The Apprentice's Vade Mecum: or, Young Man's Pocket-Companion*, The Augustan Reprint Society, Publication Numbers 169–70, William Andrews Clark Memorial Library (Los Angeles: University of California, 1975 [London: 1734]).

Ridpath, George, *The Stage Condemn'd* (London, 1698).

Rogers, Nicholas, 'Confronting the Crime Wave: The Debate over Social Reform and Regulation, 1749–1753', in *Stilling the Grumbling Hive: The Response to Social and Economic Problems in England, 1689–1750*, ed. Lee Davison et al. (Stroud: St Martin's Press, 1992), pp. 77–98.

Romilly, Samuel, *Observations on a Late Publication Intituled, Thoughts on Executive Justice* (London: Cadell, 1786).

Rousseau, Jean-Jacques, *Politics and the Arts*, trans. Allan Bloom (Ithaca, NY: Cornell University Press, 1960).

Rymer, Thomas, *The Tragedies of the Last Age: Consider'd and Examin'd by the Practice of the Ancients and by the Common Sense of All Ages in a Letter to Fleetwood Shepheard, Esq.* Part 1, 2nd edition (London, 1692).

Sedgwick, Eve, *Between Men: English Literature and Male Homosocial Desire* (New York: Columbia University Press, 1985).

Shakespeare, William, *The Illustrated Stratford Shakespeare* (London: Chancellor Press, 1982).

Shaw, George Bernard, *The Quintessence of Ibsenism* (London: Walter Scott, 1891).

'Preface to *The Shewing-up of Blanco Posnet*', in *Prefaces by Bernard Shaw* (London: Constable and Company, 1934 [1909]).

Skyrme, Thomas, *History of the Justices of the Peace*, vol. 2: *England 1689–1989* (Chichester: Barry Rose and the Justice of the Peace, 1991).

Smith, Adam, *An Inquiry into the Nature and Causes of the Wealth of Nations, abridged* (Indianapolis, IN: Hackett, 1993 [1776]).

Smith, Irwin, *Shakespeare's Blackfriars Playhouse* (New York: New York University Press, 1964).

Spens, Henry, *The Republic of Plato: In Ten Books*, trans. Henry Spens (Glasgow, 1773).

Stubbes, George, *A Dialogue on Beauty in the Manner of Plato* (London: W. Wilkins, 1731).

Thomas, David, David Carlton, and Anne Etienne, *Theatre Censorship from Walpole to Wilson* (Oxford: Oxford University Press, 2007).

John Thelwall, 'On the Political Prostitution of the Public Theatres, Part 1. With a Digression on the Character and Fate of Socrates', in *The Tribune, a Periodical Publication, Consisting Chiefly of the Political Lectures of J. Thelwall*, Volume III (London, 1795), pp. 279–98.

Thurmond, John, *Harlequin Sheppard* (London: J. Roberts and A. Dodd, 1724).

Tindal, Matthew, *A Letter to a Member of Parliament Shewing, that a Restraint on the Press Is Inconsistent with the Protestant Religion, and Dangerous to the Liberty of the Nation* (London: J. Darby, 1700).

Underwood, Dale, *Etherege and the Seventeenth-Century Comedy of Manners* (New Haven, CT: Yale University Press, 1957).

Vanbrugh, *A Short Vindication of the Relapse and the Provok'd Wife, from Immorality and Prophaneness* (London: H. Walwyn, 1698).

Waugh, John, *The Duty of Apprentices and Other Servants; A Sermon Preach'd at the Parish Church of St. Bridget, alias Bride, August 24th, 1713. Being the Festival of St. Bartholomew* (London: G. Strahan, 1713).

Weber, Harold, 'Thc Rake Hero in Wycherley and Congreve', *Philological Quarterly*, **61**:2 (1982, spring), 143–60.

The Restoration Rake-hero: Transformations in Sexual Understanding in Seventeenth-century England (Madison: University of Wisconsin Press, 1986).

Weber, Samuel, *Theatricality as Medium* (New York: Fordham University Press, 2004).

Webster, Jeremy, *Performing Libertinism in Charles II's Court: Politics, Drama, Sexuality* (Basingstoke: Palgrave Macmillan, 2005).

Whately, William, *A Bride-Bush, Or a Wedding Sermon Compendiously Describing the Duties of Married Persons: By Performing Whereof, Marriage Shall Be to Them a Great Helpe, Which Now Finde It a Little Hell* (London, 1617).

Wiles, David, *Theatre and Citizenship: The History of a Practice* (Cambridge: Cambridge University Press, 2011).

Wilkes, John, *English Liberty: Being a Collection of Interesting Tracts for the Years 1762–1769, Containing the Private Correspondence, Public Letters, Speeches, and Addresses, of John Wilkes, Esq.* (London: T. Baldwin, 1769).

Wilmot, John, *The Works of John. Earl of Rochester: Containing Poems on Several Occasions*, fourth edition (London: Jacob Tonson, 1732).

Winton, Calhoun, *John Gay and the London Theatre* (Lexington: University Press of Kentucky, 1993).

Woolf, Brandon, 'Toward a Paradoxically Parallaxical Postdramatic Politics', in *Postdramatic Theatre and the Political: International Perspectives on Contemporary Performance*, ed. Karen Jürs-Munby, Jerome Carroll, and Steve Giles (London: Bloomsbury, 2013), pp. 31–46.

Yates, Frances, *Theatre of the World* (Oxon: Routledge, 1987).

Pamphlets

A Refutation of the Apology for Actors (London: W. White, 1615).

The Lawes Resolutions of Women's Rights: or, The Lawes Provision for Woemen (London, 1632).

The Actor's Remonstrance, or Complaint: For the Silencing of Their Profession, and Banishment from Their Severall Play-Houses (London, 1643).

Remarques on the Humours and Conversations of the Town (London, 1673).

A Letter to the Right Honourable Sir Richard Brocas, Lord Mayor of London: By a Citizen (London, 1730).

The Means of Effectually Preventing Theft and Robbery (London, 1783), unpaginated.

Lillo's Admirable Tragedy of George Barnwell: Or, the London Apprentice. Since the First Institution of the Theatre to the Present Day, No Dramatic Piece Has Been of More Service to Society Than This Admirable Tragedy, and If to Point Out the Allurements of Vice, as a Warning for Unthinking Youth to Avoid the Snares of Debauchery (London, 1790).

Major and Minor Theatres, a Concise View of the Question, as Regards the Public, the Patentees, and the Profession, with Remarks on the Decline of the Drama and the Means of Its Restoration. To Which Is Added the Petition Now Lying for Signature. By One of the Public (London, 1832).

Newspapers and Periodicals

Blackwoods Edinburgh Magazine
The British Architect
Caledonian Mercury
The Country Journal or the Craftsman
Court and Fashionable Magazine
The Daily Gazetteer
Daily Post
The Drama or, Theatrical Pocket Magazine
Hibernian Magazine, or, Compendium of Entertaining Knowledge
The Intelligencer
London Chronicle or Universal Evening Post
The London Journal
London Evening Post
Middlesex Journal or Universal Evening Post
The Mirror of Taste and Dramatic Censor
Mist's Weekly Journal
The Monthly Mirror: Reflecting Men and Manners. With Strictures on the Epitome, the Stage, vol. 6
Morning Chronicle and London Advertiser
The Morning Post
The New Monthly Magazine
The New Monthly Magazine and Literary Journal
Public Advertiser
Sentimental Magazine
St James Chronicle or the British Evening Post
The Times
Universal Magazine of Knowledge and Pleasure

Parliamentary Reports

Report from the Select Committee on Dramatic Literature with Minutes of Evidence: Ordered by the House of Commons, to be Printed, 2nd August, 1832 (London, 1832).

Report from the Select Committee on Theatres and Places of Entertainment: With Proceedings; Minutes of Evidence; Appendix; and, Index, 1892. Great Britain. Parliament. House of Commons (Shannon: Irish University Press, 1970).

Report from the Joint Select Committee of the House of Lords and the House of Commons on the Stage Plays (Censorship) – Ordered by the House of Commons, to be printed, 2nd November 1909.

'Reports from the Select Committee on Theatrical Licenses and Regulations; together with the Procedures of the Committee, Minutes of Evidence, and Appendix', in *Reports from Committees: Eleven Volumes; Theatrical Licenses and Regulations; Trade in Animals, Session 1 February–10 August, 1866*, vol. 16 (London, 1866).

Archives

Metropolitan Board of Works

Theatres and Music Halls Committee in London County Council Minutes of Proceedings of the Council

Theatres and Music Halls, Licensing Sessions, Printed Papers

Online Archives

www.nationalarchives.gov.uk

Index